Partition's First Generation

Islamic South Asia Series

Series Editor Ruby Lal, Emory University

Advisory Board

Iftikhar Dadi, Cornell University
Stephen F. Dale, Ohio State University
Rukhsana David, Kinnaird College for Women
Michael Fisher, Oberlin College
Marcus Fraser, Fitzwilliam Museum
Ebba Koch, University of Vienna
David Lewis, London School of Economics
Francis Robinson, Royal Holloway, University of London
Ron Sela, Indiana University Bloomington
Willem van Schendel, University of Amsterdam

Titles

*Sexual and Gender Diversity in the Muslim World:
History, Law and Vernacular Knowledge*, Vanja Hamzic
*The Architecture of a Deccan Sultanate: Courtly Practice and
Royal Authority in Late Medieval India*, Pushkar Sohoni
Sufi Shrines and the Pakistani State: The End of Religious Pluralism, Umber Bin Ibad
*The Hindu Sufis of South Asia: Partition, Shrine Culture and
the Sindhis in India*, Michel Boivin
*Islamic Sermons and Public Piety in Bangladesh:
The Poetics of Popular Preaching*, Max Stille

Partition's First Generation

Space, Place, and Identity in Muslim South Asia

Amber H. Abbas

I.B. TAURIS
LONDON • NEW YORK • OXFORD • NEW DELHI • SYDNEY

I.B. TAURIS
Bloomsbury Publishing Plc
50 Bedford Square, London, WC1B 3DP, UK
1385 Broadway, New York, NY 10018, USA
29 Earlsfort Terrace, Dublin 2, Ireland

BLOOMSBURY, I.B. TAURIS and the I.B. Tauris logo are trademarks of Bloomsbury Publishing Plc

First published in Great Britain 2021
This paperback edition published in 2022

Copyright © Amber H. Abbas, 2021

Amber H. Abbas has asserted her right under the Copyright, Designs and Patents Act, 1988, to be identified as Author of this work.

For legal purposes the Acknowledgments on p. ix constitute an extension of this copyright page.

Series design: Adriana Brioso
Cover image © Margaret Bourke-White/The LIFE Picture Collection/Getty Images

All rights reserved. No part of this publication may be reproduced or transmitted in any form or by any means, electronic or mechanical, including photocopying, recording, or any information storage or retrieval system, without prior permission in writing from the publishers.

Bloomsbury Publishing Plc does not have any control over, or responsibility for, any third-party websites referred to or in this book. All internet addresses given in this book were correct at the time of going to press. The author and publisher regret any inconvenience caused if addresses have changed or sites have ceased to exist, but can accept no responsibility for any such changes.

A catalogue record for this book is available from the British Library.

A catalog record for this book is available from the Library of Congress.

ISBN: HB: 978-1-3501-4266-4
PB: 978-0-7556-3541-2
ePDF: 978-1-3501-4268-8
eBook: 978-1-3501-4267-1

Series: Library of Islamic South Asia

Typeset by Deanta Global Publishing Services, Chennai, India

To find out more about our authors and books visit www.bloomsbury.com and sign up for our newsletters.

For my family: here, there, and everywhere.

Contents

Acknowledgments	ix
Preface	xii

	Introduction	1
	Oral History and Partition	6
	Voices from Aligarh Muslim University	9
1	Defining the Aligarh Muslim University	19
	The Founder's Context	21
	Creating a Victorian Muslim Education	26
	Pillars of the Moral Community	29
	Discipline and Place in AMU	32
	Conclusion	37
2	Self-Realization and the Nation: AMU Student Activism	41
	Education and Politics: Continuity and Change 1898–1937	43
	From Muslim Nationalism to the Two Nation Theory 1937–47	47
	The League Period at AMU, 1940–7	53
	Aligarh Students and the 1945–6 Elections	55
	Conclusion	61
3	Pushing the Boundaries: Partitioning and Aligarh Muslim University	63
	The Inner Circle of Discipline, 1946	66
	Outer Circles, Other Sites of Disturbance	72
	Conclusion	80
4	The Muslim Question in India after Partition	83
	Continuity and Slippage after 1947	85
	The Nationalist Turn: AMU in Independent India	90
	Telling Moment: January 30, 1948	92
	The Muslim Case in India	95
	Pakistans, Pakistanis, and India	97
	Conclusion	101

5 Muslimness and Pakistan	103
When Minority Becomes Majority	104
AMU, Pakistan, and Bangladesh	108
Two Nations, Three States: 1947/1971	114
Conclusion	120
Conclusion	123
Redemption	128
Epilogue: The Babri Masjid, AMU, and Indian Muslims	135
The Babri Masjid Verdicts and AMU	136
The Citizenship Amendment Act/National Register of Citizens	139
Appendix of All Interviews—Alphabetical by Narrator	143
Pakistan (2005–10)	143
India (2008–9)	152
Bangladesh (2010)	160
Notes	163
Interviews Cited	205
Bibliography	207
Index	222

Acknowledgments

This project has occupied my life in large and small ways for two decades, and my intellectual and personal debts are many. First, my humblest gratitude extends to the seventy-two individuals whose narratives form the foundation of this analysis. They and their families invited me—a veritable stranger in most cases—into their homes, offering tea, snacks, and stories. The interviews often blossomed into rich conversation that provided the comfort of family when I was far from home. I am grateful for their hospitality and their stories. Without them, this project would not be.

Aligarh alumni the world over helped me to build the connections to narrators. I am indebted to the moderators of the Yahoo Groups AMU Network (and its moderator Shaheer Khan), WorldofAligs, and VoiceofAligs. Syed Ali Rizvi, a leader among American Old Boys, was tireless in his support of this project. He offered advice, connected me to narrators, and even once met me on a moving train! Similarly, independent scholar Afzal Usmani functioned as a network hub, linking me to Aligs everywhere I went. Naved Masood, son of Masood-ul Hasan, frequently helped me out with contact information and additional, (sometimes unpublished) materials. It is a testament to the global network of Aligs that I was able to engage such a geographically broad group of narrators.

I owe my gratitude above all to my extraordinary Ph.D. supervisor, Gail Minault, in the History Department at the University of Texas at Austin. Her scholarship set the bar high for her students, and I aspire to do justice to her reputation. In addition to expertise, she modeled the ways of scholarly generosity, and I will always be grateful for her guidance and friendship. My dissertation committee, Kamran Asdar Ali, Martha Norkunas, Wm. Roger Louis, and Philippa Levine guided and shaped the earlier form of this project. In addition, scholarly mentors have constantly reminded me of the value of the work: David Lelyveld, Yasmin Saikia (herself an Old Girl of AMU), Lucy Chester, and Neilesh Bose. Many friends in graduate school and during fieldwork in India helped me to generate ideas, refine analysis, and stay motivated! Special thanks to Max Bruce for his help with the title.

In India, my Aligarh Muslim University (AMU) adviser Shireen Moosvi of the Department of History and the Center for Women's Studies at AMU made me welcome and guided me when I was doing the field work there in 2009. I spent a lot of time in the History Department and faculty including Irfan Habib, Iqtidar Alam Khan, and Gulfishan Khan helped to connect me with narrators in Aligarh and Lucknow. I am also indebted to the staff of the Maulana Azad Library, especially Ramesh in the Sir Syed Room, and Dr. Shayesta Khan and S. M. Mohsin Jafri in the Manuscripts Section. In addition, Shan Mohammad and the staff at the Sir Syed Academy supported my access to their collections. In Pakistan and Bangladesh, it was the friendly staff at the National Archives that made my daily work possible. In Pakistan, too, the scholars of the Nazaria-e-Pakistan Foundation in Lahore, under the direction of Dr. Rafique Ahmad, spent long hours in interviews and sharing resources with me.

To the many organizations who funded my research, I must acknowledge my gratitude: the Department of History and the South Asia Institute at the University of Texas, the American Institute of Indian Studies, and the American Institute of Bangladesh Studies. My research in India was funded by a Critical Language Scholarship in 2008 and a Fulbright-Hays Doctoral Dissertation Research Award in 2009. Many thanks to the USIEF Staff in Delhi and to Adam Grotsky. My initial interest in this project was facilitated by an IIE Fulbright to Pakistan in 1999.

My colleagues at Saint Joseph's University have sustained their enthusiasm for this book. The members of the Interdisciplinary Writing Group have read many drafts and have made it better with their feedback. I feel lucky to have such dedicated colleagues offering sustained intellectual community. In addition, my thanks go to Tikia Hamilton at Triple Ivy Writing and Educational Services, LLC, for her invaluable editing and suggestions in the final stages of revision. In Philadelphia, my life and my scholarship have been enriched by the community around the South Asian American Digital Archive (www.saada.org), particularly the friendship and leadership of Samip Mallick.

Over the years I have been developing my practice as an oral historian, the scholars and thinkers that lead the Oral History Association (OHA) have become a community of steadfast allies. As a scholarly community, my friends in the OHA are fierce in their dedication to ethics of our practice and I have learned an immense amount from them. Brooke Bryan, Troy Reeves, Kathy Nasstrom, and Doug Boyd, in particular, have read drafts and encouraged my scholarship. At Doug's invitation, I am grateful to have been able to deposit the oral history interviews at the heart of this book in the *Partition's First Generation Oral History Project* at the Louie B. Nunn Center for Oral History at the University of Kentucky Libraries.[1]

My thanks to the Institute for South Asia Studies at Berkeley, Munis D. Faruqui and the committee members for awarding me the inaugural S.S. Pirzada Dissertation Prize on Pakistan in 2015. I am grateful to the editors, staff and anonymous reviewers at I.B. Tauris who have been steadfast supporters and have worked with me to make the book better.

My family has always been at the core of this project. My paternal grandmother crossed the India-Pakistan border in 1947 with three children and raised seven altogether in Pakistan. My father migrated to the United States, where he met my mother in Oklahoma. My parents and my two remarkable sisters supported me every step of this journey with emotional support, funds, nourishment, and long conversations about triumphs and trials. Aaron Jakes, my friend turned family, has been a constant ally. My father, who died in 2013, would have loved to see this book in print. He was only five years old when he became a partition refugee, and he spent his whole life seeking to create a secure future for those he loved.

My extended family in Pakistan lived the experience of leaving Aligarh and settling in Pakistan, and I was driven by my desire to understand their experience. My great uncle and initial interlocutor, Major General Wajahat Husain (Ret'd)—Poonan Mama—spent dozens of hours speaking with me in his study, and this relationship meant the world to me. My thanks are also due to his family, Talat Mami, Kashif, and Atiqa. My grandmother, Begum Birjis Abbas, was in many ways my muse, and I worried after her death in February 2007 that I might lose my way. But this story is driven by survivors; they provided the inspiration to keep going. My aunts, uncles, and cousins in Lahore fed me, taught me, and put up with me during several research visits to Pakistan. I know I did not always make it easy. Thank you. In Karachi and Islamabad, too, my relatives always gave me a home, and sometimes a car, as well as company, encouragement, and conversation.

Many friends and families took me in when I was no more than a friend of a friend. Sumer, Parul, and Sanat Datta invited me to call their (quite incredible) Gurgaon home my home. More broadly, the Bindaas Gang—too numerous to name here—made my life in India the best kind of adventure with endless Bollywood dance parties. By extension, Bindaas Pakistan made it all possible by setting the original example for hospitality: Shandana Mohmand, Miguel Loreiro, and the Bandey family. In Delhi, Theresa, Olivier, Sasank, Martin, and Ryna were a gateway to the rest of the world with music, laughter, late nights, and mince pies. Of course, James supported all of us. In Lucknow, the whole crew at the AIIS Urdu program, led by Ahtesham Sahib, supported my Urdu and introduced me to narrators in addition to providing a classroom to which former students, like me, can always return.

In Aligarh, when I arrived alone, knowing nobody, a phone call went around the world and Dr. Maqbool Alam appeared at the guest house to pick me up. He, Raffia Aunty, and their daughter-in-law Asra helped me to get settled and became my local family. Without their support and advice, I might not have been able to stay. It was Maqbool Uncle who finally helped me find my family's ancestral home in Aligarh city as I detail in the Preface.

Stateside, many friends have touched this work and shared the journey. Sylvia Gale and Alistair Jones, our friends-like-family have held me throughout the journey of this work. Sylvia deserves special mention for understanding so much more than I ever could, and for sharing her wisdom with me.

Of course, the support of these colleagues, friends, and institutions has been significant, but the ideas here, the mistakes, and responsibility for them are mine.

Finally, Jamison Warren deserves more than thanks. He embodies true partnership. His love and patience has made it possible for me to become, over our years together, a scholar, a professor, and a mother to our precious Ruby. His spirit of adventure tells me that there is much more to come.

Preface

Early on a Sunday morning in 2009, I rode my bicycle from my hostel near the university, across the railroad tracks, and into the city of Aligarh, India. I carried a bottle of water and a map of the city my uncle had drawn for me. Though it had been sixty-two years since his family left Aligarh for Pakistan—my uncle was only in the third grade at the time—he assured me that the map was "perfectly correct." I had been living in Dodhpur, a Muslim neighborhood near AMU, for a couple of months prior to embarking on this search for my family's prepartition home. The home was located on Amjad Ali Road, which was named in honor of my paternal grandmother's grandfather (my great-great grandfather), who had been a "leading lawyer advocate of Aligarh."[1]

The streets were deserted, free of the choking traffic that I had experienced on earlier forays into the city. "I'm looking for Amjad Ali Road," I told a concerned-looking traffic officer. "Amjad Ali Road? *Nehin*. Doesn't exist!" the officer insisted. Undeterred, I approached the local roadside juice sellers, who simply shrugged their shoulders, before suggesting that I ask a man passing on the street just then. According to the juice vendors, the man had "been around for a long time," but, when I asked him about the place, he also seemed bewildered. Agitated, he exclaimed, "If you want to find that place, go ask in Pakistan!" I was startled. Of course, the map I carried *was* from Pakistan, but I didn't want to reveal my connections to the place. The man, however, was gesturing toward Upperkot, the Muslim neighborhood with a congregational mosque on the hill.

Feeling defeated, I abandoned my search. I rode my bicycle back down the hill to the Grand Trunk Road, tracing it past my uncle's old primary school and across the bridge still known as the *kat pulla* (wooden bridge), though it has long since been cemented. I continued back into the Civil Lines, past the university, and to the *ghoshtwalli galli* ("Meat Lane," since butcher shops lined the street). Upon arriving at the girls' hostel where I was renting a single room, I overcame my frustration with a nap. The hostel was quiet in the afternoons. Most of the other residents were young teenage girls, busy studying for their entrance exams, hoping first to secure admission into Muslim University Girls High School and, subsequently, AMU. Later, I returned to transcribing the oral history interviews I had collected from AMU graduates who lived through the Indian partition of 1947.

I initially heard stories about the Aligarh home from my great uncle, Major General Wajahat Husain, in June 2005 in Lahore, Pakistan. It was my first interview for my graduate research, and I was a little bit nervous. Though I had always known Wajahat by his family pet-name "Poonan" and found him warm and loving (I still cherish an emerald ring he gave me when I was seven or eight years old), he had a reputation in our family for being a bit stern and overly concerned with punctuality. As a British-trained officer, he maintained an almost-intimidating dedication to decorum, even in the comfort of his own home. Perhaps it should not have surprised me when I turned on the recorder, and he began reading from a short document he had already composed:

> At Aligarh in my father's house, we were a large family and as for custom and traditions in those days we lived on what is known as the joint-family system. My parents, nine of us: five sisters and four brothers . . . [We lived in] a large, big house in three portions. The front portion was the *mardana* where we had the traditional drawing room, dining room, guest rooms, and my father's office. He was initially a civil servant and later a lawyer. Then the rear portion, which was the lower portion, was where the boys lived. We had our own rooms and my uncle lived with his family. Upstairs was the *zenana*, the third portion of the main house where my mother and my father had their bedrooms. We all dined together and stayed together. And at night we used to come down and sleep in our bedrooms downstairs. Outside was a big garden, servants' quarters, driveway, garages and stable for the horses. We had a car. There were only two or three cars [in Aligarh] at the time. We had a 1935 model Overland Ford which was kept but taken out very seldom. Mostly we used the horse-drawn carriage. All children used to go to our school and colleges in the carriage. They used to drop us and then collect us in the afternoon one by one. In the evening we played cricket with our parents and amongst ourselves and hockey while the girls played badminton among themselves. It was a very happy family and my mother, my parents, kept very strict control and discipline ensuring that a) we got the best possible education and b) we were all kept under tight discipline. Truthfulness, straightforwardness, obedience to our elders and, of course, love and affection between all the boys and the girls and, of course, to our parents were the cardinal points of our upbringing.[2]

Horrified by the fact that he was reading directly into the lapel microphone attached to his shirt, I didn't truly hear much of what he said. As soon as I could, I tried to shift the narrative. As a newly trained oral historian, I knew I did not want narrators to read from written documents. I wanted to draw out memories and meaning through conversation, reflection, and a thoughtful exploration of the past.[3] Milquetoast descriptions such as, "We were a happy family," contained little substance, and I shuddered to think about the other bland platitudes my great uncle might offer. I eventually convinced him to dispense with the written statement, altogether. Over the next several years, we embarked on a series of fourteen interviews that became the basis of his own 2010 memoir, *1947: Before, During, After*. Our interviews also established the foundation for my own research on the experiences of AMU students throughout the period of partitioning that created the independent states of India and Pakistan.[4]

Like his eldest sister (my paternal grandmother), Wajahat had been born and raised in the house he described during his reminiscences. After studying Qur'an at home, he began his formal education, as a day student, in Minto Circle, the AMU-affiliated secondary school, and completed all of his schooling in the university's affiliated institutions. He graduated from the university in 1944, during the height of the Second

World War. Eager to contribute to the war effort, that same year, Wajahat joined the Air Force. However, just as he was set to begin flight training, the war ended, and he "became surplus."[5] In 1946, he entered the first postwar officer's class in the Indian Military Academy, Dehradun. As he explained that June day, "I finished up in the top three in the passing out order. Then [I was] taken in the Royal Indian Armored Corps and my regiment was the King George V Central India Horse, a very fine Indian Armored Corps. We passed out on 22nd December 1946. And then joined our regiments." He further recalled that, a few months later

> it had been decided that Pakistan would come into being and then a circular was sent to me by the Adjutant asking for my option. Those of us [Muslims] who did not belong to what is now Pakistan had the option of staying either in India or going to Pakistan. Those who belonged to what is Pakistan had no option. They had to stay. I had the option and then I opted for Pakistan.

His regiment was divided, and the Muslim men transferred to the 19th Lancers in Pakistan. However,

> on 14th of August there was the night when Pakistan was coming in to being, Pakistan Day or Independence Day. My Colonel, a British officer, said that he would collect me to celebrate Pakistan day at the local Ahmednagar Club. He said, "I'll collect you and then we'll go together." It was very nice of him—a young 2nd lieutenant being taken by the Colonel of the regiment. So he took me and, as we were driving, he told me that "You are leaving for the Boundary Force in two days' time. A squadron of the regiment is proceeding to East Punjab where the troubles are going on and you will be part of the Boundary Force."[6]

Wajahat spent approximately six weeks serving on the ill-fated Punjab Boundary Force, escorting both trains and columns of Muslims who were heading West into Pakistan, and trains and columns of Hindus and Sikhs who were migrating East into India. Some were attacked. As the only Muslim officer leading a squadron of Jats and Dogras, some of whom hailed from the disputed border area of Gurdaspur, Wajahat witnessed some of the horrific violence surrounding the 1947 Partition.[7] As the operations of the Boundary Force wound down—it was disbanded in September—and the Jat Squadron was deployed to Kashmir, Wajahat began planning his move to join his regiment in Pakistan. In the meantime, however, he learned he had been appointed as an instructor in the Indian Military Academy, and though he could not accept the posting (having opted for Pakistan), he traveled there first. For a few days, he helped to divide the Academy's assets. "They were counting how many bicycles would go to Pakistan, and how many this and how many that," he recalled.[8] Subsequently, some British officers arranged a loan of a 1,500-weight truck and he proceeded to Aligarh to collect his family so they could accompany him to Pakistan.

Wajahat returned home one afternoon in October in that army truck. He had been out of contact for a few months, since his Boundary Force deployment, and the family had no way of knowing whether he was alive or dead. Yet, the excitement of his return was brief, as Wajahat explained to his family that he could transport them in the truck, but they would have to leave immediately.

> My mother, God bless her, was very upset because there was so much stuff and she didn't know what to take and what not to take, Wajahat remembered. I said, "I'm very sorry, you can only take a couple of suitcases each, of the most essential things, otherwise everything will have to be left." She was very brave and so was my father. And they, in a few hours' time, organized everything.[9]

As he remembered it, his younger siblings, just children at the time, "were all shouting and crying because they wanted to take their things." Though he initially hoped to remain with them there until the next day, the entire family fled in the wee hours of the morning, fearful that, having opted for Pakistan, Wajahat might be arrested if he tarried too long in India.

My father, who was only five years old at the time, also fled India in a truck, perched in the back with his mother and three younger siblings. My grandfather, who had earned an L.L.M. from AMU, remained in Moradabad to settle his legal practice; he reunited with them later. The journey carried my grandmother, father, my aunt, and my uncle across North India, through Lahore, and all the way to Peshawar—by truck and train. After my grandfather joined them, they settled in Lahore. Wajahat's elder brother Intisar, who served in the Indian Railways, had already secured a home in Lahore, the former residence of a High Court Justice. Fortunately, the home was large enough to suit the entire family. My father spent the rest of his childhood residing at 47 Jail Road, right up until he left to study in the United States in 1960. The house exists in my memory merely as a ruin, but members of our extended family built new residences on the site and continued to live there until recently.

Despite my initial frustrations, I didn't permanently abandon my quest to find the home in which my grandmother and my father were born in Aligarh. With the support of both a local friend and a long-serving and elderly imam of a mosque in the area, shortly after my disappointing solo venture, I located Amjad Ali Road. Still, the police had been right; Amjad Ali Road no longer existed. In the mid-1990s, in the wake of the destruction of the Babri Masjid in Ayodhya by Hindu zealots, Hindu-Muslim riots spread to Aligarh. They tore through the historically Muslim neighborhood, and no Muslims lived there any longer. The road marker bearing my Muslim great-great-grandfather's name was torn down, and the street was later renamed. However, the auto mechanic, whose stall occupies the corner lot, saved the stone road marker engraved with my great-great-grandfather's name. He showed it to me. Overturned, it now serves as a part of the stoop in front of his shop.

Farther down the lane, we found the house. It now belongs to a Hindu family who fled Lahore in 1947 and received it as Refugee Property. The large gardens had been transformed into an apartment complex with a small Hindu temple in the car park. A Sikh Gurudwara flanked the other side of the house. The homeowners operated a business manufacturing tin and brass pots, along with other sorts of cookware. They used the old garages as storage for their inventory. In the business office located on the ground floor, we met a member of the family. When my guide explained who I was, the man appeared agitated. Though born after his family's migration, he clearly bore the trauma of their displacement. Apparently, he feared that my return was merely for the purposes of making a claim on the property. I assured him that this was not my intention.

Still, he made it clear that he did not want to speak with me. As he explained, twenty years prior, the house itself had been divided; the family who lived in the other section was not scarred by partition. "Perhaps they would be willing to show you around?" he suggested. To my delight, the family welcomed me, inviting me into the second floor living room, which previously had functioned as a *bara darwaza*, or a semi-open terrace, which many families used in the days before indoor cooling to allow the wind to waft through. The terrace was now an enclosed living room; children sat there completing the evening's homework. The family escorted me from this front section, or the *mardana* that Wajahat had described, through to the *zenana* and up to the roof. The rooftop crenellations my uncle had captured in his descriptions had disappeared, but from the large roof, we absorbed a spectacular sunset view of the Upperkot Mosque, the same view my grandmother and her large family most likely enjoyed while residing there. When we departed, the current residents packed me a box of *besan ka laddoo*, a traditional sweet, to carry to my family in Lahore.

Walking around the neighborhood a bit later, we encountered a man in his seventies, who remembered my family and their great love of kite-flying. Indeed, Wajahat's uncle, Fasahat, whose family also lived in the house, had imparted to his children a dedication to kite-flying that persisted along with our celebrations of spring and summer in Pakistan. It was Fasahat's son, Nayyar, who had given me the map.

Over the months I lived in Aligarh, I learned more about how the events of 1947 continued to influence daily life and the relations among the city's residents. For instance, I came to understand what the man I encountered on the street meant when he told me to "Go to Pakistan!" He was referring to the Muslim neighborhood around the mosque, not the state created in 1947. In other words, the creation of Pakistan, which many Indian Muslims imagined as a homeland, had extended its influence in Aligarh. As such, all Muslims, even those who, unlike my family, had chosen to stay in India, still became "Pakistanis," while their neighborhoods morphed into little "Pakistans." Tensions continue to run high between the two states, giving these labels profound implications for the city's Muslim residents. Though Aligarh sits far away from the borders that define the margin between the two states, the city retains important symbolic value in their shared history; in addition to being the home of many Muslim families, it remains the home of the AMU.

Since its founding in the late nineteenth century, AMU has been the premier educational institution for the sons of India's elite Muslim families and a center for developing Muslim leadership. In the 1920s, Aligarh students displayed anti-imperialist zeal by joining the Khilafat Movement and supporting Gandhi's non-cooperation movement. In the 1930s and the 1940s, as India sought independence from the British, it became a hub of pro-Pakistan activism, and its students fanned out across the country to support Muslim electoral candidates. Even after partition, the university's influence has been broad. Since 1947, AMU graduates have served as heads of state in India, Pakistan, Bangladesh, and the Maldives. Today, it stands as a

Central University, located in a Hindu majority city, and welcomes students from all backgrounds. Yet, because of the institution's perceived connections to Pakistan, it also has emerged as a contentious site for India's volatile communal politics.

I first became interested in AMU because of my own family's experience there. Their stories led me into a more complex network of experiences, and it was through exploring the stories of AMU students that I grew to appreciate the ways in which partition has transformed Muslim lives in the subcontinent through shifts in everyday experience that affect access to spaces and places, and even concepts of belonging.

As it turned out, that first interview I conducted with my great uncle, Wajahat, contains the structure and seeds of my larger inquiry. During his interview, he described the culture of his home, while emphasizing the importance of discipline; he spoke about the university and outlined its relationship to the surrounding city; he revealed the ambivalence of religious practice at the university; he shared his impressions of All-India Muslim League leader Mohammad Ali Jinnah, who frequently visited AMU, and he boasted about the impact Jinnah had in fomenting pro-Pakistan feelings throughout the university; he explained his own decision to migrate, a decision that was based on ambition rather than compulsion. He chronicled the events that took place during partition, its resulting violence, and the methods he pursued in the hopes of protecting his family and securing a prosperous future. The first interview became the basis of a five-year oral history collection project that transported me throughout Pakistan, India, and, finally, Bangladesh, to interview former university students who lived through the activism of the 1940s, the 1947 Partition, and the university's adjustment to independence in its wake.

Starting in the university, this study follows the paths of the students who settled throughout the region. It crosses the boundaries of India, Pakistan, and Bangladesh to uncover histories of partition as yet unheard. As my travels and interviews transcended the political geography of partition, a variety of unexpected histories emerged. I was surprised to discover narratives of trauma from those who never left, who never migrated far from home. Rather, narrators revealed that alienation from the safety of familiar places disrupted their expectations of belonging. These oral histories constitute a fresh partition archive that is defined, not by borders and migrations, but by disturbances within networks of relationships that were rooted in place. They revealed that whether a place was disturbed was not necessarily tied to physical violence, but to the disruption of relationships and community patterns that gave place meaning. These histories encourage a framing of partition that draws attention to the ways narrators experienced ongoing changes associated with what I will call "partitioning"—the process through which familiar spaces and places became strange and sometimes threatening—and they highlight specific, never-before-studied sites of disturbance distant from the borders.

The seventy oral history narratives I collected from AMU students now settled in India, Pakistan, and Bangladesh convinced me that, to understand the contemporary challenges of national belonging that Muslims face in South Asia, it is vital to consider the impact of the 1947 Partition of India and creation of Pakistan. Seventy years after independence, Muslims—who constitute India's largest minority, but Pakistan and Bangladesh's majority populations—must compete for political space and influence throughout the region. Despite their centrality to the politics that forced the partition, Muslim voices remain silenced in scholarship that focuses overwhelmingly on Hindus displaced from Pakistan areas.

The AMU and its students were integral to the creation of Muslim nationalism from its earliest days. By the 1940s, the students were serving as advocates for Pakistan, and they experienced the disruptions of partition, despite their distance from the newly created borders. These narrators came of age and built their lives under the circumstances this partitioning created. They were partition's first generation, and are now the oldest living generation in South Asia.[10] Their stories differ substantially from existing partition histories in that they illuminate repercussions throughout the region, not just on the borders. These stories also offer new insight into the enduring impact of partitioning on the lives of South Asian Muslims. The oral histories I collected over five years and that I explore in the following pages demonstrate that, for South Asian Muslims, partitioning has been a profoundly local experience that has left people feeling displaced on all sides of the borders.

I am deeply indebted to those who shared their stories. They kindly welcomed me into their homes and bequeathed their histories. Many have since passed away, and I feel their loss personally and intellectually. There are many more questions that I wish I had asked, but I hope that by preserving their voices, I have honored the legacy of their individual experiences. As an oral historian, I am a part of every interview I conducted. The narrators shared their stories, but I applied an interpretive lens in the hopes of drawing out meaning from their memories. My interpretation may only be one of many, and since the interviews are archived at the Louie B. Nunn Center for Oral History at the University of Kentucky Libraries, they are available for others to discover.[11] Inevitably, when they are read under different historical circumstances, the anxieties and meanings that seemed so important to the narrators and to me will appear different—and indeed they will be different. The oral history interview is a co-created historical document. The narrators generously shared their experiences, their memories, and their truths with me. The analysis here and its flaws are mine.

Introduction

When violence occupies the center of partition history, as it has in the rich body of historiography that has emerged since the late 1990s, all migration appears to have occurred by compulsion.[1] By contrast, in AMU, the disruption of partitioning was distinct from the actual experience of violence, but intimately connected to the *fear of violence* and the disturbance of a sense of belonging. In oral histories, AMU students narrated these disruptions through descriptions of specific campus spaces that suddenly felt unsafe. They detailed fears about how they imagined that the university would be unable to extend its protections to the students, especially as Muslim authority would inevitably diminish in the wake of Indian independence. The disruption of this power left them feeling exposed and vulnerable throughout the process of partitioning, and these feelings guided their choices about migration. In AMU, partition disrupted the "institutional underpinnings of everyday life," leaving students disoriented. Dreams were both realized and deferred, familiar worlds were rendered strange, and as new sources of authority replaced traditional ones, safe places became threatening.[2]

The August 1947 Partition of India that accompanied independence from British colonization created the new state of Pakistan, initially apportioned into East and West wings. By 1971, the fledgling Pakistan had fractured into the two independent states of Pakistan and Bangladesh, and so the end of empire in India set off a chain of events that have had a profound effect on all of the citizens of South Asian states. Typically, these events have been narrated through a restricted geography and set of images. The enduring picture is of Punjab, and sometimes Delhi, wracked by senseless violence, train massacres, abduction, rape, and betrayal. Disbelief that such violence could occur runs through many narratives. Scholars frequently characterize the partition as a singular event, a *moment* of violence in which communal passions overwrote the idealized history of peaceful coexistence between communities. To examine the 1947 Partition merely as a moment in history denies it historical continuity and context, and places it outside the pale of South Asian history.[3] Everything that predated the moment of division, including the independence movements that necessitated it, and everything that followed, including the 1971 independence of Bangladesh, must then belong to distinct historical narratives.[4] A reconceptualization of partitioning, with attention to continuities and not just cleavages, creates space to examine the various communities who experienced what historian Vazira Zamindar has called a "long partition," which, in many respects, is ongoing.[5] In the oral histories I collected from former AMU students, the process of partitioning began in March 1946 and continued to shape their everyday lives some seventy years later.

During the months of violence that spanned the early years of partitioning, millions of people fled their homes in fear of losing their lives. Political and communal violence swept through North India in waves, beginning in August 1946 in Calcutta, Bihar, and Noakhali; in March 1947, it exploded in Rawalpindi, and by late summer the flames of communal violence whipped through Lahore, Amritsar, and Delhi. In 1950, violence overwhelmed communities in East Pakistan and drove many Hindus into India.[6] By this time, throughout the region, many had witnessed violence directly, while others certainly were aware of its threat. Tens of thousands of women became victims of sexual violence, abduction, and rape, and many still bear its physical and emotional scars.[7]

Stories retold by groups of people who migrated for other reasons, whose lives also were disturbed by partition's refiguring of states, help us to develop an ever more complex understanding of the partition experience. These stories also reveal much about other sites of disturbance. As David Gilmartin has suggested, the problems associated with narrating partition should encourage historians to "place the tension between multiple realities and the production of shared moral meaning at the very heart of the partition story."[8] These are the multiple realities of partition: even as people fled for their lives, others considered their career choices, examined their options, and imagined their futures. Arthur Kleinman has argued in *Violence and Subjectivity*, the volume he coedited with Veena Das, that the violence of everyday life—structural violence—affects people throughout social hierarchies, not just the poor or marginalized. For this reason, Kleinman argues for a more inclusive concept of "everyday violences" that incorporates an examination of social disruption and the trauma of delegitimization by state practices.[9] These social processes breed fear, and living with terror "not far below the surface of the ordinary" can fuel rage, cowardice, and even betrayal, Kleinman contends. In the AMU environment, though the narrators whose stories I preserved did not speak directly of trauma, the patterns through which they narrated their experiences of partition clearly demonstrated the social dislocation and alienation typical of traumatic experience. Whether they chose to migrate or not, partition's disruptions continued to resonate in their narratives, even if they experienced no actual violence.

Distant from the borders, AMU persists as a key site of partition, not because of its location but because of its meaning *as a place*. Located only ninety miles from New Delhi, India's modern capital and the historic center of Muslim rule, AMU was a key site of development for a distinctly Muslim nationalism and home to many leading intellectuals and reformers. In the years leading up to Indian independence and partition, it was a hub of pro-Pakistan activism. As a result of Partition, its population, too, was divided by the boundaries that separated India and Pakistan. Many students, staff, and faculty migrated to Pakistan to pursue the promises of the Muslim homeland envisioned by the All-India Muslim League. Despite widespread enthusiasm for Pakistan at the university, however, most of those associated with AMU remained in India. From there, they had to learn to navigate Indian independence as members of India's largest minority community, whose loyalty was cast in the shadows by that looming "Muslim homeland" on both India's Western and Eastern borders (until 1971). In particular, students carried with them the experiences, values, and histories that had defined their lives at AMU, a self-consciously Muslim environment surrounded by a non-Muslim majority. They experienced the independence and partition of India and Pakistan as a dynamic interaction of local and national priorities, of public and private worlds.[10] Drawn from oral histories and oral geographies, this study explores an archive of lived experiences that links contemporary challenges of belonging in South Asia with the disturbance of particular sites of meaning before, during and after the 1947 Partition.[11]

Though scholars have been collecting oral histories from partition survivors for two decades, the oral narratives I collected shed new light on our understanding of partition in several ways. They record Muslim voices, which are discernible only faintly in most partition historiography. As I detail below, the effort to collect oral histories originated in Delhi and Indian scholars have established the field. Among the earliest investigators, Urvashi Butalia recounts her visit to Pakistan but she did not systematically collect oral histories there; in *Remembering Partition* Gyan Pandey notes the impossibility of securing a visa for Pakistan. The realities of a partitioned subcontinent weigh heavily on our field. As recently as 2014, Devika Chawla acknowledged that until she hired a Muslim driver to transport her to interview appointments with Hindus displaced from Pakistan in 1947, she had "never spent this much time in the company of Muslims."[12] Her driver came from a Muslim family that did not migrate in 1947, but during her childhood in India, she rarely, if ever, interacted with Muslims, and she had extremely limited knowledge of Muslim Indian experience, even within the city of Delhi, where Muslim monuments decorate the landscape.

The narratives I collected also preserve experiences that, in the absence of violence, find no place in official or even institutional archives. During periods of disruption, the absence of violence may not be notable enough to be preserved. Only when there is an expectation of noise does quiet merit attention.[13] While most histories of partition focus on its disruptive violence and displacements, these narratives focus on lives affected by "everyday violences" of other kinds that rendered familiar places suddenly strange. Additionally, they focus on places not typically included as sites of partition because they are far from the borders drawn in 1947 and 1971. Instead of a border, the site of partition might be a cinema, a railway car, or even a medium-sized town in the hinterlands. Rather than focusing on those periods of upheaval easily identified by mass migration or warfare, these narratives trace the longer processes of partitioning that made partition feel necessary to young Muslim men, and that continue to affect their lived experience and daily lives throughout the subcontinent. Given the increasing marginalization of Muslims in India, their experiences often occupy center-stage in this analysis. These narratives of partitioning are part of longer life histories that reveal that AMU students sought to navigate partition's challenges as they simultaneously faced their own decisions about their futures and adopted new roles in the transition from child to adult and from subject to citizen in the three new states that emerged out of the 1947 independence from Britain: India, Pakistan, and Bangladesh.

AMU students emerged as a segment of a larger group that was caught in the middle of the vociferous state-making that lay at the heart of the partition drama: the Muslims. The "Muslim Question" presented the central conflict of the independence movement and the stumbling block in the negotiations that forced the partition in the first place. How should the state deal with a substantial minority population (linked at least nominally by their shared faith), who felt entitled to a share of power, but who would be marginalized demographically in a parliamentary democracy? The solution to this conflict was, ostensibly, the creation of Pakistan, an outcome that means that Indian independence cannot be separated from Indian partition. However, that solution not only failed to answer the Muslim Question (for those Muslims who remained in India) but also spawned a whole new set of Muslim questions for both India and Pakistan. Yet, the voices of Muslims are silenced in many histories of partition that center on violently traumatic narratives of those who migrated from Pakistan areas and who witnessed, even if not personally, the seemingly senseless violence plaguing Punjab and Delhi.[14] These narratives of displacement highlight the "vivisection" of India and often fail to investigate other experiences and repercussions of India's partitioning, ones that may not have been driven by physical violence or forced migration. As Joya Chatterji has pointed out, these ground-level histories continue to focus overwhelmingly on the border in Punjab to the exclusion of the unique circumstances in the Bengal borderland.[15] I would add that these histories fail to account for any site beyond Delhi that is not a border at all.

The foundational academic works on partition, which prominently feature oral histories, tend to focus on "high profile" and "disturbed" places like Delhi and Punjab. However, people living in places that may not have been as wracked dramatically by violence faced significant choices about belonging, nonetheless.[16] Whether a place was "disturbed" by partition was not only about physical violence but also about the rearrangement of community patterns and the introduction of new forces and new faces into these communities that changed the ways in which they operated. These kinds of changes were obvious in places like Amritsar, Lahore, and Delhi, but they also took place in Aligarh and in the towns in the United Provinces (now Uttar Pradesh (UP)) from which many AMU students came.[17] The disturbances that began in the mid-1940s disrupted their sense of place as individuals and as a collective community in India and continue to affect them today in both their lived experiences and memories.[18] AMU remains a "high-profile" site of Muslim organization, but scholars have neglected to examine it as a critical site of partition. This is due in part to the fact that, as every former student of that era told me: there was no violence in AMU.[19] This did not limit partition's impact, for as Bangladeshi scholar Meghna Guha Thakurta has suggested, the "fear of being dispossessed [and] the fear of not belonging" caused people to flee, even if they had not witnessed a single act of violence.[20] As a site for examining the disturbances of partition, AMU was a place that defined and was defined by a group of Muslims whose community was and remains deeply disturbed by the changes partition wrought.

By decentering Punjab as the dominant site of partition, other partition stories have the chance to emerge. The question of choice, for instance, looks entirely different in cities that did not emerge as sites of significant violence. In 1947, when Aligarh native and graduate Wajahat Husain, then a "one pipper," a lowly Indian Army second lieutenant, had the option of choosing between India and Pakistan, he shared, "Well, to be honest, I thought that there was probably very little future in the Indian Army as a Muslim. Well, probably [that] may or may not be wrong, but that was the impression."[21] Wajahat felt his family's fortunes decline after 1938, and he sought to establish a strong basis for his own career.²² Based on their religious background, soldiers in the army and other government servants were offered a choice as to whether to "opt" for settling in India or Pakistan. Muslims who resided in areas that would become India could opt for service to either state, as could Hindus who lived in areas allotted to Pakistan. However, Hindus in India and Muslims in Pakistan would be naturalized to that state: they were offered no other options. Guha Thakurta has noted that, for many, there was a matter of conscious choice. Many families whose members worked in government service "were given the option to take up equivalent work on the other side. Some families, however, had to decide in a very short period of time, so that people who exercised the option also had to reach a hurried decision."²³ My interviews revealed, too, that the entire family could be affected by one member's decision. Wajahat returned to Aligarh in an army truck to collect his family and convinced them to board it before daybreak. In contrast, Ather Siddiqi's elder brother was an active Muslim League partisan who left for Pakistan, but his father "was a government servant and he didn't want his second son, only two sons, to go."²⁴ Though his brother and later his sister and parents settled there, Ather Siddiqi never migrated to Pakistan. The borders of the states divided his family permanently.

AMU Professor Emeritus Irfan Habib, who is an Aligarh native, albeit not an AMU graduate, suggested that opportunism motivated educated Muslims to leave for Pakistan. According to him, they had "the idea that they [would] get high posts in Pakistan . . . they would get recorded property of Hindus in Sindh, and if they were Punjabis, in Punjab. That had begun to have its own attraction."²⁵ Nevertheless, once the Indian state developed public sector engineering services, he told me, this sort of relocation came to a halt. Indeed, Zafar Mohammad Khan recalled that, since he got a job in the Public Works Department after he passed out of AMU in 1955, he never considered Pakistan (though two of his sisters migrated for marriage).²⁶ Pakistani narrators, particularly those who graduated with engineering degrees prior to the late 1950s, detailed an almost identical chronology of events. Those who graduated later located jobs in India and pursued successful careers in the public service sector. Thus, Indian narrators recognized the attraction of Pakistan as a suitable location for career advancement, and Habib even recognized the difficulty India encountered in their efforts to provide equally appealing employment opportunities. However, those who remained in AMU as professors felt a powerful affinity with the university. Accordingly, they felt privileged that they had been able to stay.²⁷

On all sides of the borders, narrators constructed self-justifying narratives that linked their own experiences to that of the state. While conducting interviews, I did not encounter moments of outright regret, like those documented by Butalia, Guha Thakurta, and Zamindar. Nevertheless, many accounts reflected a tinge of disappointment. Because I approach the question of "choice" seriously, I also interrogate narrators' choices for signs of coercion. Women's choices, in particular, were often circumscribed by their family's desire to see them well-married at a time when so many educated and eligible young Muslim men had relocated to Pakistan.²⁸ Among the narrators who participated in my oral history research, only one participant described his family being "forced" out of his home in the Western UP city of Saharanpur.²⁹ A few others mentioned riots, including Ather Siddiqi, also from Saharanpur, Zahida

Zaidi from Delhi, and several from Meerut. But even Siddiqi described his family's relocation to Moradabad (farther east in UP) as a "migration" rather than an escape.[30]

Scholars certainly have begun to publish more nuanced and expansive accounts of partition experience. Rita Kothari's *Unbordered Memories* incorporates the voices of Sindhi Hindus into the canon through the short stories of partition survivors, a project complemented by Natasha Raheja's growing "Sindhi Voices" oral history collection.[31] Joya Chatterji and Uditi Sen draw attention to displacements in the Bengal borderland, and Sen has also pursued the histories of Bengalis resettled in the Andaman Islands.[32] Additionally, Anna Bigelow argues that, in the town of Malerkotla, in Indian Punjab, residents have invested deeply in a narrative of *bhaichara*, or brotherly affection, which challenges the narrative of communal hatred and violence that characterizes many partition discussions.[33] Through his ground-level exploration of partition in Sialkot and Gujranwala, Ilyas Chattha's *Partition and Locality* also offers much-needed specificity to the experience of partition in the Pakistani Punjab.[34] Ranabir Samaddar's edited collection, *Reflections on Partition in the East*, highlights the linguistic and cultural connections between East Bengali Hindus and Muslims that span the national boundaries.[35] Meanwhile, Pippa Virdee has observed that partition historiography tends to neglect Pakistan, and Pakistani women, especially. Her own work on Pakistan addresses this gap, and Pakistani scholars, such as Furrukh Khan and Nighat Said Khan, also focus on the often-marginalized voices of women.[36] Ravinder Kaur and Devika Chawla have investigated the Punjabi refugee experience in Delhi, and their work reveals how individuals and families continue to cope with partition's transformations over the course of several generations.[37] Many of these studies address the particular histories of local places and the ways in which the destabilizing uncertainty of partition altered them. The picture of partition grows increasingly complex, as the Punjab borderland comes to mark only one of many sites of partition experience.

Partitioning therefore must include more than the official history of boundary creation and the division of assets—more than the history of unbridled violence. The history of the subcontinent's partitioning also must include a history of the Muslim nationalist movement that inspired young, elite Muslims to fight elections for Muslim candidates, as Mohammad Ali Jinnah implored, "even if they be lamp posts."[38] Furthermore, it is critical that scholars begin to interpret the students' activism historically, and to take seriously the possibilities that the demand for Pakistan suggested to them *at the time*. We must also separate student activism from its outcome: the creation of Pakistan. The creation of Pakistan held long-standing implications for all South Asians, especially Muslims, and the Partition altered boundaries among and between communities, not just states. To access these histories, I have pursued stories beyond the archives and have discovered a rich source of meaning in oral history narratives.

Oral History and Partition

In the 1990s, scholars endeavored to collect oral histories of partition, hoping their work would serve as a corrective to the official, sanitized histories that documented high-level diplomacy, political negotiations, and military activity. Two early works, by an Indian Judge (1949) and a British government official (1961), initiated the effort to represent on-the-ground experiences of partition survivors. While they sought to quantify and describe the carnage of partition and its resulting migrations, they nonetheless conveyed a sense that a reader was looking down on the bloodbath from above.[39] Apart from these, the first Indian remembrances to emerge out of partition were unofficial ones. These include the many short stories and poems that explore the issue of partition and its associated violence, and which also acknowledge the terrifying inconsistencies and disruptions that public officials were unwilling or unable to see.[40] Fictional stories comprised the only narratives that expressed people's ambivalence toward the decision to divide the country, until researchers including Urvashi Butalia, Ritu Menon, Kamla Bhasin, and Gyanendra Pandey began to collect oral histories more systematically. The sentiments and memories narrators shared betray but little connection to the activities and priorities of the leaders who negotiated the end of empire. Oral histories filled the historical record with lived experiences and represented the first public efforts by scholars and survivors to make sense of partition and its violence. They have inserted much-needed South Asian voices into the imperial histories of what the British have called the "Transfer of Power."[41]

Scholars pursued these efforts as a direct response to the eruption of violence that targeted Sikhs following the 1984 assassination of Prime Minister Indira Gandhi at the hands of one of her Sikh bodyguards. Delhi-based scholars immediately connected the anti-Sikh violence to the riots of 1947, wherein people were targeted for their religious identities (arbitrarily and not always accurately).[42] The recognition of this continuity between the present and the past triggered a sense of déjà vu for these scholars, yet their inquiries have exposed partition's ruptures primarily. These histories seek to understand the sources of partition's disturbances and the consequences of the rupture in moral continuity that sustained the violence. Through their scholarship, partition became "Partition," monolithic and unique.[43]

In contrast, I examine the continuities that persisted throughout the experience of partitioning, which still is unfolding, more than seventy years later. The narratives I have collected respond dynamically to past and present circumstances and point to a variety of experience not typically included in earlier studies. They belie interpretation that focuses on Partition as a unique and terrible event that occurred primarily in Punjab and Delhi. For this latter reason, I explore the construction and disruption of sites of meaning in and around AMU. Narrators' strategies of remembrance illustrate how the meaning of the university and the surrounding sites determined the nature of partition's disruptions for AMU students. The stories they shared were marked by concerted efforts (and the sometimes failure of those efforts) to create continuity between the present and the past. It is clear that they hoped to place their own experiences within a historical context that illuminated the conditions under which they lived during the time they participated in the interviews. As narrators described and defined their pasts, they also described and defined themselves in relation to that past.

Oral histories, like documentary and archival sources, serve as a permanent record of the past.[44] Well-designed oral history interviews rely upon careful research, and must be interpreted as a source for understanding the past. Still, the production of personal history in oral histories is a process that is both deeply rooted in past experiences and reflective of present ones. It is both "cumulative and presentist."[45] Therefore, the refashioning of the past is both continuous with it (determined by the nature of past experience) and constructive of it (recast by present circumstances). As oral historians have long argued, "subjectivity is as much the business of history as the more visible 'facts.'"[46] That is to say, in oral history, the importance of historical facts lies in their meaning to the narrator. The fact that they believe and remember certain experiences as true is as significant as "what really happened," even as much as the facts stashed away in archives or recorded in newspapers.[47] For this reason, oral history brings both depth and breadth to historical understanding by opening up the events that make up the conscious past of individuals and communities.

When I first began to collect oral histories of partition experience from among former AMU students, I constantly had to remember that memory is not a straightforward source of historical knowledge. As my oral history collection grew between 2005 and 2010, I reckoned with the ways in which the stories narrators recounted were different from those in the existing scholarship. Indeed, my first interviews in Pakistan left me feeling disappointed and frustrated, as narrators "failed" to incorporate the standard topics of partition historiography: border violence, displacement, and train journeys. But when I really began to consider them in full, I discovered many similar themes, which participants recast in the context of AMU and as part of the transformations in daily life that partition caused for Muslims, even if they had not experienced the violence of the borders.[48] Rather, these oral histories connected partition's meaning to the long process of mobilization that brought independence to the subcontinent, and to the formation of Muslim nationalism that motivated the demand for a separate Pakistan. Furthermore, they contextualized these concerns within the rich context of life at AMU. These oral narratives provided rich material in which to search for moral meaning, "shared" or otherwise, causing me to view Indian, Pakistani, and Bangladeshi independence within the context of shifting boundaries of community and belonging, and not just as the outcomes of lines too hastily etched on a map. To make sense of their true meaning, I had to gaze through the political lenses that narrators used—sometimes communitarian, sometimes communal, both individual and collective—to understand how Muslims saw themselves and to see how others regarded them throughout the subcontinent.

Though personal narratives might seem to belie the existence of collective memory, in fact, "collective memory is the framework in which historical remembering occurs."[49] In fact, argues Susan Crane, relying on Maurice Halbwachs, "'what remains' has more to do with who is acting as a witness and who is remembering lived experience than it does with whether a narrative adequately sums up a historical event."[50] Therefore, the "who" of history determines both the "what" and the "why." Michel-Rolph Trouillot has argued that "the collective subjects who supposedly remember [the past] did not exist as such at the time of the events they claim to remember. Rather, their constitution as subjects goes hand in hand with the continuous creation of the past."[51] In the narratives I collected, at the moment narrators incorporated themselves into a group—here, the Muslim community embodied in AMU—they formed self-justifying narratives based on that group and began to use its memories and language to define their outlooks.

The creation of new states altered that subjectivity by introducing citizenship, and my interpretation thus warranted a continuous reading, because the subjectivity of Muslims in AMU and throughout the subcontinent still is being constituted through the process of partitioning. The role of Muslims in the struggle for freedom, the fight for independence, the pursuit of liberation, and the definition of citizenship in the three post-1947 states that emerged from the former British India is far from settled (as I explore in greater detail in the Epilogue).

By looking at the shared formative university experience of AMU graduates, who have contributed so much to the trajectory of South Asian history, I examine the points of convergence and divergence in their stories, which illuminate the demands of the process of partitioning. Ultimately, the slippage evident in the stories they shared regarding personal, communal, and national memory serves to highlight the "multiple realities" of partitioning. The national stories that these narrators applied to their experiences during and after 1947 make it possible to examine the same story through multiple lenses. Thus, it is possible to discern a continuity of priorities and values between stories and across borders, even as the discontinuities caused by the drawing of boundaries may be impossible to ignore. When the temporal and spatial framework expands, South Asian partitioning emerges more clearly as a set of lived experiences. This allows a shift away from a few high-profile sites, where partition may appear as an anomalous moment, inconsistent with a narrative of national realization and state formation (as it appears in India), or as a triumphal accomplishment marked by heroic sacrifice (as it appears in Pakistan). These oral histories suggest that it might be both and neither, less and more. They expose the fact that how those who lived through partition continue to perceive it may be as significant to historical understanding of it as the events that transpired and that have been defined "Partition."[52] In remembered histories, partition appears "incomplete,"[53] "conjured,"[54] exclusive, placed, gendered,[55] bigoted, vital, temporary,[56] "ever-present,"[57] failed, promising, inevitable, and accidental, but certainly not singular.[58] These histories bring into view the complexities of partition's multiple realities.

Voices from Aligarh Muslim University

As I detailed in the Preface, I initiated my interviews in 2005 in Lahore, when I first interviewed Major General (retired) Wajahat Husain, my great uncle. Through him, I met others of his generation who filled in my scholarly understanding of the university's significance with their own stories. I followed as many leads as I could, often cold-calling by phone or in-person to set up a visit. Between 2005 and 2008, I traveled twice to Karachi, where I met many former Aligarh students of partition's first generation, including the founders of the Sir Syed University of Engineering and Technology. Thereafter, I visited Islamabad and Rawalpindi, where I engaged with the founders of the Sir Syed Memorial Society. I spent hours visiting with and interviewing the scholars at the Nazaria-e-Pakistan Foundation in Lahore. Though they were not AMU graduates, they have dedicated their scholarly endeavors to understanding the history and meaning of Pakistan. In 2009, I lived in Aligarh,

Lucknow, and Delhi, where I researched in the archives of the university and met many AMU graduates through the vibrant online communities of AMUNetwork and WorldofAligs.[59] By 2010, I understood that it was vital to incorporate the story of East Pakistan into my research. I traveled to Bangladesh and worked closely with the Aligarh Old Boys' Association to locate individuals who had graduated during the 1940s and 1950s. Everywhere I went, in loosely structured interviews, I first asked narrators to establish the details of their life histories. We talked, often over a cup of tea, about their backgrounds and childhoods, how they made their way to Aligarh (both literally and figuratively). They subsequently shared their memories of partition and its aftermath, the challenges they faced, how they decided where to live and which career options to pursue.

In the earliest interviews I conducted in 2005 and 2006 with narrators in Pakistan, participants appeared quite keen on helping me understand the entire trajectory of Pakistan history. They wanted to ensure that I collected the "correct" story.[60] In these interviews, I found myself interrogating narrators about how they related to their own history. When did Pakistan's history begin? What type of monument should commemorate Partition and Independence? During the five months I lived in Aligarh, I spent my days in the archive of the Maulana Azad Library and my evenings in conversation. My interviews were more driven by an attempt to understand the atmosphere of the university during the 1940s and 1950s. Therefore, I posed many questions about each person's participation in university and political activities. This was when I came to understand the diversity of political opinion and allegiance in AMU, both during the period I was researching and today. And while conducting interviews in Bangladesh, I was curious to learn about how AMU received the Bengali/Sylheti students, how they coped in their new surroundings, and how life changed for them after 1947. As such, each body of interviews projects a distinctly different texture. While my own interests determined my initial questions, I learned to listen and follow up on the topics that seemed most important *to them*. From the interviews, I learned to see partition differently, to recognize its broader geography and longer scope, and reframe its continuities and its ruptures.

As a researcher, I am grateful to those who opened their homes and shared their histories with me. I remain deeply concerned with their personhood, and I recognize that they may appear as unlikely candidates to narrate oral histories of partition. Scholars who typically rely upon oral history as a research methodology tend to emphasize the experiences of underrepresented groups whose voices are absent in dominant narratives, particularly women, and those of lower social and economic status. In that sense, oral history is a social justice practice; its aim is to restore marginalized voices to history. Partition oral history has focused overwhelmingly on recovering the stories of women and people residing in places that have been affected by the violence that Gyan Pandey has argued *was* Partition.[61] By contrast, the narrators in my study are mostly elite, educated men who were unmolested by partition's ravaging violence. However, what has emerged clearly since I launched the project are the ways in which the intersectional nature of their identities has determined their trajectories so completely. No matter what their political affiliation, social or economic status, or geographic location, they were always *Muslims*, and therefore, they were required to examine their circumstances very carefully in 1947.⁶² Suddenly, however, those circumstances were dramatically altered by whether they chose to settle in India, Pakistan, or Bangladesh. On the surface, it may appear that migration to the Muslim majority state would solve problems of belonging, but within the boundaries of those three nation states, narrators still had to navigate a delicate web of identities and allegiances as they came of age. Their stories have been absent in the historiography. Moving with the privilege of a foreign citizen, I crossed the borders created in 1947 and 1971 to collect them. Indeed, no other single study of partition and independence includes such an international collective.

This group of individuals emerged from the tightly regulated social, educational, and political environment of AMU at a formative time in their lives and in the histories of their various nations and states. AMU thus persists as the central organizational node of analysis, though among these narrators many identities persisted within this collectivity. When I started interviewing, I expected nationality and national narratives—allegiance to the state narratives of India, Pakistan, and Bangladesh—to define these groups, but each individual narrative bears the imprint of many different attachments. In addition to those obvious divisions, groups were defined further by the political perspectives they held in their youth—the leftists at AMU, for instance— by their experiences of partition, or by their individual choices to remain attached in some way to the university (or to establish a life separate from it).⁶³ How each imagined their place within these collectivities affected how they remembered their experiences during the disruptions of partitioning. Their identities are relational, determined through experience, memory, and comparison. It is critical to understand who these narrators are and what drew them together.⁶⁴

First, they are Muslim.⁶⁵ For some, Islam defined a religious practice, and for others, Islam encompassed a collectivity with which Muslims felt a sense of commonality. Arguably, self-definition as Muslim transcends one's personal faith, though the sense of "belonging" to a Muslim collectivity undoubtedly affected the decisions of these interview participants to attend AMU in the first place, as well as their experiences during and after their tenure at the university. Yasmin Saikia, in her ethnography of the Abdullah Hall of the Women's College, goes so far as to call it "religion-neutral."⁶⁶ Despite the centrality of "Muslim-ness" to the university's name and identity, only two narrators spoke at any length about experiencing any personal religiosity during their time in AMU: the leftist professor of history Iqtidar Alam Khan who said he would "go to the mosque and pray there and give *azan* also," but, later disavowed this behavior; and Zafar Mohammad Khan who told me he was a "regular goer to the mosque" because he was interested in reading and translating the Qur'an.⁶⁷ Instead, many others described their efforts to evade the religious regulation in AMU. Wajahat Husain explained that, while there was only one mosque, Sunni and Shi'i prayers were separated. "The students used to say, 'Which session are you attending? Are you going to the first show or the second show?' The first show used to be the Sunni congregation the second show used to be the Shi'a congregation."⁶⁸ This mischievous description upends the perception that AMU students were religiously inclined. Mosque attendance was an obligation they fulfilled, as and when it fit into their lives. Still, during our interviews, however, in both India and Pakistan, many narrators used religiously charged language and some made a special effort to demonstrate their devotion or describe its importance in their adult lives.[69]

Second, they are Aligs.[70] They each attended the AMU or its affiliated institutions (including the Women's College) during the 1940s and 1950s.[71] Almost all of the narrators shared the experience of residential life in AMU. The residential system was a unique institution in India, core to the AMU identity. Those who were nonresidents (day scholars like Irfan Habib, Wajahat Husain, and Iqbal Shafi) were formally affiliated with residence halls, and they also understood the significance and dynamics of the residential experience. Though the female narrators did not attend AMU as full-time students, they attended under various schemes of separation and integration over this time period, with many residing in Abdullah Hall in the Aligarh Women's College and attending postgraduate classes at the university (like Zahida Zaidi and Saeeda Kidwai).[72] Whether male or female, during their stay at the university, almost all of these narrators possessed an awareness of the political changes afoot in the country. Generally, they concurred that the Muslim League agenda was broadly persuasive at AMU, though many denied sympathy for its utopian ideals.

In the tradition of the institution's founder, Sir Sayyid Ahmad Khan, most of the narrators originated from families who were in government service (including Ather Siddiqi, Masood-ul Hasan, Mohiuddin Khan, and Waheeduddin Choudhri) or landholding, some of whom possessed massive estates, such as Riazur Rahman Sherwani. Others held small estates, like Majid Ali Siddiqi and M. A. Rashid.[73] Only two narrators were born into families where education represented the main profession, such as Iqbal Shafi and Irfan Habib.[74] Many became educators and professors, including Asloob Ahmad Ansari, Ather Siddiqi, Fatima Fari Rahman, Iftikhar and Iqtidar Alam, Irfan Habib, Masood-ul Hasan, Saeeda Kidwai, Shahid Rashid, Wazir Ahmad Razzaqi, and Zahida Zaidi. Few stemmed from families with military backgrounds (the police was more common), though many of the narrators themselves served in the military, particularly those I interviewed in Pakistan. Many first served in the British Indian Army and later in the Pakistan Services, including Major Generals Ghulam Umar and Wajahat Husain, Brigadier General Iqbal Shafi, and Wing Commander Baaquie, among others. In East Pakistan, Habibur Rahman tried to join the Pakistan Air Force in 1949, in the hopes of becoming a pilot, but, weighing only ninety pounds, he was deemed too small! He subsequently pursued a career in law. Abdul Rasheed Khan revealed that he was the first in his family to opt out of police service, though he did remain in government service, and he retired from the Karachi Development Authority. At the time of our interview, he was serving on the engineering faculty at Sir Syed University of Engineering and Technology, an institution the Pakistan AMU Old Boys' Association established in 1993. Many of these informants worked as professional engineers, and whereas the men who served in the military resided primarily in Pakistan and the professors primarily in India,[75] engineers resided in all three countries. Among those who lived in Pakistan were Abdul Rasheed Khan, Z. A. Nizami, and Zakir Ali Khan; in Bangladesh, Mohiuddin Khan, Salahuddin Choudhury, and Engineer Waheedudin Choudhri; in India, Ahmad Saeed, Majid Ali Siddiqi, and Syed Saghir Ahmad Rizvi. Whether they resided in India or Pakistan, the women I interviewed were primarily educators. These included

Fatima Fari Rahman, Saeeda Kidwai, Zakia Siddiqi, and Zahida Zaidi (who was also well known as a poet).

The few women I interviewed had attended the Aligarh Women's College, which Sheikh Abdullah originally founded in 1906. Despite the protestations of Sir Sayyid Ahmad Khan against women's education, in 1937, the college became an accredited undergraduate institution and an affiliate of AMU. By the late 1930s, women had begun to participate in postgraduate classes on the men's campus. Although AMU boasted Her Highness Nawab Sultan Jehan Begum of Bhopal as its first chancellor, it was not until after partition that the university finally admitted women. Known to everyone as Saeeda Apa, Saeeda Kidwai was the first woman to attend postgraduate geography courses. Kidwai graduated from AMU in 1939, during the first convocation to include women.[76] Today, there are many women studying there, though in 2014, the vice chancellor restricted female undergraduate students from using the university's Maulana Azad Library, and women are now segregated in certain reading rooms with more limited hours than those available for their male peers.[77] Though much has changed in AMU since the 1940s, women's education has never been central to AMU's corporate life. Women's hostels remain spatially marginalized as was true when Abdullah Hall, two and a half kilometers from AMU's center, was the only option for female students.

Though advancing in age, each narrator could recall vividly the events of 1947, and, for many, the moment of decision—whether to pursue their futures in India or Pakistan—marked a critical turning point in their lives. Of the seventy-two individuals I personally interviewed, thirty-two chose Pakistan between 1947 and 1965 (two originally hailed from Lahore), with the majority relocating between 1947 and 1948. Following family members who had settled in Pakistan and urged them to come, others migrated later.[78] Some of the women migrated after they married men in Pakistan (who may have had roots and family connections in UP).[79]

Another twenty-eight narrators chose not to leave India. Many of these individual never supported the idea of Pakistan, as was true for professors Irfan Habib and Riazur Rahman Sherwani. For some, family circumstances (such as an attachment to land or community, or a father's attachment to Congress nationalism), or their own nonage prevented them from making an independent decision, as in the cases of professors Ather Siddiqi and Masood-ul Hasan. Among these twenty-eight existed a significant divide that colored their perspectives on many of the issues we discussed: on one side were those who remained in Aligarh and attached to the university; on the other were those who located employment beyond Aligarh's protective boundaries. Seventeen have remained close to the institution. Among those who remained in Aligarh, many repeatedly talked about how lucky they were to be there and about how, once employed as AMU faculty, they were set and didn't have to worry about their futures (Ather Siddiqi, Masood-ul Hasan). Eleven lived in Lucknow and New Delhi, where many worked as engineers, scientists, or educators. Those outside of Aligarh seemed more willing to discuss the adversity Indian Muslims face in independent India (such as Ahmad Rashid, Majid Ali Siddiqi, Mohammad Amin, and Saghir Ahmad Rizvi).[80]

Finally, there was a small group who settled in East Pakistan—the majority of them were ethnic Bengalis or Sylhetis—and these narrators later supported Bangladeshi independence. Their ethnicity marked a difference not only in their post-1947 experience, but it also meant that their identity in Aligarh was objectively different from those students (and narrators for this study) who largely hailed from the Urdu-speaking areas of UP.[81] The former students who were of Bengali heritage offered a unique perspective on the culture of tolerance and brotherhood at the university, and while they generally remembered their experience positively, they were aware of "difference" in a way that Urdu-speaking, *roti*-eating UP-*wallas* were not.[82]

Throughout this analysis, one or two narrators potentially represent the different groups cited earlier; their intersecting identities means that the definition of these groups is in some ways fluid. The Muslim identity itself means different things to different people. While, in the case of my interview participants from AMU, there may have been an expectation that they remain observant, Irfan Habib has reminded the Indian public in an interview with the online newspaper *Scroll.in* that even the All-India Muslim League, the political party that commanded the allegiance of many at AMU, "was not orthodox. They were communal, but not religious."[83] In addition, some East Pakistanis shared leftist sympathies with their North Indian fellows, but shifted to Pakistan, nonetheless. It is key to recognize that AMU's environment has long been rife with factional allegiances, and whereas I might have presumed that the pressures of family and community would affect the decisions these young people made during the independence movement and the demand for Pakistan, their actions also were influenced by their attachments to local people and places.

For many narrators, it was the most intimate of relationships that determined their choices. Fathers loomed large in stories of Aligarh and partition, but their roles were not uniform. Sir Sayyid was the father of the institution, whose priorities guided student activism throughout the institution's history.[84] But, as David Lelyveld has demonstrated, Sir Sayyid himself was raised in the home of his maternal grandfather and three of the most influential members of Aligarh's first generation grew up without strong fathers.[85] Some narrators, like Wajahat Husain and Ghulam Umar, represented their choices to migrate to Pakistan as independent of their fathers and families. Wajahat noted that he did not discuss his decision with his father and that, for some time in September and October 1947, his family remained uncertain of his whereabouts. Wajahat's family's roots were deeply embedded in Aligarh, and it was only after he traveled to Aligarh to fetch them that his family decided to shift to Pakistan.

Irfan Habib, Riazur Rahman Sherwani, and Ahmad Saeed all made note of the relationship between their father's political allegiances and the allegiances they adopted. Habib's father was a moral leader who guided many students toward Marxism, including his son. Saeed claimed the identity of the Congress primarily because his father was a staunch nationalist.[86] But Sherwani disavowed his father's close ties to the Muslim League and became a committed Congress worker, instead.[87] The political leaders, too, became fathers. In the Habib household, Gandhi was *Bapu*, father.[88] Jinnah was the father of Pakistan, and as Sarfaraz Hussein Mirza recalled, when he died, the women in his family lamented, "*Baba mar gaya!*" or "Our father has died!"[89] For many Indian narrators, after partition, it was Nehru's protective power, as the father of the modern Indian state, that saved Aligarh from destruction.

My own father's story was the only partition story I heard as a child. He was born in Aligarh and migrated to Pakistan when he was just five years old, and remembered bouncing around in the back of a truck, and cutting his leg on a jagged metal edge.[90] As I have traced the stories of so many from Aligarh, I have also filled in much of the context of his skeletal memories. I conducted much of my work by interviewing other people's fathers and grandfathers, all of whom welcomed me into their homes as if I were family. This, too, might be read as an effort to build social continuity through the rupture of partition.

I conducted these interviews during a time of tremendous social change in the subcontinent. In the years following the September 11, 2001, terrorist attacks in the United States, Pakistan was increasingly drawn into a theater of war on the country's western border. Violence sometimes spilled into Pakistan, an ally of the US-led offensive in Afghanistan. When I arrived in Lahore in January 2008, right after the assassination of former prime minister Benazir Bhutto, I could sense that the unrest in the country was affecting the tone and topics of the interviews. By the time I returned to Pakistan to conduct interviews in 2010, the turmoil that followed the Pakistan People's Party and Asif Ali Zardari's assumption of power had created such terrific anxiety that it became difficult for my interview participants to maintain their focus on my research topics. In processing them, I tried to remember that interviews are works-in-progress, sites "in which narrators revise the image of their own past as they go along."[91] This was incredibly important, because narrators' anxieties about contemporary Pakistan emerged in their recounting of its creation. The history they were remembering was colored by what they were experiencing as they spoke.

Similarly, I arrived in India during a time of palpable tension between India and Pakistan. In November 2008, terrorists from Pakistan held Bombay hostage for three days while they attacked a number of sites associated with foreigners (the Taj Palace Hotel) and Jews (Nariman House). These horrifying events and others altered the relationship between non-Muslim Indians and their fellow Muslim citizens in that they created an impression that terrorist violence stemmed from outside, rather than inside India. This lifted some pressure off India's Muslims, whom, for decades and particularly in the 1990s, many Indians suspected of perpetrating anti-state violence (even when its primary victims were other Muslims, as I discuss in Chapter 4). However, the attack deepened tensions between India and Pakistan, and this affected many of my interviews with Indian Muslims.

Whereas, in Pakistan, I had been quite open about my own family's links to Aligarh, along with the fact that my grandfather and several uncles attended AMU, in India I remained wary of revealing this information. I sometimes didn't mention it until quite late in the interaction, when a narrator became curious about me and my motives for collecting his story. Then I would tell him, "My father was born here, but now my family is outside." "Outside" is a euphemism for "abroad," and in this case, use of the term allowed me to mask the fact that much of my extended family lives in Pakistan.[92] What most often followed was a brief investigation into family origins, although given the fact that my father migrated when he was only five, none could recognize my father's name. Occasionally, a narrator might remember Wajahat (who was friends with Nawab Sahib Ibn-e-Saeed Chhatari), but more often than not, our conversations ended with shrugged shoulders and the reminder that "it was a big university." In the context of the personal interaction, it was never a problem that my family was in Pakistan; however, I feared that if I revealed this information too early, it might affect people's willingness to share their true feelings about the state's creation and their assessment of the people who moved there. In fact, while sometimes begging my forgiveness in advance, many proceeded to express their opinions frankly.

In Bangladesh, I also felt apprehensive about sharing my connections to Pakistan, but since the Aligs there were so few in number, I wanted to share with them the fact that I recently had lived in Aligarh and was particularly curious about their experiences there. The Bangladesh chapter of the Aligarh Old Boys' Association was instrumental in locating narrators willing to speak with me. However, I was surprised to find much less animosity toward Pakistan and Pakistanis than I expected. While active in the movement for Bangladeshi liberation, this older generation had earlier been active in demanding an independent Pakistan. They believed in its ideals, but grew disappointed by its realities; several still held hope for a broad South Asian political unity.

As I reread and reevaluate the interviews now and in the wake of Narendra Modi's rise to power, I cannot help but be moved by the anxieties with which Indian Muslims continue to struggle, as their identities are increasingly battered by India's shift to the right. Meanwhile, tensions with Pakistan continue to flare. The experiences of Aligarh Muslims during partition may grow in importance as we recognize the damage that identity politics are wreaking on South Asian communities. Oral history narratives open up the possibility for reflexive analysis of the past, for the present is always present in them. None of the narrators I interviewed cast themselves as partition's victims, even if they gave up land, jobs, and history to migrate to Pakistan; even if they recognized that Muslims have faced more difficult paths to success in India; even if they acknowledged the failures of the state to secure and serve their interests. Nonetheless, their narratives betrayed the anxieties of traumatic experiences: slippage in carefully constructed identities, insecurity, vulnerability to state power. These elements have persisted long after the migrations of partition have ended, and they reveal as much about the meaning of the present as the past.

Oral history interviews are unstable; they are highly dependent on context, but this should not be read as a weakness. Rather, they convey the textures of individual and collective experience. Once written in response to a particular context, a document may be interpreted differently over time, but its content remains the same.[93] An interview, even the same questions, would be different if conducted under different circumstances. Oral history interviews are inherently dynamic, determined by the positioning of the interviewee, the interviewer, and the context that surrounds them both. As a young female, foreign, non-Muslim researcher (along with any number of other identity markers that people may have understood), my experience differed from that of any other researcher. If reconfigured, any combination of these variables would create a different outcome. As it stands, I was often welcomed as if a long-lost member of the family, though many narrators saw fit to remind me of my duties to community, family, and faith (sometimes explicitly as narrators read me passages from the Qur'an). All of this served to deepen my commitment to the story I sought to tell: their story.

That story begins with the origin story of the AMU. Founded as the Mohammadan Anglo-Oriental College in 1875, the institution ultimately became the AMU in 1920. Chapter 1 examines the conditions of the university's founding, the personality and symbolic valence of its ever-present founder, and the environment of the university that instilled in young Muslim men a sense of solidarity backed by a distinctly masculine, Muslim identity. This was the environment that nurtured the narrators whose stories appear throughout the book. Chapter 2 focuses more closely on the AMU environment in the 1930s and 1940s—a place that remains unexamined in histories of partition and a period that earlier studies of the institution neglect. Through a combination of oral and archival sources that expose the nature of student life in the university, I reconstructed the texture of that period and the impact and meaning of the Pakistan Movement on its students. Chapter 3 explores the experience of the 1947 Partition at the university. Narrators recalled that the university was perpetually under threat; they described the conditions there by sharing stories about disturbance to particular sites of meaning and about their daily experiences in and around the campus. They lived with a siege mentality that bred an atmosphere of intense fear and, under those conditions, the students sought alternative sources of authority. Chapters 4 and 5 examine the experiences of AMU students in the three post-partition states by connecting their experiences to broader, contemporary questions of belonging that minorities face in India, Pakistan, and Bangladesh, including Muslims. The chapters examine how multiple events—from the 1952 anti-Ahmadiyya riots in Lahore to the 1971 Liberation of Bangladesh, and finally to the 2019 verdict in the Babri Masjid case—have contributed to the growth of both sectarian tension in Pakistan and right-wing Hindu nationalism in India. In this book, I show that the emphasis on Muslim solidarity so actively supported at AMU since its earliest days, which motivated the political activity of its students, proved to be dangerously homogenizing. Even as Muslim nationalism sought to consolidate an imaginary mainstream Muslim identity based on the norms and language of the North Indian elite, it simultaneously led to the exclusion of others. The ongoing politics of inclusion and exclusion portend significance for everyone in the region, not just the narrators whose stories animate these pages.

1

Defining the Aligarh Muslim University

From portraits in nearly every room at AMU, Sir Sayyid Ahmad Khan (1817–98) gazes down on the institution that he founded, and his presence sometimes feels as material as that of its current administrators. Though long dead, his reputation as a thinker and a reformer has persisted, and is nearly unassailable in the minds of those associated with AMU. He represents a legacy of Muslim empowerment, and whatever difficulties the Muslim community may have faced are attributed to a failure to uphold the ideals he proclaimed. Sir Sayyid's idea for the Muhammadan Anglo-Oriental College (MAO), founded in 1875 (that became AMU in 1920), was to groom a generation of Muslims who "would be in a position to do good to their country"[1] through attention to "knowledge, skills and values necessary to qualify them for public leadership."[2] The college was to be a residential environment where students lived together as brothers and learned to interact and organize themselves in preparation for their lives beyond the confines of the campus. Sir Sayyid's gaze is an ever-present reminder of AMU's ideal Muslim: faithful, educated, generous, masculine, and cosmopolitan.

Former student and retired professor of English Asloob Ahmad Ansari told me, "I think he was the greatest benefactor of the Muslims in the last several years, or centuries I should say."[3] Ansari's memory instinctively drew Sir Sayyid into the present, for the passage of time has not diminished his importance. In Ansari's memory, the period of Sir Sayyid's leadership and the values he represented were not distant in time, but occurred "in the last several years." This contemporaneity fortifies the link between AMU now and AMU then; it is the thread through which the traditions of the past remain relevant for Aligs in the present. University students, faculty, and administrators are constantly measured against the ideals of Sir Sayyid's vision. Alumni—known as "Aligarh Old Boys," even if they are women—throughout the world seek to sustain his legacy through their financial and ideological support of AMU, and through creating new institutions that mimic its values.[4] Branches of the Old Boys' Association exist anywhere there is a presence of Aligs worldwide, though they are only loosely connected to one another. Zakir Ali Khan, who was general secretary of the Aligarh Old Boys' Association-Pakistan from 1960 until his death in 2012, explained to me that the goals of the association were "exactly what Sir Sayyid has taught us: to establish educational institutions, to impart education, to make education available to those who cannot afford to pay."[5] The Association in Pakistan founded the Sir Syed University of Engineering and Technology and the Association in Dhaka, Bangladesh, has purchased land for a similar, though otherwise unrelated, project. The world over,

Aligarh Old Boys gather to celebrate Sir Sayyid Day, on the founder's birthday, October 17, with food, fellowship, and recitations of poetry. Sir Sayyid's symbolic presence unifies Aligs across time and space, and is a benevolent but constant force in the lives of students, administrators, alumni, and "well-wishers" of the university.[6]

Through an exploration of AMU's founding, this chapter argues that the identity that draws AMU students together was a distinct product of the late nineteenth-century colonial experience. It was heavily influenced by the personality, priorities, and symbolic valence of Sir Sayyid himself. From its earliest days, environment of the university instilled in young Muslim students a sense of solidarity backed by a late Victorian, and distinctly Muslim, masculine identity.[7] The enclosed environment of the MAO College proved to be fertile ground for cultivating Sir Sayyid's ideas of Muslim manhood, as the residential institution trained boys for public life.[8] The values on which the institution was founded combined the priorities of British schools and universities, especially Cambridge and Oxford, with those of elite Muslim households like the one in which Sir Sayyid grew up. The outcome was the creation of a set of norms of comportment and hospitality, erudition, and faithfulness that came to represent the Aligarh ideal, but codified the particular expectations of the late Victorian colonial experience. To Aligs, these values appeared timeless, and continued to represent the ideal values of the institution throughout the period under study here (1935–50). The residential campus environment bred an elite masculinity and cultivated men who would be prepared to represent Muslims as a body in the British colonial establishment.

At the end of the nineteenth century, the formalization of British power and the influence of technologies of enumeration, like the census, caused religious communities to identify themselves politically in ways they never had before. The census served to mask the internal diversity of encompassing categories like "Muslim" and "Hindu," which aligned with British sensibilities about "great faiths" of the world (led, of course, by Christianity).[9] Sir Sayyid's quest to develop an Indian Muslim identity was part of a mission to develop and advance Muslim interests by resisting the certain political marginalization of a demographic minority. His goal was to resist the outcome that the 1873 census suggested: that Indian Muslims would be a permanent minority in the subcontinent and thus alienated from power. Rather, he sought to associate Muslims with the ruling establishment. To enjoin Muslims to his agenda, Sir Sayyid invoked the history of Muslim power in the subcontinent, but mobilized a narrative of decline that urged Muslims to work together to restore the social status they enjoyed before the British took power. Over a long period of time, from the 1860s to the 1930s, just such a narrative was used again and again to rally Muslims to the institution's causes and to rally the institution to the causes of India's Muslims.

The institution's identity was closely associated with the norms of the North Indian service elite, Sir Sayyid's own community. Despite compelling evidence to the contrary—that is, that the student body was always complex and heterogeneous—the residential model facilitated a narrative of similarity and solidarity that has remained sacred to Aligs, who have sought to protect it and therefore to protect the founder's legacy. The residential environment defined an enclosed campus in which young men, removed from their family homes, shared the experience of training for public life.

While Sir Sayyid's vision was bound to the contours of the colonial establishment, by the 1930s, when the anti-colonial movement was well underway, AMU's priority of Muslim unity became a cornerstone of Muslim political empowerment. By 1940, the All-India Muslim League focused on Muslim solidarity in its demand for independent statehood on the principle that Muslims constituted a unique nation within India. AMU students were key actors in generating enthusiasm for a Muslim homeland called "Pakistan"—thus inextricably linking the worlds of education and politics at AMU.

The Founder's Context

Sir Sayyid Ahmad Khan emerged as a prominent reformer in the late nineteenth century. He was a mid-level colonial officer, serving in Bijnor, who gained recognition for his loyalty during and after the uprising against British power in 1857. The events of the 1857 rising—that culminated with the British exile of the last of the Mughal emperors to Burma—highlighted for Sayyid Ahmad the vulnerability of the Muslim position. He set about trying to rehabilitate Muslims who, as a whole, he felt were in a state of decline. In his view, the mighty ruling class that had yielded formidable kings and dominated the subcontinent in part or in whole since the early thirteenth century had descended into a low ebb in its civilizational history because of complacency and declining attention to the principles of respectable or *ashraf* culture. Sir Sayyid's efforts relied on this perception of decay, of "relative deprivation" that became essential to the identity students took on at AMU.[10]

The perception of deprivation spurred a shoring up of elite Muslim values in the period after the 1857 Revolt, and Sir Sayyid used it to generate support for his reformist religious and educational ideas. This consolidation fed a homogenizing narrative that privileged the Muslim elite of North India as the hereditary leaders of Indian Muslims, but risked excluding others who did not fit into this narrow identity. There are aspects of Sir Sayyid's perspective that scholars have been willing to ascribe to "his time and place," including his conservative ideas on educating women outside the home.[11] Less examined, however, has been the influence of this elite narrative of unity on the attitude of exceptionalism that developed within AMU. Sir Sayyid's ideals have been seen as progressive within the AMU community, and indeed he resisted the prevailing anxieties of his time, particularly with regard to Muslim reluctance to pursue Western education. Still, they were in part determined by his unwavering loyalty to British power and the fear that any hint of disloyalty would lead to the permanent marginalization of Muslims in India. These two narratives were interwoven in the institutional environment of AMU, where it has become difficult to separate the value of his educational mission and the dangers of his political prejudices.

Sayyid Ahmad Khan was in many ways well-suited to his role as a culture broker between the Muslim service gentry and the growing British colonial establishment. In the late nineteenth century, both classes were coming to terms with shifting realities of power.[12] He enjoyed the high status of the Delhi *ashraf*—those families who claimed heritage outside the subcontinent and who were considered respectable—and his family had a long association with both the Mughal court and the British bureaucracy.

Sayyid Ahmad was raised in the home of his maternal grandfather and had been trained in the subjects of a traditional Indian Muslim education; he knew Persian, Urdu, and Arabic. His grandfather, Khwaja Fariduddin Ahmad, had been *vazir* (prime minister) in the court of the Mughal emperor, Akbar Shah II (r. 1806–37), and also served as a British-appointed envoy to Persia and as its agent in Burma.[13] In addition, Khwaja Fariduddin was a pious Muslim, devoted to Shah Ghulam Ali, a *pir* (saint) of the Naqshbandi Sufi order. Sayyid Ahmad later credited both his mother and his maternal grandfather with shaping his cosmopolitan sensibilities. Though he was a prominent follower of the Muslim reformer Shah Wali Ullah, he participated in a variety of religious festivals and commemorations, including that of Holi, the Hindu festival of color.[14] This distinctly Indian upbringing, characterized by overlapping cultural and religious experiences, prepared him for his critical role in guiding his contemporaries through a process of adaptation to their altered circumstances after 1857 as the British heaped blame for the uprising on the Muslims, India's former ruling class.

What has traditionally been called the "Mutiny" of 1857 plays a pivotal role in most histories of AMU. In the collective memory, this history tells of the devastation of Muslims and their communities—especially of Delhi and Lucknow—of the erosion of Muslim social status, the usurpation of land and the alienation of landholders.[15] For Indians, and for Muslims in particular, the uprising of 1857 has taken on the valence of a national trauma, because it permanently disrupted the institutions of Muslim power, represented by the moribund Mughal imperium based in Delhi.[16] Disruptions to everyday life, such as 1857 (and later, partition), become, in the collective memory, moments of coherence for a moral community and provide "a close link between self-identity and national identity."[17] For the Muslim elite, 1857 provided the impetus for the formation of a concept of a unified Muslim identity closely linked to the intellectual leadership of Sayyid Ahmad Khan, and embodied in the institution he founded in Aligarh.

The 1857 Revolt was an uprising of Hindu and Muslim soldiers who feared that the British were trying to "take away their caste and convert them forcibly to Christianity."[18] Discontent over wages and the expansion of British power into daily life had been spreading in the armies of the East India Company for decades, but the trigger for the revolt was a rumor that cartridges for the new Enfield rifle were greased with a combination of beef and pork fat that, if ingested, would strip one of caste.[19] Since the soldier had to pull the cartridge from its case using his teeth, he would certainly ingest the grease and it would pollute, and thus destroy, his caste.[20] Thus alienated from his community, a man would be vulnerable to forced conversion to Christianity. This controversy erupted at a time of increasing suspicion of the British in the East Indian Company Bengal Army, and the uprising quickly spread from Meerut across North India.[21] In the end, however, the mutineers—who had installed the ailing Mughal emperor Bahadur Shah Zafar as their leader—were subdued and the British regained control.[22] Many Indians and Pakistanis imagine it as a foundational event in a narrative of anti-colonial resistance by remembering the event today as "the First War of Independence." This reframing was first suggested by V. D. Savarkar in his 1909 publication, *The Indian War of Independence of 1857*, in which he advanced a triumphal narrative of resistance that de-emphasized the cartridge controversy (among others) as a mere catalyst that roused the "real spirit of the Revolution": love of religion and love of country.²³ It is not at all clear that the mutineers had a consolidated objective as Savarkar implies. Furthermore, it is critical to remember that the Indians *lost* this First War of Independence. As a starting point for a history of solidarity, it is a foreboding one.²⁴ Considering Savarkar's own efforts to foreground Hinduness in Indian identity, it is ironic that Muslims, even in today's India and Pakistan, have adopted his framework. However, it is not the actual uprising of 1857 that marks the beginning of the period of Muslim regeneration. In the AMU version—in contrast to the Indian nationalist one first outlined by Savarkar—the discontent of the *sepoys* (soldiers) is not remembered as a proto-nationalist impulse that led to the movement for independence from the British and ultimately culminated in the victory of independence in 1947. Rather, in the AMU version, 1857 exposed the weakness of Muslims, their educational backwardness, and their lack of access of positions of power, the conditions that necessitated Sayyid Ahmad's heroic intervention.

The meaning AMU well-wishers have attributed to 1857 has less to do with the content or the events of the revolution itself, than with the perception of decline and rejuvenation that followed it. In other words, the revolt that might be identified as the First War of Independence is less significant in itself than the outcome that Muslims were finally alienated from power with the exile of the Mughal emperor, the revolt's nominal leader.²⁵ The effect of the national trauma was not, therefore, that it disrupted an existing collective identity, formed, for example, under Muslim rulers or fortified by religious confession that drove the rebellion, but that the grievances exposed by the rebellion and its aftermath *created the conditions* in which a collective identity formed. Thus, 1857 was the origin of the collective Muslim identity that formed around the institution at Aligarh, at the core of which was a sense of decline, and the valorization of the succeeding regeneration led by Sir Sayyid Ahmad Khan.

During the uprising in Bijnor, where Sayyid Ahmad was posted, he protected the family of the British Collector and Magistrate, Mr. Shakespear, thus establishing himself as steadfastly loyalty to British rule. In the wake of the rebellion, Sayyid Ahmad did not see any potentially sustainable impulse that might indicate a larger revolutionary motive among the mutineers, or the potential for a systemic change that would mark the end of British rule in India. He felt, rather, as he suggested in his 1859 *Asbab-e-Baghavat-e-Hind* (*The Causes of the Indian Revolt*), that the rebellion reflected the confluence of "many grievances [that] had been rankling in the hearts of the people."²⁶ In his estimation, the rebellion was haphazard, rag-tag, and neither the outcome of a sophisticated conspiracy nor simply a reaction to contaminated Enfield cartridges (and here Savarkar agreed with him). Still, the Indians lost: Muslims and non-Muslims alike.

The formalization of crown rule in 1858, as Queen Victoria adopted the title Empress of India, became the substance of Muslim grievance in the post-Mutiny period. Sayyid Ahmad Khan positioned himself as a leader of the much-maligned Muslims, and by responding to the crisis in the language of loyalism, sought to recover the position of privilege that Muslims had enjoyed, and that had been marked by the tenure of the Mughal Emperors in Delhi (symbolic though their reign had become by the nineteenth century). Sayyid Ahmad Khan's loyalty to Mr. Shakespear during the uprising earned him a pension in perpetuity, and in 1869 he was awarded the title of C.S.I.: Companion of the Most Exalted Order of the Star of India.[27] His properties in Delhi were pillaged during the fighting, but the British extended their support. He therefore came to believe that traditional Indian systems of patronage were losing social currency in the changing environment of British India.[28]

As the British sought explanations for the rebellion, the issue of Muslim "backwardness," emerged as a particular problem in Bengal, the original site of British conquest in the eighteenth century and home to many of the rebelling troops. In 1871, W. W. Hunter, a civil servant and historian in Bengal, focused on this problem his post-Mutiny treatise *The Indian Mussulmans: Are They Bound in Conscience to Rebel Against the Queen?* in which he questioned the very possibility of Muslim loyalty to the British.[29] Sir Sayyid Ahmad Khan was appalled. More than a decade before Hunter's critique, in 1859, he had clearly argued in *Asbab-e-Baghavat-e-Hind* that the 1857 uprising was neither a conspiracy nor compelled by the Islamic faith. Still, with Hunter's query, Sir Sayyid again found himself having to respond to accusations of Muslim disloyalty. In his rejoinder to Hunter, a review published in *The Pioneer*, Sir Sayyid cautioned that "writers should be careful of their facts when treating of any important subject, and having got their facts, ought to avoid all exaggeration or misrepresentation" lest the ideas of one Englishman be interpreted as those of the "whole English community."[30] In 1860, he published *An Account of the Loyal Mohomedans of India*, documenting the activities of loyal Muslims, and concluded with the wish that his work had "satisfactorily demonstrated . . . that there was really no foundation whatever for the calumnies which would lay upon Mohomedans [sic] the blame of originating the Rebellion in 1857, as an act sanctioned or countenanced by their religion!"[31] Through these written excursions into the British public sphere, and his unabashed support for the legitimacy of the British ruling establishment, he earned their favor, and had their ear as he became a vocal advocate for the needs and rights of Muslims both educationally and culturally.

Sir Sayyid Ahmad Khan ventured into educational reform with the formation of scientific societies that brought Western science to Indian readers in translation. Eventually, he settled on English as the most valuable tool for educational advancement. Though he did not speak it himself, he became determined to demonstrate to Indian Muslims that English was not only vital for a career in public service, but that it presented no threat to their faith or traditional values. Hindu enrollments in English schools grew after 1860, but Muslims were reluctant to access English education, fearing that it would create "disbelief of religion in the minds of the pupils."[32] Furthermore, in these schools, *ashraf* Muslims worried that their children would have to mix with "vulgar people," by which they meant both Hindus and lower-status Muslims.[33] Instead of risking this social contamination, Muslims continued to patronize traditional institutions and networks and remained aloof from British education.

Though Hunter's book was nominally an analysis of the plight of Bengali Muslims, as Sir Sayyid rightly pointed out in his response, the book "abounds in passages which lead the reader to believe that it is not merely the Bengal Mohammedans that the author treats of, but the Mohammadans throughout India."[34] Hunter's report became the basis for a "perception of decline" that persisted in Muslim reformist thinking through the late nineteenth century and beyond. Despite this negative narrative, the period after 1857 was actually one in which the ideals of the middle classes in North India were consolidated through the reformist efforts of Sir Sayyid and others. As Anil Seal has shown, the Muslims in the Northwest Provinces and Awadh (later the United Provinces, today Uttar Pradesh (UP)) did not suffer the extreme alienation of the Muslims in Bengal. The Muslim population in these Northern regions was urban; many were landholders or professionals. As late as the 1880s, "Muslims continued to hold more than 45 percent of all of the uncovenanted and judicial posts in the provinces."[35] Even "the Muslim student population in modern high schools was generally proportionate to the Muslim numerical strength" in most of the provinces, *except* Bengal.[36] Despite Sir Sayyid's critique of Hunter, he employed examples of alienation in Bengal just as tendentiously to support a declensionist narrative that generated support for his educational reforms.

Another significant development critical to this tale was the shift in understanding about the relationship between the metropole and the colony that surrounded the uprising, and, in particular, the shift in perception about the relationship between colonial administrators and colonized peoples. In England, after the Mutiny, there was a distinct shift in conceptions of masculine identity that were a direct result of the presence of the Empire as a space of masculine rule. The subjects of that rule, too, were implicated in gendered hierarchies that associated loyalty with masculinity and, to some extent, similarity, and cast revolt as cowardly and effeminate. Fears of disloyalty rocked the empire after 1857, consolidating the need to preserve the superiority of the British "race." These efforts valorized militarism and the virtues of physical fitness and athleticism.[37] As Heather Streets argues, the theory that some Indians belonged to "martial races" expanded during this period as the British cast the mutineers of 1857 as "treacherous, faithless, deluded and easily incited to passion," in contrast to the loyal martial groups that she identifies as Scottish Highlanders, Sikhs, and Gurkhas.[38]

After the revolt, the ratio of British soldiers to Indian *sepoys* in the Indian Army shifted from 1:6 to a more even ration of 1:2.[39] This shift buttressed the authority of British soldiers and created an increase in demand for British soldiers and officers in the empire. British rule was expanding into the hinterlands and required more British hands to manage it. As Muslims tried to position themselves advantageously after 1857, they were particularly troubled by the encroachment of British power. In the space between the "unmanly" Bengal Army, and the "martial races" fell the Muslims, closely associated with the subcontinental power the British now assumed, but also with fighting against the British in Delhi and Lucknow. Overwhelmingly, the Muslims were held responsible in its aftermath.[40] Even in Sir Sayyid's eyes, post-1857 British contempt for Muslims and their heritage displaced centuries of honorable Muslim leadership.[41]

Sir Sayyid's educational movement combined two powerful myths—of deprivation, and alienation from power—as the basis of a Muslim awakening that mobilized "Muslim national will for a competitive coexistence in the future."[42] He hearkened back to the precedent for Muslim power and facilitated a desire to recover it. He worked to protect the existing pillars of the community, and to create new ones designed to foster modern (read: European) values and learning. His experience with the British had taught him that to garner their favor, he would have to represent an interest "which the government believed existed, [and with] which it imagined would need help."[43] He set out to groom a class of boys who could become successful in the British system even beyond the boundaries of traditional government service.

Creating a Victorian Muslim Education

In 1869, Sayyid Ahmad's younger son Mahmud won a scholarship to study in England, at the University of Cambridge. Sayyid Ahmad joined him there for seven months, and it was during that trip that many of his ideas for constructing modern educational institution in India began to germinate. Sir Sayyid was taken with the ancient university model, and he came to believe that the British had earned their power and achievement in the subcontinent through superior technology and information systems. As David Lelyveld has shown, Sir Sayyid believed that a superior education system that prepared men for "social leadership" drove the empire's advancements.[44] As it turns out, Cambridge in the late nineteenth century was itself in the midst of a significant transition, and what Sir Sayyid and his son saw there had deep and enduring implications for the development of the educational model at AMU.

As the empire expanded in the nineteenth century, the conception of masculinity at Oxford and Cambridge became more muscular, predicated on notions of competition, physical strength, racial superiority, and action.[45] Cambridge prepared men for public life by taking them out of the climate of the domestic environment, encouraging competition on the sports fields and valorizing militarism and "imperial adventure."[46] At the same time, education at Cambridge shifted from concentration on the subjects of classical learning to new academic disciplines: science, language, history. The university became a training facility for fit, confident, and capable public men. Boys were, in other words, groomed for power in the classroom and on the athletic field.

Sir Sayyid sought to exploit these strategies to uplift Indian Muslims, to prepare them to compete within the British system. He imagined a new educational institution that would combine the models of the ancient universities of England and the traditional education of Indian Muslims. His efforts to rejuvenate Muslims focused on educational uplift designed to combat the reluctance of Muslims to enroll their children in government-sponsored institutions through which, they feared, children would be separated from their religious heritage and upbringing. Upon his return to India, Sir Sayyid started a journal intended to offer advice and guidance to Muslims. This journal *Tehzib ul-Akhlaq* (Social Reform) sought to revive attention to the tenets of Islam, facilitate social harmony, and encourage the dismissal of folk superstitions among Muslims.[47] His educational reforms were met with skepticism, even when he sought to build consensus by soliciting the opinions of other thinkers. Upon his return from England, he sponsored an essay contest on "The Progress of Education Among Indian Muslims" designed to discover the real reasons that Muslims declined to take advantage of British government education in India.[48] Assessing the results of the contest, Sir Sayyid found some of the reasons Muslim families gave for avoiding government education to be "absurd." Still, he determined that even if the government were to make changes to the existing system, it would remain insufficient to their needs. Thus, he wrote, "Muslims should themselves make arrangements for the education of their children if they want to preserve their ancient learning, secure benefits from modern learning, and to bring up their children according to the requirements of the age."[49] In 1875, he founded the MAO in Aligarh and argued against the idea that the institution was a foreign transplant, but rather that it was an "indigenous creation."[50]

The curriculum at the MAO College included the subjects of traditional Muslim education and recognized the importance of the study of Qur'an, Urdu, and Persian, but it emphasized Western scientific subjects. By shifting the value of education from the traditional to the modern, Sir Sayyid sought to align the qualifications of Indian Muslims with those of English school boys. In this way, Indian and British boys should be eligible for the same privileges of leadership.[51] In both Cambridge and Aligarh, the educational environments were distinctly and deliberately gendered. Young men were prepared for public life in environments dominated by a sense of sexual difference enshrined in the "separate spheres" ideology. Paul Deslandes notes in his study of Oxbridge men between 1850 and 1920 that the undergraduates complained that women—their mothers and sisters—simply could not understand what it was like to be in the university.[52] Similarly, it was key to Sir Sayyid's agenda that young men be separated from the enclosed spaces of the *zenana*, where they were exposed to corrupting superstitions, and brought into the world of men. Not only had the young men left home, but they were building unique and separate societies within their colleges.

As the century drew to a close, conceptions about masculinity continued to change in Britain. Whereas in the mid-Victorian period women were seen as companions— and indeed many of them benefited from a secondary education—by century's end, women were closely identified with a stifling domestic environment, and men increasingly sought independence away from home. The public school system became normalized in this period, and boys were often sent away to school in their early teens. After a stint in the university, as John Tosh argues, "Disillusionment with domesticity and the hankering after a racing men-only world were what attracted many to careers overseas."[53] It was no accident, therefore, that the first principals of the MAO College were recent graduates of Oxford and Cambridge. In fact, Syed Mahmud was sent back to England to locate a principal with "cosmopolitan sentiments."[54]

Theodore Beck, the second and by far the most important principal, began his tenure in 1883. Two other Cambridge graduates, Harold Cox and Walter Raleigh, followed him as professors two years later. Beck, with his deep attachment to the legitimacy and supremacy of British authority, tended to the growth of Aligarh's first generation. They were loyal to their institution, one another, and to the British. He supported Sir Sayyid's goal to develop a generation of Muslim men who could find a place within "the authoritarian framework of British rule" by replicating the Cambridge environment and its masculinizing agenda.[55] He welcomed social interaction with Indians, and detested "the Englishman who sneers at the natives."[56] Nonetheless, he embraced the hierarchy that placed Englishmen above Indians of all sorts and rejected the possibility that Muslims at Aligarh should be allowed to debate the validity of the existing hierarchy.

Beck was adept at imagining how the model of the Cambridge man might be adapted to the Indian environment. He felt that in their roles at the MAO College, Cambridge men must

> reluctantly abandon the cultivation in the majority of our students of the poetic, artistic, or philosophic temperament, and devote our attention to turning out men who in appearance are neatly dressed and clean, of robust constitution and well-trained muscles, energetic, honest, truthful, public spirited, courageous and modest in manner, loyal to the British Government and friendly to individual Englishmen, self-reliant and independent, endowed with common sense, with well-trained intellects and in some cases scholarly tastes.[57]

As an authority figure in the college, his role was to maintain strict boundaries within which the students could express themselves verbally and physically. Students were to be active in campus life, and engaged with current issues, but they should remain separate from broader politics.

In 1886, reflecting on his tenure at the college, Beck heralded the introduction of the Union Club at Aligarh. It had been modeled on the Cambridge Union, of which he, Cox, and Raleigh had each served as president. Beck saw the Aligarh Union as the quintessential site for the cultivation of gentlemen and wrote that "if every recent president of the Oxford or Cambridge Unions had gone into the Indian Civil Service 'what a capital set of fellows the last 4 or 5 years at Cambridge would have sent out.'"[58] Beck's authoritarian paternalism marked his approach to his role in Aligarh, and in the debating union one topic was strictly off-limits: British rule in India. Beck invoked the history of 1857 in his determination that the Aligarh Union not become a forum for "Bengali-style sedition."[59]

Sir Sayyid, too, sought to distance MAO students from the "seditious" Bengalis who had instigated the rebellion in 1857. However, in modeling the educational environment at MAO College on the British one, he mimicked and reified ideological structures of gender and power that were being cultivated at Cambridge to ensure the superiority of British men over women and colonized people throughout the empire. Thus, although Sir Sayyid's educational reforms have typically been seen as progressive, and he suffered criticism for them in India, the model he emulated was defined by the particularities of late Victorian Imperial England. The MAO College was a distinctly Indian institution, and at the moment of its founding, it was also a profoundly colonial one.

The Viceroy and Governor-General Lord Lytton laid the foundation stone of the College in 1877, setting in stone the relationship between the institution and the Government of India. The seal of the college, set in marble above the entrance to the original quadrangle, exemplified the union of East and West that Sir Sayyid envisioned. On each side of a lush palm tree are a crescent moon (the symbol of Islam) and the British crown. Sir Sayyid's speech on the occasion praised the beneficence of the British establishment in supporting Muslim education. He expressed his aspiration that the educational agenda of the MAO would encourage Muslims to appreciate the blessings of British rule and "to dispel those illusory traditions of the past which have hindered our progress; to remove those prejudices which have hitherto exercised a baneful influence on our race."[60]

Pillars of the Moral Community

The changes of the late nineteenth century in British India did present new challenges for the Indian educated classes. As the British formalized their rule, transferring sovereignty to the Crown in 1858, their strategies for governing India's diverse populations increasingly focused on technologies of knowledge gathering that might deepen their understanding of Indian society. Enumerative technologies, like census taking, were tested in India, with dramatic consequences for the codification of political categories. The codification of census data created a link between numerical and demographic statistics, religious affiliation and political power.[61] As a result of the 1873 census, Indian communities began to organize themselves into political categories, and the Muslims were no exception. Startled by the numerical disparity between Hindu and Muslim populations that the census revealed, Muslim leaders feared becoming a permanent minority in Indian politics.[62] The British system of classification focused on broad religious categories that would determine the constitution of social and political units of governance. Thus, although the Muslim community in India was fractured by sectarian and class divisions, Sir Sayyid recognized that an inclusive organization would magnify its influence. To draw Muslims together, he formed the Muslim Educational Conference, a political organization to correspond to the Indian National Congress (formed in 1886).

Sir Sayyid feared British retaliation against Muslim political agitation, and because he accepted the inevitability of British rule in India, he opposed the Congress and favored differentiating the Muslims from it.[63] In Sir Sayyid's view, if Muslims joined the Congress, they risked losing the special concessions they had received in the past through British beneficence. He remained intransigent in his opposition to Congress, despite the willingness of some Muslims to join its ranks as a way of finding a political voice.

Though Sir Sayyid claimed that his goal in founding the Muslim Educational Conference was nonpolitical, intended rather to foster the social, educational, and economic uplift of Muslims, his actions responded to political trends of the time, including the claims of the Indian National Congress to represent all-India interests. Francis Robinson argues that the MAO College "was the arena in which Muslim opinion was created and United Provinces Muslim leadership assembled. The [Muslim Educational] Conference was the means by which this opinion was disseminated among Muslims in the rest of India and this leadership imposed upon them."[64] Indeed, even if the effort to unify the Muslim community in opposition to Congress was simply a way of encouraging Muslims to recognize their plight, David Lelyveld notes that the college itself "was a profoundly political enterprise." The rationale for its existence was bound up with an analysis of "being Muslim and the nature of political power in British India."[65] For Sir Sayyid, the power of the Muslim community lay in its differentiation from Congress, the recognition of the *qaum* as a distinct identity with unique needs, and the maintenance of the social standards of the *ashraf*.

The effect of this organizing was the construction of a Muslim "moral community" drawn together by common history, values, language (Urdu), ancestry, and status.[66] Sir Sayyid used the Urdu word *qaum* to define this moral community, and though its meaning in different contexts has been contentious, for him it connoted the Muslims of India, differentiated from the greater body of Muslims worldwide by their unique interaction with the Indian environment.[67] His ideas of *qaum*, a broadly unified group of people with similar interests, helped him to invest the Muslim community with the strength and power generated by common interests. Faisal Devji has pointed out that Sir Sayyid's usage of *qaum*, rather than "*ummat* or *millat* [terms] used for specifically religious groupings that were localizable neither in time nor in space," implied that among Indian Muslims there was a "natural belonging together."[68] His was not a nationalism linked merely by religious confession or territory, but by shared social status and experience. This conception of *qaum* did not necessarily exclude North Indian Hindus, of the same social status, including landholders and regional princes. He famously described the two main communities of India to be "two eyes of a beautiful bride," an image that suggested the two communities needed to work together.

It remains a point of pride for Aligs that Hindus were always part of the student community, that though special arrangements were made for their dietary and residential needs, they looked and dressed just like the Muslim students. Still, Sir Sayyid saw the emergence of a majority Hindu political group as a threat to his efforts. Loyalty to the British was vital to the success of his efforts to support Muslim education and development. The MAO College, the hub of his organizational efforts, could not survive without British financial support.[69]

Sir Sayyid's reforms shored up Muslim identity and aligned it with the ruling class by consolidating it under the values of the *ashraf*, though this group represented only a small segment of Muslim society. One of the pillars of this community was its language: Urdu. Prior to the mid-nineteenth century, Urdu had primarily been a spoken vernacular, a hybrid of the official Mughal court language of Persian and the local Hindustani. Urdu had replaced Persian as the language of the courts, and though elite Muslims were traditionally educated in Persian, they often spoke Urdu at home.[70] It was an institution unique to the North Indian service gentry, who occupied these overlapping milieux, and Sir Sayyid felt it was under attack by advocates of Hindi (written in the Devanagari script).[71] Without Urdu, Sir Sayyid feared, students would be cut off from "original sources of knowledge as well as languages of political power."[72] The privileging of Urdu as a Muslim language neglected the linguistic diversity of Muslims throughout the subcontinent (and as would become critical later, especially in Bengal). It marginalized the regional languages spoken by many rural and lower-class Muslims. However, the destabilization of Urdu as an official language would certainly mean further alienation of elite Muslims. Support for Urdu was one of the key issues that exposed Sir Sayyid's animosity toward the ascendance of Hindus in public space.[73] He questioned their eligibility to fill positions of power previously held by Muslims and sought to hinder their arrival at every step.

Sir Sayyid feared that newly educated Hindus, especially those without hereditary status, would excel in the competitive examination for the Indian Civil Service, to the exclusion of Muslim men of "good breeding."[74] He resisted open competition for government jobs between Hindus and Muslims out of fear of social transgression, the upheaval that might occur if "weakly" Bengalis attained positions of power not determined by their hereditary social standing. In 1888, he asked an audience to image the consequences of the competitive examination system:

> Over all races, not only over Mahomedans but over Rajas of high position and the brave Rajputs who have not forgotten the swords of their ancestors, would be placed as rule a Bengali who at the sight of a table knife would crawl under his chair . . . I am delighted to see the Bengalis making progress, but the question is—What would be the result on the administration of the country? Do you think that the Rajput and the fiery Pathan, who are not afraid of being hanged or of encountering the swords of the police or the bayonets of the army, could remain in peace under the Bengalis?[75]

Sir Sayyid's gendered rhetoric indicated that the most threatening aspect of Bengali ascendance was the threat of their perceived effeminacy. He raised the possibility that other "races" of the country would not tolerate their rule and that chaos would ensue, which they would be unable to control because of their irrational fear of confrontation. Ultimately, he found them unfit for public leadership. The empire demanded strong leaders with well-established community institutions. Theodore Beck emerged on the side of the Muslims in this controversy as well, raising the fear of "quick-witted Bengalis" who would flood the civil services to the detriment of both Muslims and British.[76]

Even while Sir Sayyid supported a kind of Hindu-Muslim unity, he differentiated the political agenda of Muslims from that of Bengalis and urged Muslims to resist alliance with the Bengali-dominated "National Congress."[77] He often used the term "Bengali" interchangeably with "Hindu," but he associated Bengalis with a particular political identity with which Muslims could never find favor. A key shortcoming of Sir Sayyid's logic, and the elision of "Bengali" with "Hindu," was his inability to see Bengali Muslims as those most in need of the rehabilitation he sought to facilitate. This was primarily an issue of class: the majority of Bengali Muslims were cultivators, not landowners. His contempt bears a hint of the taint of "backwardness" (described by Hunter) that Sir Sayyid had worked so hard to prove should not apply to the Urdu-speaking elite. However, it rendered Bengali Muslims invisible. Hindus, for their part, might be students or well-wishers of Aligarh, and their financial support was meaningful, but as political actors the interests of "Bengalis" (read: Hindus) were, in his estimation, diametrically opposed to those of Muslims.[78] The effect of this prejudice was to resist associating "masculine" Muslims with "effete" Hindus, and to avoid the pitfalls of being associated with a nationalist movement that might be seen to be opposing or undermining British authority.

Despite the aggressively communal political rhetoric that took hold of the Aligarh Movement in the waning years of the nineteenth century, there was a sense that the institution at Aligarh could only be successful if it remained open to all of India's people. Sir Sayyid's oft-quoted remarks, in which he referred to the "two eyes of a beautiful bride" or called himself a "Hindu" by virtue of being a resident of Hindustan, laid the foundation for the attitude of inclusion at MAO, and later AMU, that persisted through many generations. Though the political agenda Sir Sayyid established for elite Muslims was increasingly divergent from that of the Hindu-led Indian National Congress, on an individual level Hindus and Muslims should get along.[79]

One first-generation Alig, political activist Mohamad Ali Jauhar, reinforced the ideal of inclusion in a 1904 pamphlet.[80] He quoted from the educational scheme for the university which proclaimed its goal to send its graduates "throughout the length and breadth of the land to preach the gospel of free enquiry, or large-hearted toleration, and of a pure morality."[81] This agenda encompassed the "original and fundamental principles of the aims, objects and policy of the Mohamedan [sic] Anglo-Oriental College" and were etched in stone at the entrance to the College Hall.[82] These aims were naturalized, linked to familiar Victorian values, and set in stone.[83]

Discipline and Place in AMU

The college Sir Sayyid founded was residential so that students would be removed from the folk influences of their households. As at Cambridge, the geography of the MAO College created a masculine private sphere, bounded by walls that physically shut out those who were not eligible for access to this elite environment, including women. These walls also kept the boys in, where they could be monitored and disciplined into the men that they would be when they emerged from this chrysalis.

The residential campus was a transitional environment, a liminal space between home and the world outside. Thus, it was important that it appear familiar and cultivate the same priorities of home. The campus was explicitly designed after Cambridge, but preserved the bond to the *ashraf* households in which the boys grew up. The original quadrangle was designed in the image of a *haveli* (mansion), with a courtyard surrounded by residential spaces. Students were thus sheltered from the outside world, but had space to move around, with easy access to the mosque and the college's central academic gathering space, the Strachey Hall. The college was a healthier home where boys would not be spoiled, but brought up "properly."[84] Both at Cambridge and MAO, women's schools and colleges were outside the boundaries of the men's colleges.[85] The walls of the campus protected boys from the influences of the world outside and the customs of women. Removal from the private sphere of the home was a crucial step in preparing boys for the public sphere of the empire. Isolating students in this environment, where they lived, ate, and played together, encouraged in them a feeling for the importance of the community. This community operated like their family, but without the mitigating customs that originated in the domestic sphere and that could corrupt masculine identity.[86]

The campus of the MAO College was the prime site in which students learned to become part of the moral community Sir Sayyid had envisioned. The residential system occupied the core of the moral and disciplinary order. Vice Chancellor Aftab

Ahmad Khan, a first-generation graduate, wrote in 1926 (two and a half decades after Sir Sayyid's death) that the residential system persisted as the

> most distinctive and the most important feature of our institution from its very start.... Residential system is an organization according to which young men are kept together under a system which is best calculated to develop and bring out all that is best in human nature. This is only possible if the lives of young men are regulated according to principles and methods which have stood the test of time and experience. Such principles and methods are the basis of discipline without which no residential system, in the real sense of the term, is possible. Hundreds of young men, coming from different and distant parts of the country, and representing all sorts of ideas and manners, virtues and vices, if kept under proper control and effective discipline, gradually evolve a corporate life and character which leads to success. But if they are left unregulated and uncontrolled, the result must be disastrous.[87]

Aftab Ahmad Khan resisted allowing students to reside outside the formal campus, with the few exceptions of the day scholars who lived with their own families in the city. Even those students raised his suspicions, however, and this anxiety draws attention to how important the institution's isolation appeared to its faculty and administration. Within the campus, the students could be controlled, and were seen as a unified and disciplined group. When outsiders penetrated this hallowed ground, it was never clear what contamination they might bring, and what might happen if they could not be conditioned by the residential system. As a result, Aftab argued that "with the exception of those who live with their parents or very near relations, no student coming from outside should be permitted to reside in the city."[88] Day scholars were affiliated with a university hostel, marking them as insiders.

Hindu students, however, were for some time, "accommodated either in the thatched bungalows, or in hired Railway bungalows outside the University compound."[89] This arrangement was necessitated by overcrowded conditions in the hostels. In 1926, Vice Chancellor Aftab Ahmad Khan proposed the construction of the first Hindu hostel inside the campus since the days of Sir Sayyid.[90] In the early days, Hindus themselves resisted sharing accommodations with Muslims, fearing that "it would be much resented by their relatives & caste-fellows,"[91] and in 1896 there were twenty-seven Hindu day scholars in the college, but no Hindu boarders.[92] Considering the importance of the university's residential environment, the dislocation of Hindus made it more difficult for them to be incorporated into the student body seamlessly. While the residential system was the primary disciplinary mechanism for forging the Aligarh man, in practice it was insufficiently constructed.

In the early years of MAO College, due to a lack of funding, the walls themselves did not fully enclose the campus and were thus ineffective at maintaining the boundary with the outside. Nor were they effective in keeping students in; this situation was further complicated by the willingness of the *chowkidar* (gatekeeper) to let the students in and out during the night.[93] By the 1940s, the walls formed a physical barrier, but one that students still found opportunities to cross. Students were permitted to go into the city, but had to return to their hostels by 9:30 p.m. Restrictive though this system may seem, Zakir Ali Khan and others remembered with pride that the "whole system was organized—the policing of the university system—by the students and staff only. No police were involved. They were so competent that no quarreling was going on . . . the proctors, they were all students."[94] Echoing Aftab's 1926 remarks, many narrators referred to the disciplinary environment as a key aspect of the university's celebrated *mahol* (atmosphere). Narrators placed a high value on the independence of the institution in managing matters of discipline.[95] They imagined AMU as isolated, set apart from other institutions and sources of authority. They remembered a self-contained environment, defined by norms and meanings that were impervious to outside forces.

As Zakir Ali Khan indicated, senior students were selected to become the proctorial monitors, responsible for maintaining student discipline on the university grounds and off. Irrespective of the campus boundaries, AMU students were expected to uphold the institution's norms of dress and behavior anytime they ventured into public. An excerpt from the *Aligarh Magazine* in 1934 links these norms with the cultivation of the brotherhood at AMU:

> It is under [the Proctorial Monitor's] guidance that the City, Railway Station, Cinemas in the Town and other places outside the University area are patrolled by these representatives of our law and order who can haul up any student who misbehaves himself or is guilty of any breach of University discipline or commits an act which is likely to lower the prestige of his fellow-students.[96]

The statement defines a circle of protection within the purview of the university's disciplinary regime that includes several sites in Aligarh city, where the university's disciplinary power would be made visible through the presence of proctorial monitors. In these places, each boy's behavior would reflect on the reputation of his brothers; he was wise to keep this in mind.

The intimacy between discipline and brotherhood rested at the heart of the meaning of an AMU education. For narrators, the disciplinary regime was a key trigger for memories of life before and after partition, and it bred a powerful sense of collective identity that marked their belonging to the institution. It became clear through the oral histories I collected that AMU was a conceptually and physically bounded environment in which students shared experiences, and became a brotherhood, a *biradari*, that bound them to one another and to place. The university exerted its protective disciplinary regime over them and extended the university's reputation even beyond its walls. The collective identity formed at AMU was deeply influenced by conceptions and use of space. This applied even in the spatially separate, but equally enclosed, Women's College, dominated by the Abdullah Hall. Yasmin Saikia has noted that "the experience of being with others . . . enables those within the space to negotiate a mutual relationship."[97] This friendship, cultivated in place, created a lasting sense of "responsibility to those with whom one shares the space," and deep connections to place.[98] The places that held meaning for the men and women of AMU extended beyond the campus and defined the very landscape of North India.

The proctorial system of discipline defined the ways that the university both maintained isolation for students and managed its relationship with the world outside. While women remained largely enclosed in the "fortress" of Abdullah Hall, for men the surveillance of the proctorial system reached into the city, extending norms and expectations for student behavior even when they left the visible confines of the campus.[99] The disciplinary system thus organized the space within and around AMU into layers, throughout which the university's authority projected. As former students narrated the their experiences, they imagined three concentric "circles of safety" that radiated out, with the campus as the center.[100] Geographer Yi-Fu Tuan has argued that the creation of boundaries, most intimately at the margins of the body and the home, defines spaces within which "material or conceptual" security becomes enforceable.[101] These imagined circles clearly defined the boundaries of belonging, meaning, and safety: the campus surrounded by the boundary wall; the town of Aligarh defined by the extension of the proctorial system (including railway station, movie theaters, and cafes); and the region beyond Aligarh adorned by the Muslim-influenced towns of the United Provinces (Agra, Bareilly, Delhi) and the students' homes.

Throughout these circles, the uniform AMU students wore clearly marked their association with the institution. The uniform itself was a curious mix of Eastern, Western, and Turkish elements. Despite the punishing heat of Aligarh during much of the year, the full uniform consisted of a black *sherwani* (a long, heavy tunic with a banded collar), white straight pajamas still known as "Aligarh pajamas," cotton socks, shoes, and the red Turkish fez. This costume represented Sir Sayyid's efforts to align the identity of Aligarh men with the "highest level of culture," by combining elements from India and the West, thus rescuing them from contemptibility in the eyes of the British.[102] When a boy donned the black sherwani and Aligarh pajamas, he began the transformation of becoming an Aligarh man.

During the 1940s, Professor of History and Pro-Vice Chancellor A. B. A. Haleem was remembered especially as the administrator who enforced the rules of conduct and etiquette. Students remember him as a stickler for the uniform. Despite his high regard for the British, and the fact that most teachers had dispensed with it, he still wore *churidar* (tight) pajamas and sherwani with Turki Topi (fez).[103] As Zakir Ali Khan told me, "That was the recognition of Aligarh. Looking from every angle, you can see that he is from Aligarh."[104] Some narrators even pointed to the uniform as a leveling agent—both Hindu and Muslim students wore it—so "you could not distinguish. [The Hindu] was wearing the Turkish cap, he was wearing that sherwani and he was behaving exactly [as we were]. He was given vegetarian food ... There was no fighting, there was no prejudice, there was nothing."[105] The uniform was fundamental to the identity of AMU students because it was not just attire, it communicated commitment to AMU's norms of behavior, irrespective of background. That all students wore the same uniform signaled the absence of communal feeling.

Retired AMU professor of museology Iftikhar Alam Khan remembered that his first exposure to the Aligarh sherwani was when AMU students arrived in his hometown to campaign for the Muslim League in 1945-6. They stayed in his father's village home in Fatehgarh. He remembered, "They had come from Aligarh, the university sent them ... And they used to say this that [the Aligarh boys] were outstanding speakers ... I was small but I remember that they were in black sherwani." Growing up in Farrukhabad, he had been educated in Christian schools where the boys wore khaki short pants and white shirts. Though his parents bought him several sherwanis to wear, he resisted wearing them after he was sent to Aligarh in 1948 and preferred his white shirt and khaki "knickers."[106] Still, he remembered being disciplined into wearing it by the older boys when he was a student in Minto Circle School in Aligarh.

> *One day I went to Shamshad Building* [adjacent to campus] *wearing khaki knickers and a white shirt. And a senior boy asked me, "Are you a student?" and I said, "Yes." "Where?"*
> *"In Minto Circle."*
> *"What dress is this?"*
> *"What's wrong with it?"*
> *He sent me back with another boy. He sat me on the back of a bicycle and said, "Take him back, put him in a sherwani and bring him back."*[107]

Young Iftikhar encountered the power of AMU's disciplinary agenda. The older students took it upon themselves to ensure that the younger boys conformed to the Aligarh way, most visibly in matters of dress, even in the markets beyond the campus walls.

The system of seniority, and the tradition of grooming younger boys to respect and obey their elders, is considered one of the hallmarks of the disciplinary regime in AMU. The older boys held power over the younger ones, and those who had been at the university longer had power over newcomers (even, oddly, if the longer-tenured student had failed his examinations and not advanced through his degree). Many narrators remembered that as juniors they were compelled to say "salaam" to elders before the elder greeted them. Professor Nasir Ali, who joined AMU in 1939, wrote that the system

> upheld the healthy traditions of Aligarh which constituted Aligarh culture. Any lapse on the part of their youngers elicited a stern admonition. These words were not uncommon, "Partner, this is not done here." The well-meaning authorities could justifiably bank upon their good office in maintaining discipline. The student community in general held such seniors in high esteem and followed their advice unswervingly.[108]

This self-enforcing disciplinary regime held prime place in the memories of narrators, and its priorities were the offspring of Sir Sayyid's priorities. The MAO and later AMU relied on the strictures of hierarchy and discipline within the circles of safety that emanated from Aligarh to develop the Aligarh man. In their memories of the period prior to 1947, discussions of the system of discipline pervade narrators' memories. Most speak glowingly of the system, but Saghir Ahmad Rizvi first saw it as sinister.[109] He told me that when he first arrived at AMU as an intermediate student, he was upset by the culture of seniority, and the fact that he had to obey the senior boy who occupied the rear portion of his suite in Sir Syed Hall. "He was the senior, so he used to dictate and so I have to obey him. So I passed this way, three or four months, and then I got tired of it."[110] Rizvi left the university and completed his intermediate degree in Lucknow. By contrast, Abdul Rasheed Khan told me that this system helped to build the solidarity of a familiar environment. "It was such completed brothership there, and my senior loved me like a younger brother and I respected him like an elder. Even in front of my 'elder brother'—I didn't smoke in front of him, in his presence. So that culture building was there."[111] That "culture building" was key to the creation of the powerful moral community that developed at AMU; its coercive aspects created a sense of vulnerability in the students, but once drawn into its fold, they discovered strength and support.

In a 1942 address to students, A. B. A. Haleem stressed

> the need for the maintenance of a high standard of discipline and explained that the most successful nations of the world to-day are those which have realized the value of discipline. Discipline is bred in the bones of the English, and we should not have any hesitation in learning from them whatever is good in their national life. Self-discipline is the noblest and highest form of discipline and it is only where self-discipline is wanting that it becomes necessary to impose it from above.[112]

Haleem reminded the students of their place in the hierarchical order of empire (though it reads anachronistically now, as the Pakistan demand had been articulated two years prior). The English were at the top, with discipline bred in their bones, but their standard was attainable. By maintaining self-discipline, students could avoid punishment. Two features stand out in Haleem's formulation. First, that civilization marked by discipline could be taught. Indeed, this was Sir Sayyid's mission for the institution. Second, that maintaining inner discipline would preclude the intervention of any outside authority. Haleem focused on the distinction between the world inside the university and the value of remaining isolated from the outside. At the same time, it was the strict adherence to the norms of the inside world that prepared boys for the world outside. Zakir Ali Khan emphasized the point that inner discipline built the resilience and self-assurance that students would need outside.

> We are proud of it and that it brought a lot of self-confidence in us. We can go anywhere, you give us any problem and then we will try to solve the problem . . . We will undertake the responsibility and we will try to resolve this according to the best of our ability. That is the lesson of Aligarh.[113]

Conclusion

Sir Sayyid's educational reforms were rooted in his own late nineteenth-century values and expectations. He wanted to free students from the bonds of the traditional (thus backward) domestic environment, but his residential plan appealed to conservative and respectable families by protecting the institutions that were important to them. In both curriculum and spatial design, the MAO College, which became AMU in 1920, embodied links between England and India. British and Indian faculty taught Western subjects alongside traditional Muslim ones. The spatial layout of the university itself both mimicked that of Cambridge and reflected that of Indian *havelis*. The enclosed environment of the campus facilitated the growth of the highly gendered ideals of gentlemanly comportment, dress, Urdu language, and Muslim faith. Inside the boundary walls, the students of the college became a "brotherhood" a *bradari* based on the shared values of the *ashraf*. Lelyveld points out that this *biradari* functioned in different situations, whether as a religious confession or a political interest group, and ultimately as the basis for an independent national identity.[114] The residential system and the extension of the proctorial system of discipline beyond the formal boundaries of the campus provided both formal and informal training for the world outside.

The "men-only" realm of the campus was distinct from home; it was a place where classmates and teachers stood in for family, where allegiance transferred from "home and mother to the broader world of manly responsibility" and to the institution itself.[115] However, the educational institution itself did not constitute the public sphere. It was a substitute domestic environment in which masculine values replaced feminine ones, in which young men could focus on their transition to the outside world. Only upon leaving its confines and facing the trials of the world beyond could they truly become men.[116] The boundary walls set the institution apart from the distinctly different world outside. They kept its wards in and the rest of the world out. But of course, they had to leave sometimes, for local forays into the city, or to return home for holidays. When students left campus, they were identifiable by their dress: black sherwani and white trousers. Thus attired, they remained both committed and subject to the university's norms. In the best of times this system offered stability, safety, and comfort.

However, when A. B. A. Haleem spoke to the students in 1942 about the necessity of self-discipline, political ferment was the order of the day. By 1942, the majority of students were becoming involved in political activism, many on behalf of the All-India Muslim League (AIML). Despite Sir Sayyid's efforts to keep education and politics separate, his efforts at organizing a Muslim constituency meant that Aligarh frequently appeared at the center of efforts to organize Muslim opinion and action. Sir Sayyid's Muslim Educational Conference was the first entity designed to unite the interests of elite Muslims. The anti-colonial non-cooperation movement found fertile ground there as students walked out and founded the purely nationalist Jamia Millia Islamia (JMI) on the steps of the Aligarh mosque. The All India Muslim Students' Federation was also founded at AMU. As politics encroached on the university's isolationist atmosphere, and students were compelled by the political opportunities that were sure to accompany the end of empire, the question of discipline became critical. During the 1940s, student were torn between the model of isolation and discipline that Sir Sayyid and Beck had created (and Haleem sought to perpetuate, at least with his rhetoric) and the allure of expressing themselves publicly. This tension between the priorities of the university inside and wider politics outside highlighted the meaning of the boundary between. Though students had always found ways to challenge Aligarh's strict discipline, during the period when the AIML's influence was dominant (1938–47), the lure of the broader world of politics was strong. During the 1940s, a time of intense political activity in Aligarh, students pushed beyond the university's boundaries—both social and physical—drawing criticism from both internal and external sources. Since its founding, the institution at Aligarh had been a hub of meaning and the source of protective authority for its students. The political ferment of the 1940s challenged that authority as students sought a place in a world where they would no longer be British subjects, but fully independent citizens.

2

Self-Realization and the Nation

AMU Student Activism

For students, AMU was well established as a place, a location that was bounded by meaning. The university's physical and emotional boundaries were coterminous with those of home. Faculty possessed a parental authority—often challenged—that sought not just to educate but to protect and guide. Students upheld the university's moral order and authority by sustaining their commitment to discipline and brotherhood.[1]

Within this unique environment, tension persisted between the ideals Sir Sayyid envisioned and the pressing realities of late-colonial India. The late nineteenth and early twentieth centuries were periods of dramatic transformation, of which Aligarh and AMU had been a part. The university had been founded in the upheaval of post-1857 British India. By the early twentieth century, too, periods of political tumult in India and on the campus created opportunities to test both the resilience of Sir Sayyid's ideals and the boundaries of the institution's mission. Increasingly, as students became involved in a variety of political movements, they strained against both. University administrators attempted to rein them in, by insisting on the distinction between the university as an educational environment, Sir Sayyid's ideal, and its value as a site for mobilizing Muslims as a political constituency, the vulnerability against which Sir Sayyid had fortified the campus. Despite their putative isolation, the potential of political change inspired students and they yearned to have a role. Political ideas gained currency in Aligarh especially in the face of an external threat. There were three key episodes when the fates of the community and the institution were particularly tightly linked: when it was founded (1875), when it became a university (1920), and when it became a political tool of the Pakistan Movement (1940s) that led to the independence and partition of the country.

The thread that runs through all three major political moments at Aligarh prior to 1947 is that of solidarity—Muslims at Aligarh came together to support one another for the advancement of the community as a whole. The persistence of dissenting voices within the Aligarh fold is a characteristic that has survived all of its political upheavals despite the efforts of the institution's well-wishers to convey an image of unity. Rather, it is the constant pursuit of an ethos of unity that has driven all significant political mobilizations on the campus. This continuity is important because it created a shared field of reference for all of Aligarh's major political moments. This solidarity creates context within which these moments can be read together, rather than as isolated, unique, and distinct. Compartmentalization renders Aligarh's politics vulnerable to claims of exceptionalism, it can easily push certain periods aside as anomalous. Isolating any of these episodes might provide fodder for state-centered narratives, but when they are read together, historically, the real meaning and intentions of the students' enthusiasm—to build and sustain Muslim solidarity—emerges.

This chapter connects Aligarh students' activism in the 1930s and 1940s to its antecedents, and decouples it from its outcome—the creation of Pakistan—to expose the students' motives. The Pakistan demand can therefore be read as part of a continuum of political action at AMU that began in its earliest days. Thus, the central priority of Muslim uplift emerges clearly as a separate objective from that of independent statehood. The concern of the student activists, particularly those at AMU, was for the community, its integrity, safety, and advancement. Those values sustained Sir Sayyid's objectives, but were in no way selfless or idyllic concerns. Aligarh boys fully expected that they would be the leaders of the Muslim moral community for which they worked. Their own welfare was tied to the community's fortunes.

Sir Sayyid first argued for the institution's value on the grounds of "relative deprivation" and post-Mutiny persecution. In his eyes, Muslims' resistance to English education would leave the community deficient; they would be excluded from consideration for prestigious posts, commercial opportunities and social interactions with "European fellow subjects."[2] Sir Sayyid envisioned closed spaces within which the students would be trained before emerging as actors in the colonial environment. It became clear, by the time of Sir Sayyid's death, however, that his loyalist views were not wholeheartedly shared by all Aligs, or even by all the founders of the Aligarh Movement.[3] In 1906, Muslim leaders came together to found the AIML in Dhaka. Though many of the League's founders had been part of the Aligarh Movement that sustained the reforms and funded the institution, the party was spatially and philosophically distinct. Significantly, early leaders, including the Aga Khan, hailed from cities outside the Urdu-speaking North Indian belt.[4] As Faisal Devji has argued, the founding of the AIML itself can be read as a reaction to Aligarh's loyalist conservatism. Still, from its early days, the League was concerned with Aligarh's well-being, and made a priority of raising funds to sustain the institution.

Shortly after the League was founded, students on the campus began chafing against British leadership there, and by the late 1900s and early 1920s the institution was actively grappling with the changing political environment of British India. As the hegemony of British power declined, and the leadership of MAO campaigned for it to be endowed as a university, Aligarh students and Old Boys became involved in both the anti-colonial Khilafat Movement and the non-cooperation resistance. AMU students refused to remain apart from the political agitation; they stood poised to direct the collective strength of the AMU brotherhood toward the larger world of anti-colonial politics. These efforts involved projecting the priorities of AMU outward and pulling the priorities of the nascent freedom movement inward.

Whereas during the 1920s AMU students were at the vanguard of non-cooperation, the administration retained British loyalties. Mubarak Shah Zuberi, the grandson of the long-serving vice chancellor Ziauddin Ahmad, illustrated these tensions when he remembered, "Mohamad Ali Jauhar came to Dr. Ziauddin, sent by Mahatma Gandhi, asking Dr. Ziauddin to close the university during the Khilafat movement or, 'If you don't close the university then you stop teaching English.' Dr. Ziauddin refused. And he said 'Why don't you ask Mahatma Gandhi go close Banaras Hindu University also?'" Ziauddin feared that resistance to British power and abandoning the instruments of Western education would merely serve "to put Muslims a century behind Hindus."[5] In fact, Banaras Hindu University did not embrace the calls for non-cooperation. Ziauddin, too, rejected the Ali brothers' anti-colonial stance and supported establishing the university with British government funding.

By the late 1930s, however, Muslims perceived their status to be compromised. The Indian National Congress held several provincial ministries, including in the United Provinces, and Muslims feared being disenfranchised as a minority. By the 1940s, the AIML, intent to rejuvenate support for Muslim nationalism after the return of Mohammad Ali Jinnah to Indian politics, exploited the tension between Hindus and Muslims and specifically recruited Muslim students. The League's message was well-received in AMU, and throughout the 1940s it held political dominance there.

Enthusiasm for the Pakistan demand tolled the death knell of the ostensible separation between education and politics that Sir Sayyid felt it was so important to establish. Archival and oral sources reveal the persistence of political activities, and even institutional support for them over a long period of time. The political atmosphere in AMU was rife with interpersonal and political frictions, though they have largely been obscured by selective historical concentration on individual episodes of political activity. As they engaged in political activities, students crossed and recrossed the physical and affective boundaries of the campus, both reifying and eroding them. With each transgression they altered the relationships between inside and outside.

Education and Politics: Continuity and Change 1898–1937

Despite Sir Sayyid's allegiance to British power, anti-British sentiment first became visible on the campus only a decade after his death in 1898. The tension that grew between the institution's trustees, students, and the English staff echoed growing anti-British sentiments in India and internationally but were rooted in much more local grievances. Whereas Theodore Beck, Aligarh's second principal (1883–9) had been a true devotee of the Aligarh project, and Shaukat Ali remembered Beck's "easy familiarity toward Indians," his successor, Theodore Morison (1899–1905), embraced a "stiff" policy toward the students.[6] Beck had frequently interacted with the students, even in games, whereas Morison maintained a boundary between himself and the students, even refusing to meet them at his bungalow.[7] In an unpublished pamphlet, Hameed-ud-Deen Khan, who arrived at the MAO College in 1909, remembered his disappointment at discovering that the English staff were not as friendly or "intimate with the students" as he had expected from hearing tales of Beck. Rather, he "gradually realized that the general atmosphere [in Aligarh] was definitely anti-British . . . I cannot say how far we were influenced by the political tempo, steadily rising in the country, but we had sufficient sources of irritation of our own."[8] The scene he described in his pamphlet was one motivated by its internal characteristics. In the words of S.

M. Tonki, a second-generation Aligarh student, who was drawn into the nationalist movement, "The struggle continued between the self-respecting trustees and the all powerful [sic] principal til [sic] 1919, when the last of them, Mr. Towle, resigned with the European staff following him **en bloc**."[9] The conflict with the English staff was emblematic of student discontent with imperialism, and "created a highly favorable atmosphere . . . for the reception of Mahatma Gandhi's non-cooperation movement."[10] That is, when the leaders of the nationalist movement, including Mohandas K. Gandhi and Aligarh Old Boys Mohamad and Shaukat Ali, urged Aligarh students to join the non-cooperation movement, they did so as much because of local implications as global ones.[11] As Hameed-ud-Deen Khan emphasized, however, localized concerns drove students to action. Discontent with the British staff coincided with more explicit political agitation on the campus surrounding the negotiations to transform the MAO College into AMU.[12]

The campaign for the Muslim university was a cause dear to the hearts of all associated with Aligarh, but the visions for the form and leadership of the institution varied widely. As Lelyveld and Minault have shown, the campaign itself became the battleground for factional rivalries; a deep fissure opened between anti-imperialist nationalists and pro-British loyalists. That the leadership of both the conservative and the progressive factions of Aligarh Old Boys, Ziauddin Ahmad, the principal of the MAO College, and Mohamad Ali Jauhar, the famed Khilafat leader, had been contemporaries at Aligarh in their student days, serves as a reminder of the diversity of perspectives that emerged from that enclosed and protected environment. Whereas loyalist Muslims sought comfort in the educational traditions that linked the university to British patronage, nationalist Muslims looked outward from the university into the broader world of India and the Empire.

A confluence of national and international events in 1919 and 1920 resulted in an agreement between the Congress, the League, and the Khilafat "in favour of non-cooperation," which put Aligarh, as a government-supported institution, under the spotlight.[13] The early twentieth century saw a rush of inaugurations of new universities, including Osmania, Dhaka, Lucknow, and Agra, that encroached on AMU's singularity.[14] No longer did its dedication to the secular education of Indian Muslims set it apart. A prominent group of Old Boys who had laid claim to Sir Sayyid's legacy, but come to see the loyalist aspirations of their alma mater as anti-national, led many students into sympathy with the pro-Turkish Khilafat Movement and anti-imperialist forces of nationalism. Mohamad and Shaukat Ali looked to the example of the Deoband Madrasa's insistence on eschewing government grants to argue that the university should remain free of British funding.[15] Despite the Ali brothers' vociferous resistance, "the ambitions for Aligarh as a central institution in an independent, Muslim, all-India educational system," characterized by affiliated junior institutions throughout the country, fell by the wayside.

The Ali brothers were loathe to abandon their goal, and in October 1920, Mohamad Ali convinced some of Aligarh's students to walk out in protest. Together, they founded the JMI, the "Muslim National University" in the Aligarh mosque. Other leaders, however, including MAO principal Ziauddin Ahmad, accepted a pared-down university model and moved to incorporate the AMU with government support. As it turned out, the Ali brothers' nationalist challenge accelerated the creation of the AMU, but the JMI, that "lusty child of non-cooperation," cast a shadow over the occasion.[16] The two new institutions of learning were inextricably linked during this period. They laid claim to the same intellectual history, yet they held opposing philosophies sacred. Their temporal and spatial coincidence tied education in Aligarh to trends in national politics, even if only by its resistance to them.

The defining moment of the nationalist period at the university has become the founding of the JMI, but the initial revolt did not have enough momentum to keep the institution alive. It was not long before many students returned to the newly founded AMU—in the interest of completing their education—though many retained their nationalist sympathies.[17] The League had held its annual session in Aligarh in 1925, and since then it had tried to draw students into its fold. Professor Mohammad Habib was successful in persuading more students to join the Indian National Congress during this period, though, and the party dominated the Students' Union. Congress influence indicated a rejection of the loyalist policies that the Union upheld under British leadership when discussion of British rule in India was strictly off-limits.[18] K. G. Saiyyidain, an Aligarh Old Boy and well-known Indian educationist, fondly remembered the great Union Jubilee debate in 1926 "when the students of the University endorsed with great acclaim, a policy of united nationalism."[19]

Long after the events surrounding the founding of the two institutions, nationalist sentiment remained evident in student publications, including *The Aligarh Magazine*. In 1930, an appeal for donations to the Sahibzada [Aftab Ahamd Khan] Memorial Fund was couched in nationalist rhetoric. The appeal called on donors to support AMU with funds because of its impeccable nationalist credentials. The appeal argued that students from all provinces of India met in Aligarh and

> on one side we are placing into the crucible the Hindus, the Musalmans, the Christians, the Sikhs and the Parsees of India and beating them all on the furnace of Aligarh to fashion out of this mixture a common substance purged of the alloy thereby creating the typical man—that future citizen of India on whom would rest the task of building the nation of this great land, and perhaps of the world as India promised to be the future leader of humanity.[20]

The appeal heralded the universal Indian citizen, a composite of many cultures that, once mixed, created a "typical man." Aligarh was cast as a forge for creating this typical man: one who, above all, held dear the unity of the nation and would forego the communal or sectarian allegiances that had become increasingly meaningful since the late nineteenth century.[21] The Aligarh man, in this formulation, was stripped of the defining characteristics of his religious identity. He had been homogenized in the hot fires of the furnace, purified, "purged of the alloy," and forged as an Indian. The Aligarh ideal elided difference as students emerged with a uniform set of ideals, ready to serve India, irrespective of their heritage.[22]

Throughout the 1930s, the Congress spirit remained evident in the university publications, the *Muslim University Gazette* and the *Aligarh Magazine* as writers frequently appealed for "understanding cordiality between Hindus and Muslims."[23]

They emphasized the contributions that Muslims broadly, and Aligs in particular, made, not just to Muslim educational and cultural advancement, but "to the country in general."[24] AMU was, for several decades, a testing ground for ideas as students explored alternatives to the state in which they had been raised. A distinct tension began to arise between the interests of the university, which had gone to some lengths to isolate its wards from the world outside, and the interests of the students who insisted that their contributions to that larger world be recognized. These tensions also exposed the variety of political opinion that had emerged from Aligarh over the decades.

Well-wishers of the Aligarh Movement argue that it "sought the intellectual and cultural regeneration of Muslims" and that "the essence of the movement lay in its spirit of freedom of thought and expression, and in the urge to keep pace with changing times," therefore producing "figures of all political shades and hues."[25] This rosy assessment should not obscure the fact that deep and enduring conflicts of values have fueled disputes over the direction that Indian Muslims should go. These trends were evident in the earliest days, and remained present during the campaign for the Muslim university and persisted into the post-nationalist 1930s and 1940s. Retired Kashmir University professor of Arabic Riazur Rahman Sherwani emphasized this point to me when I first interviewed him on the terrace of his Aligarh home in 2008:

> I want to tell you one thing, not only during this period, even from an earlier period when there was no Muslim League, even from that time, there has always been a section of teachers and students in this institution, when it was MAO College as well as when it became University, who thought on different lines from the administration of the university, or from the majority of the students. . . . Through all the phases, there have been students here and teachers also, whose line of action was different from that of the majority. I also belonged to that minority.[26]

The distinctions between political factions became distinct in the late 1930s as the devolution of power into Indian hands raised the stakes of political representation. In 1937, the Indian National Congress' election success allowed the party to form provincial ministries under the Government of India Act of 1935. This was a politically polarizing time, as Muslims came to grips with the reality of parliamentary democracy. In particular, although the League and Congress had worked together during the elections, generating nationalist enthusiasm, visible at Aligarh, once the ministry was seated, Congress declined to form alliances with the League. League partisans saw this as a breach of faith and used it to fuel support for their political movement.[27]

As a consequence, AMU students turned to the League for political expression, and Congress' influence waned. This transformation once and for all challenged the ethos of political passivity that the administration had attempted to preserve since Sir Sayyid's days.[28] In this context, the May 5, 1937, issue of the *Muslim University Gazette* took up the issue of the university's role in politics explicitly. Addressing the role of the university in the lives of the students, the editorial, "University and Politics," evoked the separate nature of the university itself and the dangers of the temptations of the world outside. While in the university—an enclosed space, apart from practical life and strictly bounded—students were being prepared for life outside, but they were not in it yet, and to become involved would mean a dangerous distraction from their educational priorities. Thus, the editorial reminded students, "the Muslim University allows fullest liberty to the students to discuss all social political and economic problems of the day and form into groups on that basis provided that the rules of discipline are scrupulously maintained and the strictly academic nature of these activities is not violated."[29] The May editorial further acknowledged that among the staff of the university there were a variety of views, but that all AMU staff "act as a body" to exert a wholesome influence on the students and to guide them in their studies and "they are always anxious to see that the academic atmosphere of this institution is not disturbed by forces outside this sphere."[30] The editorial raised two significant issues in its closing lines, one was the tension between education and politics—that would increase in significance throughout the ten years that followed—and the other was the idea that the forces of distraction and corruption come from outside the university.

The Muslim League activity indeed put both of these premises to the test. Whereas in 1937, nationalist sentiment was still strong, by late 1938 the pro-vice chancellor (academic head of the university), A. B. A. Haleem, went so far as to estimate that "about 90% of the students of the University have strong Muslim League sympathies and it is no exaggeration to say that out of 114 members of the staff about 100 at least are Muslim Leaguers."[31] Haleem's testimony placed Aligarh at the leading edge of the rapid expansion of Muslim League membership that followed its 1937 Lucknow meeting, and it put to rest the notion that education and politics could be kept apart in Aligarh.

From Muslim Nationalism to the Two Nation Theory 1937–47

As the Congress ministry in the United Provinces took its seat in 1937, the *Muslim University Gazette* published a supportive piece welcoming the leadership of Chief Minister "Pandit Pant and his co-workers, who are the right men in the right place, and who have been chosen by the people to govern in their name."[32] The same piece criticized "minority Government" as antithetical to the spirit of democracy, and therefore "unwholesome." It expressed trust in the motives of the Congress ministry to protect Muslim interests because Congress was "not a communal body and therefore it does not look at things from the communal point of view."[33] The author urged the new Congress ministry to recognize that "a backward Muslim society is a drag on the general advancement of the nation" and thus to make provisions for safeguarding the interests of Muslims, particularly with regard to education, culture, language, and religion. Ultimately, the author argued, consistent with the strategy that the *Gazette* had adopted during this period, the fate of Muslims was inseparable from the fate of the nation. It made no sense for the Congress ministry to abandon its Muslim constituents because although Muslims may have been "backward," they were part of India, and their lot was India's lot.

Significantly, the editorial cast Muslims as a minority, deserving of safeguards. The editorial rejected the concept of a "minority government" and urged the elected government to extend care to the minority. The minority, however, was subject to the whims of this government, and there was a mild but implicit threat that just as Muslims who received safeguards could help to ameliorate social ills, were the Muslims to find themselves empty-handed, they could prove an equally disruptive force. The role of the minority here was not to govern, but to hold the government accountable for its promises.

Beyond the university, in March 1937, Jawaharlal Nehru had issued a call to Congress to "make a special effort to enroll Muslim Congress members" and to engage them in practical politics while protecting the "religious, linguistic, and cultural rights of minorities."[34] The resulting Muslim Mass Contact Campaign was a reaction to Congress' poor performance in Muslim areas in the 1936 elections, and endeavored to draw Muslims into Congress based on common economic concerns rather than on the basis of Congress sympathy for Muslims' parochial issues, as it had done during the Khilafat Movement.[35] The Muslim Mass Contact Campaign targeted Aligarh and other cities in UP, and Mushirul Hasan reports, it "had a favorable impression" on students at AMU.[36] But Congress activity also galvanized the AIML, an organization then seeking to expand its franchise. Congress action in Aligarh and other Muslim strongholds in UP appeared to be an assault on the League's territory, leading it to redouble its own efforts.

By the end of 1937, it is clear that discontent with the Congress ministries had grown quickly both in the university and outside of it. Sir Harry Haig, the British governor, worried that Congress was establishing a parallel authority and that local Congress committees were undermining the district administration.[37] British concerns about Congress influence grew alongside the concerns of Muslims. An almost-frantic anxiety pervades an article on "National Education" in the year's last issue of the *Muslim University Gazette*. Since August, the *Gazette* had been grappling with the ideas at the heart of Mahatma Gandhi's Wardha Scheme of Education, primarily its emphasis on craft/industrial production.[38] Whereas Gandhi (and K. G. Saiyyadain, the scheme's chief architect) saw an opportunity for craft production to generate independent funds for educational development, the editor decried the notion, arguing rather that the state should direct more money and resources toward education.[39] But it was Pandit Madan Malaviya's Convocation address at Allahabad University that betrayed how threatened Muslims at AMU felt about Gandhi's educational scheme. The story heavily criticized Malaviya's use of Sanskritized Hindi in front of an audience conversant in an Urdu-ized Hindustani. According to this report, "when a gentleman tried to express his feelings of bewilderment, he was hooted down by the more vociferous section of the house, and no one questioned the despotic rule of the majority."[40] Only a few months after the magazine welcomed Congress ministries and expressed trust in their intentions to safeguard Muslim interests, this story cast majority rule as "despotic." It went on to attack Aryan Hindu claims of Indian nativity that would exclude Muslims, and argued aggressively for an inclusive system that would recognize the contributions Muslims made to India.

December 1937 saw two meetings of the Muslim Students' Federation, both held in Calcutta, one under the leadership of nationalist Humayun Kabir and one under Mohammad Ali Jinnah.[41] The All India Muslim Students Federation (AIMSF) had been founded at AMU, despite significant resistance from the still-nationalist Union; the double meetings suggest that tensions persisted within the Federation.[42] Remarkably, the speeches that each leader delivered in Calcutta appear to be in almost-direct conversation. Kabir chastised Muslim leaders for relying on a narrative of weakness and decline that provided the impetus for political organization; Jinnah deployed just such a narrative even as he urged the students to organize. He said that he had "failed" with the Hindus and that there was now "no other course open to us except to organize ourselves through separate organizations like the All-India Muslim Students' Federation."[43] Kabir called students to the nationalist cause, and urged them to "rise above their personal or their class interests" and work for the emancipation of their motherland.[44] It was a mistake, he argued, to believe that Indians or Muslims or the youth were weak, but it was obvious that by combining forces they would undoubtedly be strong. Jinnah argued that Muslims would no longer be "camp followers" and would never "be subdued or be camp followers or slaves or the subject race of 'Hindu Raj.'"[45] Citing the failure of the All India Students' Federation—over whose meeting he had presided the previous year—to include Muslims among the executive leadership and its failure to facilitate communal unity, Jinnah urged the students to "organize for self-defence and self-help."[46] The *Muslim University Gazette*, for its part, avoided taking sides between the two new organizations, but did not miss the opportunity to criticize the mainstream press for failing to cover the meeting led by Mr. Jinnah arguing that the press did not "attach much importance to the problems which immediately concern Muslims."[47] Thus, while resisting the urge to take sides, the paper articulated a call for an independent Muslim press, a move toward separate representation in the public sphere, a theme that would emerge again and again as the Muslim League ought to control its own propaganda/narrative through the 1940s.

Controversy erupted over the actions and agendas of the Congress ministries from the singing of the Bengali anthem *Bande Mataram* to the failure of Congress governments to protect Muslims from harm during communal riots.[48] Muslims felt threatened by the Mass Contact Campaign, which appeared to them to be an effort to drive a wedge between the Muslim masses and their traditional leadership. This was especially acute since much of that leadership had turned to the League in large numbers by the end of 1937.[49] The Wardha educational scheme had further frightened Muslims—already conditioned to fear assaults on their traditional systems of learning—with its apparent priority of teaching Hindu values, and even dancing (this came on top of the 1921 Vidya Mandir scheme, which sounded to Muslims as if schools would be turned into temples).[50] This close link between education and Muslim solidarity placed AMU at the heart of the tension. Shortly before his address to the inaugural meeting of the All India Muslim Students' Federation, Jinnah came to recognize the political value of Muslim anxiety. Sarfaraz Hussain Mirza suggests that Jinnah resisted the formation of a separate organization for Muslim students until late 1937 when he came to understand that "if the Muslim League intended winning the battle of Muslim freedom it must secure the cooperation of Muslim students."[51] Muslim students were critical to the success of the Muslim League's rejuvenation because of the power of the education-political nexus.

Whereas in the late 1930s, Jinnah mobilized student support by appealing to the idea that Muslims were a minority community that required concessions and safeguards in a democratic state, his speeches to student groups reflected, over time, the transformation in his mind from conceiving of the Muslims as a Minority to insisting that they be recognized as a Nation. One former AMU student described Jinnah's appeals to students as being the result of the fact that "he knew what revolution can a student bring in the masses. That is what actually happened."[52] The concept of belonging together that had been implicit in Sir Sayyid's efforts to develop the *qaum* at Aligarh now acquired power as a modern political category, even if it remained largely aspirational.

In 1938, the Muslim League published the *Report of the Inquiry Committee Appointed by the Council of the All-India Muslim League to inquire into some Muslim Grievances in Congress Provinces*, known colloquially as the Pirpur Report. In the minds of North Indian Muslim readers, the Report put paid to Congress' claims to communal fairness. Though many still suspect that the episodes it described were at best exaggerated, at worst "imaginary," the Pirpur Report stimulated Muslim mistrust of the Congress ministries and provided fodder for a clearly articulated common grievance.[53] The Pirpur Report alleged all manner of violence and disregard for Muslims on the part of both regular citizens and the authorities in Congress-governed provinces. It ultimately argued that communalism was driven by the majority community.[54] Part III of the Report is a detailed accounting of "Muslims' Grievances" in the six Congress-governed provinces: Bihar, UP, Orissa, Central Provinces, Madras, and Bombay. As might be expected, the Report was received with terrific anxiety, appearing as it did at a time when Muslims had already begun to lend their support to the League and its mission. It was the widely publicized Pirpur Report that finally turned the tide at AMU, and the League, with its updated message of empowerment, began formally to establish itself there.[55] Though he belittled the significance of the events listed in the Pirpur Report ("What were the atrocities? Nothing as compared to—two people killed there, one head broken there"), former student and retired Aligarh University professor of English Masood-ul Hasan described the allure of the League.[56] He remembered, "The Congress volunteers had their Young Men's Corps. Even the Khaksars, they had theirs. The ordinary young student, the ordinary young man, he was left out." The League seemed to present an opportunity to fulfill the students' desire for "self-manifestation."[57]

Mohammad Ali Jinnah visited AMU in March 1940 to make an important speech to the students just before he traveled to Lahore for the Muslim League session at the end of the month. During that visit, he spoke about the difference between Minority and Nation. The Muslim India of which Jinnah spoke in March was the same as the differentiated Nation that became the heart of the Pakistan demand. Since the advent of separate electorates in 1909, he noted, most people assumed that the Muslims were a minority requiring safeguards and governmental or legislative protection of their rights. In fact, this was the political strategy Jinnah himself had used throughout the 1930s. Now, however, he argued that when "we used this term . . . what we meant was that the Muslims were a political entity and that must be preserved at all costs."[58] Jinnah had turned away from the earlier rhetoric of decline, so ably deployed by reforming Muslim leaders before him, most notably Sir Sayyid Ahmad Khan, and turned a sense of exclusion into a call for action. Whereas the concept of Minority had given Muslims a false sense of security and Hindus a false sense of power, the concept of nationhood made possible a demand for political equity. This demand for parity would guide the League through the next seven years.[59]

The AIML leaders, for their part, especially Jinnah and his right-hand man, the Alig Liaqat Ali Khan, repeatedly reminded AMU boys of their centrality to the League's strength and Muslim life in general. Jinnah taught them that they represented India's Muslims and hence that India's Muslims were like them, regardless of their regional or linguistic origin. Major General Ghulam Umar remembered meeting Jinnah in March 1940 when he spoke before the Muslim University Union:

> On the eighth of March 1940, Quaid-e-Azam, Mohammed Ali Jinnah—he was not yet [known as] Quaid-e-Azam—he visited Aligarh and I was a student there. He addressed the students and during his address he used the word "Muslim India." One of the students got up and asked him, "Where is Muslim India? There are some provinces where Muslims are in the majority, four or five provinces, but otherwise, Muslims are in Bengal, in Madras, everywhere. What is this Muslim India?" And [Jinnah] said, "There is not a corner of India from which a Muslim student is not present here. This is Muslim India." In other words, that was his concept of Muslim community.[60]

Jinnah's words reflect the earlier explanation of the AMU identity, as one purified and forged in the fires of Aligarh's furnace, but the source of the material was here reduced to "Muslims." The image was so compelling to Umar that he held onto Jinnah's words verbatim for sixty years. The Urdu-speaking elites subscribed wholeheartedly to the idea that Jinnah inherited from Sir Sayyid, that the Muslims were a united moral community, which he now labeled a nation, because when they looked at its values, they saw themselves reflected. Mohammad Ali Jinnah further empowered the students with the words, "What Aligarh thinks today, Muslim India will think tomorrow."[61] This Muslim nation, and its claims, heralded at AMU just prior to the passing of the Lahore Resolution that articulated a claim for statehood, became the object and goal of the Muslim League Demand for Pakistan. For as in earlier attempts to mobilize the Muslims for change, Jinnah's demand that the League exclusively represent the Nation, paradoxically, was based on his desire to create a Nation, a political force strong enough to command attention at the center.[62] He missed no opportunity to convince the youth of this and to impress upon them the need to be self-reliant. "It was no use," he said, "depending on anybody. We must depend on ourselves. I am willing to be friendly with all but I depend upon my own inherent strength."[63] Jinnah understood his audience; his declarations affirmed AMU students' beliefs.

In 1941, before the students of Punjab, he berated the Congress for not catching on to the new paradigm: "Hindu leadership is still harping on the same old story that we are a minority and that they are willing to give all the safeguards according to the principles laid down by the League of Nations."[64] Jinnah tried to draw the students away from a narrative of dependency and into one of self-reliance. A critical part of this was an appeal for solidarity within and among Muslims themselves. Jinnah recognized, and it was clearly apparent to him in his political work in the provinces, that Muslims, though unified at least nominally by their shared faith, were divided by a variety of factional loyalties. His claim to nationhood could never stand without at least apparent internal cohesion within Muslim communities. And the students were key to this appeal. He reminded them, "Muslims must remain in complete unity and solidarity amongst yourselves. Nobody can help you if you quarrel among yourselves."[65]

A key question about Jinnah's intentions persists, however, and that is how he expected a Muslim identity comprising Muslims from all over the country to transform into the "independent states" outlined in the Lahore Resolution of 1940. The resolution called for the aggregation of areas in which Muslims were numerically in a majority in the Northwestern and Eastern parts of India. By 1940, Jinnah and the League interpellated territoriality into the idea of nationhood—the strategy marked a departure from the fluid contours of Sir Sayyid's *qaum*—as represented by Muslim majority areas that the Lahore Resolution demanded. In an address to the Punjab Muslim Students' Federation in March 1941, Jinnah unambiguously declared, "We are a nation and a nation must have a territory," a nation "must have a territorial state and that is what you want to get."[66] Was the Pakistan demand understood to be territorial? I believe there is sufficient evidence to make clear that it was. However, the question of completely separate statehood remained unresolved until very late in the negotiations for Pakistan.[67] In 1945, for instance, Fayazuddin Tariq, a student at AMU, wrote a letter to Jinnah seeking AIML support for the foundation of a Medical College at the university. He noted his return address as Maris Road, Aligarh, Pakistan. Pakistan did not exist in any form in 1945, but on Tariq's imagined map it included the familiar ground of home in Aligarh. Contrary to the arguments that Aligarh Muslims expected to be connected to Pakistan via a corridor linking the Northwest and Eastern zones, Tariq's mental map suggests a different understanding of Pakistan's territoriality.

There was already a precedent for semiautonomous statehood with which the students of AMU were familiar. The support of local landholders and nawabs had been instrumental to the establishment of the educational institution in Aligarh. One narrator went so far as to suggest that the location of the institution was strategically linked to their investments. "Sir Sayyid was a great visionary and he has chosen a place which is very near to Delhi and it is surrounded by small Muslim states. Small states you could call them, but they were all feudal lords. They were very helpful in establishment of Aligarh Muslim University."[68] Indeed, the small Muslim states of UP encircled AMU. And, even farther afield, leaders of AMU and the princely state of Hyderabad in the Deccan had long maintained these links by serving in one another's institutions. The Nizam of Hyderabad was the chancellor of the university, the Nawab of Rampur its pro-chancellor and a significant financial patron.[69] Nawab Ali Hasan Khan of Bhopal "was a great admirer of Sir Sayed and . . . helped Aligarh college with money and support."[70] The Nawab of Chattari, a local *zamindar* (landlord) and Aligarh patron, was the prime minister of Hyderabad State from 1941 to 1943 and again in 1947; he also served as chancellor of Osmania University in Hyderabad. It was not inconceivable that a Muslim state could exist within a larger Indian polity, and Aligarh's links to Hyderabad, Rampur, Bhopal, and other Muslim states proved it. The presence of Muslim majority states, princely and otherwise, too, lent power to the idea that Muslims represented a political entity, "or to put it in words that Jinnah would use from 1940, Pakistan already existed in colonial India."[71] There was no conflict between a Pakistan demand that was both territorial and part of India, because its component parts were joined by an ethos of solidarity through which Muslims were forged into a moral community of shared values. AMU students saw in the Pakistan demand the familiar terms of the Aligarh Movement. Pakistan, for them, was not merely a territory where Muslims would occupy the majority, but a consolidation of the priorities of their founder. Pakistan, for them, meant empowerment through solidarity.

This narrative of solidarity resonated at AMU, an institution built on an ethos of unity, a place that even now zealously guards its legacy as a place free from communal or factional strife. This is, of course, a fiction, and while the AMU environment may not have been dominated by Hindu-Muslim strife, the student body was far from monolithic.

The League Period at AMU, 1940–7

During the League period, other political groups continued to function on the campus. In particular, the leftists, led by Professor Mohammad Habib, resisted League hegemony. One of them, Indian graduate Nasim Ansari, described in his memoir a university where among the students were "representatives of every province in India and followers of every party" where "whether differences between them were based upon class or upon theories, they were not concealed in any way."[72] This assessment fits very neatly into the image of AMU as a diverse yet harmonious environment, but several narrators described surprising levels of political bullying and coercion aimed at enforcing the League's agenda. Certainly the Congress and the leftists continued to operate on the campus throughout the 1940s (and both have remained powerful there since 1947), but it was at risk of attack by the League. Irfan Habib, Mohammad Habib's son, withdrew from the Muslim University High School after being bullied and pushed into a ditch because of his family's politics.[73] In an off-the-record exchange, one narrator described the arrival of several Communist Party activists near the English House hostel at AMU. When the young students realized who the representatives were, he told me, they began shouting abuses and catcalling. The narrator is not alone in remembering the exclusivity of the League sympathizers. Riazur Rahman Sherwani recalled:

> During the earlier days, leaders of various parties used to visit the university. Pandit Nehru was very popular among the new generation of that time. And he visited the university in early 1930s . . . Gandhiji also visited this university. All those people used to come here. But when Muslim League had a sway, it had hold of the university, the leaders of other parties stopped coming here. Not stopped, they were not allowed to come here. Only leaders of the Muslim League, they used to visit the university and no leader of any other party could come here.[74]

The Muslim League monopoly during this period extended to personal relations, and as Sherwani was a nationalist and Congress supporter throughout this period, he told me, "My father was always anxious that I may not be harmed physically due to my views. Because the majority of the students were of a different point of view, so his main anxiety was my safety."[75] The League enforced its position through all manner of persuasion, not all of them peaceful. They took over the Students' Union and became what Jinnah called "the arsenal of Muslim India" when they later fanned out across the country working for the Muslim League in the 1945–6 elections.[76]

As a result of the Muslim League influence, the university continued to struggle with the relationship between education and politics within the university. Former student Hameed-ud-Deen Khan argued in 1967 that the campus had always been immune to the "communal virus" because no matter what the political views of the college and university leadership, "they never allowed the students to take any active part in politics."[77] Even Irfan Habib confirmed that whatever the beliefs of the faculty, their teaching did not betray their politics.[78] Time and again the *Gazette* harmonized on this point: students were in the university for training, not to get involved in political action. The frequent reminders to students that their job was to stay focused and to study, but not to agitate, betrays a formidable anxiety over their disruptive potential. Hameed-ud-Deen Khan argued that faculty had remained aloof by refusing to lecture to AMU students "about Muslims' fears and aspirations," but by 1938 Pro-Vice Chancellor A. B. A. Haleem was proclaiming the strong Muslim League sympathies of students and faculty. In fact, the engagement of the faculty and staff of the university with the League agenda was a key distinguishing feature of the League period. By 1945, as Muslim League leaders at Aligarh, including Haleem and Manzar-i-Alam, attempted to secure their claims on leadership positions within the party, Aligarh students wrote letters to Jinnah advocating for them.[79] The boundary between education and politics had been all but totally eroded, with dire consequences for the institution and its leadership.

Vice Chancellor Ziauddin Ahmad had shown, throughout the terms of his leadership, that he opposed student involvement in politics.[80] This was clearly on display in the dispute over non-cooperation in 1920, and as late as 1942, during the Congress Quit India Movement. Students in other universities, particularly Allahabad, Lucknow, and Banaras, actively responded to the Quit India agitation, but, as Irfan Habib remembered, AMU remained quiet. Mukhtar Zaman, as a student of Allahabad University, clearly remembered seeing the Hindu students form a procession to protest the spontaneous arrest of the Congress Working Committee.[81] Both at Allahabad and at AMU, however, the Muslim students remained apart. Certainly, by 1942, the League had gained significant traction at the university and the discipline of the students may also be seen as a reluctance to associate themselves with Congress' movement. However, the British credited the calm to the willingness of Ziauddin Ahmad to cooperate with the authorities.[82] Ziauddin actively encouraged the students' passivity. In a Central Assembly debate in 1942, he declared, "I very much deplore that some political organizations are using the students for political propaganda," and he went on to lament the collusion of the teachers.[83] While this could be a reference to League activity in AMU, considering the timing it is far more likely to be a direct attack on student involvement in the Quit India agitation. Jinnah, too, praised the students' restraint in a speech before the AIMSF at Jalandhar in November 1942, congratulating "the Muslims that they in a body, from one end of India to the other, had kept completely aloof from the mass civil disobedience."[84]

League leaders both enjoined the students to join the League and work on behalf of its ideals and urged them to focus on their education, and not to be distracted by the temptations of national politics. Valuable though they were, the students were a volatile and potentially fickle constituency. In the early years of the AIMSF, Jinnah and other Muslim politicians had urged the students to focus on their studies, to support their community, and to prepare themselves for the "future responsibility" that would fall on their shoulders as leaders of the Muslim community.[85] Jinnah guided the students, through his appearances, at once encouraging them to prepare for their future role in Pakistan and simultaneously cautioning them against being swayed by sloganeering and "catch words."[86] He retained their allegiance throughout this period with his long-held promise that when "the time comes, and when you are ready, I will tell you what to do."[87]

Aligarh Students and the 1945–6 Elections

Throughout the 1940s, the League developed its values among AMU students and elsewhere, but it was not until the occasion demanded, in the 1945–6 elections, that Jinnah moved to deploy his arsenal. Muslim League politicians impressed upon the students that the elections were "life or death" for the League and the Muslim Nation; the results of the elections would determine the viability and influence of the Muslim political community.[88] Jinnah urged students to do everything they could to support the League. They participated in fund-raising, propaganda and pamphlet distribution, voter canvassing, and the establishment of polling stations.[89] "Even at the cost of one academic year," Liaqat Ali Khan, Jinnah's right-hand man, told them, the time had come "in the life of the nation" that academic sacrifice was deemed appropriate to ensure independence.[90] For the first time, Ziauddin Ahmad, the vice chancellor, facilitated groups of students leaving the university to campaign for the League; he began actively to encourage student involvement in the freedom movement activities that he had previously opposed. The League organized a special training camp at AMU in October 1944 to educate student activists about the specifics of the Pakistan demand. The agenda of the training course included lessons on Islamic history, Muslim League history, and Pakistan, as well as lectures on the "Art of public speaking, and Manning [sic] the polling booths."[91] The students who participated in this course were then dispatched outside of Aligarh to work on behalf of the League. Under the banner of the AIML, the students embraced Jinnah's call to action.[92] Students were indispensable to the League during this time. They traveled the countryside spreading the message about Pakistan and garnering support. The students joined in droves, leaving the protective environs of the campus, of Aligarh, of the purview of the proctorial system of discipline. The students described a sense of freedom, of "spaciousness" that contrasted with the sense of sometime stifling security they felt in the university itself.[93]

Liaqat Ali Khan was instrumental in organizing the students for election work. Pakistani Brigadier General Iqbal Shafi recalled that Liaqat personally visited the campus and interviewed the groups who wanted to go electioneering. Seeing the young Shafi, then only a fifteen-year-old boy, Liaqat asked,

"*Mian Sahibzada aap kya karengey?* What the hell are you going to do? . . . *Mian Sahibzada, aap kya karengey?*"
I said, "Sir, I recite the poems of Iqbal."
"Which poems do you recite?" I said, "*Utho Meri Duniya [ke garibon ko jaga do]!* (Rise and arouse the poor of my world!)"
So he said, "Fine! Fine! Don't waste my time.". . . what he meant was, we were passed! You see, "Alright, you go."[94]

The League provided minimal financial support and sent this group to Punjab and the Northwest Frontier. The boys encountered resistance there as both provinces were officially opposed to the League.[95] Still, Shafi argued, "That was the thing. Government against you, but the masses with Quaid-e-Azam. That was the atmosphere! We were in between."[96] The giddiness with which Shafi remembered his deployment came through in his memory. This was the moment that he became a full-fledged participant in the Pakistan Movement! Many narrators spoke excitedly about those experiences.

While on those electioneering trips, students spoke to gatherings of people, particularly after the nighttime prayers.[97] Abdul Rasheed Khan, now teaching in Karachi's Sir Syed University of Engineering and Technology, recalled, "We went to towns and villages to convince the people to vote for Pakistan. In those days we were very staunch supporters."[98] In the students' minds, their election work made a significant impact on the outcome of the elections, even in minority provinces, where Muslims were not expected to shift to Pakistan territory. Nonetheless, recalled Khan—who worked in the Hindu state of Balrampur in UP—"My feeling is that Pakistan could not be formed without their vote. They voted 100% [for Pakistan]." Mukhtar Zaman, himself a student activist and the author of an important monograph *Students' Role in the Pakistan Movement*, suggested, "The youthful zeal of the student workers created a good impression on the electorate . . . the students' participation in the campaign improved the image of the Muslim League . . . and the words uttered by the students were heard with attention." AMU boys, in particular, he wrote, "looked impressive" in their black sherwanis and Turkish caps, and "left a mark on the imagination of the masses."[99]

Many of the AMU students who fought these elections hailed from minority provinces, though it was not obvious that they would be required to shift to Pakistan to enjoy the benefits of Pakistan's autonomy. Jinnah aggressively propagated the idea that minorities in India would be protected by the mere presence of a Muslim state—what has become known as the "hostage nation" theory.[100] According to this theory, both minority Hindus in Pakistan and minority Muslims in India would be protected by the presence of their co-religionists across the border. In 1945, however, the locations of those borders, or how they would function, were not clear to anyone. Still, as Abdul Rasheed Khan put it, "that was the aim, that Pakistan will look after the interests of Muslims in the minority in India."[101] Ultimately, however, many of these families, including those of AMU students, did migrate to Pakistan during or shortly after the mass migrations of 1947 when Pakistan and India were permanently divided. Rather than creating connection, these migrations created a fissure between the Muslim communities on either side of the border.

The involvement of Aligarh students in electioneering on behalf of the Muslim League has persisted as the most resilient image of Muslim student activism for Pakistan, and was the "high point" of their association with League politics.[102] Indeed, AMU students have been credited with galvanizing rural support for Pakistan.[103] Their enthusiasm, as seen from the Pakistani side of the border, establishes their credentials as transparently nationalistic. From that angle, it appears that AMU students, as a whole, shared enthusiasm for Pakistan and the League's goals. Indeed, Bangladeshi jute expert Salahuddin Chowdhury told me that the idea of Pakistan was "more or less not controversial" when he was a student at AMU. Pakistanis hailed the influence of youth in the elections. For many of the young men who supported the League and ultimately chose to migrate to Pakistan, the emergence of the League fulfilled a hitherto nascent desire for action. It was an exciting and inspiring time to be at AMU.

Indian narrators spun the same events in the opposite direction, and even decried their involvement in the elections.[104] Masood-ul Hasan, one of a very few Indian narrators willing to speak in some detail about his experiences in Muslim League electioneering, represented League activity as an "occasion for self-manifestation." In retrospect, though, he dismissed student electioneering activities as inconsequential, overblown in the students' memories. With some bitterness, he noted that because Aligarh boys played an active role in electioneering, "Aligarh had to pay heavily later on, we still have to pay for it."[105] In contrast to Ghulam Umar's clear and glowing recollection of the transformative power of Jinnah's visits to AMU for consolidating the identity of Muslim India, and Iqbal Shafi's glee at being allowed to join an electioneering group, Masood-ul Hasan's memories were tinged with hostility. Jinnah had adopted a phrase to empower AMU boys that has remained the most powerful marker of the intimacy between AMU and the Muslim League activism for Pakistan; on March 10, 1941, in a speech before the Aligarh Union, Jinnah cried, "Aligarh is the arsenal of Muslim India and you are its best soldiers!"[106] Remembering this, Masood-ul Hasan remarked, "Here is Jinnah Sahib, he coined that phrase 'arsenal.' 'My arsenal.' 'Arsenal.' Anybody would feel puffed up! Okay? We were nothing."[107] The League harnessed the enthusiasm of the young men and, in Masood-ul Hasan's opinion, used them to accomplish its goals. He remembered with some regret that "Aligarh's boys came in handy. Why? Did they come in handy because they were committed to the cause? I tell you! Not so. I speak as an insider. Not so."[108] Throughout his recollections, Hasan reiterated that he thought support for the League was childlike and ill-advised. But he had been among the many students who fortified the League organization in the late 1930s and early 1940s, at a time when many forces came together to galvanize Muslims in solidarity and action.

Delhi University professor of History Mohammad Amin resisted the suggestion that there was any coercion on the part of League sympathizers to draw in others. Rather, he told me, if a student didn't want to go electioneering for personal reasons, there was no pressure to do otherwise. "If one is thinking, fifteen or twenty days, that would be a loss," then one might decide not to go.[109] Amin pointed to the debate on the fundamental conflict between education and politics: electioneering interfered with the academic agenda of the university. If students went away, they might not be able to keep up with the content or meet the requisite attendance minimums to be allowed to sit for their exams. At first, League leaders toed the university's line; they encouraged students to spread the League's message only during their vacations. Later, Liaqat Ali Khan urged them to give up even a whole academic year, if necessary, to fight for Pakistan. Iqbal Shafi, then only a student of the Intermediate, was unfazed by the potential effect on his academics. Whereas Amin had worried about meeting attendance requirements, when Shafi realized that his attendance would be insufficient for his year to count, he began to look forward to the further adventures he might have instead of attending classes! Imagine his disappointment when the vice chancellor Ziauddin Ahmad (remembered as always an advocate for students) allowed students to sit for their annual exams despite the ostensibly disqualifying poor attendance.[110]

Many of the interviews I conducted addressed this period, and there is a wealth of correspondence between League leaders and AMU leaders that reveals a much more complex and fractious relationship between the university and the League that can complicate straightforwardly nationalist perspectives on student activity. State-supported teleologies in Pakistan, for instance, cast AMU men as the quintessential Pakistanis, but in India state narratives cast them as perfidious. The correspondence between League and university leaders reveals a close intellectual relationship, but also some tensions financially and culturally. For all the attention paid to the image of AMU students as the foot soldiers of the Pakistan Movement, an examination of the correspondence reveals surprising ambivalence. It seems that the glorified image is largely retrospective. In fact, student activism was dominated by the same kinds of factional concerns that characterized all political activities at the institution.

The university administration—from the Union to the teaching staff to the vice chancellor to the pro-vice chancellor—was not only sympathetic to the demands of the League, but obviously complicit in its expansion at AMU. Though the vice chancellor and the pro-vice chancellor were rivals for power at the university, both Ziauddin Ahmad and A. B. A. Haleem were actively corresponding with Mohammad Ali Jinnah and Liaqat Ali Khan about League activities.[111] Khan Bahadur Obaidur Rahman Khan Sherwani was, at the time, the honorary treasurer of the university, and responsible for managing the funds that the AIML sent directly to the Muslim University Muslim League (MUML). These funds were disbursed through Sherwani and the accounting was documented by the chief accountant of the university.[112]

The MUML, which gained official recognition as a City League in 1945—and thus was officially affiliated to the Parliamentary Board—"in recognition of the services it [had] rendered ever since 1937" worked feverishly to organize students for election work in the closing quarter of 1945. Letters to Jinnah cite a variety of election activities undertaken by large numbers of students: "500 student workers were sent by our university Muslim League for all the provinces but largely for UP";[113] "700 selfless warriors" demonstrated the "untiring zeal of the Muslim youth";[114] "600 students and 20 members of the teaching staff" were able to help the League in the Central Assembly elections.[115] After the stellar showing of the League in the Central Assembly elections, MUML president Manzar-i-Alam began to organize for the Provincial Assembly elections. He leveraged the official position of the MUML to appeal directly to Jinnah for funds.[116] There was a flurry of correspondence in late 1945 between AMU Leaguers and M.A. Jinnah as Jinnah himself tried, from a distance, and at this late stage, to begin to manage the League affairs at AMU. A rift between Haleem and Ziauddin Ahmad divided the League forces at AMU, and pitted Manzar-i-Alam and League propagandist Jamil-ud-din Ahmad against A. B. A. Haleem after Jinnah asked the latter to chair an election work committee. Jamil-ud-din resisted Haleem's appointment and recommended Manzar-i-Alam out of concern that the students would undoubtedly reject any person who appeared to be usurping the power of the MUML.[117]

The students, the foot soldiers of the League's electioneering team, here became leverage in the aspirations of university officials to acquire their own political power. The students were a potentially disruptive force as much as they were a potentially mobilizing one. The university officials understood this dynamic well, and Jinnah appeared to have his own anxieties about it, which might explain his unwillingness to involve them in the world of active politics in the first place. Even as Jinnah authorized up to Rs. 30,000 for student League work, he cautioned his acolytes to work together. Their unity would be rewarded with his attention and support.[118] Ahmad and Alam succeeded in officially displacing Haleem as the chairman of the Election Funds Committee, forming on December 11 a "responsible committee after full consultations with the Vice-Chancellor Dr. Sir Ziauddin Ahmad and all others who are genuinely and actively interested in Muslim League work." The committee was led by Dr. M. B. Mirza of the Department of Geography. Khan Bahadur Obaidur Rahman Khan Sherwani, honorary treasurer of the university was to serve as the manager of the funds Jinnah sent, and the remaining two committee members were Ahmad and Alam themselves.[119] Within ten days, Jinnah sent ten thousand rupees and ardently requested that Jamil-ud-din, as convener of the committee, keep in close touch with him in regards to its use, seemingly in addition to the accounting that Sherwani was to send. The committee leapt into action, immediately dispatching "225 students to Punjab, 25 students to NWFP, 22 students to Sind, 10 students to Assam, 7 students to Bengal, and nearly 75 students to United Provinces and other provinces of India" despite the fact that the university had already closed for the winter break.[120]

On January 19, 1946, Haleem's contingent fired back. A fourth-year bachelor's student, a resident of Aftab Hostel, wrote to Jinnah to inform him that the real election committee, led by A. B. A. Haleem and consisting of "responsible members of the staff aided by enthusiastic students," was carrying on League work and organizing the students. In contrast, he argued, Ahmad, Alam, and others were doing nothing but "making propaganda on their ownselves [sic] and using the League for personal advancement but obstructing sincere League workers in the university area."[121] The student thus appealed to Jinnah to unseat the current committee and replace it with a committee led by Haleem. It is important to recognize that all of the officials on both committees were involved in League work, and some of them, including M. A. H. Qadri (Haleem) and Jamil-ud-din Ahmad (Alam), were working to create and distribute League propaganda through official channels. Throughout this dispute, Jinnah played his cards close to his chest, repeatedly urging the complainants to work together for the good of the League.

The entire affair came to a head over the allotment of the Aligarh legislative seat for the provincial elections. The UP Muslim League Parliamentary Board allotted the seat to an Aligarh businessman (and League worker) in January 1946. However, most correspondence in protest of his appointment does not even refer to the nominated candidate. It is evident that the real power play—at least as it appeared in AMU—was between A. B. A. Haleem as president of the UP Muslim Students' Federation and Manzar-i-Alam, president of the MUML. Both Haleem's and Alam's partisans argued that the seat rightfully belonged to their leader. This was the first time that the realm of active politics acquired relevance in the workings of the League partisans at AMU. Until that point, the factional bickering had seemed to revolve around internal issues. It now became clear that all of the League leaders, on both sides of the dispute, sought to leverage their involvement into greater political prestige in representing the new Pakistan.

It was here that the League edifice at AMU began to crumble. It may have been the fulfillment of AMU's anxiety about the infiltration of active politics into the academic environment, or perhaps it was just the outcome of unbridled youthful enthusiasm. The significance of all this bickering lies in the role of the students, long held to have been the "arsenal" of the League elections. AMU's disciplinary responsibility had been complicated by the empowerment of the students as political agents. As the vice chancellor's anxiety about this grew, he repeatedly attempted—ineffectually—to reel the students in. Irfan Habib remarked that Ziauddin "was very afraid of taking action against hooligans," even if this meant manipulating the rules in their favor.[122] In 1946 (as I examine in greater detail in the next chapter), their behavior began to get out of hand. By mid-1946, that arsenal turned mercenary and Jinnah's fears were realized. Hameed-ud-Deen Khan, then professor of Persian at the university, reported that when Ziauddin realized that Pakistan would finally be created, he withdrew his support for student political activity. He called a closed-door staff meeting and "said that it was time that there was a shift in Aligarh's political role. Aligarh had to remain in the Indian Union and had to adjust and adapt itself to the situation. Political realism demanded that Aligarh [withdraw] itself from the political forefront."[123]

As far back as 1920, Ziauddin had been resistant to student political activity, but throughout the 1940s he had defended students against charges of indiscipline— even beyond the campus boundaries—and he had permitted students who had gone electioneering to sit for their annual exams. His rededication to disciplining student activity manifested in several ways. The best known is that he withdrew from publication an issue of the student *Aligarh Magazine* over the charge that it contained an inflammatory, anti-Hindu article on the aftermath of the 1946 Bihar communal riots.[124] In addition, Ghayurul Islam, honorary secretary of the Muslim University Union, complained to Jinnah that Ziauddin Ahmad had threatened to dissolve the League organization.[125] In late 1946, as he tried to temper separatist League enthusiasm, students agitated against him. Masood-ul Hasan recalled that students organized a "demonstration in front of the VC's office. Schoolboys on their way to Minto Circle also joined the procession and they marched to the office. Offensive slogans were raised, glass-panes smashed, and the VC was forced to tender his resignation. It was unbelievable that a popular VC like *Dr. Ziauddin Ahmad* could be treated by the students so disgracefully."[126] His tolerance may help to explain how the students gathered so much power in such a short time. After a long struggle between the political worlds inside and outside the university, the educationist in Ziauddin won out, but the students, energized and politicized, ousted him. Discipline broke down completely. Ziauddin, perhaps, had also been drawn in by the promises of Pakistan. They sounded so consistent with the cause to which he had devoted his life. He participated in empowering a body of students with such a sense of entitlement that it seemed they would be able to pluck the ripened fruit of Pakistan. Just then, he withdrew his support, and they drove him from his position as their leader.

In a letter to Jinnah in January 1947, Ziauddin blamed "communist students exploiting the name of the Muslim League," by which he meant the Muslim Students' Federation, led by his old rival A. B. A. Haleem. He conceded, "On account of the impossible demands of the students, and absence of support from the staff, I did not like to continue." The choice of the next vice chancellor, Ziauddin noted, would be in Jinnah's own hands.[127] This authority in reality belonged to the Aligarh Court, comprising members from many walks of Muslim life, but it was a key site of factional posturing, and Ziauddin acknowledged the reality that many members took their marching orders from Jinnah. In that moment, it appears, six months before the official creation of Pakistan, that its boundaries were coterminous with those of Aligarh, though Aligarh would never officially become part of Pakistan.

By separating the outcome of the Pakistan demand from the political mobilization that made it possible, it becomes clear why the League's rhetoric appealed to the AMU students. There was no suggestion that the students would be required to migrate elsewhere to enjoy Pakistan's fruits. Rather, the Pakistan Movement, driven by Muslims bound together by common interest, led by Aligarh students, would give "expression to the hidden feelings of the Muslim nation."[128] In his speeches before the Aligarh Union, Jinnah frequently emphasized the rapid growth of the Muslim League since 1938. In November 1941, he told them that in 1939 the League had become big enough, influential enough, that it had become impossible for the British to ignore it. But as he spoke, the League had become strong enough "to make as big a hell, if not bigger, as Congress can."[129] This is a significant declaration considering the impact of the League's political losses in the 1937 election, and it primed the students to keep working for the League; the outcome of political action was strength, and it was measurable, and it was growing. In case the students had not fully grasped the implication of the rhetorical shift from minority to nation, Jinnah clarified: "It is not a question of concession or compromise, protection or safeguards. It is a question of the inherent birthright of Mussalmans to self-determination as a national group inhabiting the sub-continent to establish their own states in those zones where they are in the majority."[130]

Conclusion

The official narratives that unproblematically incorporate the narratives of Aligarh's Muslim League to serve particular national agendas have both deliberately overlooked the actual content of political ferment at the university during the 1940s. The students were mobilized by the terms of the demand for Pakistan, drawn to the empowering ideal of representing themselves as a nation to be reckoned with, rather than as a minority to be protected. This critical shift in the Muslim League rhetoric drew the students in, even before the formal passing of the Lahore Resolution in 1940. They were spurred toward this choice by the criticisms of the Congress ministries in the late 1930s that made it appear that Hindus were abusing Muslims in every corner of India. The election campaign, organized through the university, appeared to be the modern way of responding to this oppression, and the students enthusiastically traveled, sometimes very far afield, to educate Muslims in towns and villages about their new political power. When they returned to the boundaries of the campus, utterly distracted from their studies, they did their best to maintain the momentum of electioneering in an environment overflowing with youthful energy. League leaders took advantage of this energy and deployed the students to advocate for their own political aspirations. Having built themselves a constituency, they now appealed to it for support.

Aligarh in 1946 was tumultuous and roiled. When the university administration began to withdraw its support for the Muslim League's Pakistan agenda, the students, aware of their own persuasive powers, mounted a revolt. Pakistan, for them, was very real, even if they didn't understand it to mean that they would have to move to a specific territory. Pakistan, to them, was an obligation to educate and uplift other Muslims, to draw in and protect their own and to attain a measure of political power and influence. Ziauddin's ambivalence for this agenda, and his ultimate refusal to condone the rhetoric of hatred that came with it in the wake of communal rioting in Calcutta and Bihar, marked the high point of unrest. Having exhausted their energies, the students got back to preparing themselves for Pakistan. Even Jinnah rarely visited during 1945 and 1946. He had been so active there in the early part of the decade, inspiring the students to work for Pakistan, and once they were consolidated, he left them to work under the leadership of their own; once they had proven their worth in the Central Assembly elections of 1945, he funded them for the provincial election work. But Jinnah had stepped into a hornet's nest, and though he always sought to calm the tensions and controversies at Aligarh, it undoubtedly caused him some anxiety to see how unpredictable his arsenal could be.

3

Pushing the Boundaries
Partitioning and Aligarh Muslim University

I often wonder how the young feel, who, at the threshold of their lives have seen and experienced catastrophe and disaster. They will, no doubt, survive it, for youth is resilient; but it may well be that they will carry the mark of it for the rest of their days.
—Prime Minister Jawaharlal Nehru, Aligarh Muslim University, January 24, 1948[1]

During the communal riots and disturbances of 1946 and 1947 in India, for the first time AMU students felt afraid. During this time, growing communal tensions disrupted the sense of isolation and safety so integral to the university's identity.[2] As Ahmad Saeed remembered, "in '47 . . . these communal riots [were] all around us. We used to read it in newspapers. Naturally we were scared. And we were in the center of it. All around there were people belonging to the other community. So we were scared! And there were threats also. At least we felt so, I don't know how real they were. So, naturally, there were threats."[3] The landscape of fear and threat that Saeed described, in which AMU appears surrounded, defined a dramatic shift in meaning for the university. This amounted to a profound *"loss of context"* that created "a feeling of extreme contingency and vulnerability in carrying out everyday activities."[4] By virtue of their faith and heritage, and their allegiance to the highly visible Muslim university, the students were "naturally" threatened when communal identities redefined the meaning of Indian space. In the face of this threat to their sense of place, AMU students began to fear the world around them.

AMU was never attacked during the violence of partition.[5] Yet fear, what Yi-Fu Tuan has identified as a combination of "fear and anxiety," permanently rearranged the relationship between AMU students and the world around them. As Tuan argues, "Alarm is triggered by an obtrusive event in the environment, and an animal's instinctive response is to combat it or run. Anxiety, on the other hand, is a diffuse sense of dread and presupposes an ability to anticipate."[6] This definition aptly applies to AMU in the mid-1940s. A growing sense of dread, fed by the publication of Muslim League propaganda like the Pirpur Report, created a tense anticipation that Muslims would be targeted if they ventured beyond the safely constructed environs of the university. At the same time, Tuan argues, anxiety can drive an effort to seek either security or adventure fueled by curiosity. As the example of student electioneering has shown, students thrilled in the "spaciousness" it offered, but when they returned to campus, they were reluctant again to be contained within the disciplinary regime that had a been "a jealous guardian and protector of their rights and privileges outside the University area."[7] In 1946 an episode of violence in Aligarh city that involved AMU students triggered the "alarm" that transformed persistent anxiety into fear. As violence threatened, or appeared to threaten the campus, from the outside, students retreated into the boundary walls of the university, ever more starkly defined against the non-Muslim world outside. In Saeed's explanation, AMU was "in the center" of all animosity directed toward Muslims.

Throughout 1946–7 mounting violence beyond the campus altered the AMU boys' view of the world. It was "not to be measured by external acts of murder, loot, or abduction" but the "state where a sense of fear is generated and perpetuated in such a way as to make it systemic, pervasive and inevitable."[8] This was a new paradigm, one governed by a "fear of not belonging" in a place where one had always belonged before. Students discovered, throughout the period of partitioning, that places that previously seemed safe, protected—from cinemas to trains to the city of Delhi—were no longer accessible. The narrators who betrayed a sense of having been traumatized were not those who moved away from the institution—even into places that were "disrupted," like Delhi, or Punjab, but those who remained intimately attached to AMU and all that it symbolized, who had to renegotiate the circles of safety once so clearly associated with the institution. Indeed, as Salman Khurshid has suggested, for those who chose "to stay at home," it has become difficult or impossible to "speak of the trauma, the injury or the insult."[9]

To understand the trauma of partitioning in AMU requires an interpretive shift away from a narrative that suggests that violence "was" Partition (isolated and singular), and toward one that can incorporate "everyday violences" that caused the disruption of particular sites of meaning.[10] Experiences of partitioning Indian space started before August 1947, and continued long after. In AMU, trauma was intimately connected to place and the university's ability/inability to ensure students' safety in the spaces beyond the boundary walls of the campus by expanding its disciplinary regime.

The story of partitioning in Aligarh was not a story about national borders, but it was about boundaries and the effects of transgression.[11] As Edward Casey has argued, the state border's power is "restrictive and foreclosing."[12] In the particular context of partition's borders, Vazira Zamindar's *The Long Partition* has shown exactly how newly drawn state borders between India and Pakistan served to restrict movement and belonging in the years after the 1947 Partition.[13] The boundary around Aligarh, however, was more "pliable and porous," and therefore distinct from the "cartographic or legal entity" of the state border.[14] The boundary, in Casey's formulation, "facilitates the movement ... of bodies across it"; thus, the boundary defines the place, or as Casey puts it, "*boundaries are where places* happen."[15] The margin that connected AMU to the world outside did have protective power, and the institution's reputation spread beyond the campus and the town. However, as students crossed this boundary and ventured into the world beyond, as they frequently did during the 1940s in support of the idea of Pakistan, its protective power diminished.

This chapter examines the former students' narratives closely and shows the impact of the disruptions partitioning has exerted on everyday life in and around the university. I explore the experiences of AMU students throughout the 1940s: how they interpreted the changes taking place and the effect those changes would have on their own lives. As Nehru noted in 1948 during a speech at the university, AMU graduates were starting out in the midst of "catastrophe and disaster"—the disruption of the moral order of the university, and, by extension, the credibility that this moral order had promised to provide as they built independent lives. As they narrated their experiences of the 1940s, they drew their narratives through particular sites in and around the campus. These sites once formed the context of their daily experience, but were rendered strange by the destabilizing uncertainty of partitioning. The sites of social violence that former students referred to, which became sites of terror, were previously places where their safety was ensured by the marks of their belonging to AMU.

Those narrators who remained in India described the disruptions to their lives by speaking primarily in terms of how the new paradigm of distrust born of communal politics affected their relationship to place. During the electioneering, students took risks by crossing out of AMU's formal boundaries, and beyond the reach of proctorial monitors, as they boarded trains bound for Assam, Punjab, and distant towns in UP. The AMU uniform and identity was their ticket to explore this broader world. But, by the middle of 1946, as AMU's identity was increasingly politicized, the power of access the unique AMU identity gave them began to diminish. The political activism of the mid-1940s caused a recentering of AMU as a hub of Muslim nationalism. In the context of the anti-colonial movement, this parochial identity increasingly came into conflict with the Congress' aspirations for a united India. While the Indian National Congress officially proclaimed its commitments to secular nationalism, AMU students experienced heightened levels of tension with the non-Muslim communities surrounding the campus. The risks of boundary-crossing transformed into objective dangers as AMU remained in India and its students, readily identifiable by their dress and comportment, were held partially responsible for the outcomes of partition.

The importance of AMU, for its students, was that it constituted an "organized world of meaning" that layered their understanding of home and family with their aspirations for the future.[16] It was a bounded place within which they could develop their ideals, and despite the protestations of the university administration, could even sustain political opinions and activities with growing confidence throughout the 1940s. When former students described their lives in AMU before 1947, they drew attention to it as a place, defined by behavioral expectations and predictable social relations. They also spoke of the space beyond, an outer circle of protection that connected them to sites of importance in the city and the broader region of the United Provinces (now UP). Taking their unique perspectives into account, this chapter argues that the disruption of AMU's isolation thrust students into the heart of the disturbances of partitioning, even before the drawing of the distant borders. These are ironic stories: Indian narrators, many of whom have remained close to the university, the source of protection and prestige, tell stories of disruption and discontinuity, whereas Pakistani narrators emphasize continuity, even as they experience physical dislocation from the university they remember. AMU students enjoyed the benefits of the university's special prestige before partition, and anticipated promising futures. Partitioning disrupted the moral order that supported this prestige in the context of the social violence that is the source of their trauma.[17]

The Inner Circle of Discipline, 1946

As they remember the period surrounding the 1947 Partition, narrators described a university under siege by hostile communities. Mohiuddin Khan, now settled in Bangladesh, told me that "the atmosphere was also tense. Sometimes we used to feel that maybe we may be attacked by Hindu majority people around . . . at night we used to remain very careful."[18] By describing their efforts to protect it, these narrators affirmed their allegiance to the university. They had patrolled its boundaries and kept watch from the rooftops. They rallied to defend the campus against potential attackers, "wielding—many of them even trembling with fear—the sticks of the mosquito nets."[19] There is a persistent narrative of threat, but some students remembered responding with a show of strength, as when Zakir Ali Khan told me, "We used to guard the university. We used to travel in trucks and whatever transport all around the university periphery. We spent nights together guarding the university."[20] The students were determined to protect their own safety within the boundaries of the university against any threat of outside attack from what Zakir Ali Khan called "mobs," and they never referred to engaging the outside authorities to maintain peace.[21] Since AMU's earliest days, and in the memories of many of these narrators, the university's independence from the civil authorities was a source of pride. Zakir Ali Khan told me that there was no need for police intervention because AMU's own disciplinary system operated so effectively.

However, in reflecting on the events of 1947, several narrators referred to the deployment of a military regiment around AMU during the disruptions.[22] In Mohiuddin's memory, "the government protected [the university] with Tribal People Regiment, Gurkha Regiment or something, they were guarding the university."[23] Khan's pride in the memory of the disciplinary regime contrasts with the sense of security Mohiuddin described as a result of the presence of troops on the boundary of the campus. There is an almost imperceptible silence here in the story of partitioning in Aligarh. That AMU would relinquish control over its safety to the Indian military shows that something significant had changed on the boundary between the campus and the non-Muslim world around it. While at first glance this may appear to be a reaction to the scale of the threat, further investigation revealed that the arrival of the troops marked a shift in AMU's relationship to the city and to state power as a result of the disciplinary breaches that were allowed during the League period.

One episode, in particular, emerged from interviews, to mark the collapse of confidence in the disciplinary regime at AMU that had been so meticulously upheld throughout the 1920s, 1930s, and early 1940s. The episode, in March 1946, revealed the impact of transgression across the boundary between the city of Aligarh and the university through an act of student indiscipline and university administration's response to it. Though the original episode commenced as a show of student strength, it enabled the possibility of retributive violence by city dwellers that established the precedent for the fear of attack that animated the university in 1947. As much as the political environment at AMU had been determined by local concerns, in this case violence loomed from the outside, but the fear emanated from a disruption to the familiar, local environment.

In the spring of 1946, as students returned from electioneering, there was an attack on a local market in response to which the government deployed a company of military police. As Irfan Habib recounted the event to me, "In 1946, Aligarh students, in a large mob, went to the grain market of U.P. and burnt it. And five villagers were burned to death."[24] Iqtidar Alam Khan told me that this was the first episode of violence that "disturbed" him, and it ultimately led him to leave the university and to pursue his intermediate education elsewhere. His memories of it were not vivid, because he was a boy, and "living inside the university." However, he did "remember some persons who were serving the students living with us in the hostel used to pretend they were participating in the events. I don't know how far it is true. To the extent that sometimes I used to feel very afraid."[25] Khan's memory that the hostel staff bragged about being involved with the burning of the grain market in the town indicates that Muslims were in a position of power in this riot. Despite the power of Muslims in the conflict, the riot left students feeling vulnerable, and this sense of vulnerability persisted in their outlook throughout the years of partitioning. There was no precedent for a Hindu attack on the university that would justify deploying troops to protect the campus. Rather, as the memories above reveal, AMU students threatened the residents of the city. In fact, the military police were not deployed to protect the students from the city dwellers as they remember; they were deployed to protect the city dwellers *from* the students. How then, did this episode become the source for a narrative of fear and anxiety among AMU students that characterized the transformations of partitioning in Aligarh?

On March 29, 1946, there was "an altercation between AMU students and the proprietor of a Hindu cloth shop, in which students beat up the shopkeeper."[26] This incident, occurring as it did, in the heated environment of the 1945–6 elections and growing communal tensions, sparked a riot, the burning down of the grain market, and the deaths of at least four individuals. The *Times of India* reported property damage valued at about Rs. 650,000.[27] The British governor[28] blamed student indiscipline for the riot, and noted that the "Hindus in the town always live in a kind of half panic" under the threat of the sometimes-unruly students.[29] To mitigate student threat, the government created a Riot Scheme for the posting of a military police company at several points along the railway line "through which the students are likely to enter the city."[30] The government's Official Inquiry Report, published in May, stated that the best place to stop the students was at the *kat pulla*, the bridge over the railway tracks.[31] The official report noted that due to the "strong corporate spirit" of AMU students, it would require a great force to stop their rowdy behavior. Therefore, the report suggested bypassing the university's proctorial staff, typically the first responders in incidents of student indiscipline, and punishing those involved in the riot with a fine.

The university responded to the incident by increasing its defensive power, acting on the sense of threat the students also remembered. Without calling upon the services of police or military, the university increased the number of *chowkidars* (watchmen) and armed them with sticks. Faculty and staff were enlisted to help in "patrolling the area with guns and being present in batches of 2 every night."[32] The university fortified the boundaries, even though the students had instigated the violence, and in the eyes of the city dwellers and the authorities, the students were the aggressors. In a meeting of the Academic Council during which the resolutions to increase protections passed, there was no discussion of sanctioning the student culprits.

The British governor was concerned that the local authorities were ineffective at controlling the students and that the incoming Congress administration would respond vindictively to the event. Congress Muslim Rafi Ahmad Kidwai did harbor some concerns that the collective fine would be too broadly applied, and potentially harm Muslims, including city residents, who had not been involved in the riot. Nonetheless, as home minister in the UP Congress ministry, he noted derisively, "In the past whenever there was some trouble the matter was referred to the university authorities and they somehow managed to let the students free."[33] The incoming Congress leaders favored taking legal action against the students. Paul Brass argues that a conflict with Francis Wylie forestalled Congress action on the matter, but Irfan Habib explained that the intervention was much closer to home. His father Mohammad Habib, at the behest of AMU vice chancellor Ziauddin, convinced Congress chief minister Govind Ballabh Pant to use restraint in his response to the students.

> So actually, Rafi Ahmad Kidwai was Home Minister and he issued a statement that there will be prosecutions and imprisonments. You can't kill people. So Dr. Sir Ziauddin, Vice Chancellor, came to our house... My father was enraged at this [and argued] "They must be punished!" And Ziauddin said, "You know, Habib Sahib, it's useless talking to Kidwai Sahib. Talk to Pantji. He was your leader in the Swaraj Party. We are prepared to do everything they tell us. But prosecutions? What will happen?" So my father went to Pant, went to Lucknow, and he told us later that Pantji was very annoyed. Very annoyed. [Pant] said, "Rafi Sahib is right, we shall have prosecutions and we have witnesses. They shall go to prison!" And they had put military police, not in the university, but at the clocktower. And all the students, the moment they saw the military police at clocktower, totally there was demoralization in the university. Silence. My father said, "Alright, I'll tell [Ziauddin]." But as he reached the door, Pant said, "Habib, come back. After all, they are our children. We don't want to see them in prison. So tell Ziauddin it should not happen. But I'll tell Rafi Sahib to tell the police to withdraw the cases." So that's 1946.[34]

These explanations radically alter the narrative of perceived threat in AMU. For one thing, they show that AMU students had the capacity to threaten other Aligarh residents, despite the geographic boundary of the railway tracks separating the two communities. For another, they do show the power of the university to affect policy. Finally, they show Ziauddin's approach to student discipline; he was primarily concerned with protecting them from a threatening outside world, even at the expense of punishment and those hurt by their behavior.[35]

Though all of the details of the episode show that AMU boys were in a position of power, perpetrating violence and getting away with it, still narrators emphatically repeated their fear that Hindu mobs would cross the *kat pulla*. It is critical to remember that no Hindu group had yet done so (and did not do so in 1947); rather, the Muslim students frequently crossed over into the town. The transgression of this boundary was deeply symbolic; it was the vein through which students accessed the town, but in the minds of the students, traffic on the bridge must be unidirectional. The fear that Aligarh Hindus would breach the boundary incited terror in the students and betrayed their belief that the university might be unable to continue to protect them.

This episode demonstrates why, despite the distance from the disturbed border areas in 1947, AMU students did feel so afraid. The actions of a few of their number left people dead in 1946, and though there was no retribution then, legal or otherwise, the possibility that the mostly Hindu residents of the town would exact revenge was again aroused during the communal disturbances of 1947. AMU students also understood that the student body as a whole would be held responsible for the actions of a few— this was the darker side of their commitment to the AMU brotherhood. Masood-ul Hasan has written specifically about the students' anxiety during this period, though he omits the role of the students in provoking the anger of Aligarh's Hindu residents:

> In 1946 when communal riots had broken out on a large scale in the country, one evening a rumour got 'round that the University was to be attacked that night. Some night patrolman got panicky, and the University siren was sounded as a warning. But the students took it as a challenge, and rushed out of the hostels, wielding—many of them even trembling with fear—the sticks of the mosquito nets. Some of the more prudent strategists were even said to have chosen the ground under the dining-tables as a more advantageous field of operations. The Proctor had a hard time of it, and it was with considerable difficulty that he could send the boys back to their hostels.[36]

Hasan's explanation characterizes the university as the victim of undifferentiated communal hatred, but he also shows students ready to respond with a show of force. The students rose up to defend their institution against "challenge" (he does not classify the potential act as retributive), though the show of strength and the fear of victimization are closely linked. Even those running out to meet the challenge trembled, a biological response to fear. Others simply ran to hide! This explanation, and its silences, clearly shows the difficulties the university faced in 1946 and 1947. The students' violent behavior had provoked a potential response much too large for the university to defend against. Both the state and the students had lost faith in the university's proctorial system (with the state seeing it as an impediment to discipline), and each adopted a defensive stance against the other by fortifying the boundary between.

Irfan Habib remembered that during the 1946 deployment the students were "chastened" by the presence of the troops, indicating the power of external authority to modify their behavior in a way that internal discipline had been unable or unwilling to do. The presence of the authorities at the clocktower in 1946 would have been an unambiguous signal that if AMU's students were to continue causing trouble in the city and with local residents, the university's traditional sovereignty would be subject to challenge by the authorities. However, in the memories of these narrators, the official presence of troops near the campus was not received as threatening, but as protective, comforting. Irfan Habib is alone in remembering the deployment as "demoralizing"; for him, it chastened the Muslim League activists, who had been his sometimes harassers. For most, this turn toward finding comfort in state protection during times of disruption was a marker of a more significant nationalist turn that began in AMU during this period. It is this nationalist reorientation that provides the context for the memories of those Aligs who remained in India throughout the disruptions documented here. Still, it is interlinked with the disruption that Aligs experienced as a result of partitioning, a process they experienced in very local and personal ways.

As former students remembered this period, the events of 1946 collapsed into the events of 1947 so that it appeared to them that the police posted near and around the campus were protective forces deployed to keep the university safe from external attack during partition's upheavals.[37] This perspective confirms the notion that the government was concerned with protecting the institution itself and, by implication, India's Muslims. Narrators read back nationalist solidarity and allegiance to the Indian state onto the partitioning of Aligarh. This effort was part and parcel of the effort of AMU Muslims to outlive the suspicions about their loyalty. It has changed people's memories, making it possible for them, in some cases, to deny allegiance to the Muslim League, to mask their desire to migrate to Pakistan, to conceal student violence against one another and against non-Muslims, and, ultimately, to seek to overwrite the League period at the university by suggesting it was little more than an anomaly.[38]

Nonetheless, the fear and anxiety that former students reported from this period was real, "systemic, pervasive and inevitable."[39] Their concern was that the boundary walls of the institution might be breached, that non-Muslims would cross the wooden bridge, enter the university, and attack the students. With the passage of time, most have neglected to remember that the attack they feared may have been retributive—rooted in the local conflict between AMU and the town—and not, as they remembered, an unprovoked attack on a helpless minority.

There is a significant difference in the tone of some of the narratives here, too, that helps to illuminate the power that national narratives exert on memory. Perhaps the most dramatic contrast appears in examining statements from Pakistani engineer Zakir Ali Khan, and AMU retired professor of English Masood-ul Hasan (cited earlier). The experiences of these two men, even during their time as students, was dramatically different. Khan was an avid sportsman and captain of the university hockey team, and he had access to the privileges of that position.[40] Hasan, on the other hand, was studious and unathletic. His allegiance to the Muslim League ideology of Pakistan had long since become a source of regret, whereas it was the core of Khan's identity. Both men were on campus during the uncertainty of 1946–7 and partitioning at AMU. Khan remembered his experiences through a distinctly "League" lens:

> When we were in Aligarh there were nights when the university was being attacked by the villages in which Hindus were living all around Aligarh. The Hindu mobs, it was a very rabid-type of organization of Hindus. They were in mobs, [organizing]

attacks on the university by villagers. We used to guard the university. We used to travel in trucks and whatever transport all around the university periphery. We spent the nights together guarding the university.⁴¹

Khan remembers two significant aspects of this experience. First, the threat to Muslims from Hindus was so real that he remembers the campus actually "being attacked" by Hindu mobs. Second, he and his compatriots adopted a position of strength in the face of this threat. They did not cower under tables or hide inside the hostel as in Hasan's recollection. They traveled the university periphery to guard it from attack.

The contrast between these two explanations is worth considering, for Khan's narrative contains a key factual inconsistency. AMU was not attacked during the 1947 Partition. Zakir Ali Khan's description of patrolling the university is, at its heart, a narrative of triumph. He and his fellow students faced the threat of attack with strength, and he has imagined an actual attack to prove that they were successful. This narrative sits easily with the Muslim League narrative of Muslim vulnerability in India, but it is fortified by the idea that Muslims could wield power, as they would in Pakistan.

Hasan's explanation, however, revealed the fact that the Muslim students felt vulnerable, more consistent with AMU's post-1947 stance, when the narrative of Muslim empowerment had worn away and AMU once again seemed a Muslim outpost in the hinterlands. Hasan's perspective represents an Indian nationalist disavowal of AMU's 1940s devotion to the Muslim League—a group seen as "separatist" in India. This disavowal seemed necessary to protect his own integrity and the integrity of the institution as loyal to the Indian state. Even as he revealed these experiences to me, Hasan betrayed his anxiety: "I don't usually speak of them for the fear—or I shouldn't say fear—that I might be misunderstood. And my credentials may be unnecessarily questioned even at this stage."⁴² Hasan's anxiety that his former attachment to the AIML, if publicly known, might impugn his credentials reveals a key anxiety lurking beneath the declaration that the Indian government has always taken care of AMU.

AMU's protective power collapsed in 1947. One narrator, who had been in AMU since 1945, revealed how his father's refusal to extract him from AMU during the disturbances reinforced for him the value of the solidarity cultivated on campus. Though first terrified, he ultimately found solace and strength with the other boys.

> I wrote to my father. "Please call me back. I am being frightened over here." He said, "Why? You are a coward, boy? No! Be there in the hostel. What happens to the other students will happen to you also! And I think nothing will happen."
> AA: And was he right?
> KPS: He refused to take me back home. He was at that time at Kanpur. So Aligarh was not so far from Kanpur. [He could have come] anytime! . . . *No, no.* Nothing has happened. It was correct, but I was a lad and so much frightened with my other students. They were from far distance so could not go there easily but I can go to Kanpur very easily. But he refused me, I still remember that thing. That gave me some encouragement. He said what happens to others, it will happen to you also!⁴³

After the 1947 borders were drawn, and refugees began to enter Aligarh, he told me, "We were asked to safeguard our university in the night and *we put a searchlight on the roof of V.M. Hall and we did duty up there. . . At night we watched so that there should not be any attack*."[44] Students had become a major line of defense against the newcomers, who could ally with the already-incited Aligarh Hindus. Here, however, there is no mention of the Indian government or military. As the transition to independence took hold, it was not clear who could protect Muslims from suspicions challenging their loyalty to the very state that demanded it.

Outer Circles, Other Sites of Disturbance

It was not only within the hallowed walls of the campus that AMU's reputation offered protection and influenced student behavior. Narrators frequently spoke of three other sites of meaning—Aligarh's picture halls, the railway platform and trains, and the city of Delhi—that occupied outer circles of safety. Disturbance of these other sites demonstrated the necessity of renegotiating the boundaries of belonging during India's partitioning. The "circles of safety" that surrounded the institution shrank as the threat grew.[45] The proctorial system could not protect the students from fear, and it could not prevent them from acting out their fear on others.

The picture halls of Aligarh had been a favorite stomping ground of AMU students. As Majid Ali Siddiqi remembered:

> As far as the entertainment was concerned. There were only picture houses. Two or three picture houses were there. You would go to the picture house. And in the picture house, also, I must tell you. There was a Proctor Seat. A Proctor Seat in the back—*there were two picture houses, there weren't so many*—in the Proctor Seat he used to sit free. That boy, he used to sit in the Proctor Seat and watch all the Aligarh boys in the cinema house, they are not doing any mischief.[46]

Because they were so popular, the university drew them into its disciplinary regime. Many narrators told me about the special seat kept aside in Aligarh's cinema halls for the proctorial monitor.[47] Under the watchful eye of the monitor, AMU boys could go to the cinema, and it became a sort of extension of the residential system. This system was designed to control the behavior of the students, to ensure they maintained the upright "character" the university expected.

However, in 1949 when Iftikhar Alam Khan arrived at Aligarh, as a student of the Minto Circle preparatory school, he described (in a mix of Urdu and English) a very different scene.

> *To go a film you had to have at least eight or ten boys together [and] because there would be the bigger boys included, you could get permission from the Warden. I never went. Because I knew that in the film houses there were stabbings and people were killed. I feel that in all of those years,* there is a cinema hall, Tasveer Mahal, which was very close to the university and I used to go to that one. *But I was most*

afraid of Royal because I knew that a lot of people were killed there in '47... I believe that in the two or three years I was there, only once I would have gone and in that because lots of students were going to see this film together, some famous film and everyone was going. But I was so scared.[48]

The sense of threat he felt in going to the cinema halls in the years following the 1947 Partition contrasts sharply with the decorum of the earlier scene and points to a significant disturbance in the moral order of the university and its relations with the town.[49] He felt safe only in that cinema hall that was closest to the university; the farther the boys moved from the campus boundaries, the less they sensed the university's protective power. No longer did association with AMU represent prestige, as it had before 1947, it represented vulnerability.

The railway station was another site under the disciplinary purview of the proctorial monitor. Like the cinemas, the railway station functioned as an extended part of the campus and AMU boys were highly visible there. As Masood-ul Hasan remembered, "The discipline within the compound of the halls, that was the responsibility of the Provost and the warden. The discipline outside—the extramural discipline you are supposed to say—it was the responsibility of the proctor."[50] The railway station was the gateway to Aligarh, a site through which almost all students had to pass as they moved between university and sometimes distant homes. "He was a big guy, [the] Senior Proctorial Monitor. He would flaunt about it. They would display badges. And they were especially prominent at the railway station where every arriving and departing train was attended upon by them."[51] The visibility of the monitor in the railway station sent a message to both students and community that the space was within AMU's bounds.

The station, as a fixed space, was within university surveillance, but the students imagined their privilege extending into the trains themselves. Prior to 1947, AMU students frequently traveled by train without actually purchasing tickets. Many narrators referred to this "Aligarh tradition," and argued that between Aligarh and Delhi, a distance of fewer than 100 miles, AMU students were not expected to purchase a ticket. Iqbal Shafi argued that it was a question of dignity:

> It was below our dignity, of Aligarh students, below our dignity to buy a railway ticket to go Delhi or Agra. It was our railway. And all these railway officials knew that these are Aligarh University students, they'll never buy tickets so nobody bothered.
> AA: What do you mean it was "below your dignity?" What does that mean?
> Iqbal Shafi: Why should we buy tickets? We are going to Delhi and coming back! You know, Aligarh was like this hub and one side was Delhi and the other side was Bareilly and the third side was Agra. Agra, about forty miles, Bareilly about sixty miles, and Delhi about ninety miles. This was a free-for-all, and nobody bought the tickets. Why should we buy tickets? We are going to Delhi, Aligarh and you know, Bareilly. Anyhow, so that was the tradition.[52]

Shafi declared that the lines that connected Aligarh, Delhi, Bareilly, and Agra were "our railway"; these were the arteries that linked the Muslim centers of Aligarh, Delhi,

Bareilly, and Agra, from which many AMU students and professors hailed. The direct rail connections between these cities affirmed that the connections between them were more than just spatial. Doreen Massey has argued that place is defined in part by networks of meaning that link it to other places, that "local uniqueness" should be understood as the sum of wider contacts.[53] Thus, the railway lines constitute the web of meaning that sustained the networks through which students accessed other cities. Shafi, here, incorporated the whole region around Aligarh into AMU's outer sphere of influence. So influential was the university that AMU students, he felt, were entitled to move freely in this are without fear of legal challenge. Although he seemed to recognize that the privilege of traveling without ticket was not strictly speaking legal, it was certainly tolerated, because of AMU's reputation for raising young men of character. However, this was to change.

During the 1945–6 elections, AMU students depended on the "privilege" of free rail travel. They put pressure on this system as communal tensions mounted all over the country, sometimes erupting into violence. Students traveled to Delhi—a journey of only a couple of hours—to AIML meetings and to meet (or to try to meet) with Mohammad Ali Jinnah. Whereas many students may not have been able to afford a ticket, the system made it possible for them to leave Aligarh in the afternoon for a meeting after the evening prayers, and to return the following day for free. Bangladeshi Habibur Rahman exclaimed that as part of their support for the League agenda, "we had to go. Regularly we had to go!"[54] As Pakistani Captain Wazir Khan put it, the sherwani was "like the license to travel, even without ticket."[55] However, in 1945 and 1946 as the League unleashed AMU students for election work, this sense of entitlement, combined with the meager financial support the AIML provided for their endeavors, created tension between the railway staff, the university, other citizens, and even other Muslims. The AIMSF sought to censure the system and to challenge AMU students' sense of entitlement. During its Seventh Annual Session, in 1945, the AIMSF passed a resolution arguing that the good name of the university was being tarnished by

> the irresponsible and undignified behaviour of those students who travel without ticket and steal eatible [sic] of the poor passengers. This so-called "tradition" and "Activity" [sic] of Aligarh boys has been too much degenerated and criminal habits are fast developing through them among a section of Aligarh students. Scenes of roudism [sic] and mal treatment [sic] have become things of daily occurrence. This session of the All-India Muslim Students Federation strongly condemns the above mentioned tradition and activity of the Aligarh students and recommends to the self respecting [sic] and dignified section of the Aligarh Students to create a strong public opinion against them.[56]

Despite Shafi's claim that the purchasing of the ticket was "below the dignity" of AMU students, here other students appealed to whatever remained of AMU students' "dignity" to end the system as it was causing problems for the reputation of Muslims. It appears that the solidarity that prevailed within AMU, in which students were responsible to one another, did not necessarily extend to others, even other Muslims, in the outer circles of AMU's influence.

The AIML, however, depended on this system as it sent AMU boys out into the countryside for election work. Iqbal Shafi remembered that as AMU Old Boy Liaqat Ali Khan gave his group their instructions, he provided a small amount of support for their travel.

> There was a *munshi* sitting with his black tin box. So [Liaqat Ali Khan] says, "There are seven of you, okay. *Munshiji, give them two tickets, from Delhi to Jalandhar.*" Do you know what that means? In seven people, give them money for two tickets. There were a lot of things understood, or taken for granted. There was no explanation. The ticket would be of third class... And why two? And from Delhi to Jalandhar. Why? Because he knew that from Aligarh to Delhi they will all go free. From Aligarh to Delhi they would all go free and from Delhi to Jalandhar, among seven people, two tickets are enough. That's enough. Don't buy seven tickets. So that was the thing that was understood. And we took it for granted. *"Okay, fine, you got the money for two tickets, and now you go."*[57]

Thus, even as the Muslim Students' Federation, who also supported the AIML demand for Pakistan, attempted to reel in AMU students, to encourage them to follow the letter of the law, the League itself was dispatching them into the countryside with meager provisions and an expectation that their status as Aligs would secure them special privileges on the trains.

Even Ziauddin, in his annual address in 1945, complained about growing indiscipline in trains and the railway station:

> All sorts of men, Hindu or Muslim, not connected with the University in any way, including even middle-aged men, have been treated by the railway staff as University students and all their misdeeds have been attributed to indiscipline in the University... To fortify ourselves against irresponsible criticism we have introduced the system of identity cards. We are tightening the system of permits, and are adopting other administrative measures for the still better supervision of our students.

Ziauddin made the move to fortify surveillance seemingly out of disbelief that Aligarh boys could actually be responsible for the acts of indiscipline of which they were accused. In contrast to the appeal of the AIMSF, his permit system was not to help in identification of undisciplined Aligarh boys, but rather an effort to prove that those who were behaving badly were not Aligarh boys at all.[58]

After 1947, however, trains became sites of catastrophic violence on the borders, and their specter hung over AMU students. The sense of entitlement that students felt with regard to the trains before 1947 helps to expose why the trains became such a specific site of trauma for them after independence. The earlier system had allowed and even encouraged AMU students to flaunt their identity and relationship with the institution while riding the railways. The uniform of a black sherwani, white pajamas, shoes, and socks was the "license" AMU boys used to access certain spaces. The meaning of trains changed during 1947, Wazir Khan remembered, because "thousands and thousands and thousands [were killed]—those who could travel by train—all the trains were attacked and the people were butchered. They will not spare anybody."[59] The university's influence exerted no protective power. AMU students' fear extended into the railway cars—previously sites of entitlement—where the visibility of the uniform would now mark the boys as "other," rendering their position even more precarious. By 1947, the sherwani no longer marked inclusivity. As many narrators made clear, it marked the boys as potential victims of anti-Muslim violence.

The fear that AMU students experienced in trains and stations in 1946 and 1947 adopts the symbolic valence of their relationship to institutions of the state. As Marian Aguiar has argued, Indian trains constitute a unique social space, one that represents the state, but that is also occupied, or inhabited. Thus, it exposes "a distinctive relation between the public and the private."[60] AMU students clearly inhabited the railways in UP with a distinct sense of ownership. In the period before 1947, the state (even the colonial state) was invisible in their narratives. The source of authority in the train and station was the AMU proctorial monitor, and trains were sites of protective tolerance. After 1947, trains became active sites of negotiation in which Muslims felt highly exposed and vulnerable. The mobile environment of the train car, then, is not significant simply for its liminality, but also for its role as a boundary. This could not be more clear than in the memories of former AMU students who saw the infrastructure of the railway and trains as neutral space—colonial space—before 1947. As trains came to be associated with the contests over belonging that were redefining Indian space as Hindu space, that neutrality came into question. The same fear of mobs breaching the boundaries of AMU space by crossing the *kat pulla* is mirrored in stories about trains and railway lines. AMU students began to seek a neutral identity or an escape from the markers of Muslimness, which had come to bear a negative valence in independent India.

In fact, many students spoke of efforts, throughout India's partitioning, to hide their Muslim identity in trains and stations. Normally, they adopted one of two strategies (or a combination of both): they modified their appearance, or found company and a sense of security among other Muslims. In August 1946, Waheedudin Choudhri—a retired Bangladeshi engineer I interviewed in 2010—made his way to the university in the midst of severe rioting in Calcutta. He recounted his circuitous journey to Aligarh from Sylhet in Northeast India (later East Pakistan). He adjusted his route to avoid the riot-torn city and he sought protection in neutral dress. "I was wearing a khaki pant and khaki shirt and I tried to conceal [my identity]! Such that nobody will know whether I am a Muslim or a Hindu. I had to do it!"[61] He told me, "Once I reached Aligarh, I was safe there. The university authorities had an arrangement in the railway station for the students who were going and reaching there."[62] His memories clearly defined the sensation of safety he associated with the campus. The university staff acknowledged the threats to students' safety (only a few months after the riot) and were deployed to protect them. He illustrated the boundary between the safe space of the university and the unsafe space of the world outside through his description of his train journey. Waheedudin's first experiences of partitioning occurred in 1946, through these disruptions to his personal geographies, as he modified his route to avoid Calcutta, and his appearance to avoid appearing Muslim.

Delhi University professor of history Mohammad Amin said that he was advised "to carry a book or something like that. And in the book, write the name Mahavir Prasad or Raghav Lal or something or the other."[63] Because Hindus and Muslims are often visually indistinguishable, Muslim identity sometimes hinged on the most private marker: circumcision. Muslims therefore made efforts to mask their Muslim identity through more easily accessible markers. Waheedudin shed the sherwani, and here Amin suggested that he attempted to impersonate a Hindu student by writing a marked Hindu name in his book when he traveled by train. The arbitrary value of a name written in a book as a way of establishing identity suggested that even indelible physical characteristics, like evidence of circumcision, could be considered equally arbitrary, distinguishing only between aggressor and victim.[64] These efforts to conceal identity revealed a powerful anxiety and fear of violence. Shahid Ahmad Dehlavi remembered Muslims in Delhi seeking to conceal their identities by shaving their beards. I. H. Qureshi advised the women of his family to wear saris and Hindu caste marks as they fled their home in Delhi University in September 1947.[65] AMU boys, for generations, had flaunted their identity by proudly wearing their school uniform outside the campus. In trains, it served as their ticket. In 1947, it put them in danger.

The disruptions of 1946 and 1947 restricted AMU's "place in the world"—both spatially and affectively, and students' freedom within the outer circles of safety declined. Iftikhar Alam Khan, whose narrative more than any other revealed the depth of anxiety that fear caused the students, remembered his reluctance to wear the sherwani when he arrived at AMU in 1949. He also told me that he could not travel in the direction of Delhi after the riots of 1947. Though his father lived there, he only felt safe traveling in the direction away from Delhi, away from the specter of violence. Still, as he traveled, he sought the company of other Muslims and sought to hide his identity. Remarkably, he found an ally in the man who ran the "toddy shop" in the Hathras Railway Station.[66] Hathras was nearly thirty-five kilometers from Aligarh's protective reaches, but squarely within its sphere of influence.[67] Khan feared for his safety because he knew that as he headed away from Delhi and Aligarh, there would be "no Muslim."

So outside the Hathras station there was a store selling sharab. Sharab you know? Country-made liquor. A lot of people used to come to drink liquor over there. The bartender, the worker, he was called "Pandit," he used to have a (ponytail). But he was a Muslim. I knew that. He was from my village. He had changed his name and all that, and because he had to live there, in the liquor shop. If he wasn't a pandit, his caste was very low, then people wouldn't drink. And if he was a Muslim they would kill him, so having become a pandit he stayed there. I was knowing this. I reached there at night, and had to wait three hours [for my connection]. I used to go out, near this liquor store and look to see if this man was there or not. He used to see me and give me a signal [of recognition] I used to say something. Then I would sit near to him. Until the train would come after three hours. He used to come and ask after me "How are you doing?" "Yes, I'm well."[68]

After departing from Hathras in the direction of his hometown—Qaimganj in District Farrukhabad—Khan began to feel more comfortable. For after three or four stations, people began to recognize him as the son of a powerful family. Then, he said, "*I was in my own territory. But what was really bad was that I couldn't go towards Delhi.*" The trauma of partitioning seems to have ruptured the intimacy of connection between Aligarh and Delhi that brought Delhi, too, into AMU's sphere of influence, and made it a "Muslim" site.[69] Before 1857, Delhi had been a key site of Muslim power, the seat of the Mughal dynasties that had governed India in whole or in part for centuries. The British transformed it into the colonial capital in 1911, and in 1947 Delhi became the central site of independent Indian state power. Iftikhar Alam Khan's memory revealed the ambivalence with which AMU students approached the state. Though they relied on the state for protection—and Iftikhar Alam is one of those who actively praised the efforts of Prime Minister Nehru to "save" AMU—instruments of state power, including Delhi and the trains, retained a threatening quality. Khan did not arrive in Aligarh until 1949, and then as a young child. Still he experienced the consequences of the rupture between Aligarh and Delhi. The pride in a shared Muslim identity seems to have drawn the two cities together in the earlier period, but whereas the Indian state offered a promise of secular nationhood, the reality for Muslims was that the very symbols of the modern state provided only ambivalent protection.[70]

For Muslims in Delhi, the ambivalence of the state remained a deeply painful reality, as they remembered its failure to protect them during the violence of September 1947. In addition to migrants from elsewhere on their way to Pakistan, many Muslims fled homes in the city itself; together they gathered first in sites that represented Muslim history and power, like Old Delhi's Jama Masjid, and later in refugee camps like the ones at Purana Qila and Humayun's Tomb. The conditions in the Purana Qila camp were so poor, with shortages of food, water, clothing, and all basic necessities, that Zakir Husain called it a "living grave."[71] Gyan Pandey reports that for some time the Indian government seems to have treated the camps and their residents as though they were the responsibility of the Pakistan government, despite Gandhi's protestations that Muslims, too, were Indians, and therefore "*our* citizens."[72] Even as conditions improved for Delhi Muslims after Gandhi's attempts to mobilize state resources for their protection, his fast to secure peace in the city, and even his assassination by a right-wing Hindu zealot, Delhi's Muslims remained "besieged, demoralized, and terrified."[73]

Beyond Delhi's reaches, to combat the fear of being isolated as a target for violence, many students reported that during their journeys, in order to find the kind of strength in community that AMU symbolized, they sought out other Muslims for company and, more importantly, security. Iftikhar Alam Khan described this earlier, when a man, only nominally Muslim and masquerading as a high-caste Hindu—known as "Pandit" and selling country-made liquor—provided enough of a veil of solidarity to make Khan feel safe. Another narrator, Masood-ul Hasan, reported finding comfort sitting next to a Muslim convict on the train! Questions of dignity here were tested by questions of safety, and one effect of the exposure of Muslims after 1947 was to reify their identity as "Muslims," the problematic group that had demanded and received its own state. Masood-ul Hasan described his journey to his home in Bhopal in January 1948. Though the railway system had established "minority compartments" after the "great killings" of 1946 and 1947, Hasan, empowered in his identity as an Alig, chose not to ride in the minority compartment, as a "little assertion of self-confidence."[74]

He told me, "in those days I was religiously clad in a sherwani."[75] In other words, as he embarked in Aligarh, he was visible to others on the train as a Muslim and an AMU student. Though he did not choose the minority compartment, he settled in near another Muslim, a "hefty prisoner" who was an "Afghan" and traveling with several constables. Hasan shared his breakfast with the prisoner. At the next station, the prisoner and his constables disembarked, and Hasan eventually shifted to the minority compartment.

Zakir Ali Khan, who earlier tried to demonstrate the reality of the threat to Muslim security presented by the Hindu villages surrounding AMU by showing how the students protected their campus in a show of strength, told a story about train travel that does more to betray his own fear for his safety.

> Once when I was traveling, in my compartment, Hindus sighted two Muslims sitting there and they pointed and said, "He is a Muslim," and they tried to tease him. They threw his luggage outside the train with the result that when the first station came the poor fellow got out of the train. I sat quiet there, and they never thought that I am also a Muslim.[76]

Whereas Khan's earlier story sought to portray his strength as a member of the Aligarh community, dedicated to its welfare, when outside that community, his position was severely compromised. When he was alone, not only did he conceal his own identity, but he failed to act in defense of another Muslim who was being mistreated. Hasan and Khan seem to have swapped roles: Hasan's "little assertion of self-confidence," short-lived though it was, required courage, and depended on solidarity. By contrast, in the face of an actual threat of violence, outside of the university's protection, the gallantry Zakir Ali Khan had mustered was much deflated.[77]

Like many stories told by former AMU students about the period immediately after the 1947 Partition and Independence of India, none of these young men became the victim of anti-Muslim violence. Still, the narrators repeatedly described a traumatic sense of being out of place as a result of losing access to sites associated with a history of power.[78] One effect of the sense of isolation of AMU from the rest of India prior to 1947 was that it created a sphere of influence around the institution that created a protective boundary between them and the world outside. Furthermore, 1947 caused a recentering of AMU as its students were held in large part responsible for the division of India. The disruption of that boundary, not the national ones, left the students feeling exposed to danger. The anxiety that the former students betray came from when they ventured beyond the protective bounds of AMU, and it is worth remembering that many of these narrators have remained close to the institution since independence. Ironically, those who never left home felt less safe than those who navigated the uncertain national borders that were sites of violence. The destabilization of notions of safety and danger reveals the disruption of the meaning of AMU as a place in a larger network of meaning marked by the university, its extended disciplinary regime, and its links to other sites of meaning in UP.

AMU's proximity to Delhi and other Muslim centers was particularly important. Before 1947, students had used the trains and railway lines to mark out the boundaries of territory that they considered "their own," by imagining a network of cities, connected by railways, through which they could freely and safely move. As they traveled along railway lines—to and from home, or Delhi (where they sometimes met AIML leaders), or on electioneering trips—they inscribed a network of meaning upon the landscape.[79] During the disruptions, as narrators described their relationship to the university and the university's relationship to the world that surrounded it, AMU's geographic location seemed to shift. Zakir Ali Khan described AMU's proximity to Delhi as a significant marker of the university's importance; retired AMU English professor Asloob Ahmad Ansari described Delhi as "not very far off"; several former students, including Habibur Rahman (Bangladesh) and Ghulam Umar and Iqbal Shafi (Pakistan) emphasized AMU's proximity by demonstrating its centrality in the AIML organizational structure. Delhi's closeness to AMU during the AIML period was clearly enhanced by ideological connection, but after 1947, several narrators identified Delhi as a source of disruption. It was as a result of refugees coming from the direction of Delhi and Dehra Dun that one narrator participated in setting up a searchlight on the roof of V.M. Hall; he and other students took turns keeping watch.[80] Asloob Ahmad Ansari told me that while AMU was "immune" from communal disturbance, riots were happening "round about Aligarh and Delhi."[81] Delhi was the place, he told me, where people were "victimized." In all of these memories, Aligarh and Delhi are tightly linked in a historical network of power relations deeply embedded in the AMU narrative. It was from Delhi that the last Mughal emperor was exiled, that the Muslims were held responsible for the mutiny, and, after the demise of the empire, that Delhi native Sir Sayyid Ahmad Khan rose to lead the Muslims into the future. In 1947, Delhi itself seemed displaced. It became a site of refuge as Muslims fled to Pakistan and Hindus and Sikhs poured in from Punjab. Refugee camps (liminal by definition) were sites of despair. It is not difficult to see here that Delhi's proximity and vulnerability to such disturbances altered its meaning and the students' confidence in the notion that they would be safe there.

For AMU boys throughout partitioning, fear and anxiety arose from a serious disruption of the sources of authority that had previously served to protect them. The meaning of the places in which they had learned to feel safe, and to build solidarity—from the local cafes and cinemas of AMU where students gathered; to the railway station that linked home and university; and the very geography of their institution in India—now changed irrevocably. When external authority deteriorated, the safest place appeared to be within the campus itself. The campus was the tightest circle of safety. Electioneering had taken them out beyond the farthest circle, but fear drew them back in. While they feared attack, no one actually crossed the boundary into the university, and whether they defended it with trembling hands or with shows of strength, the university itself represented a powerful continuity in the midst of traumatic disruption all around.

Conclusion

Though distant from the standard borders of partition history, AMU is nonetheless a critical site through which a new history of partitioning becomes visible. The experiences of the very foot soldiers of the Pakistan Movement reveal that the primary experience of partitioning, even for those who did not migrate to Pakistan was intimately related to space and place, and the boundaries that defined them. The oral histories through which narrators recounted these memories might also be considered oral geographies—remembered histories of place and meaning.[82] The sense of belonging to place was a key element of AMU's identity, and the proctorial system of discipline expanded that sense of belonging into a variety of sites beyond the formal boundaries of the campus: into cinema halls, cafes, and the railway station. These places formed an additional circle of safety in which the students could move freely, albeit under the watchful eye of the university's disciplinarians. Beyond the city, AMU narrators imagined the university as a center in a broader landscape of Muslim history. The railway lines connected the campus to Delhi, Bareilly, Agra, Bhopal, Lucknow, all centers of historical Muslim power and significant Muslim communities in Hindu majority UP. Partition disrupted the meaning of belonging within these concentric circles of safety as familiar places were rendered strange by the threat of violence and the experience of alienation. Whereas standard histories of partition have examined the disrupted borders, these stories revealed partition's "multiple realities," and showed that far from the borders Muslim lives and communities were deeply disturbed by the everyday violence of the spatial marginalization that was an outcome of the 1947 Partition.

The boundaries that surrounded AMU were always dynamic. They defined both the inside and the outside, keeping students in and others out. They were both physical and conceptual, defining the campus and the aspirations of Muslim unity embodied by its values.[83] As Edward Casey has theorized, the boundaries of place serve as "the matrix of historical action."[84] In the 1940s, as students engaged actively with the politics of the world beyond the campus boundaries, and experienced its spaciousness—both thrilling and terrifying—they redefined the meaning of the place to which they returned. Through crossing the boundaries as they went electioneering, AMU students eroded the boundary's protective power and in 1946 neither the students nor the local authorities any longer trusted the disciplinary system to maintain the delicate separation that had governed the relationship between university and the city. The erosion of these boundaries created insecurity in the university—fear—as AMU became more exposed in a highly sensitive political environment. Thus, even as the boundaries became more porous, they also came to define an increasingly stark sense of difference and antagonism between the Muslim students with their attachment to Pakistan (read as separatist) and the non-Muslim majority of the city. Ultimately, the boundary that was drawn between India and Pakistan came to mark a new spatial framework that redefined the place of Muslims both inside and outside the university. That many AMU students crossed that new boundary into Pakistan in a final act of transgression permanently altered the place of the university itself. Whereas in earlier decades, AMU students had projected their identity outward, seeking to define Muslim India with their values, after 1947, they sought to take on the identity of the whole of India and to adapt it to the AMU environment.

In AMU, rather than fortifying Muslim solidarity as the League promised, the creation of Pakistan compromised the university's political influence as Muslim identity was reduced to being "merely religious."[85] The university's disciplinary regime was rendered moot and students began to look to the state for protection. The symbolic isolation within which young Muslim men had been inspired was destroyed, replaced by alienation, both from co-religionists who had shifted to Pakistan and from non-Muslim Indians. Those Muslims in India who described their fear and insecurity repeatedly enacted the role of the threatened minority, the very identity that Mohammad Ali Jinnah and the Muslim League demand for Pakistan sought to displace with the language of the Muslim Nation. As I argue in the following chapters, it is impossible and unwise to ignore the outcomes of partition when considering the experience of South Asian Muslims after 1947, for the partition of India was a paradoxical outcome of the Pakistan Movement that reduced the power of the Muslim minority in India precipitously, rather than fortifying the solidarity that gave the movement its power.

4

The Muslim Question in India after Partition

The narrators included in this study shared the formative experience of coming of age at AMU, but their identities have since been formed in opposition. Indian Muslims, facing threats to their safety and autonomy in India, looked derisively across the border. The ramifications of Pakistan's creation continued to affect them. Since 1947, their futures have been dependent upon the goodwill of the Congress and the non-Muslim majority. The benefits of citizenship have not been evenly distributed among India's populace.[1] The creation of Pakistan has raised "Muslim Questions" throughout all of British India's successor states and exerted terrific power on the memories of AMU narrators. All narrators engaged national narratives but localized their memories in the institution of AMU as they reconciled their post-partition experiences with their earlier allegiances.

The narratives of the nationalist movements in India—whether the "composite culture" narrative of the Indian National Congress or the "Two Nation Theory" of the Muslim League—sought to define the boundaries of identity within the state(s) they demanded from the British. While the "composite culture" narrative appears broadly inclusive, and the Indian state has been more effective at recognizing the multiple identities of its citizens (linguistic, regional, religious), Muslims have struggled to advance since independence.[2] India, as a non-Muslim majority state routinely confronts issues around Muslim belonging, and, despite their privilege, Aligs have not been immune. Ather Siddiqi argued that India was the most tolerant country, and that Hindus had never "shown anger or intolerance." He noted that they "allowed" Muslims to remain in India. In this formulation, Muslim success is evidence of the "large-heartedness of the majority community."[3] Siddiqi, like many Indian Muslims, accepted with gratitude the space "allowed" for Muslims. Significantly, despite the success of Siddiqi's entrepreneurial daughter in establishing a commercial bakery, Muslims overall have not kept pace as a community even with more socially marginalized groups like Dalits.[4] In addition, marginalization of Muslims has been endemic, and since the Bharatiya Janata Party (BJP) came to power in 2014, attacks on Muslims have increased in frequency.[5]

My objective here is to examine the experiences of Aligs and other Muslim citizens of all the post-partition states. Aligs are representative of the larger Muslim minority in India. Though they are set apart by class and education, AMU's historical connections to Pakistan have mitigated the differences of class and meant that AMU Muslims identify as part of an embattled minority. In the Muslim majority states of Pakistan and

Bangladesh, however, Aligs are tied to assimilationist narratives that have the potential to oppress other minorities. Therefore, their position can be seen as alternately exceptional and unexceptional. Aligs have been involved in large and small ways in the establishment of all three states, and their experiences and perspectives cast some light on these contestations over belonging. The position of Aligs has been malleable: they take on different positions depending on their vantage point, and each individual's experience of partition and independence inevitably shaped his experience. There is not one story here; there are many stories of discrimination, assimilation, acceptance, resistance, and cooperation. The disputes over identity and belonging that made partition seem necessary created a complex web of identities that Aligs and South Asians more broadly continue to negotiate.

As partition slips further into the past, it continues to have a transformative effect on the way people perceive themselves as citizens of states. It would be folly to try to isolate contemporary politics from the narratives of inclusion and exclusion that predominated during the movements for Indian independence and Pakistan when narratives of unity were constructed to politicize loosely linked groups in pursuit of a particular agenda.[6] Likewise, regional and ethnic identities can still be mobilized in order to secure political space in the face of the homogenizing narrative of the state. Narratives that proclaim a space of unity for those with shared characteristics (as distinct from priorities)—ethnic, religious, linguistic, or national—are mirrored by narratives of exclusion that define who cannot be included. These narratives are interwoven parts of the larger fabric of South Asian identity. To understand them, we must see how they are connected.

The 1947 Partition of India placed AMU in a difficult position. Though it had a long history of association with nationalist politics, during the 1940s it had been drawn fully into the Muslim League fold. But never was there a real possibility that AMU would be part of the Pakistan for which its students enthusiastically campaigned. In independent India, then, it appeared to be a traitorous outpost, and indeed Pakistan continued to recruit AMU graduates until the 1960s. Those who wanted to, and who could, left for Pakistan. Others stayed. AMU was in India, and in India it would remain. The challenge of independence was to forge an identity for the institution that both honored its historical legacy and charted a path for a sustainable future.

After independence, Muslims officially became "the minority community" in India, even, as Gyan Pandey has argued, in places where they occupy the numeric majority. Leaders like Sir Sayyid Ahmad Khan, and later Mohammad Ali Jinnah, sought to cultivate a sense of moral community among Muslims, but the processes of partitioning ultimately set them apart as subjects of suspicion. In Aligarh, in a celebratory speech to over 200,000 people on the occasion of independence, the secretary of the All India Congress Committee announced that minorities in India would enjoy "full protection and privileges if they remained faithful citizens of India."[7] Thus defined, the conditions of Muslim citizenship were predicated on the submission of Muslims to the independent state. Even Ahmad Saeed, whose father was a nationalist, and who claimed to have no sympathy with the Muslim League or its agenda, described the threats to Muslims as "natural." This turn of phrase indicates the depth of the anxiety in Muslim communities as a result of this ongoing partitioning. His choice to remain in independent India, and his belief that Muslims could be fully engaged citizens seem to contradict his straightforward recognition of the threats to Muslim security. By the time of our interview, Saeed recognized Muslim vulnerability as an inevitability of Indian life, even as he argued that hard work would propel Muslims to greater heights of success. The slippage between these positions illuminates the tension embodied in Muslim citizenship in India and how profoundly it was affected by the events of the 1940s.

Continuity and Slippage after 1947

Among those narrators who remained in India, the university, though changed, remained a powerful site of continuity with their prepartition lives. Their narratives betrayed the effort required to establish continuity between the institution and the Indian narrative of citizenship. Even as they revealed the traumas of disruption during the partitioning of 1946 and 1947, they declared the importance of AMU as an exemplary site of India's composite culture, and credited AMU's nationalist leaders with saving the institution. The tension evident in these complex narratives should not suggest that there is a problem of loyalty among AMU Muslims, but that in their effort to establish their position as unproblematic Indian citizens they have had to reimagine AMU's place in Indian history. This required excising the problematic phase during which the AIML dominated campus politics and minimizing their attachment to its erstwhile ideals. Thus, many of these narrators both (a) emphasized continuity at the university and (b) marked the post-independence period with enthusiastic declarations of allegiance to the nationalist agenda and its leaders. Narrators established continuity in two ways: first, they minimized the impact that the 1947 Partition had on the normal functioning of the university; and second, they lavished praise on Zakir Husain, the first significant vice chancellor after independence, for "saving" the institution.

By minimizing the disruptiveness of the partition, and even the impact of the out-migration of students and faculty to Pakistan, Indian narrators suggested that for all of the League's self-importance during the period of its dominance in the institution, it did not have the power to permanently disable the educational institution. The focus on Zakir Husain established continuity with the pre-Muslim League nationalist period of the 1920s. Zakir Husain's appointment as vice chancellor rehabilitated the university's earlier nationalist identity. Therefore, narrators excised the League period as an anomaly and focused their attention on getting back to business after the disruptions of 1947.[8] Those who were not League partisans during the 1940s had a comparatively easier time thinking through partition in this way, but those who felt sympathy with the AIML agenda attempted to cover their tracks with expressions of regret and even guilt. For both groups, there is evidence that Muslim identity remains in conflict with Indian nationalist identity, and in the latter case there is a sense that in the wake of partition AMU Muslims felt responsible to the larger body of Indian citizenry for the deeds of fellow Aligs and other Muslims.

Riazur Rahman Sherwani, whose family were large landholders in Aligarh, told me that "so far as the working of the university was concerned, it was not affected by [partition]. The doors of the university always remained open for the non-Muslims as well, even during the time when that movement [the Pakistan movement] was in full force."⁹ This statement set the stage for establishing the continuity of AMU's nationalist orientation. He defended the institution's nationalist credentials by arguing that the League influence was not powerful enough to displace the inclusive agenda, and that the division of the country had not had a marked effect on the functioning of the institution."¹⁰ Irfan Habib, too, emphasized continuity in the academic realm when he suggested that "one of the strengths of the institution [was] we didn't notice, the admissions were on time, classes were held, a teacher disappears [and] was replaced immediately by another teacher."¹¹ Despite the image of teachers spontaneously disappearing, Habib insisted that students "didn't notice" any change. Both of these narrators, however, proved that within the boundaries, AMU's values and priorities were resilient. Was this enough to prove that the university was "not affected" by the transformations of partitioning?

In fact, the tenor of narratives describing the post-1947 period differed distinctly. In narratives of the earlier period, academic life occupied an inferior, and sometimes practically invisible position relative to social, residential, and even political life. After 1947, as the above statements show, narrators emphasized the continuity of the educational agenda. Whereas during the League period, politics edged out education, after the nationalist turn academics became ascendant in the memories of former students. Thus, by directing attention away from the disruption to residential life— exemplified by the emptying of the AMU hostels after a period of severe overcrowding— these narratives rebalanced the scales by arguing that very little changed on the campus.¹² Ather Siddiqi, who arrived at AMU in the immediate aftermath of the partition migrations, was highly cognizant of the effect of the disruptions. He applied for admission in early 1947 but could not secure a place because the hostels were too crowded. After the creation of Pakistan, however, "students left en masse. From six-seven thousand—that was a big number in those days!—[the student body] was reduced to two thousand. There was no difficulty in getting a room in the hostel."¹³ Despite his awareness of the significance of this disruption, Siddiqi also tried to establish continuity with life before 1947 despite the fact that he was not then present in AMU. Nonetheless, he argued, "life continued and new teachers were appointed and our studies resumed." Siddiqi's determination to capture the continuity came despite the fact that he was not actually on campus before August 1947.¹⁴ He clearly implicated himself as a participant in the events.¹⁵ That Siddiqi's narrative suggested the importance of continuity with life before, but consistent with the nationalist turn, also implied that the disruptive forces disappeared from AMU in 1947 and life carried on peacefully after that.

Many narrators, though, described the empty hostels, the absence left by their friends and classmates. Indeed, between 1946 and the 1947–8 academic years, the student population of AMU and its allied institutions, including the Muslim University High School and the Minto Circle School fell from 6,061 to 4,613.¹⁶ The annual vice chancellor's report noted that many teachers and students had been "lost" as they could not join "through lack of communications" during the disruptions of 1947. In the Engineering College, "the number of students returning for the Session 1947–49 was about 50 per cent of normal" and the number of undergraduates in the Faculty of Science dropped by about 40 percent.[17]

Mohiuddin Khan, now settled in Bangladesh, told me that the remaining students felt this "loss of students" because "the whole university campus became very quiet!"[18] Iftikhar Alam Khan noticed this quiet in 1949: "When I arrived in the hostel, there were six boys, only six boys in the whole of the [primary school]. There were ... three hostels. Three big hostels means three hundred, or two-fifty capacity. So there was a total capacity of five or six hundred and in this there were only six boys."[19] Narrators advanced a common explanation for this loss that, unfortunately, is not well supported by the available evidence. Mohiuddin explained that before 1947 "the students used to come from Punjab, Northwest Frontier Province, and also Southern India; they did not come [back]."[20] In other words, those students from "Pakistan areas" did not return to the university. This explanation undermines to idea that North Indian Muslims who supported Pakistan migrated to Pakistan alone or with their families. Many narrators, including Irfan Habib, Ather Siddiqi, Saghir Ahmad Rizvi, and K. P. S. (anonymized), argued that the depletion of AMU's population came primarily from the fact that no students from "partition provinces turned up at AMU" after 1947 and even that students from Hyderabad were airlifted out of Aligarh during the disruptions.[21]

This argument suggested an effort to read back Pakistan's geographic identity onto her ideological one, creating a false sense of continuity. Despite their insistence, leadership of and support for the Pakistan Movement was embedded in UP, the very region they defined in imagined concentric geographies surrounding AMU. In addition, since its earliest days AMU had attracted the majority of its students from these Muslim minority regions of North India.[22] Indeed, students hailed from throughout the subcontinent (and the world), but Urdu-speaking North Indians dominated. The explanation that only students from "Pakistan areas" ultimately chose to settle in Pakistan, however, helped to establish AMU's nationalist credentials by highlighting two equally important features about AMU's student body. First, it proved that all those students who had been affiliated with the AIML's demand for Pakistan were originally from those areas that were to become Pakistan: Punjab, Northwest Frontier Province, Sindh, Balochistan, Kashmir, and Bengal. Their allegiance made sense; their homes would be incorporated into Pakistan. It made sense for them to seek opportunities and build their futures in Pakistan because of geography, not because they had experienced or feared discrimination from Congress or Hindus more generally. Second, this explanation proved that partition purged those students who had been loyal to the AIML agenda. They did not remain in AMU, and, therefore, it was unreasonable to worry about disloyal elements in the student body. Although students from "Pakistan Areas" did not return to the university, many students and faculty who did not return were North Indians. Despite an absence of evidence, this argument persisted, at least anecdotally, as a major feature of the AMU explanation of the impact of partitioning.

It is not difficult to understand why this narrative has become so well established in AMU. In the immediate aftermath of the creation of Pakistan, even politicians like Sardar Vallabhbhai Patel cautioned Muslims that "mere declarations of loyalty to the Indian Union will not help them at this critical juncture. They must give practical proof of their declarations."²³ Hindus regularly urged AMU students to join their fellow Muslims in Pakistan, and indeed this heckling remains a feature of Hindu supremacist speech. Indeed, it was under those pressures that migrations to Pakistan continued at least into the 1950s (when there were severe communal riots in Aligarh) and perhaps until as late as 1965 (when India and Pakistan fought an all-out war). Zakir Ali Khan, who settled in Pakistan, remained at AMU until 1951, and described the efforts of the State of Pakistan to recruit from AMU's Engineering College.²⁴ It was one of the few in India, and the only one that admitted large numbers of Muslim students.²⁵ Ather Siddiqi reported that Pakistan continued to draw students from AMU for many years. "Everybody at that time thought that he should get a degree and go to Pakistan, so for the first maybe ten, fifteen, twenty years maybe, this went on. AMU was producing graduates, but they were all going to Pakistan because there was great demand. For engineers and civil services bureaucracy, et cetera."²⁶ Pakistan represented a powerful opportunity to AMU graduates, and especially engineers. Thus, despite the insistence that the migrations of partition stripped AMU only of those students who remained home in "Pakistan Areas," the facts show that migration stretched on for decades.²⁷ Irfan Habib reported that AMU graduates finally stopped going to Pakistan "after 1960 with the [establishment of] public sector engineering services [in India]. They got higher pay here, why should they go?"²⁸ This acknowledgment of the continuing migration from AMU even after 1947 puts up an explicit challenge to the notion that Pakistan created very little disruption there.

The defining moment of narratives that discussed life in AMU after 1947 was the arrival of Zakir Husain as vice chancellor in 1948. His arrival was heralded as the turning point in the university's deliberate reorientation toward the secular Congress government that was underway by 1948. Unlike Ziauddin, Obaidur Rahman Khan Sherwani, or Nawab Ismail Khan, who all served as vice chancellors during the early years after independence and were partisans of the Muslim League, Zakir Husain's nationalist credentials were unsullied. He had abandoned MAO College in 1920 during the non-cooperation agitation and been a founder of the JMI. He remained loyal to that institution throughout the independence struggle and was closely associated with Congress leaders Jawaharlal Nehru and Maulana Abul Kalam Azad. Nehru appointed Husain, who served as vice chancellor of AMU from 1948 to 1956 before moving back into more active political life.²⁹ These were critical years, and Zakir Husain's connections within the Congress government undoubtedly drew in support for the institution, and drew the institution into "the national stream."³⁰ It was under his guidance that the government increased the grants to the university, and though he was not remembered for large infrastructural development as Ziauddin has been, he ensured the university's survival during a period of intense uncertainty.³¹

The students recounted his influence with a sense of tremendous gratitude. As Ahmad Saeed described him, Zakir Husain "was sort of a screen which almost saved the university from adverse days that it was expecting to see after partition."³² Mohammad Amin reiterated that "it was primarily Nehru and his choice of sending Zakir Husain Sahib as Vice Chancellor that saved Aligarh University. Otherwise, for all purposes, it would have disappeared."³³ These anxieties of targeting and annihilation, expressed by narrators in Lucknow and Delhi respectively, contrast sharply with the insistence by those closer to AMU, that it was "not affected." Rather, as one narrator argued, AMU was targeted such that "whenever any popular person emerged from AMU or in other fields, people branded him as not a true nationalist in that respect. This is very unfortunate."[34] Nehru and Husain both came to the aid of the university during its time of need, facilitated a shift in the institutions orientation, and became a protective screen for it. The language of "screening" engages the significance of the university's boundaries. The students imagined Zakir Husain and the nationalists as a boundary that, like its physical boundaries, would protect them and connect them to the non-Muslim world of independent India. Thus, even as Nehru emphasized the shared environment of secular India, the boundaries remained critically important sites for Muslim engagement. Saeed saw Husain as an agent of the central government's benevolence and, above all, consistent with the memory of the protective power of the military police posted around AMU in 1946, he credited the government for protecting the university.

Despite the enthusiastic support for the nationalist reformation that emerged from the memories of India's Aligs, slippage persists in their explanations of their post-1947 experiences. Many narrators, significantly, expressed a sense of guilt as they reflected on this period. Iftikhar Alam Khan, for instance, explained his fear and anxiety by clarifying: "*my problem was that I was also feeling guilty.*"[35] This guilt pointed to an incomplete imagining of a post-partition Indian Muslim identity, and though these narrators repeatedly denounced the Muslim League and disavowed those who migrated to Pakistan, guilt linked them together. It revealed the solidarity that tied them to other Aligs and Muslims during the heady period of Muslim unity and the heyday of the Two Nation Theory, even if, as in the case of the Alam brothers, they were not Muslim League sympathizers. In addition, it revealed the expansiveness of the question of Muslim belonging; Muslim citizens embodied the guilt of India's "vivisection."

For some, the sense of guilt had morphed into fury over a serious betrayal of the ideals of solidarity that had been fostered at AMU. The students together fought to achieve Pakistan, but then the few who chose to stay were betrayed and abandoned by the many who left. Ather Siddiqi identified a "guilty conscience" as the reason that his brother, who had been a Muslim League supporter, chose to migrate to Pakistan. Though Siddiqi was a vocal supporter of the Indian secular state, he told me, "I also wanted to go! But my father would not allow me to go. He was a government servant and he didn't want his second son—only two sons—to go. He forbade me to go. So, I didn't know what to do. So I worked for a year, but I wanted to do higher studies so I returned to Aligarh and I worked so hard."[36] At the time, he was too young to make the decision on his own, and his father was not keen to leave because he was only three years away from retirement (Siddiqi's father did finally migrate to Pakistan in 1965). But Siddiqi described a turnaround in his sentiment that he portrayed as an experience of coming-to-his-senses. He told me, "Our sentiments and emotions were pro-Muslim League-y but when rational thinking increased . . . I realized that Pakistan was the wrong thing."[37] Professor Siddiqi was not alone in claiming that support of Pakistan was irrational or senseless. Several narrators described this sensation, and how their enthusiasm was compounded by youth. An exchange I had with Professor History Iqtidar Alam Khan, now a well-known leftist historian, displayed this very well:

> Iqtidar Alam Khan: What happened was that, this idea that there should be a Pakistan that would be good for Muslims and it would guarantee a good future for Muslims, that idea was all around. And perhaps I was also influenced by that because I remember that once or twice there was a procession taken out from the hostel, I don't know why and how, but I was also a member of that procession! And fifty or sixty boys they were just raising slogans "Pakistan Zindabad!" Going round the university campus. For nothing! I don't know why, who took out that procession! So this kind of atmosphere was there, and I was also influenced by that.
> AA: Did you have an idea about what that meant—"Pakistan Zindabad?" What did Pakistan mean to you? Do you remember that?
> Iqtidar Alam Khan: Yes! Something where the Muslims would be in a state and the Muslims would be in a dominant position, they wouldn't be oppressed. Really I was not a very, very thinking person. I was not able to analyze. I didn't have any idea of the institutions that were being created. But general frenzy was there and I was a part of that frenzy.[38]

Masood-ul Hasan echoed this sentiment when he suggested that "Maybe I am trying to rationalize or justify something. Maybe it is a mature man in me who is speaking now," and that mature man has since realized that "no doubt the very demand for the partition of the country was not a very sane and wise call."[39] The Indian narrators, even those who had sometimes been involved in the Muslim League campaigns, remembered their experiences as though they had been duped. Their activities were driven by a desire to fit in, to be involved, to be a part of something bigger than themselves. By 1947, however, the power of AMU's brotherhood had become too large to be contained within the university's bounds. The departure of students and faculty for Pakistan was the ultimate transgression of those carefully drawn boundaries. It left AMU isolated and vulnerable. The fear generated by the threat of communal violence during this period had a chastening effect and fostered a nationalist turn that the remaining students embraced.

The Nationalist Turn: AMU in Independent India

The first issue of the *Aligarh Magazine* in 1948 opened with a photo of Mohandas K. Gandhi in his funeral shroud. The still face of India's fallen leader appearing there marked a significant shift in the composition of the editorial board of the magazine and, more importantly, the university's outlook. It was an explicit sign that the events of 1947 and 1948 had transformed AMU's *mahol*, despite its distance from the newly drawn borders. A panegyric essay "In Memoriam" served as a memorial to the life of Mahatma Gandhi and as a call to AMU students to "pledge ourselves anew to uphold steadfastly, by exercising a strenuous moral discipline and working incessantly for a just social and economic order, the ideals of universal human brotherhood and peace for which he lived so single-mindedly and laid down his life so heroically."[40] Whereas Gandhi had been inducted as the first Life Member of the University Union in 1920, throughout the 1940s both the *Aligarh Magazine* and the *Aligarh University Gazette* treated Gandhi as the representative of a Hindu parochial movement that threatened Muslims. His appearance in the magazine as a national hero and a friend to the Muslims signaled a nationalist turn, an effort to harmonize AMU's values with those of the secular Indian state. The call to students to rededicate themselves to "moral discipline" resonated with the values of the AMU residential system, such that the ideals of Gandhi's *Hind Swaraj* mixed with the ideals of Sir Sayyid in the service of social and economic justice.[41] The remembrance enjoined students to embrace the universal brotherhood that connected them to Indians beyond the university's boundary walls. The political activity surrounding the Pakistan demand had eroded AMU's vaunted isolation, but the boundary walls had assumed prime importance for ensuring the students' physical safety. In its first issue after independence, the *Aligarh Magazine* suggested that the boundaries between AMU and the rest of India should effectively dissolve. The most important brotherhood was that of Indians, within which Aligs must find a place.

This issue of the *Aligarh Magazine* demonstrated a particularly clear and poignant example of the shifts in outlook and orientation that were taking place in AMU in 1948 as it sought to reestablish itself as a nationalist institution. This reorientation sought to excise the period of Muslim League domination since 1940 by reengaging with nationalist ideals that had been influential in the 1920s and 1930s.[42] In a coincidence of timing and publishing, the issue also contains a much less prominent lament on the death of Dr. Sir Ziauddin Ahmad, the former vice chancellor of the institution, who passed away in London in December 1947. Ziauddin had been one of the Pakistan partisans who facilitated the Muslim League's political organizing on the campus as part of his commitment of Muslim solidarity, but he also represented Aligarh's first generation, and his death closed a chapter in the university's annals. The transition that is marked in the *Magazine* between the League period and a restored nationalist period is well captured by the laments for both Gandhi and Ziauddin.

This new era brought other changes, too. The uniform of the sherwani was disappearing, and with it, worried editor Syed Zainul Abedin, Aligarh pride. In "The Flying Fez," he lamented that "There is a diversity in our unity; what a motley crowd of various fashions we are. But surely not the one we were intended to be."[43] He evoked and inverted the composite culture narrative of the Indian state—unity in diversity became diversity in unity—thus establishing his nationalist credentials and acknowledging the challenges surrounding AMU's identity. The sherwani had come to mark AMU students as members of a problematic minority, but the fez also signaled links to other Muslim lands. The meaning of these vestments would have to be reestablished within the newly defined nation-state, for, as he regrets, the community was not one "intended" to give up its unique markers, even when consigned to a minority identity. Abedin called on the university authorities to reestablish the meaning of the boundaries by restoring the expectations of the residential system, especially for new students arriving as migrants from Punjab and other disturbed areas.

The nationalist turn was buttressed, in the same issue, by the publication of the 1948 Aligarh Convocation speech delivered by Prime Minister Pandit Jawaharlal Nehru only six days before Gandhi's assassination. An editorial lavished praise on Nehru's leadership, noting:

> Side by side with the Father of the Nation, Mahatma Gandhi, he withstood unflinchingly the irrational frenzy which in its devastating sweep over some parts of the country extinguished all the human values of civilized life. During the dark days of spiritual distemper and social disintegration he held aloft, undimmed with a finely tempered equipoise, the torch of reason, tolerance and good-will among the various communities of the Indian Union. We have every confidence that he will continue to justify the faith his people generally and the minorities in particular have in his enlightened statesmanship.[44]

Nehru's speech addressed the challenge that AMU faced as a result of its recent political orientation, but he magnanimously invited the university and its students to find solidarity of feeling with other Indians.

> All of us have to be clear about our basic allegiance to certain ideas. Do we believe in a national state which includes people of all religions and shades of opinion and is essentially secular as a state, or do we believe in the religious theocratic conception of a state which considers people of other faiths as something beyond the pole? [*sic*; read: pale].[45]

Thus, even as Nehru made a point to make Aligarh students feel welcome as Indian citizens, he acknowledged the pull of Pakistan. Pakistan's allure continued to affect the students for many years (some say until 1965) but officially the institution began its about-face in 1948. For the students, however, Gandhi's assassination in January 1948 provided a terrifying reminder of what was at stake as they took on the responsibilities of citizenship.[46] Nehru sounded a note of caution, but Gandhi's assassination forced Muslims to recognize the precariousness of their position in independent India. By 1949, when the arrival of Zakir Husain as vice chancellor was announced in the *Aligarh Magazine*, its official transformation was complete.[47]

Telling Moment: January 30, 1948

The partition of India and the creation of Pakistan undermined the solidarity and power of the Muslim elite, cultivated at Aligarh during the 1940s. However, the unlikely event that confirmed the sense of difference that would define their experience throughout the period of partitioning in independent India took place in Delhi, the center of historical Muslim power. Retired Delhi University professor of history Mohammad Amin suggested that the assassination of Mahatma Gandhi on January 30, 1948, "tells you most" about the disruptions of partitioning.[48] Whereas Aligs felt targeted and afraid on campus during the events of 1946 and 1947, the possibility that a Muslim might have been responsible for Gandhi's assassination awakened Muslim terror, no matter where they found themselves that day. Returning to the sites of meaning around AMU through which they narrated partition's disruptions, many of the narrators with whom I spoke about their experiences on January 30, 1948, narrated their experiences of being in trains or train stations on that day. Regardless of where they found themselves, however, they all described their apprehension on hearing of the assassination and fear that the assassin was a Muslim.

In every interview I conducted, when I asked about the assassination of Gandhi, the response was the same: Muslims feared that the assassin had been one of their community and knew that if it had been, the consequences for Muslims would be terrible.[49] Similarly, they all credited Nehru and Patel with making the identity of the assassin, Nathuram Godse, a Hindu fundamentalist associated with the Rashtriya Swayamsevak Sangh (RSS), known as quickly as possible. Then, the community heaved a collective "sigh of relief."[50] The narrators' attachment to the role of Congress leaders in saving Muslims by quickly making the assassin's identity known reflected the shift in the attitude of AMU students, from feeling threatened by the Hindu-dominated UP Congress government, to feeling that it was only Congress leadership that could protect Muslims.

Masood-ul Hasan was traveling by train from Aligarh to Bhopal on January 30, 1948, clad in his Aligarh sherwani. During this journey, as I discussed in Chapter 3, he had asserted his self-confidence by choosing not to sit in the minority compartment, though he did find another Muslim on the train for safety and comfort (albeit an Afghan convict). The prisoner and his constables disembarked at Agra and after they did, Hasan noticed an "uncanny silence" on the platform. He heard someone say that Gandhi had been killed, and he was instantly struck by the thought that it must have been a Muslim who was responsible. His response, he said, was that "I lost nerve, and I also shifted to the minority compartment."[51] In the liminal space between Aligarh and home, Hasan sought the protective confines of the minority car and its protective solidarity. The anxiety created by the assassination marked him out negatively as Muslim, and he feared sitting among his fellow Indians, lest he should become the target of their grief, or worse, rage.

S. M. Mehdi, then a communist activist in Bombay, was preparing to board a train at Victoria Terminus, when he heard the news of Gandhi's assassination.[52] His fear for his own safety precluded his ability to grieve for the slain leader. When I asked him how he felt about the death of the great leader, he responded with surprise,

> Emotionally, about Gandhi I thought, I mean, we thought less, I suppose, than ourselves. What is going to happen to us? Presuming someone is going to stab us, kill us. Who has killed? The whole thing was, who can it be? And it always came down, it must be a Muslim, it might be a Muslim, it must be a Muslim, it might be a Muslim, that's all. It must be a Muslim.[53]

Mehdi described himself as a person who did not believe in communal division, in essential differences between Hindus and Muslims. He associated with a mixed group of leftists, socialists, and communists, including erstwhile Alig Ali Sardar Jafri, who had disavowed these labels, he said, "as we heard this news that a fanatic Hindu has killed Gandhi . . . I mean, just imagine! We, who did not believe in this nonsense of Hindus and Muslims, when we heard that a Hindu had killed Gandhi, we felt relieved, that at least a Muslim has not killed Gandhi."[54] A lone, potentially Muslim assassin became a metonym for the whole community, and, for a few tense hours, Mehdi's identity was reduced to only one aspect: his Muslimness. This episode betrayed a serious disruption in the social fabric of Mehdi's chosen community. Though he normally would not identify as a Muslim first—preferring the less parochial veil of his political identity—the communalization of Indian life created by the partition determined his reaction to the tragedy of Gandhi's assassination and he knew it would similarly determine the reaction of others toward him. In fact, in the quiet after the assassination, when no trains ran and no taxis were available, he hitched a ride with a Sikh man.

> We asked him, "Sardarji, where are you going?" He said, "I am going to Pakistan. And come along, you also come with us!" Meaning: Muslim areas. He was going to kill. So we laughed, and said, "No, no, we have got some work to do, etc. etc. So please you drop us near the Opera House. He said, "Alright." So he dropped us and he went away.[55]

Not until he got back to the home of newlywed Sardar Jafri did he tune into the radio news to discover that the assassin was "a fanatic Hindu," and he was overcome with relief.

In other places, too, the possibility of a Muslim assassin kept Muslims off the streets for fear of reprisal. The small group of Hindu conspirators responsible for Gandhi's death did not occupy the same metonymic space, for their disloyalty could be cast as transparently exceptional. Gandhi's assassin was identified as a member of the RSS and any retributive actions were directed at that right-wing political party. Two narrators described anti-RSS sentiment in the wake of the assassination. Irfan Habib recalled that as Aligarh students marched toward the city, "There were communists also demanding execution of RSS leaders. 'Hindu Sabha, *nehin*!' (No to the Hindu Party!) RSS and Hindu Sabha, *Phansi Do! Phansi Do!*' (Catch the RSS! Hang the Hindu Party!) I forget the title, the slogans."[56] Iqtidar Alam Khan recalled that RSS members were targeted and offices attacked in "a nationalist frenzy in which everyone was hating RSS like anything."[57] These memories were the exceptions, in that most narrators did not associate the aftermath of Gandhi's assassination with anti-RSS violence; they clearly remembered the threat of anti-Muslim violence, for as Irfan Habib remarked, "Of course, Hindus are not marked out."[58]

The politics of partitioning essentialized identities throughout North India, especially in places most affected by the migrations and resettlements of 1947. At AMU this process was magnified by the symbolic separation that already developed between the university and the town. The procession that Professor Mohammad Habib led toward the town, across the *kat pulla*, was intended as a show of solidarity, or possibly a show of strength by a community seeking to establish itself solidly on Indian ground. As Muslim students and faculty crossed the boundary that divided university and town, they asserted themselves in that public space as fully privileged, not cowering, citizens of India. The procession became possible only once Muslim innocence had been established. It was a rare opportunity for Muslims to demonstrate their loyalty to India by joining non-Muslim Indians in critiquing the exclusionary politics of the RSS, a Hindu nationalist, and anti-Muslim organization.

The Muslim Case in India

On January 15, 2011, India's *Tehelka* magazine published an article on several rounds of bombings that had targeted Muslims from 2006 to 2008. These blasts had earned notoriety in India and many Muslims, members of the so-called radical organizations, were rounded up and charged with committing the crimes.[59] Ashish Khetan argued in *Tehelka* that "since the first horrific blasts in Mumbai in 1992, there has been an automatic and damaging perception amongst most Indians that there is a Muslim hand behind every terror blast" and that this bias has been shared by the security forces who were quick to look for Muslims rather than actual perpetrators. Khetan's article, "In the Words of a Zealot. . ." built the case against this assumption. As he pointed out, over the last several years, further investigations had begun to break down the artifice of this discriminatory assumption, and revealed radical Hindutva activists hiding behind it. Based on the leaked confession of Swami Aseemanand, the article illuminates the real culprits behind these infamous blasts, and suspicion has fallen on activists throughout the RSS hierarchy, right to its highest ranks. Swami Aseemanand admitted to helping to conceive of the blasts and to identify targets, though the blasts themselves were organized and executed by others. Significantly, Aseemanand also identified other potential targets, including AMU.[60]

Aseemanand's confession sparked enough concern at Aligarh that it prompted a request for additional security, perhaps a reasonable one considering the fact that most of the other targets had already been hit: Malegaon, Mecca Masjid (Hyderabad), the Ajmer Dargah.[61] All of the targets were selected to injure Muslims and two of the targets, Hyderabad and AMU, were selected because of their perceived connections to Pakistan. The persistence of suspicion that Muslims broadly and Aligs specifically harbor anti-national sentiments is remarkable when since 1947 Muslim intellectuals have worked tirelessly to undo this perception.[62] The larger question relevant to independent India persists here, as Gyan Pandey so aptly put it, "Can a Muslim Be an Indian?"[63] This question has vexed the issue of citizenship for Muslims in the ostensibly secular Indian state.[64] Pandey has shown that the creation of Pakistan, which may have appeared as a solution to the Muslim Question by granting political autonomy to Muslim constituencies, in fact, because of the rigidity of the territorial solution, *confirmed* political "difference" and fixed the notion of the "Muslim minority" even in "districts, cities, or towns where they were in a numerical majority."[65] The friability of this notion of belonging has had a profound impact on the status of the Indian Muslims today whose loyalty is now not questioned by the Queen—as in Hunter's earlier query *Are They Bound in Conscience to Rebel against the Queen?*—but by fellow citizens of a secular and independent India.[66] The migrations of partition served to remake local environments, like Aligarh, both exposing the raw wires of communal sensitivity and providing the current running through them. As the tale of Swami Aseemanand shows, Muslims are seen as potential, even likely, perpetrators of violence, but they remain vulnerable as the targets in riots and pogroms. Omar Khalidi has shown that "in every riot since independence, no matter when or where, or how the riots take place, no matter who starts the riots, in the end the victims are mainly Muslims, whether in numbers of people killed, wounded or arrested."[67]

Mosque destruction and mob lynchings in the name of cow protection are but the most visible incidents that target Muslims. These explosions of hatred have embarrassed and shocked many Indians who, by and large, take the question of secularism seriously. However, the 2006 Sachar Committee Report, commissioned by Congress prime minister Manmohan Singh, and led by former chief justice of the Delhi High Court Rajinder Sachar proves that Muslims throughout the social hierarchy in India lag in a variety of Human Development Indices.[68] They are less educated, less wealthy, and less secure than others in similar positions. In some cases, this was true before partition, though the assumption, earlier fronted by Sir Sayyid, that Muslims were backward relative to Hindus, particularly in education, has largely been disproven.[69] At the time of independence the gap in graduation rates between Muslims and All Others was relatively low. However, since that time, and especially since 1970, the gap has widened markedly and unemployment among Muslim graduates is higher than that of any other group.[70] Other marginal groups, including Dalits, have reached higher levels of achievement, despite starting from a lower position.

The Sachar Committee Report lays bare obstacles to Muslim success. How AMU Muslims should understand these difficulties, or even recognize them, remains a point of dispute in the narratives I collected. Discrimination in employment, while constitutionally disallowed, has limited Muslim achievement. Whereas they are underrepresented in the professions, they are overrepresented in jails.[71] Though a variety of reports have been commissioned by the government to examine the problem of Muslim achievement, few have had any impact on government policy and many have barely seen the light of day.[72]

Stories of discrimination, or perceived discrimination, abound. One narrator told me, off the record, that in his job he overheard remarks by senior managers at his government job reluctant to give him a special project on the grounds that he was a *"karela"*—literally, a bitter gourd—used here to mean inept, and troublesome: a Muslim. Others discounted the importance of discrimination, or challenged the basis for a discrimination claim. Ahmad Saeed argued that Muslims often failed to submit their applications or to compete for positions. In his experience, he told me, even when the government "provided training arrangements for . . . scheduled caste and minority students who wanted to participate in these competitions . . . I found that there was no Muslim student. Scheduled caste students were there, but there were no Muslim students. Even with a free lunch they were not there!"[73] Ather Siddiqi, even as he decried the presence of institutionalized discrimination, told me that Muslims dominated the lower echelons of the unskilled labor economy. Though often self-employed, their labor and manufactures were critical to the industrial economy, which was dominated by Hindus.[74] Thus, the tenuous balance that Siddiqi described holds as long as Hindu "providers" and moneylenders maintain economic superiority; a challenge to this *status quo*—economically or politically—has the potential to invite retribution. All of these factors amount to a persistent anxiety in Muslim communities, that even in the absence of the "alarm"—the other element of fear—constrains their public engagement. The periodic eruption of violence adds "alarm" into the mix to remind Muslims that their place in society is determined by Hindu tolerance (or lack thereof).

Pakistans, Pakistanis, and India

In the city of Aligarh, and other non-Muslim majority cities and towns in UP, as I discovered when I went looking for my ancestral home, Muslim localities are called "Pakistan" despite the choice of the residents not to migrate. The language of "mini-Pakistans" keeps residents alert to the potentially traitorous population in their midst, and their presence is used to justify violence against Muslims.[75] As Omar Khalidi has shown, riots tend to occur in neighborhoods where Hindus and Muslim live alongside one another, and tend to be marked by concerns over Muslim economic advance.[76] Whereas it is necessary to separate the outcome of Pakistan from study of prepartition politics, it is impossible to separate it from any examination of Muslims after 1947. The process of partitioning links the social position of Muslims in India to the migrations surrounding partition and their symbolic value in the context of Indian and Pakistani statehood. The presence of Pakistan affects how Muslims experience Indian citizenship, particularly in those areas from which there was a high level of migration, including UP, Bihar, West Bengal, and Central India, that also remain the most educationally "sluggish."[77]

For AMU Muslims, the real effect of partition's migrations resonated locally as a "loss of leadership." As early as 1948, the vice chancellor's report for 1947 reported that many teachers and students had been "lost."[78] Salman Khurshid observes the effects of partition's brain drain in "the seemingly inexplicable poverty of social and political leadership" among Indian Muslims.[79] The issue of loss of leadership is especially important with relation to political power. Partition's migrations reduced the voting bloc of Muslims from approximately 25 percent of the population to more like 10 percent.[80] Separate electorates, established in 1909, were abolished in India in 1949 as a result of the perception that separate representation was intimately linked to the separatist politics that resulted in partition.[81] Choudhry Khaliquzzaman reports in his *Pathway to Pakistan* that during Assembly debates in July 1947, Sardar Patel remarked that "Those who want separate electorates should go to Pakistan."[82] Without separate electorates, Muslims are consigned to a permanent minority. In the halls of parliament, Muslims remain material during campaigns when candidates seek their support as a voting bank. However, Muslim representation has declined under Congress-led governments and with the growth of the BJP's influence. Jaffrelot and Verniers report that "Between 1980 and 2014, the representation of Muslim MPs in the lower house of India's Parliament has diminished by nearly two-thirds even as the share of Muslims in the population rose during the same period." In 2014, in UP, where Muslims constitute 18 percent of the population, Muslim representation has dropped from 17 percent in 2012 to 6 percent in

2017. In 2014, not a single Muslim won a parliamentary bid.[83] The BJP, in power at the center, fielded no Muslim candidates in the 2019 election. This has created a sense of powerlessness within the Muslim community, because issues concerning Muslims are unlikely to be entertained if there are no Muslims to represent them. This is especially devastating in AMU, a site designed to be an incubator for Muslim leaders.

The narrators at the heart of my study in India, have, overall, an ambivalent relationship to the question of the position of Muslim Indians. There was a palpable sense of loss in this community for the cultural elite, the educated class who departed. While few of these narrators would conceded a desire to migrate themselves, and have aggressively embraced the identity of India citizenship, even looking across the border with frustration and pity, they also attributed some of the difficulties that Indian Muslims have faced to the departure of their co-religionists.[84] One Alig (of a 1970s generation) I met called them "cheaters"—who betrayed their Indian brethren by shifting to Pakistan.[85] Though many of the narrators with whom I spoke came from divided families, meaning that they had relatives in Pakistan, they compared their own experience and achievement to that of their family and friends on the other side, who they believed had changed as a result of their departure.

Relative to non-Muslims, Indian Muslims may have had a qualitatively different experience, lagging behind in observable indices. However, in comparison to Pakistani Muslims, narrators considered themselves better off or were aggressively critical of those in the neighboring country, and with the intention of proving their own success, sometimes used the examples of the exceptional to define the rule. For some narrators, Indian Muslims appeared as the preservers of truly Muslim, or truly "good" values and they linked these directly to the Indian environment. While Muslims lamented the departure of so many "good" families, leading to overall decline in Indian Muslim society, they also made clear that those families who left were no longer "good," having been corrupted by their migration.

Consider, for example, Zakia Siddiqi's critique of her husband's family in Pakistan, who she considered to be unnecessarily materialistic. "I used to go there my mother-in-law used to say, 'Put on some jewelry,' and this and that. And people would recognize me, 'Oh! She has come from India! Look at that. Poor India!'"[86] While at first glance, this may seem an innocuous difference in preference, Siddiqi used the exchange to show the fundamental corruption of society in Pakistan. Whereas, she indicated, modesty and simplicity were considered to be the values of AMU, or even Indian Muslims, Pakistan's culture was showy, shallow, and materialistic. Pakistan, as a place, had corrupted them, alienated them from the true values of the community. As she put it broadly, "even those people who migrated from India to Pakistan, their value system has changed."[87] In a written memoir, Hayatullah Ansari, a former resident of Aftab Hostel in the late 1930s, remembered his friend Akhtar Raepuri, a communist who "later changed his road. He became an aristocrat. When I met him in Pakistan probably about 1961, then his ideas were completely different."[88] Many Indian Muslims derided Pakistani migrants as opportunists, and this critique was at the heart of the perception that their values had changed. In this conception, Indian Muslims have made the best with the resources available to them, and it behooves them to keep a low profile.

Masood-ul Hasan similarly linked the presence of Pakistan with a betrayal of Aligarh's values. Speaking of Chaudhry Khaliquzzaman, an AMU Old Boy, Muslim League leader, and author of *Pathway to Pakistan*, Hasan acknowledged that Khaliquzzaman had been "our" leader, by which he meant not only the Muslim League's leader, but AMU's own leader. However, Hasan described Khaliquzzaman's abrupt departure for Pakistan as "stabbing us in the back!"[89] Whereas Hasan refused to criticize Jinnah, a League man but ostensibly an Aligarh outsider,[90] his continued anger at Khaliquzzaman—a "mean-minded man"—seems rooted in the same kind of betrayal of values that Zakia Siddiqi described earlier. Departure for Pakistan appeared then not just as the pursuit of choice, or self-fulfillment, or even as the culmination of the League's avowed policy (that Hasan, among others had supported in his students days). Departure was a personal and particular betrayal of AMU's values and revealed the deceit of Pakistan's partisans. The creation of Pakistan as a separate and sovereign state appeared to them as a transgression of the moral boundaries of AMU within which they had cultivated a utopian ideal of solidarity. Rather than serving to unite India's Muslims, Pakistan has permanently divided them.

Aligs in India critiqued the Muslim identity of Pakistan as "communal" and expressed pity for the experience of Muslims there. Saeeda Kidwai, the first female student to attend AMU for postgraduate classes in Geography, lamented the situation in Pakistan.

> What happens in Pakistan is such a terrible thing that Muslims are killing Muslims and destroying mosques. It is such a shameful thing. Here, if a Hindu kills, what is the complaint of the Muslim? Those people should complain because brother is killing brother. And in mosques! . . . On Fridays when more people come to the mosque. Boys also come, the younger generation also comes. Old people also come. If in Hindustan a mosque is destroyed look what a ruckus it creates![91]

Kidwai invoked the destruction of the Babri Mosque in 1992 as an exceptional event; that episode had a massive impact on communal relations in India.[92] What surprised her was that Hindu-Muslim conflict draws Muslims together in solidarity and with others too. She contrasted this with the complacency she perceived in Pakistan and her disbelief that Muslim versus Muslim violence was even possible there. Whereas Ahmad Saeed had suggested that Muslims were "naturally" targeted in the early years after independence, in Pakistan, Kidwai argued, the violence was "unnatural." It contravened the logic of the state and the identity politics that brought it into being. This situation was perplexing to Indian Muslims, and exemplified the fundamental difference they saw between their experience and the experience of Pakistanis. Kidwai's perspective on violence in Pakistan sustained the myth of Muslim solidarity as it developed at AMU. It failed to recognize that within and among Muslims many identities persist and the logic of a Muslim homeland has been insufficient to elide those other claims. Although the place of Muslims in Indian society has sometimes been uncertain, and her rhetorical question, "What is the complaint of the Muslim?" obliquely referred to the expectation that some narrators earlier expressed that it was unreasonable to believe that Muslims would be left alone in independent India. Still, she and others claimed that the bonds of solidarity that connect Muslims to one another in India remain strong. Muslim violence in Pakistan, to her, represented a world upside down, where the logic that created it had been inverted.

The irony of Pakistan as an overtly and officially Muslim state (since the passing of the Objectives Resolution in 1949) is that League Muslims in India had typically not been associated with explicit devotion to the faith. Venkat Dhulipala has recently argued that the Pakistan demand should be best understood as a vision to create a "New Medina," a sovereign Islamic State.[93] Though the passing of the Objectives Resolution, that enshrined the authority of Allah as the supreme lawgiver and Pakistani's identity as an Islamic Republic, may appear to confirm this notion, it does not hold in the AMU environment. The language of Islam may have characterized debates among the ulama, but in AMU, Pakistan's partisans envisioned a cultural home for Muslims; rarely was enthusiasm for Pakistan expressed as religious zeal. Rather, it was Muslims in the Indian nationalist movement, like Abul Kalam Azad, who represented "traditional" culture.[94] Their presence reinforced the perception of Muslims as "non-modern" and provided a necessary contrast with the modernity of the Hindu nation thereby reinforcing the boundaries of that nation. While Nationalist Muslim leaders existed and remain, they always represent the minority, the part and not the whole. As Aamir Mufti has argued, "The minority is cast as a segment only, and becomes an undifferentiated staging ground for the traditional, the premodern, the underdeveloped, the archaic."[95] Mufti's argument is useful, despite the attachment of AMU to its own "modernity." Irfan Habib confirmed this when I asked about the relationship AMU students had with Islam during the 1940s. In answering, he established that the League dominated the university and told about the difference between Congress Muslims and League Muslims. In his estimation,

> most nationalist Muslims were religious—Hakim [Ajmal Khan]. . .Dr. [M.A.] Ansari. Here was also Tasadduq Sherwani. They were all religious . . . Muslim Leaguers were not religious to this degree. Jinnah was not; he couldn't pray. They were mostly modern with a large proportion of people who were landlords. On the women's question they were iffy, but they had on their Working Committee women who didn't observe purdah. Jinnah's sister didn't observe purdah. Begum Aizaz Rasool didn't. So on these issues, purdah and so on, they were fairly modern . . . They were in this sense "modern communalists" rather than religious jihadis.[96]

Habib drew out a number of significant points here—perhaps most important is the way he layered the AMU identity of modernist Muslims and the "League" identity. Even Habib's description of his own father showed that identity at Aligarh was far from static. He said, "My father was a curious man: a devout believer in God, and his Prophet, even more devoted than Prophet to Gandhiji, and very well read in Marxism."[97] While Mohammad Habib's attachment to Marxism, especially, was not typical, he did represent a leftist contingent that grew in strength and importance after 1947.

Within the context of India's Muslims, AMU has represented a progressive strain since its inception. AMU Muslims, since Sir Sayyid's days, had been engaged in a process of mixing Western and traditional values. Although many non-Muslims in Congress had been raised in this tradition, including M. K. Gandhi and Jawaharlal Nehru, the party had begun to differentiate itself from British values and identity markers in the 1920s. Thus, in the context of the trajectory of the Indian state and the non-Muslim public, AMU appeared ambivalently anti-imperialist and archaically communal. Indian Aligs have sought to exile the accusations of communal identity to Pakistan by arguing that it was League Muslims who embraced the destructive communal politics. It must be clear, however, that this, too, was used as evidence that Indian Aligs perceived a distinct "change" in those who migrated to Pakistan. By embracing a communal identity, they abandoned the ethos of tolerance that had always been part of the Aligarh environment in favor of the opportunistic pursuit of wealth and power. The effect was to "confirm difference" by reducing the identities of Aligs to their Muslimness.

Conclusion

It is critical to consider the influence of the reality of Pakistan—no longer an ethos, a theory, a persuasive, and perhaps multiply (but not insufficiently[98]) imagined place—for the presence of Pakistan exerts influence on the experiences of Muslims throughout the region. As Saeed Naqvi suggests, "divergence of views on Partition conditioned differing attitudes towards Pakistan and consequently towards Indian Muslims."[99] Masood-ul Hasan put a finer point on it, "What soured our relations? The bloodshed."[100] The bloodshed of 1946–7 made indelible the line that separated the two states. This line seemed arbitrary to many, and came with an expectation of permeability. It was never imagined as a permanent definition of identity but as one that would become "blurred" with time.[101] Instead, it was reified by partition violence.[102] It now put a boundary not only between Muslim and non-Muslim Indians, but between Muslims in India and Pakistan. Saeed Naqvi argued that the Muslim who remained in India was "less ambivalent than the majority community in his opposition to the two-nation theory" and therefore "a shared hatred for Pakistan became the acid test for loyalty."[103]

Memories serve as the link between the past and the present to create a continuous narrative through 1947, but these connections are not always straightforward. Faisal Devji has argued that Muslim League nationalism depended upon the rejection of history, and that Indian nationalism depended on it, but I believe the case of partition poses an exception. In India, statehood is linked intimately to the inheritance of the past, increasingly coded as explicitly Hindu. In that narrative, the 1947 Partition is almost always read as a permanent rupture, the destruction of an ancestral Hindu land that included the areas that became Pakistan. In Pakistan, among narrators with connections to AMU, and even in some official channels, the values of the state—including its attachment to Muslim identity and Urdu—are often constructed as being continuous with the past, and with AMU itself.[104] Devji notes, as I have, the peculiar contradiction in Pakistani narratives that sometimes suggests that Pakistan was not just a triumph, but somehow must be blamed on some one. Thus, he writes, Pakistan can seem like an "unwanted or accidental consequence" of Indian politics.

It was the establishment of a territorially defined nation-state, designed to ensure the political survival of the Muslim nation once conceived of by Sir Sayyid that forced the profound disruption of Muslim institutions: educational, cultural, and religious. By relocating much of the AMU community, and cutting off access to the physical space in which its values were embodied, partitioning dislocated and de-emphasized "the dense networks of interrelationships that defined the particularities of place."[105]

AMU narrators have found it difficult to resolve questions about belonging, for proximity is irrelevant to the connection they feel to AMU *as a place*.[106] AMU taught them to believe in the possibilities of integrated communities within India, *and* they felt threatened by Hindu communities surrounding the university. They promoted Muslim solidarity *and* struggled to accept the diversity within Muslim communities from the Northwest Frontier to Bengal. These "Muslim Questions" have persisted beyond the immediate territorial reality of independent India because the removal of so many Muslims to Pakistan creates a whole new set of Muslim questions.[107] India provides the most explosive example of the challenges of integration, and AMU stands out as a powerful symbol.

Indian Muslims have recognized that the burden of tolerance rested on the Hindu majority. Ather Siddiqi, Zakia Siddiqi's husband, who was a student at Aligarh in the 1940s, and taught in AMU for most of his career, laid this argument out most clearly. At the outset of our recorded interview, which was the second of our conversations, he told me, "*So I want to prove this that India,* as a nation, *has limitless tolerance and resilience, persecution as a concept does not exist.*"[108] The very presence of Muslims in India today, Siddiqi argued, was evidence of Hindu tolerance, "they could have chucked us out" during partition, he told me. As Wazira Zamindar has recently elucidated, his words echoed Hannah Arendt in his assertion that Muslims have no "right to have rights" or a "right to belong."[109] Rather, Hindus "allow" Muslims "use" of the country. Siddiqi, despite his earlier admission that he wanted to migrate to Pakistan, laid the blame for the 1947 Partition squarely at the feet of Muslims.[110] He did not conflate the Muslims with the Muslim League, or attribute the creation of Pakistan to League politics. Rather, he argued that Muslims, as a people, should bear the responsibility for partitioning India. His is a broad indictment that grows from a sense that "*Muslims cannot live together.*"[111] This inability, as Siddiqi saw it, to live together, to live without conflict, was a foil to India's self-evident history of tolerance. The evidence appears in everyday life when the early morning call to prayer is broadcast over loudspeakers. The fact that Hindus do not interfere with this loud, public reminder of Muslim presence, is a testament, he argued, to the depth of the majority's commitment to secular inclusion. As Aamir Mufti argues, "To function successfully as a minority vis-a-vis the state is to accept this ambivalent status, on the latter's terms, as emancipation."[112]

5

Muslimness and Pakistan

For Pakistanis, the border transformed India into the spectral Other. It remained, in their memories, the site of oppression of Muslims, even as it was home to many Muslim religious and cultural sites, including AMU. Their attachment to the place froze in time. AMU became the site of youth's perfection, the place that nurtured ambition, rewarded loyalty, and laid the foundation for a successful career. That AMU remained in India meant that Pakistanis were cut off from it physically, but they could not be separated from it affectively. They imagined Pakistan, by contrast, as the site of opportunity. In their youthful aspirations, it would embody the "spaciousness" they had experienced while campaigning, that unbridled excitement of a future laid out before them. Pakistan's formation had been a near miracle, and AMU students received credit for turning villages throughout North India into "Pakistan" villages, by getting out the rural vote.[1]

Still, in spite of their focus on Pakistan's unlikely formation, narrators remained critical of its failures, of the inability of the state to uphold its promises of Muslim unity. This critique, ironically, linked the stories told by former Aligs in both Pakistan and Bangladesh. With independence, the Muslim identity touted by the Muslim League ceased to be a minority category in Pakistan, even as it defined a permanent minority in India. However, the assumption of majority did not alleviate tensions over belonging and meaning among and between Muslims of different sects and orientation. The Muslim identity projected outward from AMU and embodied in Jinnah's declaration, "This is Muslim India!," which became central to the experience of AMU students, was insufficient to contain the community's actual diversity. It was not long before Pakistanis returned to the comfort of those other identities, challenging the territorial and ideological integrity of the state. Though the fault line of Bangladeshi liberation divided the narrators, all agreed that the problem with the Pakistani state was that it had rejected the values from which Muslim identity in AMU derived. Pakistan exerted terrific power on the memories of AMU narrators on all sides of the post-1947 borders. All narrators engaged national narratives but localized their memories in the institution of AMU as they reconciled their post-partition experiences with their earlier allegiances.

In addition, Muslims and other minorities have not always coexisted peacefully in Pakistan and Bangladesh. The Two Nation Theory, by the force of which the Muslim League demanded a separate homeland, posited a fundamental difference between Hindus and Muslims but also suggested that all Muslims were united by their common faith. This homogenizing narrative deliberately obscured the diversity of India's Muslim communities in favor of an elite, Urdu-speaking, faith-driven narrative of solidarity. Ethnic, linguistic, or sectarian supremacy movements by majority communities have targeted the minorit(ies) repeatedly in Pakistan since its earliest days. These reactionary movements seek to shore up majority identity against that of the minority.[2] Pakistan's founder declared that the state would support religious freedom, and the white band on the flag was to represent Pakistan's minorities, but Hindus and Christians have faced persecution alongside minority Muslim identities like Ahmadis, Shi'a, and Ismailis.

When Minority Becomes Majority

Whereas Muslimness posed a problematic in India as a label for the suspect "other," it has formed the core shared characteristic that defined citizenship in Pakistan. During the period of reform and regeneration from 1857 to 1947, when the leaders of the Muslim community sought to unify it in opposition to British and Hindu domination, the needs and values of the elite were broadly interpreted and portrayed as the values of the community as a whole. Within the religiously defined nation-state, however, communities cohered around different issues, those that had been overwritten by the demand for statehood: class, sect, regional, and linguistic identity. The institutions that were established to service North India's Urdu-speaking elite, even those—like Urdu—that survived the disruptions of partitioning in some form, proved manifestly insufficient to serve the ultimately diverse community.

The most profound challenge to the Two Nation Theory that justified Pakistan's creation as a Muslim homeland was the secession of East Pakistan/independence of Bangladesh in 1971 after a brief, but devastating war with West Pakistan. However, the challenges to the homogenizing logic of citizenship in Pakistan have persisted with the recurrence of regional, ethnic, and linguistically identitarian movements. Aligs in Pakistan, however, who hailed primarily from North India, did not recognize more localized identity markers and imagined themselves as the standard of Muslim identity that developed in a straightforward and uncomplicated way at AMU, and that they believed led to the establishment of the Pakistani state. In other words, the image of Muslim identity that survived in their collective memory, one that collapsed difference, was constantly in conflict with the reality of Pakistani identity, which was, and remains, much more aggressively diverse.

In our interviews, Aligs like Wajahat Husain lamented the emerging fractures along lines of alternate identities.

> I am a firm believer that it is the commitment to the country that is the main thing. Everything else is secondary. That is our main problem right now. It wasn't, in our first few years after formation of Pakistan. The spirit of Pakistan at the time of its establishment was quite different from what it is now. At that time we were only concerned with doing our best, hard work, get down to building the country, establishing the country, and getting the country moving forward. We were not concerned with anything else. It's only afterwards when these feelings

of provincialism or ethnicity started entering. That has eaten up the country and has done a lot of damage, it is doing a lot of damage. That is our major problem.³

Husain's critique of identitarian politics pointed to an anxiety that other groups would seek recognition and autonomy and thus undermine the salient unity of Muslimness. His fears though, were belated—a reaction to the 1971 loss of East Pakistan, and the more contemporary provincial tensions that continued to threaten the unity of the state as he aged. Furthermore, as the power of Sunni supremacist militant groups grew in Pakistan in the early 2000s when we spoke, the consequences of those fractures were highly visible.

Dedicated observers of the scene in Pakistan have been aware of the problem of sectarianism and discrimination against minorities for some time, and have recognized the challenges minorities face in finding space within a hegemonic and homogenizing Muslim national identity. In the months before the partition, anxiety developed about the place of minorities in both the Indian and the Pakistani states. Jinnah addressed this concern repeatedly with assurances that minorities would be fully privileged citizens of the Pakistani state with full religious freedom.⁴ His most famous declaration came in his August 11, 1947, speech to Pakistan's Constituent Assembly. He addressed the nation with the immortal and oft-cited words, "You are free; you are free to go to your temples, you are free to go to your mosques or to any other place of worship in this state of Pakistan. You may belong to any religion or caste or creed." Despite these, Pakistan's minorities have faced an uphill battle for inclusion.

The story of Pakistan's minorities has received international attention because of highly publicized cases involving its blasphemy laws.⁵ Though the blasphemy laws have been on the books since the British period, military dictator Zia ul-Haq was responsible for refining the language and increasing the penalties. Pakistan's blasphemy laws assign penalties for defacing the Qur'an, defaming the Prophet of Islam, or proclaiming Muslim identity outside of mainstream sects.⁶ These laws have led to tendentious and erroneous accusations against minorities and women.⁷ In a dramatic test of Pakistan's blasphemy laws, Asia Bibi, a low-status Christian woman, was accused of maligning the prophet in a dispute with higher-status Muslim women in her village. Asia Bibi was beaten, arrested, imprisoned, and sentenced to death for her crime despite her claims of innocence. In 2010, Punjab Governor Salman Taseer stood up for the abolition of blasphemy laws in support of Asia Bibi. On January 4, 2011, Taseer was assassinated by Mumtaz Qadri, one of Taseer's own security personnel. Though Qadri was showered with rose petals by supporters as he arrived at his first court appearance, he was sentenced to death and hanged for the crime in 2016. Only a few months after Taseer's assassination, Shahbaz Bhatti, the Christian minister for minority affairs, was also killed by armed militants. The two assassinations brought the issue of Pakistan's non-Muslim minorities to the fore in a complex and quickly changing political and religious conflict.⁸ In 2018, the Supreme Court of Pakistan finally overturned the verdict in Asia Bibi's case (for lack of evidence) and she was freed from prison and ultimately left the country. Qadri's supporters protested the outcome for days. According to Pakistan's Centre for Social Justice: "There have been 1,549 known cases of the most serious charges—either blasphemy against Muhammad or desecration of the Koran," though no one has been executed. Seventy-five of the accused were "murdered before their trials" either by mobs or in police custody.[9]

The events surrounding the Asia Bibi case signaled a shoring up of majority identity—increasingly defined as Sunni Muslim—against any others who might have made a claim of legitimate belonging. Despite Jinnah's promises of inclusivity, Pakistan's minorities are well aware of the deep tensions around belonging, even if the rest of world has been ignorant of it, content to believe the official myth of Pakistani identity: that it is all Muslim. The ostensibly Muslim identity of the Islamic Republic of Pakistan has been accepted as homogenous and undifferentiated. In an unlikely foil to the experience of India's Muslims, partitioning has meant that the identity of Pakistani Muslims, too, was reduced to their "Muslimness."[10]

People belonging to minority communities have frequently referred to the plight of other minority communities, sometimes expressing solidarity with them. Pakistan's minority communities anticipated the protection of the majority Muslims by virtue of the fact that they had an experience of minority identity in India, and would therefore be sympathetic. However, as research on trauma has shown, and I think the South Asian case of ongoing partitioning exemplifies well, one of the effects of trauma is "you can't then see what you are capable of doing. You are always repeating a situation in which you are threatened and potentially destroyed."[11] The majority community in Pakistan reenacts the trauma of threat (experienced in pre-1947 India) through repeated attempts to define the boundaries of the majority by pushing the minorities outside of it. As Pakistani Christian and decorated Air Force pilot Cecil Chaudhry put it, Pakistan's minorities expected that "the Muslims would remember the problems faced as a minority and would not perpetuate the same fate for other minorities" but have confronted the reality that "it turned out to be the opposite."[12] The repetition of trauma, suggests Jacqueline Rose in the context of Israel, is the result of the "distressing overlap between the need to feel safe as a nation and the need to believe in yourself" and is the "the most historically attested response to trauma."[13] Thus, despite the good intentions of the founders of both India and Pakistan, Jinnah's protestations of the intimacy in relationship between minorities and the state in Pakistan, and Nehru's determination that the essential quality of the Indian state was its composite identity in which distinctions between majority and minority communities had no meaning in the eyes of the state, a variety of other identities have become important in India, Pakistan, and Bangladesh. These identity politics, worked out in an environment of mutual potential threat, sometimes called the "hostage nation theory" did little to create an environment of equal opportunity for minorities in either Pakistan or India. The persistence of identitarian politicking that marks citizens in relationship to one another rather than by their relationship to the state has challenged the founding narratives of all three post-partition states.

Perhaps the most potent case of religious discrimination against citizens who fell outside the fold of the mainstream Sunni Muslim identity in Pakistan is the case of the Ahmadis. Whereas the fundamental rights of non-Muslims in Pakistan have been protected under the law, the Ahmadis have been singled out for a legal classification as "non-Muslim," though they self-identify as Muslims. The "alleged doctrinal deviancy" of the Ahmadi has resulted in ongoing persecution in Pakistan including periodic attacks on their mosques and leadership.[14] The roots of the conflict between the Ahmadi and those who consider them apostates dates to before the founding of Pakistan, but became a tool for the Pakistani state under successive leaders to curry favor among Pakistan's conservative ulama, especially during periods when democratic forces had been compromised.

The Ahmadi movement emerged during the same period as the reformist Aligarh and Deoband movements and employed similar strategies—the establishment of educational institutions—to facilitate outreach and to spread its reformist message.[15] Unlike in Aligarh or Deoband, however, the Ahmadi movement was largely rural and its adherents came from the middle and lower classes, and the movement particularly focused on "missionary outreach to non-Muslims."[16] Despite class differences, in its early years, the movement had much in common with other reformist movements. After its leader Ghulam Ahmad claimed to be receiving revelations and began making prophecies, however, the Ahmadis increasingly became isolated and reviled by these other movements. The critical conflict between Sunni leadership and the Ahmadis is the question of Ghulam Ahmad's claim to prophethood. After the creation of Pakistan, the Ahmadis were singled out as a threat to mainstream Islam—the threat of Hindus having largely been eliminated by the migrations. During the 1950s, Ahmadis became the victims of violent attacks from the *Anjuman-i-Ahrar-i-Islam*, a group with whom the Ahmadi had been in conflict since before Pakistan's creation.[17] Maulana Maududi, the founder of the *Jamaat-i-Islami*, emerged as a particularly virulent opponent of the Ahmadi and he demanded that the Ahmadis be declared "non-Muslims."[18]

In 1974, the National Assembly passed a resolution that was signed into law by Prime Minister Zulfikar Ali Bhutto; it vindicated Maududi's request and designated Ahmadis a "non-Muslim minority." Though Ahmadis, like other minority communities, are legally permitted to practice their faith, the law prevents them from claiming to be Muslims. Ordinance XX passed by General Zia ul-Haq, as a part of his efforts to generate support among Pakistan's ulama, added two sections to the Pakistan Penal Code directed specifically against Ahmadis. These restrictions prohibited Ahmadis from using the Muslim call to prayer, reciting the *kalima* (declaration of faith), and calling their "places of worship" mosques. Ahmadis are threatened under Pakistan's harsh blasphemy laws, restricted under the electoral code from voting as Muslims, and all Pakistanis must sign a pro forma declaring that they consider Ahmadis to be non-Muslims in order to obtain an identity card or passport. The institutionalization of this discrimination has marginalized Ahmadis and constitutionally legitimized the accusation of apostasy by enshrining the belief in the finality of the Prophet as a criterion for claiming the Muslim identity and even Pakistani citizenship. The legal restrictions placed on Ahmadis have a broad impact. They facilitate the idea that the state supports Sunni Islam as the dominant orthodoxy under which all heterodox practices including Sufism and Shiism are vulnerable.[19] In fact, the "judicially authorized" attacks on Ahmadis have opened the door to attacks on others, including Shi'a, Christians, and Hindus, even if they do not claim Muslim identity.[20]

While Muslimness soon proved to be an insufficient category for encompassing all of Pakistan's identities, the most significant crisis of belonging in Pakistan was an intrafaith one, and emerged as a result of the tensions between the Pakistan's two wings. The independence of Bangladesh proved a fundamental challenge to the Two

Nation Theory, which was betrayed by the state's total lack of sympathy for the rights of East Pakistani Muslims. The conflict exposed a deeper racialized tension and a difficult history of communalized politics that challenged the ostensible brotherhood of Muslims that had joined together to form Pakistan itself. The degradation of the foundational narrative of Pakistani national identity was a perpetual source of regret and anxiety among narrators. After 1971, Pakistan no longer embodied, for them, the priorities of unity and solidarity to which they subscribed as students. On the contrary, Pakistan divided Muslim from Muslim and the few minorities that have survived the increasingly puritanizing environment have become the subjects of a campaign of violence supported explicitly and implicitly by the government of Pakistan.

Once charged with unifying India's Muslims, Pakistan's government has become an instrument of oppression—complicit in the rise of Islamic politics that Devji has called "Pakistan's only national project"—isolating and persecuting minorities, much to the chagrin of many narrators who think of themselves as Pakistan's founders.[21] These self-proclaimed "founders," former students of AMU who were active in the demand for Pakistan, however, disdained just as equally the rise of regional, ethnic, and linguistic nationalisms that they saw as a challenge to an unmarked Muslim Pakistani identity. Thus, they blamed these identities for the disintegration of Pakistan's unified identity. This lament for Pakistan was perhaps best summarized in the words of former AMU student Abdul Rasheed Khan. "Think of those times in 1944. The aim was ... to build up culture for the Muslims. Now [in Pakistan] we are not Muslims, we are Sindhis, we are Punjabis, we are all that ... the nation-building spirit has gone."[22]

AMU, Pakistan, and Bangladesh

Even as narrators hearkened back to a utopian vision of Muslim unity that they believe was born in AMU, their own memories betray the seeds of tensions among and between Muslims. Riazur Rahman Sherwani argued that there was never any discrimination against non-Muslim students or faculty. Rather, "The fight was between Muslim and Muslim. Those Muslims who favored partition and those Muslims who were against partition."[23] Even as he reiterated the value of tolerance within the university, he evoked its internal tensions. There were many fault lines within the student body, in part because the national identity of which AMU has been so famously construed to be the home was rooted explicitly in the values of a narrow segment of Muslim society: the Urdu-speaking, educated or landed class.

Many of the narrators who contributed here belonged to that class, and most hail from Urdu-speaking North India. Still AMU attracted well-off Muslim students from throughout the subcontinent. In fact, as several Bengali narrators told me, they became aware of AMU because they knew that respected lawyers in their own communities were its products. Bangladeshi Habibur Rahman emphasized that at AMU "they don't believe in parochialism as well as localism. They would make it an international attitude, international brotherhood."[24] Still, students from Bengal did not share in all of the cultural similarities of North India's elite, and they were set apart by their more limited fluency in Urdu.

Whereas the Pakistani narrators' identity was based on the centrality of AMU, and therefore themselves, in a teleological narrative of statehood, the Bengali narrators presented a challenge to that teleology, revealing different memories of both AMU and of their time as Pakistanis. Bengali narrators remembered a fundamental sense of not fully belonging among the largely Urdu-speaking AMU students. While few would suggest explicitly that they "did not belong," they indicated a sense of alienation and recounted the methods they employed to build community, even if on the fringes of the AMU mainstream and the spatial fringes of the campus. A key distinction between the spatial framework the Bangladeshis embraced and the circles of safety described earlier, was that the widest circle of safety encompassed majority Muslim Bengal, though its great distance from AMU meant that moving in the outer circle could be very risky, especially during periods of unrest. The inner and middle circles, too, were defined by Bengali norms and experiences.

Every Bengali narrator described building friendships in AMU primarily with other Bengali students. As Salahuddin Chowdhury said, "when I went there, I was received by some people from Bangladesh and given a room."[25] His sense of belonging at AMU was determined by the initial support he found among those who also "belonged" to his region, and he even credits them with giving him his room.[26] Whereas North Indian students like Saghir Ahmed Rizvi described the uncertainty of landing in a room with an unknown person, sometimes a more powerful senior, the Bengali students materialized to help one another get settled. Mohiuddin and Waheeduddin even shared a room. Habibur Rahman belonged to the student group known as the "Eastern Association," which included students from Bengal and Assam.[27] Thus, although AMU did not believe in "localism," it was local connections that helped students to form bonds among one another.[28]

In discussions about food, the sense of displacement from home was most acute. Where many students describe the "café culture" of students gathering for cheap snacks and long conversations in the cafes of Shamshad Market alongside the campus, Mohiuddin described the effort to find a familiar culinary experience there. "Of course, we used go to the cafes. You see, in Bangladesh, we get *shingara*, we call it *shingara*—it is vegetable inside and it is rolled in a triangular shape. So somehow we used to get in Aligarh *namakpara* and potato chip, so we mixed together that and said, 'This is the taste of our *shingara*.'"[29] The intimacy between food and home, in Mohiuddin's memory, was articulated through the particularity of place, the cafes of Aligarh, sites in which the brotherhood was formed, but that lay in the middle circle of protection. In the café, students were still within the university's disciplinary realm, but they had additional freedom to explore and create their own identities. This episode illustrates the effort that Bengali students had to exert to fit into AMU's largely North Indian brotherhood. There is a sense that, more than other students, these students sought ways to retain their own culture, while engaging with the norms that dominated student life.

Every Bengali narrator described the difficulty of eating a North Indian bread-heavy diet when they were accustomed to rice and fish. Several students described enlisting the hostel servants and their wives in preparing dishes that might convey a familiar taste. Habibur Rahman shared the story of how a connection with an AMU student leader helped him to secure a room in AMU's most prestigious Sir Syed Hall. Embedded within the story, though, was his memory of finding someone who would prepare fish for him to eat. "[The bearer's] wife was *Bosey*—the Hindus said it *bosey* not *bhabi*.[30] I was saying—to appease her—we said, '*Bosey*, we like to take rice and fish!' And she used to cook very well. And he was from my area—Vikrampur, Munshiganj—it is known, probably you have heard of Vikrampur."[31] The narrative is bookended then, with stories of how connections from home—one high status, and one low status—helped Habibur Rahman to make himself at home in AMU. Mohiuddin's memories are more tentative; he took pleasure in whatever familiar elements he could find: "on Monday noon, the hostels served a little biryani, so that was one of our very fond item! At least it is rice!"[32] Thus, while AMU was an environment that welcomed India's diversity, the reality was more complicated for the students who constituted that diversity.

The institution that the Bengalis recalled was substantively similar to the one described by others during the 1940s. These narrators, too, touted the importance and uniqueness of the university's disciplinary system, and how this system lent credibility to AMU's reputation. Habibur Rahman emphasized the university's independence from the government; whereas in other universities, like the JMI, the chancellor was appointed by the government, in AMU there was "no Chancellor from government. The Nawab of Hyderabad was the Chancellor. It was completely independent."[33] These narrators also described the influence of the Muslim League, though they tended to reveal more ambivalence in their allegiance to its ideology. Salahuddin Chowdhury, for instance, described himself as basically nonpolitical, but when I asked about Pakistan, he conceded that the idea of Pakistan was "more or less not controversial" and that he was "not [a] very active member, but supporter. I had to support this, but not as an active member."[34] His comments revealed the pressure that AMU students were under to conform to the League agenda. Both Mohiuddin Khan and his childhood friend Waheeduddin Chowdhury, who shared a room in AMU, shared the leftist inclinations of the Students' Federation and attended a rally in Delhi in early 1947.[35] Even they told me that while at AMU they were supporters of Pakistan, although "there was pressure against the progressive students' group."[36] Despite these political differences, they deeply trusted the mission of the university and its ability to provide safe haven. These students traveled a great distance to attend AMU and they had no option of returning home during periods of unrest. Therefore, for them, the university's protective capacity was particularly significant.

Their stories, however, when they focused on the events of partition, were substantively different from those I heard in India. Whereas Indian narrators strove to minimize the sense of disruption in the AMU environment, Bangladeshi stories focused on disruption, both public and personal. Waheeduddin Choudhri recounted to me in a long, winding narrative the difficulty he had in reaching AMU during the summer of 1946, when the city of Calcutta, through which he would have had to transit, was in the throes of a communal conflict known as the Great Calcutta Killings. After leaving his home—Maulvi Bazaar, in Sylhet, where he was in school—he headed for Calcutta, but he recounted,

> I could not reach Calcutta. I was advised by somebody that "You don't go to Calcutta." Calcutta was very much disturbed. "You go to Bardhaman, by Loop

Line." From there, I took a train and somehow I reached Aligarh. Once I reached Aligarh, I was safe there. The university authorities had an arrangement in the railway station for the students who were going and reaching there. So ultimately, I reached Aligarh.[37]

Throughout the interview I conducted with Choudhri, he repeated aspects of this story multiple times: "there is trouble in Calcutta"; "I went to Bardhaman"; "I just used to sit down, in khaki dress"; "it was a very disturbing time." He linked the disturbances in the country very tightly to his own experience of a disrupted and dangerous train journey. He realized, traveling in the train, that his only hope for safety was to change his plans, keep a low profile (khaki dress), and not to draw attention to himself (by sitting still). Throughout the interview, this was the only reference he made to unrest in the country, and it was metonymically represented by his own disrupted train ride. As in other narratives, the train holds a primary place in Waheeduddin's memory of partition, though the experience he describes is from 1946—outside the standard time frame of partition history—and the disruption he described was in Calcutta, not strictly speaking on the border. Like others, he felt confident in the safety of AMU, the sense that once he arrived on the train platform, back within the proctorial system of discipline, he was finally safe.

Waheeduddin also described the presence of the army, dispatched by the government to protect the university. However, the chronology was difficult to follow. He incorporated experiences from 1946 and 1947 into a continuous chain. In the middle of describing his disrupted train journey in 1946, Waheeduddin began to describe the efforts of the government in 1947 to protect the university by dispatching Nawab Ismail Khan, a Muslim Leader, but close friend of the Nehru family, to lead the institution. In 1948, Zakir Husain succeeded him. Although Waheeduddin and Mohiuddin (who was present and participated in this interview) described themselves as leftists, they, too, placed their faith for the university's survival in the Indian nationalist leadership.

The values these students learned at AMU have indeed stayed with them, and Pakistan, despite its impossibility in reality, has persisted as a guiding idea that remained important to them. M. A. Rashid, the businessman, however, demonstrated how Pakistanis had "changed" by offering a critique of life in the Western state similar to that made by Indian Muslims.

> Karachi was like machines, you see. People had no time for social jobs, you see. So I never liked [it]. I always liked Dhaka. People here, my neighbor here and there, any function they come. If there is any trouble, we help each other. They are very friendly and social. But Karachi people, no! Somebody stays in one building in some flat and down on the ground floor does not know who is staying. If somebody dies, they do not go for his burial. They were very business-type people.[38]

His critique of the values of Pakistanis laments the absence of cooperation. This change can be seen at the heart of the conflict between Pakistan's two wings. In reflecting on the outcomes of the 1947 creation of Pakistan, and their own later involvement in the movement for the independence of Bangladesh, several of these narrators demonstrated that they believed in an ideal of unity and cooperation. That they discussed their feelings about Pakistan so openly was especially significant in light of the persecution that those who were seen to have allied with Pakistan during 1971 have faced in Bangladesh since liberation.[39] Despite the passage of time, and their own efforts to assure the liberation of East Pakistan from West, they still felt a connection to Pakistan. Whereas these Bangladeshis still held tight to the possibility of federation, of a system based on "mutual cooperation," and helping one another, Pakistanis did not sustain that mutuality.

Bangladeshis emphasized their support for an idea of federation, with a particular emphasis on the Lahore Resolution of 1940. Bengali Muslim League leader Fazlul Haq—known as *Sher-e-Bangla* or the Lion of Bengal—fronted the resolution, commonly remembered as the Pakistan Resolution, at the 1940 League session in Lahore.[40] It called for the grouping of "the areas in which the Muslims are numerically in a majority" into zones "to constitute 'Independent States.'" As Rounaq Jahan has noted, many Bengali Muslim League leaders emphasized the plural "states," though the Resolution was later emended to resolve the ambiguity of the plural.[41] When Bangladeshi narrators evoked the Resolution, they referred to this verbiage as evidence of an impulse to federation. The insistence in the Bangladeshi narratives on a return to the origins of the idea of Pakistan, with an emphasis on the possibility for federation, is unique among the narratives I collected. However, it mirrors many Indian narratives in the accusation that Pakistan "changed." The assimilationist narrative of Pakistan, that once had appeared all inclusive, became a tool of oppression after independence. For these narrators, the Pakistani state's unwillingness or inability to recognize and accommodate the diversity of the population rested at the heart of their grievance. These narrators, despite having twice fought for independence, continued to believe that the best outcome for the subcontinent in 1947, 1971, and today would be a collection of federated states rather than independent ones.

Many narrators maintained some allegiance to the solutions posed by the 1946 Cabinet Mission plan, in which the British government suggested a confederation of groups that would unite Muslim states in the West and Muslim states in the East. Hindu states would form a third group. Mohiuddin told me that he thought Hindus would "crash the Muslim identity if we are not saved. So I supported also partition of India." He qualified his support, however, by noting that he thought the Cabinet Mission plan was "more practical and beneficial."[42] In Pakistan, by contrast, narrators used the Cabinet Mission plan, and Jinnah's initial acceptance of it, as a critical component in the narrative that "blamed" Nehru and Patel, and, by extension, the Indian National Congress, for the outcomes of the partition.[43] As Wajahat Husain put it:

> There is no doubt about it, and now more than ever it has come out quite clearly that the responsibility for Partition lays upon Mr. Nehru and Mr. Patel. On the Congress... Responsibility for the Partition—undoubtedly Pakistan was the main slogan and we wanted it—but the Muslim League had accepted the Cabinet Plan, and [was] going along and everybody thought it would work out alright. It was the Congress. Having agreed, they went back on their word and then there was no other alternative.[44]

In Pakistan, there was a pervasive slippage between the narrative of triumph, of "liberation," and the narrative of the oppressed minority that demanded state protection and accommodation. This slippage illuminates a theme that has run throughout this argument, that if the 1947 Partition was initially designed as a response to the "Muslim Question," it failed to provide an answer. Rather, it spawned a variety of persistent Muslim and minority questions that continue to find expression as evidence of the ongoing nature of India's partitioning. Despite the powerful rhetoric of liberation that the state of Bangladesh employs to describe its separation from West Pakistan, in the minds of those Bangladeshi Aligs who fought for the independence of Pakistan first, complete liberation may not have been the ideal outcome. Rather, reconciliation with the original idea of Pakistan, as expressed in the Lahore Resolution, and as embodied in their work as students for Muslim unity in the form of Pakistan, remained a powerful counterbalance to the standard narrative of liberation from West Pakistan.

The Bangladeshis therefore used the Lahore Resolution and the Cabinet Mission Plan as components in a developing narrative in favor of federation. Habibur Rahman (describing cooperation between Pakistan and Iran over oil resources) indicated that "mutual cooperation is necessary," which, in the context of Pakistani relations between 1947 and 1971, sums up the Bangladeshi perspective.[45] It was the absence of a spirit of cooperation in the West Pakistan-East Pakistan relationship that troubled these narrators. Since 1940, they had invested their emotions in an expectation of federation that was further encouraged by the near-acceptance of the Cabinet Mission plan in 1946. In committing to Pakistan in 1947, they expected a federal system, one where some portfolios would be controlled at the center, but as Habibur Rahman described, "If there is a confederation, yes, obviously the federal government can restrict many things, but there is still some social development. Local development."[46] The measure of success of the state would be its effect in his local place; without that, Pakistan could not have fulfilled its promises.

Even the Awami League and its leader, Mujibur Rahman, professed an allegiance to the terms of the Pakistan Resolution in his 1966 "Six Points Programme." The first point demanded that "The Constitution should provide for a Federation of Pakistan in its true sense on the basis of 1940 Lahore Resolution, and parliamentary form of government with supremacy of legislature elected on the basis of universal adult franchise."[47] That the Lahore Resolution makes an appearance both in Sheikh Mujib's Six Points and in the memories of those who supported both Pakistan and Bangladesh suggests an important continuity between the 1947 Partition and 1971. This coincidence conveyed a sense of authenticity that several of these narrators sought to project: that Bengalis were the true Pakistanis, that their leaders were among Pakistan's founders, they remained true to the original ideals, and those very ideals were corrupted in Pakistan. Without federation, without even a sense of equanimity with the Pakistani system, and in the absence of a commitment to local development, these narrators turned away from Pakistan, disappointed.

Both Bangladeshi and Pakistani narrators looked to the origins of the Pakistan Movement for a sense of clarity about the meaning of Pakistan, but they derived different meanings from its rhetoric. Both groups emphasized a kind of unity, but the Pakistanis suggested a homogenized unity, one that obscured the unique differences between individuals; the Bangladeshi narrators touted a vision of unity that recognized differences and created space for them, even while acknowledging a broader unity that could draw states together based on shared priorities. Both of these visions for South Asia were rooted in notions of solidarity, the kinds that were fostered at AMU, but they also reflect the variety of experience within the AMU student body. As innocuous as they may have seemed within the boundary walls, the fault lines of language and region defined a fundamental sense of difference. Bengali students found common ground among the students whose language or dress or region of origin placed them outside of the mainstream. The students who represented the Urdu-speaking majority, however, subscribed to an identity that created little space for recognizing these other groups. They assumed that, by their presence at AMU, all would be assimilated into an already familiar mold. Such differences in outlook that emerged from different sides of the borders shed light on the problems of belonging in Pakistan, and also how deeply rooted these narrators' experience was in those years when they were fighting together for freedom.

Two Nations, Three States: 1947/1971

In Bangladesh, it is perhaps not surprising that the 1947 Partition does not serve as the central motif in the official national history. Rather, it is one of three partitions (1905, 1947, 1971) and seen as only a stepping stone on the way to full independence. This independence, or, more often, liberation, came only after the war with West Pakistan in 1971. This variation highlights important differences with the national stories of both India and Pakistan in which 1947 serves to reorient the experience of social and political relations.

1971 is the central organizing event of the Bangladeshi past, but the tensions born out of the making of the state of Pakistan in 1947 provided the fuel for the conflict that resulted in the creation of Bangladesh. The efforts of the Pakistani establishment to narrowly determine the boundaries of belonging and the content of Pakistani identity left out its Bengali minority. Deep histories of racial and ethnic othering dating to the colonial period characterized the relationship between the more powerful West Pakistani Urdu-speaking minority and the largely rural Bengali majority. As Yasmin Saikia has articulated, in March 1971, "The state declared war against the people of East Pakistan."[48] The distinction she makes between the state and its people exposes the catastrophic consequences of this marginalization. The Pakistani government and military perpetrated horrific violence on East Pakistanis that led to the severing of ties between the two wings and the demise of the myth of the Muslim homeland.[49]

Language has been elevated to the heart of the conflict between East and West Pakistan. Jinnah's 1948 speech designating Urdu as the national language epitomized West Pakistani intransigence. However, the implication that Bengalis belonged to a different nation from the North India elite who determined the "nation" in the first place foregrounds the challenge to the Two Nation Theory. Though the Awami League captured the largest number of seats in Pakistan's first democratic general election, in 1970, West Pakistani leaders refused to allow the Bengalis into the hallowed halls of the majority to form a government. This intransigence rests on more than a conflict over language; it is intimately linked to the earlier conflicts over race, caste, and class that provided the content for the initial drive to establish a differentiated Muslim constituency in North India. Bengalis could not be Pakistanis because they were seen as only nominally Muslim—mostly Hindu—and, therefore, suspect.

The narrators whose stories are collected here represent a small but unique group. I conducted several interviews with Bangladeshi men who were students at AMU during the 1940s; they supported the Muslim League and worked for Pakistan. These narrators settled in East Pakistan, and remained there throughout the 1971 war. In addition, because this collection is limited, I analyzed interviews collected in Ahmad Salim's 2009 oral history collection *Reconstructing History: Memories, Migrants, and Minorities*.[50] I have also relied on a few interviews with Aligs collected and preserved by the Citizens Archive of Pakistan, "a non-profit organization dedicated to the Cultural and Historic Preservation . . . [that has] focused its attention on the tradition of oral story-telling in Pakistan, emphasizing the importance of such narratives in a dialogue on national identity."[51] Together, these sets of stories present a complex picture of the human experience of the conflict between East and West Pakistan that resulted in the creation of Bangladesh.

The perceptions of difference that divided the North Indian Muslim from the Bengali Muslim through deeply rooted and gendered rhetoric persisted from the nineteenth century into the twentieth. Though they originated in colonial notions of "martial" and "effeminized" races, they lasted beyond the temporal boundaries of British domination.[52] Although Bengali Muslims had been enthusiastic supporters of the Muslim League and the demand for Pakistan, as Habibur Rahman attested, they were never allowed to become fully privileged citizens of an independent Pakistani state. The government of Pakistan used a variety of tactics to prevent the assumption of the political majority by the 52 percent of the population that was Bengali. The state went so far as to redraw the boundaries of the provinces—the "One Unit" scheme—and then to dismiss the parliament after the electoral victory of the Bengali-led Awami League in 1970.[53]

Indian Muslim League leaders, and, later, West Pakistani leaders, were willing to preach a message of unity as long as it fortified their own political power. However, shortly after the creation of Pakistan, the East Pakistanis came to be seen as a liability. They were spatially marginalized and seen as weak and backward. The perception of Bengali effeteness or weakness that had survived British colonialism was combined with the sense that East Pakistan was underdeveloped and unable to be self-sufficient. These perceptions fed the West Pakistani sense of superiority and paternalism.[54] As Wajahat, who served as brigadier general in 1971, told me:

> At the time of Partition East Pakistan was in a very bad way, [it was] very backward. By way of administration, there was no infrastructure and [it was] very poorly administered and of course, they had—except for jute—there were hardly any resources. We did a lot for East Pakistan. We established for East Pakistan one of the world's best inland water transport systems for inland communications. The Chittagong harbor, which was nothing, just a very small port really, at the time of

Partition, was developed by us into a first class port and harbor. Similarly, Dhaka, which was a very backward small town was developed into a modern town. All the infrastructure, post and telegraph, railways, internal water communications—and the main thing was the development of the cantonment and the creation of the East Pakistan armed forces—was done entirely by the Federal Government at the expense of West Pakistan.[55]

I quote this passage at length because it captures the masculinist rhetoric of the West Pakistanis and, here, an Alig. He characterized the East Pakistanis as weak and inept, utterly dependent on the goodwill and financial resources of the West. In addition, the services that General Wajahat so proudly claimed credit for delivering to the East were the very same ones that the British so proudly established in India during their rule.[56] He explicitly associated development with colonial modernity and military infrastructure. General Wajahat went on to claim that the East Pakistanis were ungrateful for the support of the West. Though they accused the West of stealing revenue from jute exporting, he claimed the revenue "wasn't very much" to begin with. He delegitimized the claims of the East Pakistanis and privileged the development of the military cantonment as the ultimate marker of West Pakistani generosity. Taking a long view of the tensions between East and West Pakistan exposes the impact of long-established racist theories of Bengali inadequacy that posed a challenge to the myth of Punjabi masculinity and had very concrete consequences for national unity.

In his own memoir, Wajahat Husain noted that Colonel M. A. G. Osmani, commander of the Bengali rebel *mukti bahini* forces, was his senior at AMU. He had risen through the ranks of the Pakistan Army, but "was an avid Bengali nationalist."[57] Wajahat turned back the argument that people had "changed" since the founding of Pakistan, but suggested that Osmani, *despite* being an Alig, was a Bengali nationalist. Wajahat directed his most fervent criticism of the conflict toward Pakistan's haphazard strategies and credited India's intervention with determining the outcome of the conflict. He persisted in identifying East Pakistani activities as devious or marginal. The problem was that West Pakistan's humiliation represented a fundamental failing of Pakistan's masculine identity; it would be too much to credit victory to "effeminate" Bengalis.

An oral history from Ahmad Salim's collection illustrates how perceptions of difference were operationalized during the conflict. The collection features an interview entitled "Treatment with Maulvi Tamizuddin Khan's Family" in which the story of Dr. Norul Huda of Dhaka University's Department of Economics was retold by his brother-in-law. On the morning of March 26, 1971, the Pakistan Army burst into Dr. Norul Huda's home while he was reading the Qur'an. The officers confronted him and "demanded to know his name and his religion, Dr. Huda told them his name and said, 'I am a Bengali Muslim.' The leader sarcastically remarked, 'Can a Bengali be a Muslim?'"[58] This story, which I include here anecdotally, reveals how the tensions between East Pakistanis and the West Pakistan Army determined the nature of the violence. Included in the story is the charge that the army leader took Dr. Norul Huda's Qur'an and threw it on the floor, desecrating it. This narrative authorizes Dr. Norul Huda's piety in two ways: he is characterized as a respected intellectual, though he had escaped the March 25 massacre of intellectuals and scholars, and as a devout, Qur'an-reading Muslim. It was as an act of defiance that he announced, "I am a *Bengali* Muslim," rather than simply stating his religion. He stated that he was a Bengali first, and a Muslim, an identity clearly abhorrent to the Pakistani establishment. This defiance provoked a transgression by the Pakistani Army leader as he threw the sacred text to the ground. Even as the story establishes Dr. Norul Huda's piety—it challenges the West Pakistani claim to a normative Muslim identity by describing the sacrilegious behavior of the Pakistani Army officer. We learn nothing more of Dr. Norul Huda in this narrative, but it exposes a powerful moment of conflicting prejudices: the Pakistani Army is represented as hypermasculinized, anti-intellectual, and blasphemous; the Bengali is represented as calm and collected, devout, and steadfastly loyal to his Bengali heritage, as a true Pakistani.

Consider another story, from the pen of a Bangladeshi scholar whose father was killed by the Pakistan Army in 1971. Meghna Guha Thakurta's father "met his death at the hands of the Pakistan Army in 1971 when he was accused of possessing an identity which he had always resisted, i.e. of being a Hindu. His professed identity of a humanist was not to be found anywhere in the vocabulary of Yahya Khan's barbaric regime."[59] Both the Hindu, definitively non-Pakistani in the eyes of the regime, and the Bengali Muslim were challenged on the basis of their identities. In these cases, the Bengali could not be a Muslim, nor could he be not-Hindu.[60] And in neither case could he be treated as a fully privileged citizen of Pakistan, for the narrative of the state left little space for these identities. Ultimately, as Saikia argues, the Pakistan Army's violent tactics were "driven by the desire and motivation to save Pakistan and make the Bengalis submit."[61] Many stories of this period reflect these kinds of conflicts, and from both of Pakistan's wings. It seems that the forces of prejudice, intent on defining clear boundaries of belonging, were as productive of the conflict between the two wings as any of the other conflicts over representation, language, and economics.

Indeed the Bangla Language Movement that fueled the desire for Bangladeshi independence captured the imaginations of millions of East Pakistanis and, combined with widespread perceptions of West Pakistani and particularly Punjabi oppression, served to draw in broad support for the resistance to West Pakistan. During this struggle, Urdu-speaking Muslims and non-Bengali East Pakistanis were opposed by ethnic Bengalis, who demanded recognition from the state of Pakistan.[62] The graduates of AMU with whom I spoke about their experiences during this difficult time were primarily Bengali-speaking, though several hail from Sylhet.[63] Despite their support for the Pakistan demand during their sojourn at AMU, when their loyalty to Bengali identity came into conflict with loyalty to the Pakistani state, they placed their solidarity with the Bengali people and supported the demand for liberation.

However, these narrators protested the assertion that Sheikh Mujib's desire was always for independence. Though the independence of Bangladesh was the result of armed struggle, and the Bengali people suffered extreme hardship, these narrators insisted that their demand was first and foremost a demand for social justice. Although the Bengalis were not a numerical minority, they were treated as second-class citizens by the government in West Pakistan. Although these narrators fought for the independence of Pakistan, it was, in their minds, West Pakistan's betrayal of the original dream of Muslim solidarity that led them to work for Bangladeshi independence. Their engagement in both movements reveals clear parallels, and they articulate the claims of 1971 in the context of their experiences from the 1940s.

For the Bengali students at AMU, the allure of Pakistan was tied to their perceptions of the communal disharmony in their own home state. Habibur Rahman suggested that it was the history of Hindu oppression by wealthier Hindus in Bengal that drew him to League activity. As he told me, "the Hindus generally used to neglect the Muslims. And mostly in East Pakistan."[64] He went on to explain the most significant aspect of the Bengali relationship to Pakistan, in his opinion, that "It was only in Bangladesh that all the MLAs were Muslims." Rahman himself was very involved in student activism for Pakistan after 1944 when he arrived at AMU. He even participated in training other students for election work. He credited the Bengali students with having been very influential in Pakistan work because they were "very intelligent" and "shrewd" and went so far as to suggest that the Bengalis "made" Pakistan.[65] His sentiments about Pakistan resonate with those of the non-Bengali students. Both were drawn in by the enthusiasm for Pakistan, and Rahman characterizes the goal of their work as "the hope that there will be a change of the fortunes of people."[66] The hope that the Bengalis placed in Pakistan was the same as the hope the North Indian Urdu-speakers did. Pakistan should empower the people, serve them, and bring them freedom from the oppressive Hindu majority.

After the creation of Pakistan, however, Habibur Rahman said that it was not very long before he recognized that, "unfortunately, the army of West Pakistan, especially the Punjabis, were in control" of the implementation of the expected democracy. The fundamentally undemocratic imbalance of power represented by this outcome was deeply troubling to him and to others who had fought for the independence of Muslims. He frequently reiterated to me that he was "very much in favor of the Pakistan Movement," an active participant, and one who worked hard to learn about Pakistan and to participate in activities to build support for Pakistan. It was only "when they started all these discriminations" that he felt there was nothing else he could do but join the Awami League opposition. Still, he insisted, "No one demanded complete separations."[67] Rather, East Pakistan, led by Mujibur Rahman, sought sovereignty over internal issues including Commerce, Industries, and currency, while granting Defence and Foreign Affairs portfolios to the center. In other words, the original terms upon which the Muslim League had sought autonomy for Muslim states were reengaged. Sheikh Mujib's Six Points were designed to restore the priorities of Pakistan's original charter, the 1940 Lahore Resolution, to restore parliamentary democracy and to create a "Federation of Pakistan in its true sense."[68] The Pakistani government patently refused to accede to these demands and the conflict mounted. Contrary to Pakistani opinion, Habibur Rahman insisted, the movement for liberation was not made on "the insistence of India"; it was a demand for "self-existence!" This language aligned the demands of Bangladesh with the demands of Muslims during the Pakistan Movement in the 1940s and especially with those of students seeking "self-manifestation."[69]

In fact, the extent to which the narratives of these two events, 1947's partition and 1971's liberation, are made structurally similar is worthy of closer examination. Narrator Mohiuddin Khan, president of the Aligarh Old Boys' Association, Dhaka,

2009–10, pointed out that it was not Jinnah who rejected the Cabinet Mission plan, but that after Congress rejected it Jinnah was left with no choice but to push forward for Pakistan.⁷⁰ Similarly, Mohiuddin said it was "unfortunate" that East and West Pakistan parted. But he placed the burden on Pakistan's unwillingness to treat East Pakistan with dignity. "If they only could have accommodated us, just a little bit. It would have been different. We didn't want separation. Even Sheikh Mujib did not want separation throughout."⁷¹ It was only upon Pakistan's rejection of Sheikh Mujib's Six Points that separation became inevitable. Mohiuddin, like Rahman, insisted that "we supported Pakistan. We fought for Pakistan," and this investment in Pakistan should have earned East Pakistanis the rights of full citizenship in a democratic system. As Muslim League leaders had claimed, political representation could and should take history into account. In the end, it was the unwillingness of the more powerful party to accommodate the weaker one that led to the separation.

As in the earlier Pakistan Movement, it was the experience of oppression that drove these narrators into solidarity with their fellow countrymen and against the powers-that-be. For these men, who had worked for Pakistan in the 1940s, the narrative was familiar, but the memory of Pakistani oppression remained fresh and painful. Mohiuddin described his initial attraction to AMU as motivated by "this mood of Hindu-Muslim feelings [that] was on the forefront at that time to a large extent."⁷² Motivated by his awareness of communal tension, Mohiuddin sought an environment where he might be able to contest Hindu domination. Even before he was admitted to Aligarh in 1946, he had been active in campaigning for the Muslim League candidates in Assam. Like Habibur Rahman's, his concerns were local. The political situation in Assam, where he lived, pushed him to League activism. He was influenced by the "atmosphere at that time, in the year 1946. Throughout India more of this communal politics was coming up and the British wanted to leave and the demand for Pakistan [was] growing. So, naturally," he said, "we supported the Pakistan Movement at that time."⁷³ His attachment to Pakistan was "natural" considering the political situation at the time. Even in the earliest examples of political activity in AMU, student activism was motivated by a similar attention to the dynamic interaction between local conditions and larger political possibilities that transgressed the institution's borders. Similarly, when Bangladeshis, spatially marginalized from the centers of Pakistani power, no longer felt that the state was upholding its commitments to them, they became involved in a resistance movement that ultimately destroyed the meaning of the boundaries drawn during 1947.

East Pakistanis saw West Pakistan developing infrastructure at a faster rate, and felt that their province was being neglected.⁷⁴ Mohiuddin described his opposition to the administration of West Pakistan as a "natural" result of the feeling of being "cheated some way or other by revenue."⁷⁵ This complaint against the West is enshrined in three of Mujibur Rahman's Six Points. The third point demands "effective constitutional provisions . . . to stop the flight of capital from East to West Pakistan"; the fourth point addresses uneven distribution of tax revenue between the two wings, and the fifth point addresses the need to abolish customs duties on products produced in one wing, and sold in the other. The complaint about unfair distribution of revenue and uneven levying of taxes was a persistent one, and more than one narrator expressed it.⁷⁶

Mohiuddin noticed these disparities not long after the creation of Pakistan and began "surreptitiously" (because he was a government employee) to attend "these meetings where Mr. Fazlul Huq was delivering his speech about his activities in Assembly."[77] By the time the language movement began in 1952, he told me, "I was against remaining Pakistan." West Pakistan's inability to allow East Pakistan fully to participate in the representative democracy hardened him to it, and he felt a tremendous sense of triumph upon the success of the Bangladesh liberation movement.

Engineer Waheeduddin Choudhri was less willing to concede his support for Pakistan. He suggested, rather, that Pakistan was not the fulfillment of his leftist ideals; he sought a united India from the outset. At the time of partition, he said, "I could not say at that time I am a Pakistani or I am an Indian. Everything was in a fluid state. As I told you, we neither used to support Pakistan, nor used to support India. We were leftists. In fact, we wanted to have a leftist united India."[78] He clarified that what he hoped for was a United India and a democratic state. When I pressed him on support of Bangladesh, by asking, "Did you support independence of Bangladesh?" he replied, correcting me, "Actually, we did not support Pakistan; so we neither wanted East Pakistan nor West Pakistan, but Bengal. We wanted another state." Waheeduddin was attached to a concept of Bengal as a whole, and as distinct from East Pakistan. While he would not commit to having earlier supported Pakistan or India, he enthusiastically cast his support behind Bengal. Bengal, it appeared, embodied the values for which he had been fighting all along. Indeed, as Neilesh Bose has argued, the Bengali vision for Pakistan was liberatory, aimed at freeing minorities from "imperialist governance."[79] Waheeduddin, and other Bengali Pakistanis, "maintained a commitment to self-determination through an elaboration of their own unique culture."[80]

Cast in these ways, there is immediate continuity between the demand for Pakistan and the demand for Bangladeshi liberation. Waheeduddin's anxiety about attaching himself to East Pakistan exposed his discomfort with what Pakistan represented. Undoubtedly, his memories were colored by his traumatic experiences with his family in Chittagong during the 1971 war, but his insistence that Pakistan was a misrepresentation of his ideals seems an important lens on the relationship between 1947 and 1971. The conflict of 1971 clarified questions of belonging for Bengali Muslims, even as it challenged the foundation of the identity of Pakistan.

Conclusion

As the narrators whose stories are collected here reflected on their experiences, they betrayed the complexities of their memories and experiences through imperfect attempts to align their personal stories with readily accessible official narratives. The imperfections in this process remind us of the complexities of independence, partitioning, and liberation in South Asia. Whether the questions were of belonging in space and place, triumph/failure, inclusion/exclusion, or past/present/future, they revealed deeper processes of reconciliation that narrators have gone through in trying to establish their own identities as citizens of states and supporters of certain ideological movements. The source of these anxieties can be understood on all sides of the border.

While I have argued that support for the Pakistan Movement did not necessarily imply a desire for independent statehood and that we should avoid viewing pre-1947 sentiments and perspectives through the lens of Pakistan, the situation is drastically changed with regard to events and experiences involving Muslims throughout the subcontinent after 1947.[81]

Pakistan continues to struggle with the insufficiency of its national narrative to create space for the many diverse ethnic, linguistic, regional, and even religious groups (both Muslim and non-Muslim) that live within its borders. The independence of Bangladesh exemplified this struggle. Bangladeshi informants reflected upon their involvement with the Pakistan Movement to make sense of the transitions and challenges they faced during their drive for freedom.

The East Pakistanis were unwilling to accept this bargain, however, having conceived of Pakistan within the context of their own regional interests in Bengal.[82] The Bengalis were early and ardent supporters of the Pakistan Movement, primarily because there was an already-established struggle for power and representation in East Bengal. The Pakistan demand politicized and communalized this struggle; young Muslims recognized its priorities and were drawn into its fold. When it became clear, particularly after 1952, that West Pakistani rule had displaced the domination of both the British and Hindu landlords in East Bengal, the East Pakistanis made a similar push for parity under the law as the Muslim League had made in British India. There are distinct narrative parallels in the ways that both experiences are remembered and retold: like Indian Muslims, East Pakistanis were marginalized by a group with greater political power (if not numerical); East Pakistanis sought compromise with Sheikh Mujib's Six Points, as the Muslim League did in the Cabinet Mission; the West Pakistanis, like the Indian National Congress, dismissed these efforts, shut down talks, and forced a catastrophically violent division that resulted in triumphant, though troubled, liberation.

The eventual independence of Bangladesh presented the major substantive challenge to the Two Nation Theory. This challenge to the founding narrative of Pakistan created a complicated relationship to the past, and for many narrators, it was still a bit sad, rather than triumphant. As Anwar Ahsan Siddiqui suggested in an interview collected in Karachi by Ahmad Salim, the independence of Bangladesh was "a tragic event and it tore the two-nation theory into pieces and along with it, the hearts of its people. The fact is that the two-nation theory forwarded in 1947 became the basis of Pakistan; suddenly no life was left in it. And Hindus did not do it; Muslims finished it by themselves."[83] Whereas many Pakistani narrators were deeply hesitant to confront the issue of "loss" with regard to India, they were deeply injured by the "loss of East Pakistan." It remains the most humiliating moment in Pakistan's short history, almost totally excised from official memory. It seems that when, as young men, the contributors to this project chose Pakistan, they chose the opportunity of fulfilling the promise of Muslim solidarity agenda, and chose to leave behind the challenges of exclusion that they feared in an independent India, and as members of a permanent minority. But in so many ways, that dream has remained out of reach.

All of these examples draw out the continuing relevance of the identity politics legitimized by the 1947 division of India. I have referred to these ongoing contestations as the "partitioning" of the subcontinent, situations born of the original "Muslim Question" that was not only not solved by the 1947 Partition, but that, in fact, grew out of it. In the case of AMU, the institution's values, long hailed as progressive, have been deployed in the development of exclusionary narratives of belonging that both represented the necessity of an independent homeland, and then led to its demise. The logic of the Two Nation Theory that suggested a broad homogeneity among Muslims and fundamental difference from Hindus proved incapable of incorporating variations of practices among Muslims in diverse regions of the subcontinent.

The unsettled nature of these questions about belonging illuminates the need to expand our lens as we examine the outcomes of partition/partitioning in the subcontinent. We cannot isolate the contemporary politics of hatred and exclusion currently playing out in the subcontinent from the identity politics that created the conditions for the 1947 Partition. In all three post-partition states, diverse groups compete for space and recognition while they simultaneously develop exclusionary narratives that drive other groups out. In the aftermath of 1947, life in South Asia has been characterized by ongoing partitionings that show few signs of conclusion. Partition cannot be an event precisely located in time. It remains an ongoing process that takes place and makes place through the constant negotiation at the boundaries of social and cultural meaning in contemporary South Asia.

Conclusion

AMU, with its connections to both Pakistan and Bangladesh, stands as a powerful symbol of the contested citizenship of Muslims in India.[1] Historically, AMU isolated Muslim students from Indian society and politics, and provided space for them to safely express themselves educationally and culturally. Its political history has vexed its position as the center of Muslim opinion, however, and left it at the center of debates about Muslim loyalty. This complexity forms an important aspect of AMU's legacy in South Asia and provides a lens for examining the position of Indian Muslims before, during, and after the 1947 Partition. AMU is implicated in a complex matrix of historical, ahistorical, communal, and secular forces in which it has functioned sometimes as a center and other times as a margin. My conclusions here examine some of the assumptions inherent in narratives that seek to railroad AMU's legacy to one side or the other.

The standard story about AMU, recounted by its well-wishers, places it as the center of education, organization, and uplift for South Asia's Muslims. This narrative, however, relies on a problematic, ahistorical elision that obscures the changes that have taken place there since the end of the nineteenth century. Most discussions of the institution at Aligarh conflate the early period when Sir Sayyid and his contemporaries operated the Mohammadan Anglo-Oriental College with the period after 1920 when an Act of Parliament elevated the institution to become the Aligarh Muslim University. While this elision may seem harmless, it has very real historical consequences for our understanding of the role of the institution in Indian politics. In other words, AMU may be seen as a center of education and culture, and therefore critical to Indian life and dedicated to its values, or it may be seen as a center of Muslim life only and a harbor for Indian separatism and therefore marginal in independent India. Well-wishers insist that it remains a critical site of Muslim opinion, but this endangers it in the public sphere where, for many others, including non-Muslim politicians, AMU is little more than a distracting irritation despite attempts to "nationalize" it after 1947. Well-wishers and critics have alternately endorsed its place as a former and potential center of Muslim politics or as removed from the center of Indian life.

In the context of nineteenth-century India, Sir Sayyid's vision to bring modern education to the "backward" community of North Indian Muslims has been conceived as liberal. His willingness to incorporate English and to look outside the traditionally narrow boundaries of Islamic education represented by the Deoband school were undoubtedly progressive, but in many ways, Aligarh's political environment was defined by its conservatism.[2] Sir Sayyid sought to preserve the influence of Muslims in India by nurturing an elite class qualified to take up government posts and to represent Muslims in local government. His sights were set on the public services, and many of his wards went on to pursue careers there.[3] Sir Sayyid and his compatriots argued for a separate examination for Muslims seeking positions in the services, and this movement led to a later demand for separate electorates. Though he claimed his agenda to be purely educational, Sir Sayyid continually sought political protections for Muslims. He endeavored to carve out educational, political, and social space for them even as British fears over Muslim loyalty threatened to erode these away.

Though Sir Sayyid died before the All-India Muslim League was founded in Dhaka in 1906, and Faisal Devji argues that it could not have come into being while Sir Sayyid controlled Muslim politics, many of his collaborators in the Aligarh Movement were among its founding members.[4] Devji argues that the politics of the Muslim League departed from those of Aligarh, especially because it was led by Muslims from Bombay and other places outside of North India, including the Ismaili Aga Khan.[5] Undoubtedly, in its early years, the League did not draw heavily on material support from the Aligarh community, but by the 1930s that had changed. Devji's interventions shed light on the fact that the Muslim League was not always a separatist organization, and the university students and faculty were not always in solidarity with it. It was not until the late 1930s that students and faculty were drawn to the League's agenda in large numbers, having previously been in sympathy with the anti-imperialist motives of the Indian National Congress (and even this nationalist sentiment broke with the Sir Sayyid's British loyalism).

The tendency to examine the League, the institution at Aligarh, and the Pakistan demand through the lens of the outcomes of 1947 has obscured the contours of this history. Aligarh's priorities were always driven by the concerns of its local environment: anti-imperialism was driven by discontent with British staff; League sympathy was motivated by the perception of Congress ministry abuse of Muslims enshrined in the Pirpur Report; the demand for Pakistan resonated with the institution's commitment to cultivating Muslim solidarity. Indeed, in the early 1940s, AMU staff welcomed Mohammad Ali Jinnah with a speech confirming both the historical connections between the university and the League and the growth of support for its politics after 1937. They wrote, "The College at Aligarh was the root and the Muslim League was the fruit. In shaping the policies of the Muslim League, in securing recognition of the rights and interests of the Muslims and in making sacrifices for the Muslim cause Aligarh's share has been considerable."[6] The terms of their allegiance were deeply embedded in the norms and expectations of the educational institution as a place. The staff committed their allegiance to Jinnah and the League with the following words:

> We are as ready to-day [sic] to shoulder responsibilities and make sacrifices for the good of our University as we have always been. The nature of our work as teachers is such that we cannot take any aggressive part in politics. But we assure you that you will never find us unwilling to offer, as far as lies in our power, our whole-hearted support and service for promoting the welfare of our people whose learning and culture we represent in this institution.[7]

Though this address likely dates to 1941 (less than a year after the Lahore Resolution of 1940), there was no mention of Pakistan. To view AMU through the static lens of 1947 is to freeze it in time, to disregard the environment of active debate, and to imprison the institution's future within the anxieties born of only one of its political moments.

For many in India, the significance, and even the traumas, of 1947 overshadowed all of Aligarh's earlier history save perhaps its first few years. It is here that the elision of MAO and AMU takes on significant meaning. The legacy of the 1940s and the participation of so many AMU students in the demand for Pakistan has permanently tainted AMU in the public eye as a hub of anti-national activity; hidden its history of communal harmony and tolerance (even in 1947 the AMU campus was quiet); and, oblivious to the conditions of its founding, linked it permanently to the specter of Muslim separatism. On the other hand, Aligarh insiders cast 1947 as "exceptional" and seek to link AMU today to the values of its founder with his progressive educational agenda, to reach back to a more perfect time.[8] To establish their nationalist credentials, they lionize Sir Sayyid as a representative of India's "composite culture," a great secularist who advocated peaceful coexistence of the two major communities. Both tendencies obscure the dynamic environment at Aligarh, where opposing ideologies often emerged out of the same foundation. It was not without contestation that supporters of the All-India Muslim League, the Indian National Congress, and the Communist Party coexisted, but a failure to acknowledge this possibility damages the complexity of the institution's legacy.

The trends in AMU itself since independence have perfectly established the tension between center and margin. Since 1947, it has been the explicit and determined efforts of the central government to fund AMU that have kept it running, and attempted to save it from the stigma of its intimacy with the Muslim League demand for Pakistan. As Violette Graff observed, "Aligarh has become a key-symbol [sic] of the not altogether easy relationship which has developed between the Government of India and its secular policies on the one hand, and the *Millat* on the other hand."[9] Graff's observation, now thirty years old, has aged well. In fact, the tensions between the government and the Muslim community have grown only more vexed with the growing influence of right-wing Hindu nationalism and the political power of the BJP. The tensions at the heart of this relationship are those that complicate the position of Muslims throughout India. The government is responsible for ensuring the equitable treatment of Muslims, but it must always appease the sensibilities of the majority community. Disproportionate demands for recognition by Muslims raise anxieties over the potential for the development of a separatist nationalism. These anxieties are linked immediately to the outcomes of the 1947 Partition and must be carefully handled.

There is a contingent of AMU alumni who continue to argue that AMU should be granted a special "Minority Character" enabling it to provide additional reservations for Muslim students. The outcome of the efforts in favor of the Minority Character would be to create—or to preserve—a realm created by and for Muslims, free of the meddling of outside forces. It would create "a protective nest" that some would say was Sir Sayyid's intention when he founded the MAO College.[10]

The demand for "Minority Character" brings many of the tensions underlying AMU's relationship to the Indian state and other communities to a head.[11] AMU is one of India's Central Universities, a designation that indicates its incorporation by an

Act of Parliament and marks it as a recipient of funding through the University Grants Commission. Such central universities have a provision to "reserve" seats for students from certain low-caste and tribal communities. The system of "reservation" seeks to level access for students from a low socioeconomic status, who may have been deprived of educational and employment opportunities. In some cases, Muslims are included in the "Other Backward Castes" category, thus giving them an advantage in admission. However, there is a large faction within the AMU community that desires AMU be kept apart, as an institution with "Minority Character," with the privilege to maintain a 50 percent reservation for Muslims. Keeping in mind that a large percentage of AMU's student body comprises "internal" candidates—those students who have attended an Aligarh University affiliated like the City High School or Aligarh Women's College—the vast majority of AMU students are Muslims.[12] The extension of the reservation implied by the push for "Minority Character" would go even further to exclude non-Muslims from the institution. Irfan Habib and Iqtidar Alam Khan have been vocal critics of the demand to secure "Minority Character" for AMU, and have called it communalist and undemocratic because it would do little to alleviate inequality in educational access for Muslims outside of the elite classes.[13]

Still, this demand for separate consideration reinforces the anxieties about AMU's relationship to the "separatist" Pakistan demand and draws AMU into the public eye, where it often comes under attack by those with a communal outlook. On August 7, 2010, IBN Live ran a story entitled "AMU Falsely Claiming to be a Minority Institution" that referred to the BJP allegation that AMU's claims to Minority status were precluded by its status as a Central University and its history of being incorporated by an Act of Parliament—not by the actions of the Minority community—and that it was thus delinquent in fulfilling reservations for SC/ST/OBCs.[14] Opponents of increasing reservations for Muslims say that because AMU was founded by an Act of Parliament, and not by a minority community itself, it is not eligible for the Minority Character designation. This argument reduces AMU's significance to the bureaucratic instant of creation and disavows the history of the institution.

The AMU community itself is not unified in its perspective on the value of Minority Character. The internal conflict is linked to the tension between those Muslims who would seek to blend into India's broader secular public by limiting the demands that they place as a community on the central government and those who suggest that Muslims are already "marked" by virtue of their faith and therefore deserve special protection and services from the government. The tension has been present in various guises since the earliest years of the MAO College when there was no consensus on the value of maintaining close ties with the British government. Some Aligarh partisans admired the system of financial support developed in Deoband, where the institution was supported purely by donations from the Muslim community.[15] The debates and disagreements over government loyalty came to a head during the demand for the Muslim university and it was the incorporation of the university by an Act of Parliament during the height of the nationalist movement that remains central to the debate.[16] The educational institution in Aligarh had long survived with some government support and some support from the community, but it had always remained apart from the world of India around it, an isolated environment whose residents developed familial bonds with one another, and a sense of difference with the worlds—defined by status, faith, and region—around them.

As Professor Asloob Ahmad Ansari told me in the summer of 2008, AMU has always been somewhat isolated from other institutions in India. The recognition of Minority Character would deepen that difference, a move that is distasteful to many Indians whose attitudes toward AMU have not softened much over the period of partitioning since the 1940s. In the final assessment, there are several aspects of its identity that keep AMU apart from the world outside. The relationship between AMU and the Government of India has deteriorated since the years when Zakir Husain brought his nationalist credentials to the institution and, with the support of the Congress government, restored its academic standards.[17]

Proponents of Minority Character defend it because they do not see any other institution making efforts for Muslims. This problem has persisted over a long period of time. Mohiuddin Khan of Dhaka credited his interest in AMU in 1946 to a recognition of the fact that because there were so few reservations, he "couldn't get a seat" in Shibpur Engineering College by virtue of being both a Muslim and a Sylheti.[18] As Theodore Wright has noted, "admitting students and recruiting faculty for Aligarh strictly on 'merit' would mean swamping it with non-Muslims without any compensating improvements in Muslim access to other institutions of higher education."[19] AMU has always seen its role as a unique one, designed to serve a particular class of Indians, but partitioning has called this into question.

The debates on Minority Character have waxed and waned over the last forty years, but AMU's situation has remained uniquely problematic. Other institutions have been granted the privileges of Minority Character. Even the JMI, founded in part by Aligarh Old Boys, and led for many years by Zakir Husain, was awarded Minority Character in February 2011.[20] The National Commission for Minority Educational Institutions (NCMEI) deemed the Jamia's appeal legitimate because, although it, too, became a Central University by an Act of Parliament,

> the Jamia Millia Islamia Act 1988, codified, declared, confirmed and encapsulated the continuous and preexisting factual and legal position of the Jamia by incorporating the existing institution formally under the Act as a central university . . . Thus the evidence on record clearly proves that since its inception, administration of the Jamia remained in the hands of Muslims.[21]

The Commission clarified that AMU's appeal, on the other hand, has repeatedly been denied in the wake of the Azeez Basha case in which the Supreme Court determined that "the MAO College had lost its identity by its conversion to AMU, which was established by the AMU Act, 1920. In the instant case, the Jamia never lost its identity."[22] The Jamia, unlike AMU, has an unsullied nationalist pedigree, and though it has sometimes come under suspicion of harboring extremists, it has no material connection to the taint of British loyalism or the separatist politics that led to India's division. It was in "pursuance of the NCMEI order of 2011 that JMI discontinued reservation for SC, ST and OBC students and set aside half its seats in each course for Muslim candidates."[23] However, the status of both AMU and JMI continues to be contested. In 2016, the

BJP government affirmed the Azeez Basha decision, and in 2018, the conservative BJP government filed an affidavit in the Delhi High Court opposing the Jamia's minority status.[24] That the very question of minority identity in both institutions cannot be settled places Muslim students squarely within the perpetual politics of partitioning, even within extremely competitive arenas of Indian higher education.

AMU remains a powerful symbol of Muslim rejuvenation despite the fact that Muslims today face many of the same problems Sir Sayyid Ahmad Khan sought to eliminate when he founded the institution in 1875, and despite the factions and differences of opinions and strategy that continue to hound its partisans. It follows that Muslims would seek to protect the institution which they believe was designed exclusively to serve their community. But in a society increasingly focused on assimilation, where nationalism is the new loyalism, this demand smacks of much-dreaded Muslim separatism. The fears of both parties prey on the other, and AMU remains caught, no longer "the arsenal of Muslim India," and certainly not, as its well-wisher Mushirul Hasan has argued, "the symbol of Indian secularism."[25] Or perhaps it is, for AMU embodies Indian secularism's greatest challenges.

Redemption

The 1947 Partition was the obtrusive event that has left a legacy of fear and alienation for Muslims in India and created challenges of belonging for Muslims in all three of the states it spawned. Reflecting on the historiography and narratives of partition, Mushirul Hasan said that the "preoccupation with pain and sorrow that resulted from partition has doubtlessly limited our understanding of many other crucial areas, including the political and civic fault lines of religion, gender, caste and class that still run through our lives."[26] The importance of investigating these other fault lines cannot be underestimated more than seventy years after those transformative events. Each of the narrators whose stories appear here found some kind of redemption from the terrors of displacement, alienation, and exclusion that characterized the years after 1947. Their efforts to form continuous narratives across the rupture of partition can be measured by their ability to "come to terms with it," by recognizing its "present-tense-ness."[27] I have called this "present-tense-ness" "partitioning" to draw attention to the ongoing nature of such a process of reconciliation. As an interviewer, I tried to be perpetually cognizant of the influence of the present. In interviews, it became clear that a narrator's ability to understand partitioning in the present tense depended on a sense of redemption from the past. Many narrators referred to a sense of guilt for the outcomes of 1947, but they also identified the individual or experience that freed them from this guilt's crippling effect.

Many Indian Aligs highlighted the role of Zakir Husain in saving the university from the certain demise after 1947. They expected alienation as a result of AMU's controversial attachments to the Muslim League demand for Pakistan. "Zakir Sahib's" redemptive power found a place in other testaments of allegiance to nationalist leadership as well. Iftikhar Alam Khan, retired professor of Museology at AMU and former director of the Sir Syed Academy, spoke most explicitly about the impact of fear on his experience at AMU. Immediately after describing his fear of train travel and the threat of communal violence, he told me,

> here in Aligarh, Zakir Sahib brought the changes.... Rather, I will say Zakir Sahib also because of Nehru and Maulana Azad. For Nehru, I had unlimited—that is also because of this fear complex and guilty complex—I believed that Nehru was the only one who could save us. Without limit. He started that All India Youth Festival in 1954 probably. For this 150 universities were called... every university had started cultural activities. [In AMU] also there were cultural activities. And [the] first participation of Aligarh University's contingent was in 1956, I think. The drama team that we sent, I was the hero in that drama.[28]

This narrative exalted Zakir Husain, while it elevated the role of Prime Minister Nehru. Nehru gave the convocation speech in AMU in 1948, at the moment when the university made a deliberate about-face toward nationalist ideology. Khan's attachment to Nehru was deeply personal, localized, and came largely from Nehru's support of youth and cultural activities.[29] Khan also connected his attachment to Nehru with his "fear complex and guilty complex," subscribing to the nationalist ideology that the only way to overcome these anxieties was to participate fully in India's secular endeavor, through which, as Nehru put it, "there is equality of opportunity for all and where many variegated streams of thought and culture meet together to form a mighty river of progress and advancement for her people."[30] The youth festivals that Nehru organized brought together young people from many different regions, religions, and backgrounds and from 150 different institutions. This microcosm of the secular, national state of which Nehru spoke in his convocation address appealed to Khan, though he admitted, "that fear is still with me." Indeed, Nehru acknowledged that the process of partitioning would continue to wreak havoc on the lives of young people. Nehru's efforts offered Khan an alternative to the fear he could not release, and perhaps helped to "erase the mark" of catastrophe and disaster, as he had hoped.[31]

Iftikhar's brother, Iqtidar Alam Khan, and their comrade Irfan Habib found redemption in the ideology of Communism, going further in their commitment to reimagining Indian society on the basis of true equality, not just promises of secularism. (Iftikhar described himself as a sort of "incomplete Communist" who always maintained some allegiance to the establishment, for protection. Iqtidar and Habib are Marxists.) During the League period at AMU, the Leftist Students' Federation provided an alternative ideological space to the Congress or the League. League documents, especially A. B. A. Haleem's letters to Mohammad Ali Jinnah, show a terrific anxiety about communist influence despite the fact that the Communist Party officially supported Pakistan during this period.[32] Still, the leftist and communist students were marginalized in the university during the League period and immediately after 1947.

Iftikhar Alam Khan remembered the anti-communist sentiment on the campus. Leftist students, he recalled, were "beaten up" in the Union and "til 1952, there was a practice in the university that every year, before the Union elections took place, they would take out a procession. An anti-communist procession. 'Stalin, *hai hai!*' (laughing) '*Lamazhab log, hai hai!*' (Irreligious people! Shame!) Very strong anti-communist sentiment was there in the university."³³ After the nationalist turn, however, the communist influence grew on the campus. Irfan Habib remembered that in 1951 and 1953 the Students' Federation actually won the Union elections. While conflicting ideologies divided the institution for many years in a dispute between "fundamentalists" and "progressives"—Mohammad Amin told me that "Aligarh became a center also of the liberal school which helped in the understanding of medieval India." Except, he lamented, "when, later on, it goes up completely Red . . . and [became] ideologically tainted."³⁴ The visibility of leftism represented one change from the pre-1947 period that validated the perspectives of those who had not subscribed to Muslim League ideology.

Iqtidar Alam Khan had briefly participated with the pro-Pakistan Movement, and was a sometimes-devout Muslim. In his words, "from roughly '44 onwards up till about '50, I was an intensely religious person . . . [but I shouldn't] use this word 'intensely religious' because I didn't know anything about religion. I was a believing person. That's all."³⁵ In retrospect he saw both his religiosity and his affiliation with League politics as being largely naïve. Similarly, when he discovered his attraction to Communism, he said, "I was still having those religious attitudes which I had earlier . . . I started attending those Students' Federation meetings; there I met Professor Irfan Habib also . . . he had his own commitment to Marxism. He was a much more educated person than myself at that time also."³⁶ Though Iqtidar Alam (like his brother) remembered his commitment as poorly informed, in 1951 he was arrested for protesting a visit by then UP governor Pandit Govind Ballabh Pant to the university.³⁷ During his two months in Aligarh and Agra prisons, he was converted to Communism. Many communist activists were in jail in the wake of the "Ranadive Period" when the Communist Party actively encouraged revolution and the central government cracked down on their activities. The jail (like the college had been) was an incubator for young activists.³⁸ Iqtidar Alam told me that unlike his earlier commitments which had been born of circumstance, his experience in the jail drew him closer to the ideology. As he described the experience to me, "I became a Communist party member inside jail. When I was in Agra prison, they used to hold their meetings, cell meetings. I said, 'Why are you keeping me out? I came to jail because of you and now I am quite convinced. Everything is acceptable to me. So make me a member.'"³⁹ Once he became a member and fully separated himself from the challenging politics of the League period, Khan found absolution for his "guilty conscience" and naïve (if short-lived) commitments to religious devotion and Pakistan. For each of the Alam brothers, then, the period after independence was marked by new spatial and political affiliations. For Iftikhar, the younger, the youth festivals provided a space in which he felt the safety of the government's, and especially Nehru's beneficence. As the "hero" of the AMU play sent to Nehru's youth festival, Iftikhar could finally travel safely to Delhi. For Iqtidar, his affiliation with the Communist Party, formed in the otherwise restrictive environment of the Agra jail, became core to his identity in independent India, as he permanently rejected both his earlier religiosity and attraction to the Muslim League agenda as ill-informed.

Some narrators found redemption in the vindication of the ideology to which they had subscribed throughout. In India, this stance is best exemplified by Riazur Rahman Sherwani, who defied his family and maintained his allegiance to Congress nationalism throughout the League period at AMU. In 2008, he told me, "I did not agree with the ideology of the Muslim League. I was against the partition of the country. I thought that partition was harmful to the country as well as to the Muslims because country, if it was divided, it will lose its power, it will lose its resources."[40] Sherwani predicted the decline of Muslims in independent India, anticipated a long partitioning. He did defend Muslims against the fallacy that they were responsible for dividing the country, and he was vindicated by having, from the outset, maintained his allegiance to Congress and its ideals, despite its unpopularity in AMU.

Pakistanis, similarly, engaged a narrative of justification for their adherence to Muslim League ideology. For them, the ongoing suffering of Indian Muslims that exemplifies partitioning justified the creation of Pakistan despite the suffering of Muslims during the 1947 migrations. In fact, the achievement of Pakistan must be a triumph for the Muslim community *because* they suffered for its creation. Thousands lost their lives in its pursuit. So that these lives were not given in vain, but as part of the realization of Muslim independence in the subcontinent, narrators had to support the idea of Pakistan and presume its inevitability. Indeed, many narrators deployed ideas about the suffering of Muslims in India to suggest that even today, the legitimacy of Pakistan was self-evident.

Even as they recognized the suffering of Muslims outside of Pakistan, they struggled to reconcile the disappointments Pakistan has brought in their own lives. They were reluctant to allow the possibility that the narrative of Muslim solidarity so critical to the foundation of Pakistan could also have been an instrument of oppression against other Muslims. Thus, in their memories, they marginalized the importance of other identity markers and held fast to Muslimness as the unifying characteristic of belonging. Their triumphal narrative that denied any heterogeneity of identity or politics was an essential component of their sense of citizenship. In this conception, Indian Muslims were oppressed, and they unified and established a state in which those values could be safe and where their status would not be threatened. From their vantage point, this shared experience was sufficient to constitute the nation. The failure, in their minds, of the Two Nation Theory, was a failure of the state, not a failure of the vision. In contrast to much writing on Pakistan that treats it as an unrealized idea, these narrators have lived daily with the real limitations and possibilities of Pakistan; both its triumphs and its challenges illuminate the multiple realities Pakistan embodies.

That the Pakistani state failed to create an environment in which their values were universal caused some anxiety for the Pakistani narrators, but this anxiety was acute for those from Bengal. It was clear that the sense of not belonging originated in their university experiences. The East Bengali narrators, who fully subscribed to the Pakistan ideal based on their experience (or the perception) of discrimination by Hindus, found a home in AMU prior to 1947. Yet, this home was never free of discrimination or a taint of exclusion. In matters of food and language especially, Bengalis felt "other" at Aligarh despite the powerful connection provided by the Islamic idiom. As Mohiuddin Khan put it, "We have always a difference, because we were non-Urdu-speaking people.... So this difference was there between the students."[41] These students supported the independence movement fully, Habibur Rahman even argued that the Bengali students were especially "shrewd."[42] But, they were disillusioned by their experience in Pakistan. None imagined breaking away from Pakistan, but as the movement for Bangladesh gathered momentum, they supported it. Habibur Rahman recalled that until the early 1950s, "I was perfectly, I was wholeheartedly a supporter of Pakistan. But when they started all these discriminations, then there was nothing, well, we had to go to the opposition as Awami League."[43] The demise of the cooperative spirit between East and West Pakistan left these individuals grasping at an idea of Muslim unity that no longer seemed relevant. Their attachment to the liberation of Bangladesh provided a redeeming narrative, a renegotiation of the boundaries of belonging.

Since 1948, AMU itself has deliberately allied with the secular nationalist stream in Indian politics and, in fact, Muslim intellectuals have worked to prove that those Muslims who remained in India have chosen the rights and responsibilities of Indian citizenship. The assumption of disloyalty, in any case, was founded on faulty assumptions about the motives of AMU students during the Pakistan Movement and distrust of its relationship with Pakistan after 1947. Partitioning, the result of the creation and ongoing presence of Pakistan, as Pandey writes, has confirmed political "difference," thus fixing the notion of the "Muslim minority" in India.[44] The question of belonging therefore continues to vex the issue of citizenship for Muslims and leaves them exposed to actual violence, especially with the growing power of Hindu nationalism, which has been legitimized by the election of the BJP.

In May 2018, the RSS was denied permission to hold political "camps" at AMU on the grounds that the university's tradition did not sanction the actions of any political party to "put up their candidates either for contesting the Students' Union polls or the Teachers' Association elections," and had "'no intention' of allowing any 'direct intervention' of political parties inside the campus."[45] A BJP Member of Parliament representing Aligarh then raised the question of why a portrait of Mohammad Ali Jinnah hung in the Union Hall. The university defended the portrait's presence, noting that Jinnah had become a life member of the Union in 1938. He had been a donor, a founding member of the University Court, and an advocate for Hindu-Muslim brotherhood before he became the chief architect of Pakistan. In addition, Mohandas K. Gandhi was the first designated life member of the Union and his portrait hangs alongside Jinnah's, Jawaharlal Nehru's, and those of all other prominent Indians who were honored as life members of the Union since the founding of the university.

In response, Hindu nationalist activists from the Hindu Jagran Manch (an RSS affiliate) stormed the campus to demand that the portrait be removed.[46] They targeted an event at which Hamid Ansari, an Alig and the former Indian vice president, was to speak and be honored with induction into Union life membership. In response, AMU students surged out of the campus to demand accountability for the transgression and were themselves met by police at the Bab-e-Syed, the main entrance gate of the campus. More than two dozen people were injured in the confrontation.[47] In an eerie reflection of the same fears students expressed surrounding the threat of violence in 1946 and 1947, in 2019 AMU students were demanding the arrest of outsiders who had entered the campus. But, the AMU Teachers' Association protested, "Instead of taking action against criminal aggressors, AMU students ... were re-victimised by lathi-charge."[48]

Episodes of tension on the borders of the campus over the long period of time examined here demonstrate the value of reframing the unique event of the 1947 Partition as a longer process of partitioning within which boundaries between groups continue to be contested and negotiated through the identity politics that forced the creation of three states in the aftermath of the British departure.

The stories of partitioning in AMU, and throughout the subcontinent, illuminate aspects of the 1947 Partition that have not been clearly visible before. Whereas the focus on the borders in Punjab has contributed to an understanding of partition as a deeply felt singular episode of violence, it has also constructed "Partition" as an experience of displacement and rupture. For many, particularly for Hindus displaced from Pakistan areas, this reflection is apt. However, for those Muslims living in Pakistan and for many remaining in India, partition appears as a dramatic shift in access to spaces and places that held meaning for them as Muslims. It was not only a rupture. Rather, AMU, which was a hub linking the narrators whose stories are collected here, exerted powerful meaning on the landscape of North Indian education and politics that affected outcomes for Muslims in all three post-partition states. All of these narrators came of age during partitioning, but none of them experienced any significant violence. Still, they were plagued by the "fear of not belonging," and as they negotiated their own independence, they brought the past into the present to build a future. For all of them, emplacement was key, even if they were physically displaced. For former students who lived through 1947 in AMU, the experiences of disruption and fear that they remembered from 1946 and 1947 became the foundation for later negotiations of identity and belonging once the indelible borders were inscribed on the map. Those who did not move, who remained, "in place," felt endangered, and had to renegotiate the terms of belonging. Partition marked the boundaries of home, university, and state with uncertainty. But, as these remembered histories show, the boundaries were also mobile and malleable. Even as the boundaries were marked by fear, they created opportunities for resilience and continuity.

The sense of emplacement that these narrators shared in AMU was disrupted first by the obtrusive event of the 1946 market violence, and then again by the 1947 Partition, despite their distance from the borders. Even for narrators who emerged from this shared environment, the experiences of partitioning, of choosing homes, were multiple, determined by the concerns of family, career, and identity, though not usually because of violence. Each group of narrators has negotiated national, collective, and individual identities to reconcile conflicting histories into a coherent, though often troubled, sense of belonging.

Epilogue:
The Babri Masjid, AMU, and Indian Muslims

Though the Indian National Congress has dominated Indian politics since independence, and many Aligarh narrators have expressed their sympathies with its leadership, even the Congress does not have a great track record when it comes to protecting Muslims in India. Rather, the most egregious episodes of communal violence have taken place under ostensibly secular Congress governments, including the 1987 Hashimpura Massacre that followed the opening of the Babri Masjid to Hindu worshippers.[1] Still, with the recent rise of the BJP in India and the election of Narendra Modi—a man who many believe was at best complicit, at worst responsible, for the 2002 Gujarat pogroms against Muslims in Ahmedabad—for two consecutive terms as prime minister, the position of Muslim Indians seems even more vulnerable. Hindu nationalist parties like the BJP have long been tied to Hindu supremacist violence that has targeted and marginalized minorities, especially in preparation for contentious elections.[2] Preelection violence in UP in 2012–13 conformed to this pattern and was followed by unprecedented BJP victories in the state. In 2015, too, a series of attacks on Muslims, including an arson attack on a mosque in Faizabad, ignited concerns that the violence "marks the beginning of another phase of communal politics ahead of the UP assembly election" in May 2017 in which the BJP fielded no Muslim candidates.[3] The anxieties reverberating through Muslim communities have reinvigorated the contentious politics of partitioning. In November 2019, the Supreme Court of India issued its final judgment to settle the dispute over the Babri Masjid/*Ramjanmabhoomi* and its destruction. Only a month later, the government passed the Citizenship Amendment Act, which modified rules by which undocumented immigrants can fast-track Indian citizenship. Because the act does not extend such privileges to Muslims, it sparked fears that the government sought to disenfranchise millions of Muslims, which led to months of protests and conflict between Indians and security forces.

During the decades that have passed since the destruction of the mosque, the catastrophic rioting that followed all over India, and the periodic eruption of related violence—including the 2002 pogroms in Gujarat—India's non-Muslim public has come a great distance in recognizing the fragility of the communal peace that generally prevails in the country. At the same time, the political power of Hindu nationalists has grown, and these events are potent reminders that the relations between Muslim citizens and the government in India remains fraught.

The Babri Masjid Verdicts and AMU

The Babri Mosque was built in 1528 during the reign of Mughal emperor Babur. Though Hindu nationalists have argued that it was constructed after the demolition of a Ram temple and with "temple material," archaeological evidence, collected by the Archaeological Survey of India, has not confirmed these contentious claims.[4] Dispute over the site began in the nineteenth century, and continued after Indian independence.[5] The mosque, for its part, was old, but not otherwise an especially sacred site for Indian Muslims. In 1949, idols of Ram and his wife Sita were placed inside the mosque, deepening the contestation over the structure. In this context, the gates of the mosque were sealed, until they were reopened for Hindu worship by court order in 1986. Hindu activists, led by L. K. Advani, destroyed the mosque in 1992, on the claim that the site was the birthplace of Lord Ram, the *Ramjanmabhoomi*, and should house a Ram temple. In late 2010, the Allahabad High Court released its verdict determining how the contested land on which the Babri Masjid had been situated would be allotted to those claiming sovereignty over it. Muslim apprehension in the days leading up to the verdict revealed their awareness of the possibility of violence in its wake.

On September 19, 2010, in anticipation of the announcement of the verdict, the vice chancellor of AMU issued "an appeal to staff and students" to "maintain equanimity, and desist from any form of reaction that would destroy trust between the communities."[6] In addition, alumni of AMU engaged in a lively discussion over one of several AMU listservs about how to deal with the pending verdict, including suggestions to turn the disputed site over to the United Nations as a World Heritage Site or to give the "Babri Masjid to our Hindu brethren to facilitate the construction of a Grand Temple so as to pay respect to their faith (*Astha*), leaving only a small piece of land away from *Garbha grah* [inner sanctum] to construct a small replica of the Babri Masjid."[7] When these perspectives encountered the fiery resistance of those who felt Muslims must defend their claim to the space, alumnus Islam Habib Khan (Engineering 1951) replied, "Thousands of people and mostly Muslims have been killed at the time of the destruction of the Babri Masjid. I do not wish to visualise the reaction if a verdict is made specially in favour of Muslims. There will be another round of massacres. Personally, I do not think it will be worth it and then what would have we achieved?"[8] The VC and many of those who advocated that Muslims make clear that they would accept the verdict, no matter its outcome, raised the issue of "Aligarh's tradition of communal harmony" to justify their willingness to forego contesting the verdict. The threat of violence by the majority was palpable, and the prevailing atmosphere on the AMU campus was "an uneasy calm" as the date for the release of the verdict approached.[9]

There was also a contingent of voices among former Aligs arguing for Muslim solidarity in the face of Hindu tyranny, suggesting that Muslims should defend their claim to the territory. Those voices marked the boundaries of an important divide within the AMU community. Some voices, particularly those who lived through the Indian partition, advocated docility and the benefits of communal harmony. Other voices, many coming from those who grew up in independent India, advocated for a more aggressively represented Muslim identity, particularly in the face of the perceived non-

Muslim threat. Both groups, however, recognized the threat to Muslim sovereignty in independent India; the importance of protecting the Muslim community is common to both strategic responses. Islam Habib Khan tried to temper the enthusiasm for a vigorous response with his experience,

> If I know anything about human behaviour the reaction of the other party to the court case will be immediate and severe. Their agenda ... will become firmer and not softer and you will always be in a state of clash rather than working towards a reconciliation. Wisdom tells us that the playing ground should be made softer rather than harder as the issues are many and difficult to negotiate.[10]

As one who arrived in AMU in the wake of partition, at a time when its student body was much depleted by partition's migrations, and as one who likely experienced the tensions in AMU surrounding the 1951 riots, Islam Habib Khan recommended compromise, accommodation. Muslims would not be responsible for violence, he argued, they would be its victims.

Whereas older generations are plagued by the knowledge that demands for Muslim sovereignty over Indian space have had dire consequences, the younger generations feel so circumscribed by the boundaries of their public personae that they feel it necessary to aggressively defend themselves against encroachment on these boundaries. The continuity with earlier periods of pro-Muslim activism is clearly visible here. Famously, during the mosque destruction in 1992, Hindu nationalists raised the slogan "*Babar ki santan jao Pakistan!* (Children of Babur, go to Pakistan!)" This chant linked 500 years of Muslim civilization in the Indian subcontinent to the young state of Pakistan and reflected the deep-seated distrust of Muslim loyalty.[11] The rioters treated the mosque, located in UP, as a displaced piece of Pakistan on the Indian landscape.

The verdict in the Babri Masjid case was finally released on September 30, 2010. The controversial verdict divided the disputed territory into three parcels, awarding two of them to two Hindu claimants, and one to the Sunni Waqf Board, the caretaker of the site prior to the mosque's destruction. There was discontent on many sides as a result of this "three-way partition" but it was generally hailed as one that would make an "attempt at resolution."[12] Editorials contextualized the verdict by hailing it as an expression of "India's culture of religious pluralism,"[13] as evidence that "The Allahabad High Court itself seemed to have vaguely recognised the imperative of communal harmony,"[14] and as "a compromise calculated to hold the religious peace."[15] The widespread Muslim discontent with the outcome of the verdict, which seemed to take into account matters of faith in addition to legal claims, settled down into a feeling of "sullen resignation to the inevitable."[16] As the Sunni Waqf Board vowed to appeal the decision to India's Supreme Court, and while Muslims expressed their disappointment to one another, no one took to the streets. This was a measure of India's secularism. One Indian Muslim commented to the Pakistani newspaper *Dawn*, "At least this is not the kind of a verdict that can justify any Muslim outrage . . . They'll settle for this deal."[17] Indian Muslims, as Ather Siddiqi also indicated, have settled for a place in Indian society entirely their own, but monitored and circumscribed by the non-Muslim public surrounding them. Undoubtedly there are alliances great and small, friends, neighbors and colleagues from both communities who recognize and even share the anxieties of Indian Muslims. Hindu and Muslim groups both had called for patience and restraint surrounding the Ayodhya verdict. It was telling, however, that the expectation of violence after the verdict was so widely anticipated that its absence became the heart of the story.[18]

When I interviewed her in 2009, Saeeda Kidwai cast the destruction of the Babri Mosque as an anomaly in India, but its repercussions have remade communal relations throughout the country. The riots in Aligarh following the destruction of the mosque were some of the worst in the country.[19] In 2002, in Ahmedabad, Gujarat, over 1,000 Muslims were killed in a pogrom of violence that started with the return of Hindu pilgrims from Ayodhya where they sought to build a temple on the mosque site. The train car in which they were traveling caught fire and burned. Though the source of the fire was ambiguous, the retribution that followed targeted Muslims; the ruling BJP, and then Gujarat chief minister Narendra Modi were complacent and even complicit in the attacks. Though arguably, as the Sachar Committee Report shows, Congress leadership did little substantively to support Muslims, the communal politics of the BJP have been far more deadly. The months leading up to the 2014 elections saw communal riots in UP that displaced tens of thousands of Muslims in Muzzafarnagar and that served to consolidate the BJP's leadership and to remind Indians of the "threatening" Muslim presence.[20] The BJP election victory empowered right-wing groups nationwide, and Aligarh has remained a flashpoint for Hindu-Muslim confrontation.

On December 10, 2014, the *Foreign Policy South Asia Daily* reported that in Aligarh, on December 25, the RSS—a Hindu nationalist organization from which the then recently elected BJP draws its ideological roots—planned to convert at least 1,000 Muslim and 4,000 Christian families to Hinduism under what it called the *Ghar Wapsi* program (returning home).[21] Rajeshwar Singh, an RSS regional worker, said, "Aligarh was chosen because it's time we wrest the Hindu city from Muslims. It is a city of brave Rajputs and their temples on whose remains Muslim institutions have been established."[22]

The issue, and reports of mass conversions in Agra in December, raised a protest in parliament, and by 16 December the plan had been canceled, or at least postponed.[23] The head of the Shiv Sena in UP, meanwhile, dismissed the entire effort, noting that "The Hindu and Muslim cultures do not match at all and those who consider this a homecoming, they should take lessons from the history. We welcome 'ghar wapsi' only if it means that [Muslims] are sent to Pakistan, because [Mohammad Ali] Jinnah has already created a home for them."[24] The Shiv Sena head all but quoted Mohammad Ali Jinnah's March 1940 speech in which he identified Hindus and Muslims as two distinct nations.[25] Aligarh emerged as a contentious site because, according to the right-wing activists, it should be recovered from the Muslims who built their institutions on top of destroyed Hindu ones. Though there is no evidence that the AMU was built on top of destroyed Hindu structures, his allusion to the Babri Mosque signaled that Hindutva activists sought to lay claim to the place Muslims had so deliberately constructed.

These episodes lay bare the fact that the persistent tensions in the subcontinent between Hindus and minorities broadly, and Hindus and Muslims in particular, are tightly linked to perceptions about who "belongs" in India. The notion, advanced by the RSS, the Shiv Sena, and their political representatives in the BJP, that Hindus have a primordial, natural tie to India, as a place, amounts to a specious narrative of indigeneity that marginalizes people with connections to other faiths or other cultural geographies. In addition, for Muslims, these politics cannot be separated from the reality of Pakistan's presence on India's Western border.

In November 2019, twenty-seven years after the mosque was reduced to rubble, the Supreme Court of India issued its verdict on the fate of the land, finally settling the future prospects for the site. In a huge victory for Hindu nationalists, the court empowered the construction of a Ram temple on the site. Another plot of five acres would be allotted to the Sunni Waqf Board to construct a mosque. Muslims, weary of the dispute, have accepted the verdict with resignation. Zafaryab Jilani, the lawyer for the Sunni Waqf Board, told NDTV "The judgement is not satisfactory but we respect it."[26] Muslims are painfully aware that peace is maintained not by the good behavior of their community but at the whim of the majority.

The Citizenship Amendment Act/National Register of Citizens

In their discussions in 2010, some contributors to the AMUNetwork Listserv suggested that the destruction of the Babri Masjid was not an isolated event, but part of a larger plan to marginalize Muslims more fully. They argued that if Muslims relinquished their claim to the Babri Masjid, the Hindus would build a grand temple there and go on to police Muslim communities more closely. The anxiety that they expressed over a domino effect on Muslim marginalization echoes some of the points that Ather Siddiqi outlined in our 2009 interview. These contributors argued that the strategy of holding fast to "Muslim" territory was a way of marking Muslims' legitimate presence in Indian public space. In this context, AMU is the exemplary place. They imagined Ayodhya as ground zero of a terrifying future in which the construction of a grand Ram temple would mark the symbolic foundation of an anti-Muslim Hindu state.[27] Developments in 2019 reveal that their anxieties may have been prescient.

Barely a month after the release of the Supreme Court verdict on the Babri Masjid, the government passed the Citizenship (Amendment) Act (CAA), 2019. The act, for the first time, tied eligibility for citizenship to religious identity by inserting language into the Citizenship Act, 1955:

> Provided that any person belonging to Hindu, Sikh Buddhist, Jain, Parsi or Christian community from Afghanistan, Bangladesh or Pakistan, who entered into India on or before 31st day of December, 2014...shall not be treated as illegal migrant for the purposes of the Act.... The Central Government or an authority specified by it in this behalf may...grant a certificate of registration or certificate of naturalization to a person referred to [above];... a person granted the certificate of registration or certificate of naturalization... shall be deemed to be a citizen of India from the date of his entry into India.[28]

The act fast-tracks citizenship for undocumented migrants from surrounding countries who have fled religious persecution. The act's provisions apply to those fleeing Muslim countries surrounding India, and explicitly excludes Muslims from its privileges. Therefore, the act problematically assumes that Muslims could not face persecution in Muslim majority countries, from which they might seek refuge in India, and even if they did, they would not be eligible for the privileges of Indian citizenship by virtue of their religious identity. This logic hinges on a fundamental fallacy enshrined in the 1947 Partition, that Muslims are Muslims are Muslims. While the Muslim League deployed such rhetoric, the history of Pakistan and Bangladesh reveals that the linguistic, cultural, sectarian, and social diversity of Muslims in the subcontinent was more deeply entrenched than the Pakistan Movement's leaders were willing to allow. In addition, dependence upon the Two Nation Theory defies the logic of secular citizenship at the heart of the Indian Constitution by codifying prejudices against Muslims that emerge from perceived incompatibility between Muslim identity and Indian identity.

Furthermore, by restricting access to citizenship to those fleeing only Afghanistan, Bangladesh, and Pakistan—three Muslim majority countries adjacent to India that contain non-Muslim minorities—the CAA excludes any refugees from Nepal or Sri Lanka, Muslim or otherwise. Tragically, the persecuted Rohingya Muslim minority that has been fleeing programmatic violence in Myanmar for the last decade was also left out of the legislation. Since 2017, over 700,000 Rohingya Muslims have fled violence in Myanmar to take shelter in Bangladesh and India. While the vast majority reside in massive refugee camps in southern Bangladesh, approximately 40,000 Rohingya have entered India since 2017. The office of the United Nations High Commission for Refugees has issued identity cards to about 16,500 Rohingya in India, which it says helps "prevent harassment, arbitrary arrests, detention and deportation" of refugees.[29] In fact, however, the Indian government has deported Rohingya refugees to Myanmar, where they are also denied citizenship, potentially violating the international consensus on *non-refoulement* established by the 1951 United Nations Refugees' Convention.[30]

The narrow scope of the CAA's provisions make a clear statement about the ineligibility of Muslims for Indian citizenship without denaturalizing existing citizens. In addition, though, the CAA intersected with two other government initiatives to inspire real fear of displacement and denaturalization among Indian Muslims throughout the country: the "updation" of the National Register of Citizens (NRC) piloted in Assam, and the revocation of the special status for the Muslim majority state of Kashmir through the abrogation of two articles of the Indian Constitution.

The updating of the NRC is an effort of the Indian government to identify Indian citizens and to link their identities to existing census data. Such an effort was last undertaken in 1951, and the current effort was piloted in the Northeastern state of Assam. Eligibility to be included on the Register "would be ascertained based on the NRC, 1951, Electoral Rolls up to 1971 and in their absence the admissible documents up to 24th March (midnight) 1971. The updated NRC shall contain names of persons eligible for inclusion in updated NRC by virtue of being original inhabitants of Assam."[31] Thus framed, it is clear that the NRC seeks to register Assamese residents while excluding those who might be refugees from the Bangladesh Liberation war of

1971. Those who could not prove that they were "original inhabitants"—with relations registered in 1951 or with voting records prior to 1971 when Bangladesh was formed—would be deemed illegal migrants. Human rights activist Sanjoy Hazarika argues that the demand for the NRC originated from Assamese organizations who feared that illegal migration into the state from Bangladesh would lead to "demographic changes, and adversely affect the area's cultural and social fabric as well as political representation."[32] However, as he points out, the updated NRC in Assam, published in August 2019, left nearly two million people off the list, including both Hindus and Muslims. While those excluded from the list were not immediately denaturalized, they must undertake a process of positive proof of citizenship before Foreigners' Tribunals and/or appeals through the High Court and, finally, the Supreme Court. This system is fraught with problems, and the government has been constructing detention centers for illegal migrants awaiting their certification. Thus, the effort to preserve the demographic purity of Assam has become a government priority, but its feasibility remains uncertain. Muslims fear that they will be the ultimate losers of efforts to record both "original" and "new" citizens. If the NRC is expanded nationwide, and Muslims are excluded from the rolls, substantial numbers of Muslims could be denaturalized and ineligible for citizenship based on their exclusion from the CAA.

Furthermore, it seems that the Aligs who saw the verdict on the Babri Masjid as a litmus test for Muslim inclusion were right—the efforts of the state to claim Muslim spaces and places would not end with the site in Ayodhya. Rather, in July 2019, the Indian government abrogated two key articles of the Indian Constitution that gave India's only Muslim majority state special status as a Union Territory. Article 370 assured the state of Jammu and Kashmir of autonomy within India, defining a special relationship between state and center; Article 35A protected the property rights of "permanent residents." None but permanent residents could own property, or access certain services. The revocation of these provisions opened the door for demographic change in Kashmir—in contrast to the intention of the NRC in Assam—by *inviting migration* from outside the region, likely by non-Muslims who, for the first time, will be able to purchase immovable property.[33] The efforts to transform Kashmir have been draconian. The state has long been the most militarized, but the constitutional changes were accompanied by complete lockdown, with communication cut off to the outside world for months.[34]

The Indian government has denied that the new measures intend to discriminate against Muslims. There is dispute about whether the NRC will be expanded to a nationwide level, or be tied to the National Population Register, which includes the collection of biodata. Still, taken together, these measures appear to misunderstand and devalue Muslim experience, and to muzzle dissent as part of a project to consolidate Hindu identity as Indian identity.

Indians, by and large, take their commitments to secularism seriously. Since the passage of the CAA, Indian Muslims have been at the forefront of widespread and substantial protests against the government's efforts to restrict access to the rights and privileges of citizenship in which Indians from all walks of life have joined. Protests, notably, began in Assam on December 4, after the Citizenship (Amendment) Bill was introduced. University students responded quickly after the CAA was enacted on December 12, and universities were among the first institutions to be targeted by security forces. In Delhi, protests lasted for almost four months (and only ended in March 2020 as a consequence of the restrictions accompanying the coronavirus pandemic), but they began inside the JMI, the Delhi University that was originally founded in Aligarh during the non-cooperation movement of 1920. On December 15, in response to large student protests, police forcibly entered the library, firing teargas, beating students with batons, and injuring dozens.[35] Almost immediately, peaceful protesters in AMU heard reports of the violence in Delhi, leading to clashes between students and police. The AMU VC quickly closed the university to limit violence and wrote to the campus community on December 17 to explain his actions. The violence, he argued, was initiated by outsiders, "anti-social/lumpen elements (including expelled ex-students)" who forcibly broke open the Bab-e-Syed gate to the main campus. "After crossing the university boundary, they resorted to stone pelting the police outside the campus." The mob numbered "in the thousands," and to protect the safety of the university and its students, he had to call in the police to bring the situation under control. Many students were injured in the clashes, but of the twenty-seven people arrested, only seven were current students.[36] The VC's account mobilized familiar narratives about AMU's isolation, insisting that the boundary must be maintained to ensure calm. Yet, he was responsible for engaging police enforcement, an act that AMU students always experience as betrayal. Students disputed the VC's account, and focused on the extent of the police brutality. Even though they had been sent home, AMU students continued to participate in CAA protests throughout the winter. Upon their return to campus in January 2020, despite the VC urging them to desist, students reinvigorated their anti-CAA protests, though at a distance from central administrative buildings as required by a ruling of the High Court.[37]

One inspiring feature of the anti-CAA protests was the solidarity that protesters repeatedly expressed for the most vulnerable among them. Student protesters in Delhi were sure to acknowledge the threats to students in AMU, and AMU protesters held space for students in Jawaharlal Nehru University. In Delhi, Muslim women-led protests blocked a major road in Shaheen Bagh and established a protest camp that brought many issues to national attention: anti-CAA/NRC sentiment, police brutality (including that against students), and unemployment. The solidarities built on a shared commitment to the secular terms of Indian citizenship must be sustained by the upcoming generation of leaders that these institutions claim to cultivate.

These devastating stories illuminate the tensions that Muslims face in India, but they are not the only ones I could tell. Rather, I've listened and tried to do justice to the experiences of those who told me their stories. It was they who heralded the virtues of Muslim solidarity and lamented its shortcomings, and it was they who have charted pathways through the spaces created by ongoing partitioning throughout the subcontinent. What today's events show is that the spaces and places that gave meaning to the lives of partition's first generation seem destined to remain sites of contest.

Appendix of All Interviews—Alphabetical by Narrator

All interviews conducted by Amber Abbas and unless otherwise noted have been archived in the *Partition's First Generation Oral History Project*, Louie B. Nunn Center for Oral History, University of Kentucky Libraries.

Pakistan (2005–10)

Abbas, Begum Birjis Zaheer
Location: Lahore
Date: July 10, 2005
Biographical Notes: Birjis Abbas was born in Aligarh, India in approximately 1915. She was the eldest of ten siblings. She was educated in Urdu and English at home, but never attended school. She married Zaheer Abbas, her first cousin, who had lived with the family while completing his L.L.M. at AMU. In 1947 she migrated with her three young children via truck and train to Pakistan. She became mother to seven children, raised in Pakistan, and ensured that they all received education, even when money was short. She was my grandmother, the matriarch of our family, and she passed away in February 2007.

Abbas, Tariq Azhar
Location: Austin, Texas, USA
Date: May 21, 2011
Biographical Notes: Tariq Abbas was born in Aligarh, India on July 23, 1942. He had four sisters (Roshan, Zehra, Faiza and Ghazala) and two brothers (Anis and Shams). His family migrated from Aligarh to the newly created state of Pakistan in late 1947. He completed his primary schooling at the St. Anthony's High School and his matriculation in Forman Christian College in Lahore. He won an American Field Service Exchange Scholarship to study in the United States in 1960. He completed his B.S. at Texas Christian University and his M.S. at The University of Oklahoma. He spent his career as a Petroleum Engineer with Aramco in Saudi Arabia and in Houston, Texas. He was my father and he died on November 5, 2013.

Ahmad, Qazi Moinuddin
Location: Lahore
Date: May 16, 2010

Biographical Notes: Qazi Moinuddin Ahmad was born in Sikandarabad, District Bulandshahr, on January 6, 1929, but spent most of his childhood in Aligarh. He had four brothers and two sisters, most of whom have settled in Pakistan. His father, Professor Kazi Saeeduddin Ahmad, founded the Geography Department at Punjab University. His mother, from Aligarh, died when he was quite young. Qazi Moinuddin studied in the Muslim University High School in Aligarh before shifting to Lahore, where he attended Forman Christian College and was a Muslim Students' Federation activist. He received a "Gold Medal" from the Nazaria-i-Pakistan Foundation for his work on behalf of Pakistan. He built a career as a Shell Pakistan dealer and sustained the Qazi Welfare Society for charitable work. He died on February 9, 2018.

Ahmad, Dr. Rafique
Location: Lahore
Date: August 5, 2006
Biographical Notes: Rafique Ahmad was born on February 3, 1927, in Lahore. Both sides of his family hail from the old city of Lahore and he spent his childhood there. His father, Mohammad Siddique, owned the Punjab Stores provisions store in Tollington Market on the Mall Road which served locals, foreigners, and the military. Rafique Ahmad completed his M.A. in Islamia College in 1948 and went abroad to complete his D. Phil from Oxford University in 1956. He returned to Pakistan and began teaching in Punjab University, where he also held a variety of administrative posts including pro-vice chancellor and vice chancellor. He later established the campus of Islamia University-Bahawalpur, and served as its vice chancellor. He serves as the vice chairman of the Nazaria-e-Pakistan Foundation. He lives in Lahore.

Chaudhry, Mahmood Ali Khan
Location: Lahore
Date: July 4, 2005, and July 6, 2005
*In author's possession.
Biographical Notes: M. A. K. Chaudhry was born in Wazirabad in 1923. He was the second youngest with six brothers and a sister. He spent his childhood in Wazirabad and Jullunder. He studied in Mofussil College in Ludhiana. He was commissioned in the British Indian Army in 1944. He served in Burma during the Second World War. His family, in India, was known for its support of Pakistan, and suffered somewhat for this. Thus, his whole family migrated to Pakistan. He was an important public figure in Pakistan. He served as inspector general of police in East Pakistan in the 1960s and director general Federal Intelligence Agency and interior secretary in the 1970s. After being retired by General Zia, he took up a law practice in Lahore in the late 1970s, and in the 1990s he became the chairman of the Board of Governors of the Lahore School of Economics. He died on May 29, 2011.

Fatima, Dr. Aijaz
Location: Karachi
Date: May 25, 2010
Biographical Notes: Dr. Aijaz Fatima was born in New Delhi on December 31, 1927. Her mother died when she was two years old and she spent her childhood among

various relatives in UP, before her father called her to Aligarh when she was twelve years old. She has two sisters and one brother, but they all grew up in different houses with different relatives. Her father, Dr. Sir Ziauddin Ahmad, was vice chancellor of AMU. She sometimes attended classes at the Aligarh Women's College, and completed her intermediate from there before shifting to Lady Hardinge Medical College in New Delhi from where she earned a medical degree before shifting to Pakistan. She is the founder of the Ziauddin Hospital in Karachi, where she practices gynecology.

Hadique, Colonel Mohammed
Location: Karachi
Date: May 25, 2010
Biographical Notes: Mohammad Hadique was born in 1947 during the time of partition in Assam. His father, Mohmmad Siddiq, was in the Railways and he was posted there. A month after the partition took place, they went to East Pakistan. He started his education in Bengali medium and then he went to an Urdu-medium school where he took his Matric exam. He grew up in East Pakistan and graduated from Dhaka University in 1969. He joined the Pakistani Army and relocated to West Pakistan. His father and his uncles were killed during the war in East Pakistan. His mother and five sisters escaped and crossed over to India, and on to Nepal. He, along with three brothers and one sister settled in West Pakistan. He lives in Karachi.

Haider, Zara
Location: Lahore
Date: June 28, 2005
Biographical Notes: Zara Haider was born in Dehra Dun. Her father was Syed Yaqub Shah and her mother was Sughra Shah. She was raised in Lahore by her paternal aunt, Zubaida Khatoon, because her mother was unwell. Her father was the first auditor general of Pakistan. He was posted for two years in Washington as Pakistan's representative to the World Bank, and took his family along with him. She married Khurshid Haider, who retired from the Pakistan Army as a major general and died a few years before this interview. She lives in Rawalpindi with her son Mohsin and his family.

Husain, Vice Admiral Iqtidar
Location: Naval Housing Colony, Karachi
Date: December 13, 2009
Biographical Notes: Iqtidar Husain was born in Aligarh in July 1936. He was the twelfth or thirteenth of his mother's children, the last surviving, and therefore the youngest. (Author's grandmother was the oldest, and Wajahat Husain was between them.) His father was Iftikhar Husain. His mother's family were landlords near Hapur. Iqtidar began his education at the Government School in Aligarh, a mixed educational environment. He migrated with his family to Pakistan in 1947, when he was only ten years old. His family settled in Lahore, and he had increased success in academics. After his twelfth grade, he joined the Navy and was sent to England for training, where he married his Pakistani Christian wife. He had a distinguished career in the Pakistan Navy and retired as vice chief of Naval Staff with the rank of vice admiral. He died on July 19, 2014.

Husain, Colonel Nayyar
Location: Lahore
Date: May 16, 2009
Biographical Notes: Nayyar Husain was born in Aligarh on January 16, 1936. His grandfather was Syed Tassaduq Husain, head of Intelligence in British India. His father was Syed Fasahat Husain, who studied in AMU and was captain of the Aligarh University cricket team. Nayyar Husain had ten brothers and sisters, most of whom were born in India. He did his early education in Aligarh before migrating to Pakistan in 1948. He was commissioned in the Pakistan Army in 1958, the same year that his father passed away. He married Roshan Abbas (my father's elder sister) and had four children. He retired from the Army as a colonel and went on to serve in Fauji Fertilizer before retiring in Lahore.

Husain, Major General Wajahat
Location: Lahore
Dates: 2005–8
Biographical Notes: Wajahat Husain was born in Aligarh, where his family lived in the city on a road named after his grandfather, Syed Amjad Ali. Wajahat was my great uncle, my paternal grandmother's younger brother. Wajahat did his early schooling in Minto Circle School and the Muslim University City High School before he began his university education at AMU. He passed out from AMU in 1944 and volunteered for the Air Training Corps in 1945. He was decommissioned at the end of the war and joined the Indian Military Academy in Dehra Dun. He passed out from there in 1946. Husain opted for Pakistan, but first served on the bilateral Punjab Boundary Force before settling in Pakistan and serving in Guides Cavalry. He also served as ADC to General Gracey, the second commander-in-chief of the Pakistan Army. He retired at the rank of Major General. He later served Pakistan as ambassador to Greece and then Australia. He died in February 2013.

Iqbal, Justice Javid
Location: Lahore
Date: July 13, 2006
*In author's possession.
Biographical Notes: Javid Iqbal was the son of Pakistan's poet laureate Mohammad Iqbal. He was born on October 5, 1924, in Sialkot, now in Pakistan. He was educated in the Government College of the Punjab University in Lahore, where he grew up. He completed his Ph.D. from Cambridge University and was admitted to the bar. In Pakistan, he served in the High Court and retired as Justice of the Supreme Court of Pakistan. He died on October 3, 2015.

IS, Anonymized
Location: Karachi
Dates: May 28, 2010
*In author's possession.
Biographical Notes: Mrs. IS was born in Delhi in 1929. She lost her mother when she was three months old. From then on, she lived with relatives in Meerut. Her father was

an important official in AMU. Her early education was with tutors, and she finished the Qur'an under the guidance of a maulvi and an aunt. Mrs. IS moved to Aligarh when she was fourteen years old, and completed her education there. She emigrated to Pakistan in 1948 and married a military officer. She returned to India only twice, upon the births of her children. She lived in Karachi.

Khan, Abdul Rasheed
Location: Karachi
Date: August 10, 2006
Biographical Notes: Abdul Rasheed Khan was born in Saharanpur. He completed his matriculation and started at Aligarh in 1944. As a student at Aligarh, he worked for the elections in 1945–6 and later he migrated to Pakistan in late 1947. Khan became a government servant, first serving in Sukkar District and then later with the Karachi Development Authority. He now serves on the faculty of the Sir Syed University of Engineering and Technology in Karachi.

Khan, Sahibzada Major General Yaqoob Ali
Location: Islamabad F-7/3
Date: August 7, 2006
*In author's possession.
Biographical Notes: Sahibzada Major General Yaqoob Ali Khan was born on December 20, 1920. He hails from the princely state of Rampur, where his father was the Dewan. He attended the Royal Indian Military Academy from the age of twelve and received his commission at the age of nineteen. He served in Europe and North Africa. After opting for Pakistan in 1947, he served in the military as commandant Staff College (1960) and chief of general staff (1965) before embarking on a diplomatic career as ambassador to France, Washington, and Moscow, and as foreign minister of Pakistan. He died on January 26, 2016.

Khan, Zakir Ali
Location: Karachi
Date: August 10, 2006
Biographical Notes: Zakir Ali Khan was born in the princely state of Rampur on July 8, 1926. His father served there as superintendent of police. As there was no university in Rampur, Khan was sent to Aligarh after completing his matriculation. His older brother was also there. During his stay in AMU, he was captain of the hockey team and had the opportunity to tour all over India. He graduated in Civil Engineering in 1948, and in 1949 he chose to migrate to Pakistan where there was a shortage of engineers. His mother permitted him to go, but did not follow. He initially worked in the Karachi Metropolitan Corporation until 1979 when he became chief engineer of the [Karachi] Metropolitan Corporation. He retired in 1986 as managing director of Karachi Water and Sewerage Board and had been the general secretary of the Aligarh Old Boys' Association of Pakistan from 1960 until his death. In 2009, Zakir Ali Khan was awarded the first Sir Syed Ahmad Khan International Award for lifetime achievement in support of the ideals of Sir Sayyid Ahmad Khan. He died on February 7, 2012.

Mirza, Dr. Sarfaraz Hussain
Location: Lahore
Date: July 21, 2006
Biographical Notes: Sarfaraz Hussain Mirza was born in Ferozepur, India, in 1942. His father was a policeman, and he spent his early years in the Civil Lines, in the police colony. His family migrated to Pakistan during partition, feeling the threat of violence. He is a scholar of Pakistan history and the editor of several collections of documents as well as other books including *Muslim Women's Role in the Pakistan Movement*. He is a resident scholar at the Nazaria-e-Pakistan foundation. He lives in Lahore.

Mujahid, Professor Shariful
Interviewer: Amber Abbas
Dates: May 25, 2010
Biographical Notes: Shariful Mujahid was a Pakistani Higher Education Commission Distinguished National Professor. He was born in Madras in 1926. He studied in Presidency College and later completed a master's degree in history from Madras University in 1950. He subsequently migrated, alone, to Pakistan. He received a Fulbright fellowship and attended Stanford University, where he earned an M.A. in Journalism. He returned to Pakistan and made a career there as an academic. He was the founding director of the Quaid-i-Azam Academy at Karachi University in 1976. He was an internationally known academic, especially for his work on Mohammad Ali Jinnah. He died in January 2020.

Naqvi, Mukhtar Ahmad
Location: Sir Sayyid University of Engineering and Technology
Date: May 24, 2010
*In author's possession.
Biographical Notes: Mukhtar Ahmad Naqvi hails from Sehaswan in district Badaun, UP. He was born in 1933, but his mother died when he was only two years old. He was raised by his father Rais Ahmad, a medical doctor, along with his brother and two sisters. After completing his matriculation, he began his intermediate at Aligarh University. He migrated to Pakistan in 1947, crossing the deserts of Rajasthan and Sindh. He finished his undergraduate degree at Punjab University and his M.Sc. from Canterbury University in New Zealand. He worked in the Ministry of Agriculture in Islamabad for more than twenty years and now serves as the convener of Sir Syed University of Engineering and Technology in Karachi.

Nizami, Zilley Ahmad
Location: Karachi
Date: May 24, 2010
Biographical Notes: Zilley Ahmad Nizami was born on May 25, 1931, in Amroha, India. He grew up in Meerut. He was educated at home as a child and then joined the high school and completed his intermediate in Meerut College. His family is prominently associated with Aligarh, and his was the third generation to send its sons there. He is the younger brother of Aligarh historian K. A. Nizami and their

youngest brother Taufiq taught in the Political Science Department. Z. A. Nizami was the director general of the Karachi Development Authority, president of the AMU Old Boys Association-Pakistan, and the founder chancellor of Sir Syed University of Engineering and Technology in Karachi. He died on April 7, 2013.

Qamar, Mansoor
Location: Karachi
Date: May 18, 2010
Biographical Notes: Mansoor Qamar is from Meerut, where she was the youngest of her eight brothers and sisters. Her father, Mohammad Mukrim, was a staunch Congress supporter. She attended Mohammad Ismail Girls School and Ragunath Girls' College. After completing her Matric, she went on to Meerut College for her B.A. She completed her B.Ed. at Aligarh University Training College. She secured a teaching job in Meerut and determined to stay there. However, she went to Pakistan and ended up marrying and settling there in the early 1960s. Her first marriage lasted thirteen years, and she has three children. Her husband died and she later married one of his cousins to whom she remains married today. She teaches Islamiat in St. Joseph's School and lives in Karachi.

QSM, Anonymized
Location: Karachi
Date: May 26, 2010
*In author's possession.
Biographical Notes: QSM was born in Azamgarh in June 1929. He was brought up in Banaras, but attended AMU. After partition, he traveled to Pakistan, and after holding a variety of odd jobs he joined the Army. He retired from the army but had a role in the Sir Syed University of Engineering and Technology. He died in 2011.

Rahman, Dr. Fatima Minhaj Fari
Location: Lahore (2008) and Islamabad (2010)
Date: January 4, 2008 and May 10, 2010
Biographical Notes: Fatima Fari Rahman was born in Sheikupura in Punjab. After her father's early death, her family moved to their hometown of Aligarh where she grew up and completed her education in the Abdullah College and AMU. She completed her M.Sc. in Chemistry in 1948. She taught for several years in the Women's College and later completed her Ph.D. in Organic Chemistry at the University of London. She got married in 1961 and moved to Pakistan where her husband, a Pakistan Army officer, was stationed. She worked in the Ministry of Education in Islamabad. She was the only female cofounder of the Sir Syed Memorial Society in Islamabad. She died on November 29, 2019.

Rashid, Anjuman
Location: Karachi
Date: May 19, 2010
Biographical Notes: Mrs. Anjuman Rashid hails from Rewa State (now in Madhya Pradesh). She was born in the early 1940s, and was only four or five at the time of

partition, in 1947. Her father was a medical doctor and opened his own clinic in Rewa State. She has spent her entire life in Pakistan, and believes that her father settled in well in Pakistan. She is married to Professor Shahid Rashid and lives in Karachi.

Rashid, Professor Shahid
Location: Karachi
Dates: May 19, 2010
Biographical Notes: Shahid Rashid was born in Bijnor, India, in January 1938. His father, Mohamamd Hasan, was a civil servant, the secretary of the Municipal Corporation in Bijnor. He has two brothers and two sisters. He was educated in a Muslim school and then completed his intermediate from Nagina Hindu College. He spent a year in Lucknow trying to get admission to Medical College before arriving in AMU in 1956. He was also hockey captain. He migrated to Pakistan in 1963 at the age of twenty-five after his sister married in Pakistan. After working and teaching in the United Kingdom for fifteen years and completing his Ph.D. in Bradford University, he returned to Pakistan. He is a professor of pharmacology at Karachi University.

Razzaqi, Professor Wazir Ahmad
Location: Karachi
Date: May 21, 2010
Biographical Notes: Wazir Ahmad Razzaqi was born in Meerut, a town close to Delhi, in Western UP in 1942. Most of his family migrated to Pakistan in the early 1960s. His wife is also from Meerut; they married in 1975. He initially worked as stenographer before working for the Life Insurance Corporation of India in Saharanpur and later Meerut. He is a professor of commerce and has written several books on the subject.

Saeed, Professor Ahmad
Location: Lahore
Date: July 20, 2006
Biographical Notes: Ahmad Saeed was born on July 21, 1942, in Jullunder, East Punjab, then in India. His family shifted to Lahore in 1947 via military transport. He was educated in the Government College and Punjab University He taught for many years in Islamia College, Lahore, before retiring in 2002. He has published several collections of primary documents pertaining to the Pakistan Movement. He is now a historian with the Nazaria-e-Pakistan (Ideology of Pakistan) foundation.

Servaes, Dr. Tahira Minhaj
Location: Lahore
Date: January 4, 2008
Biographical Notes: Dr. Tahira Minhaj Servaes was born in Aligarh in 1931 but spent her first ten years in Punjab. She completed her master's degree in AMU and then went to Boston University for her Ph.D. Her father, Minhajuddin, was a chief engineer in the Lahore Irrigation Department. He died when she was ten. She is the second youngest of nine siblings: three boys and six girls. She was "shipped" to Pakistan with her sisters and cousins following partition, but returned to Aligarh and stayed until 1958. She went

to Boston and completed her Ph.D. in Physics at Boston University. She married an American and settled in the United States. She has spent most of her career working in industry as a communications engineer, and she has also taught. She lives in Philadelphia.

Shafi, Brigadier Iqbal
Location: Islamabad
Date: May 9, 2010
Biographical Notes: Iqbal Shafi was born in Aligarh in 1927. His father was an Alig and a professor at the university and his mother ran a small school for the children of the university's staff. Shafi began his education in Zahoor Ward and went on to the Muslim University High School, from where he passed out in 1943 before he attended AMU. Since 1940, he was attracted to the Muslim League platform and became a member of the Baccha (Children's) Muslim League. He actively campaigned for the elections in 1945 and 1946. Shafi migrated to Pakistan in late 1947 and served as a career officer in Pakistan's army. He cofounded the Sir Syed Memorial Society in Pakistan and was active in educational development and leadership. He died on Sir Syed Day, October 17, 2019.

Umar, Major General Ghulam
Location: Karachi
Date: August 8, 2006
Biographical Notes: Ghulam Umar was born on October 1, 1922, into a family of Islamic scholars in Ambala. His father served in the Post and Telegraph Department, and Umar was mostly educated in Aligarh, but his family lived in Shimla and Delhi. He joined the army during the Second World War and opted for Pakistan in 1947 where he served in 10th Punjab Regiment (then 2nd 15th Punjab) and also as military secretary to King Faisal of Saudi Arabia. He served as a brigadier general in the Pakistan Army during the 1965 war, and he served General Yahya Khan as secretary of the National Security Council (Military Intelligence) during the 1971 war, but fell out of favor with Zulfikar Ali Bhutto and was held under house arrest in the early 1970s. After his retirement from the Pakistan Army, he has been involved in people-to-people peace diplomacy between India and Pakistan. He died on January 18, 2009.

Umar, Khadija Minhaj
Location: Lahore
Date: January 4, 2008
Biographical Notes: Khadija Minhaj Umar was born in Aligarh, India. She was educated in Aligarh, Lahore, Sargodha, and Lucknow, where she received her master's degree. She married in 1944 and settled in Lahore just before partition because her husband was based in Punjab. She taught mathematics at Islamia College, Lahore, and then at Kinnaird College, Lahore. For three years, she moved with her husband to Dhaka, East Pakistan. She visited Aligarh often throughout her life, because her mother and other family members remained there. She died on April 6, 2017.

Zaidi, Anis, and Rais Sultana
Location: Karachi
Date: May 20, 2010

Biographical Notes: Anis Zaidi was born on April 19, 1928, in Chindausi. Her sister Rais Sultana was born in 1926. The sisters were raised in Meerut where their father was an income tax lawyer. Their mother was a Muslim League activist who traveled by train to reach out to women on behalf of the League. Sultana married young and moved to Moradabad. Zaidi pursued her B.A. at Aligarh, but as she was ailing, he completed her degree as a private candidate. During partition, both sisters moved with their family to Pakistan. They both pursued higher education in Pakistan and became educators. The women are now retired and live together in Karachi.

Zuberi, Mubarak Shah
Date: May 26, 2010
Location: Karachi
Biographical Notes: Mubarak Shah Zuberi was the grandson of Dr. Sir Ziauddin, the vice chancellor of AMU during the 1940s. He was born in Meerut on October 7, 1935, and attended AMU. Zuberi's father was a civil servant who was killed in a train accident near Lucknow. After graduating from AMU, he remained in India until 1961, though much of his family migrated to Pakistan. At the request of his mother, he finally shifted to Pakistan in 1964. He was the founder secretary of the Dr. Ziauddin Memorial Society and an active member of the Sindh Red Crescent Society. He also lived and worked in the United States, in both California and New York. He died on June 2, 2011.

Zuberi, Professor Viqar Ahmad
Location: Karachi
Date: May 19, 2010
Biographical Notes: Viqar Ahmad Zuberi was born in 1938 in Lucknow. However, he did all of his early education in Moradabad before shifting to Pakistan after his intermediate. His parents ultimately migrated to Pakistan in 1966 after his father retired but his mother always lamented leaving her ancestral landholdings. Zuberi completed his higher education in Pakistan and taught zoology and environmental biology for his entire career, including two years in Iraq early on and two years in Abu Dhabi after his retirement. Professor Zuberi lives in Karachi.

Zuberi, Waqar Ahmad
Location: Karachi
Date: May 28, 2010
Biographical Notes: Waqar Ahmad Zuberi belonged to the family of Aligarh University's vice chancellor, Sir Ziauddin Ahmad, and originally hailed from Meerut. Though he never attended AMU, he was active in the Pakistan Movement as a student in Meerut.

India (2008–9)

Advani, Ram
Location: Lucknow
Date: April 4, 2009

*In author's possession.
Biographical Notes: Ram Advani was born on October 12, 1920, in Karachi. He spent his childhood in Lucknow, but earned his bachelor's degree from Lucknow University. He began teaching and serving as bursar at the Bishop Cotton School in Shimla before taking up the family business and opening a bookshop in Lahore in 1945. He fled Lahore in 1947, ultimately settling in Lucknow, where he opened a bookshop in 1948 of which he remained proprietor until his death in 2016. He was a friend to many academics and told me "A Bookshop brings people together—you meet so many people in a bookshop." He died on March 9, 2016.

Ahmad, Khwaja Shamim, and Hamida
Location: Aligarh
Date: November 19, 2009
*In author's possession.
Biographical Notes: Khwaja Shamim and Hamida Ahmad were both professors in Aligarh University. Hamida Ahmad was born in Etawah, Uttar Pradesh, on November 12, 1945. She completed her B.A. and M.A. in AMU before becoming a professor of psychology. She served as chair of the department, dean of the faculty of social science, and provost of Abdullah Hall in AMU. She died on July 20, 2017. Khwaja Shamim Ahmad was affiliated with the Non-Resident Student's Centre (NRSC Hall), which offered nonresidential students the benefits of living in halls while they were inside the campus walls. An engineering professor, he served briefly as pro-vice chancellor of AMU.

Ahmad, Syed Mohammad, and Farrukh Jalali
Location: Aligarh
Date: May 27, 2009
*In author's possession.
Biographical Notes: Syed Mohamamd Ahmad originally hailed from Hapur. His father was killed in a communal riot in 1952. Ahmad was a well-known Aligarh personality, having long served as the assistant/acting public relations officer (PRO). He completed his Ph.D. on M. Obaidullah Sindhi after retiring from the PRO office in 1996. After his retirement, he continued to live in the Old Boys Lodge, with a view of the Aligarh mosque. Many called him "Chaccha" or Uncle. He died on December 26, 2011. Furrukh Jalali was born in 1942 and his family was originally from Karachi. He was a well-respected researcher, archeaologist, and scholar of Aligarh history. He lived in Aligarh near Muzzammil Manzil.

Amin, Professor Mohammad
Location: New Delhi
Date: November 5, 2009
Biographical Notes: Mohammad Amin was born in 1928 in the United Provinces. He was a student in Aligarh during the 1940s but was not active in League election work. He earned a master's degree in history and law and became a professor in St. Stephen's College of Delhi University in 1949, where he taught for over forty years. He became a well-known medieval historian. He served as vice chancellor of Jamia Hamdard University from 1990 to 1993. He was awarded the Padma Bhushan in 2010. He is also

the father of Shahid Amin, a historian in Delhi University. He died on December 15, 2012.

Ansari, Professor Asloob Ahmad
Location: Aligarh
Date: June 5, 2008
*In author's possession.
Biographical Notes: Asloob Ahmad Ansari was born in Delhi in 1925. He passed his matriculation from Government High School, Delhi, in 1939. He joined AMU in the intermediate class the same year. He completed his intermediate in 1941, went on to earn first class in his B.A. and B.Sc. degrees in 1943, and earned a university gold medal. He also won the Marris Prize for the best marks in English in both examinations. During his tenure as a student at AMU, he was an active speaker in the University Union and won several prizes for his writing and speaking both inside and outside the university. He lived in Aftab Hostel. In 1946, he completed his M.A. in English and was appointed lecturer in the Department of English at AMU. In 1946, he left for Oxford, earning an honors degree in English Language and Literature. After returning from Oxford, he was appointed reader and, later, professor. He retired in 1987. He died on May 4, 2016.

CSI, Anonymized
Location: Aligarh
Date: June 16, 2009
*In author's possession.
Biographical Notes: CSI was born in August 1923; his family were large landholders. He began his school in 1933 in the Minto Circle School. After completing his education, he took over responsibility for the affairs of his family's state until 1952 when large estates were abolished, though he still manages some orchard operations there. During his stay at the university, he supported the Muslim League, and although his elder brother migrated to Pakistan, he did not follow. He had been in poor health and preferred to stay nearer to home. He lives in his family home in Aligarh.

Habib, Professor Irfan
Location: Aligarh
Date: June 28, 2009
Biographical Notes: Irfan Habib was born in Baroda in 1931 but grew up primarily in Aligarh where his father had been a professor since the mid-1920s. Habib began his education in Zahoor Ward and then onto Minto Circle and the Muslim University High School. His family was staunchly nationalist and close to both the Nehru family and Mahatma Gandhi. He became a professor of history at AMU after completing his D.Phil at New College, Oxford. He is currently Professor Emeritus, having retired in 1991. Still, he returns to the History Department at AMU almost daily and continues to guide students and discuss politics with his old colleagues.

Hamid, Sayyid
Location: Delhi
Date: October 29, 2009

Biographical Notes: Sayyid Hamid was born in Faizabad near Lucknow on March 28, 1920. He received his early education in Western UP. His father, Sayyid Mehdi Hassan, was a police officer. His mother was a housewife. He completed his B.A. in English Literature and M.A. in Persian from AMU in 1942. He joined the Uttar Pradesh Civil Service in 1943 and was later selected for the Indian Administrative Service in the UP cadre. He returned to AMU as vice chancellor from 1980 to 1985. He served as chancellor of Jamia Hamdard University in Delhi from 1999 to 2014. He died on December 29, 2014.

Hasan, Professor Masood-ul
Location: Aligarh
Date: March 20, 2009, and May 1, 2009
Biographical Notes: Professor Masood-ul Hasan was born in Moradabad in 1928. He completed high school from Hewat Muslim High School. His father was an employee of the Municipal Board. He completed his F.A. (intermediate) from Government Inter-College, Moradabad. He studied in the AMU from 1943 to 1947 where he completed his B.A. and M.A. in English Literature. He completed his Ph.D. in Liverpool while he was appointed as a Reader in the Department of English at AMU. He retired from AMU in 1988 after serving as professor of English, chair of Department of English, and dean of the Faculty of Arts. He also served as the proctor of the university. Professor Masood-ul Hasan has two children, Seema and Naved Masood. He died on March 9, 2019.

Khan, Professor Iftikhar Alam
Location: Aligarh
Date: June 6, 2009
Biographical Notes: Iftikhar Alam Khan first arrived in Aligarh's Minto Circle School in 1949 after his father was arrested and shortly after the partition. He found the student population much depleted by the changes wrought by 1947's migrations. His landowning family was largely split between Muslim League and communist sympathies before 1947, and both he and his elder brother Iqtidar were active in leftist student demonstrations during their tenure in Aligarh. He completed his high school in 1951 or 1952. He became a professor of museology and was active in the dramatic arts at Aligarh. He directed the Aligarh Museum and the Sir Syed Academy. He is an expert on Aligarh's architectural history, and has written several books on this subject.

Khan, Professor Iqtidar Alam
Location: Aligarh
Date: May 31, 2009
*In author's possession.
Biographical Notes: Iqtidar Alam Khan was born in a village near Qaimganj in District Farrukhabad in 1932. His father's family were landlords, though his father also maintained a small law practice. His father, Ghulam Rabbani Khan, also developed a reputation as a poet known as "Taban." His mother was a homemaker and proficient in reading Urdu and Arabic. One of his brothers, Iftikhar Alam Khan, also became a

professor in AMU, and another brother has had a political career. He first arrived in AMU in 1945, and then returned in 1950. During his first experience at Aligarh, he was initially attracted to the Muslim League idea of Pakistan, though he later became affiliated with the leftist Students' Federation. Alam became a professor of history at AMU and Department Chair. He is a well-known Marxist historian and has published extensively on medieval India. He was awarded the Itihaas Ratna Award by the Asiatic Society, Bihar, during the Indian History Congress in 2014.

Khan, Zafar Mohammad
Location: Lucknow
Date: April 4, 2009
Biographical Notes: Zafar Mohammad Khan was born in the old city of Lucknow. His grandfather came from Qaimganj, district Farrukhabad, and married in Lucknow. His father, Aziz Mohammad Khan worked in an office in the Railway Department in Lucknow and later Calcutta. He completed his early education, up to his bachelor's degree in Lucknow, and then took an engineering degree from Aligarh (1955). He lives in Lucknow.

Kidwai, Saeeda Wahid
Date: June 17, 2009
Location: Aligarh
Biographical Notes: Saeeda Waheed Kidwai was originally from Delhi but was largely raised in Aligarh by an uncle after her father's death. She had three sisters. She was admitted to the Aligarh Women's College in 1926 and was the first woman to take graduate classes in geography in AMU. She graduated in 1939 and began teaching in 1941. She taught in the Women's College and lived in Aligarh. She was widely known to those associated with Aligarh as "Saeeda Apa."

KPS, Anonymized
Location: Lucknow
Date: September 27, 2009, and October 8, 2009
Biographical Notes: KPS was born in 1931 in Hardoi. He completed his intermediate from the UP Board in 1945, and then went to AMU where he lived in V. M. Hall. He completed his intermediate, B.Sc., M.Sc., and Ph.D. by 1956. He then went to work as a scientist in National Research Institute. When I met him, he was retired and an active member of the Aligarh Old Boys' Association in Lucknow. He died in 2011.

Mathur, Arun Kumar
Location: Lucknow, India
Date: September 30, 2009
Biographical Notes: A. K. Mathur was born in 1944. He is from Jaipur. However, he moved to Aligarh in 1951 when his father became principal of Barahsini College, a local Hindu degree college. He was a student of government college until his tenth class in Aligarh city and entered AMU in 1957. He spent his career in UP State Electricity Board posted in Aligarh. His association remained with Aligarh until 1978 because his wife was teaching there. He is an engineer and lives in Lucknow, serving as senior vice president Lucknow Management Association.

Mehdi, Saeed Mirza
Location: Aligarh
Date: June 15, 2009
Biographical Notes: S. M. Mehdi hailed from Bhopal State, and was born around 1924. He received his early education through high school in Bhopal before transferring to Christchurch College in Kanpur in 1939. He later completed his M.A. from Lucknow University. Mehdi's father, Syed Mohammad Askari, was a lawyer. In Kanpur, Mehdi lived with his paternal uncle, a prominent Congress leader, but under the influence of his teacher at Christchurch College he became a socialist. Eventually he became a communist, and in Bombay in the mid-1940s he served on the editorial staff of the Communist Part of India's Urdu Weekly *Naya Zamana*. Mehdi was a member of the Progressive Writers Group and is remembered as a radical Urdu playwright. His memories of his life and community are preserved in the Door Darshan miniseries about him *Mamujan ki Diary*. He retired to Aligarh, where his daughter is a medical doctor. He died in January 2015.

Rahman, Professor Hakeem Syed Zillur
Location: Aligarh
Date: June 29, 2009
Biographical Notes: Zillur Rahman was born on July 1, 1940, in Bhopal. His father and grandfather were both Unani physicians and authors of books on the subject. He was raised in Bhopal and attended AMU, arriving in 1955. After passing out, he became a faculty member and has settled in Aligarh. He was awarded Padma Shri by the Indian government in 2006 for his contributions to Unani Medicine. In 2008, he opened the Ibn Sina Academy in his home: a library, museum, and reading room that focuses on Unani Medicine and Islamic History.

Rahman, Professor Wasi ur
Location: Aligarh
Date: November 21, 2009
*In author's possession.
Biographical Notes: Wasi ur Rahman is originally from Shamsabad, District Farrukhabad, Tehsil Qaimganj. He was born on December 27, 1927. His father was a teacher. He was the youngest of five siblings. He completed his early education in Shukohabad and his B.Sc. from Kanpur (Agra University). He first arrived in AMU in 1947–8 and completed his M.Sc. and Ph.D. He taught for some time in SUNY Albany and completed additional research work. He taught in Aligarh and was briefly pro-vice chancellor. He died on June 21, 2010.

Rizvi, Syed Saghir Ahmad
Location: Lucknow
Date: October 6, 2009
*In author's possession.
Biographical Notes: Syed Saghir Ahmad Rizvi is originally from Lucknow, the place to which his mother's relations belong. After passing high school, he joined AMU in the intermediate. He left after only a few months and completed his intermediate in

Lucknow. However, he returned to AMU to complete his engineering degree. He was active in supporting candidates in the Engineering College and Union elections and served in some posts himself. He was also captain of the Engineering College hockey team. He supported the Muslim League, but rather than migrating to Pakistan, he left for the United States shortly after completing his education. He lived and worked in the United States for several years before settling down in India.

Saeed, Ahmad
Location: Lucknow
Date: October 10, 2009
Biographical Notes: Ahmad Saeed was born in Lucknow in 1927. He was primarily raised in Aligarh and attended the Muslim University High School. He got his degree in engineering from AMU where he had served as a senior cabinet member of the Engineering College Union. He was never attracted to the Muslim League because his father was a nationalist. Saeed even read leftist and communist literature but never joined a party. During his stay at the university, he also participated in horse riding and won the Mr. University contest. He later served on the UP State Electricity Board from which he retired as director. Both of his children also attended AMU.

Shamsi, Lt. Colonel Mohsin Jalil
Location: Lucknow
Date: August 11, 2008
Biographical Notes: Colonel Shamsi belongs to Gonda; he was born in the late 1930s. His family were in business, and belonged to the Punjabi *biradari*, and were converts to Islam from several generations back. His father, Hafiz Abdul Razzaq, was a *hafiz* and a businessman, and he taught English administrators Urdu and Persian. He passed away while Shamsi was in high school. Shamsi matriculated at the Medical College in Lucknow in 1957. He joined the army and served for more than twenty-five years. He lives in Lucknow.

Sherwani, Professor Riazur Rahman
Location: Aligarh
Date: July 6, 2008, and November 20, 2009
Biographical Notes: Riazur Rahman Sherwani was born in 1923. He began his schooling in Minto Circle School in the 1930s. His family were large landholders in UP. Riazur Rahman Sherwani's early education was traditional, in Arabic, Persian, and the classical Islamic subjects. After joining school, he went on to complete his M.A. and Ph.D. in Arabic and taught both in AMU and in Kashmir University. Though his father was a well-known politician, and during the 1940s a League sympathizer, Riazur Rahman Sherwani worked on the side of Congress during the 1945–6 elections and remained committed to Indian secularism throughout his life. He lived in his family home, Habib Manzil in Aligarh, until his death on November 4, 2019.

Siddiqi, Professor Ather
Location: Aligarh
Date: May 11, 2009

Biographical Notes: Ather Siddiqi is originally from Saharanpur. He was admitted to AMU in 1947 for his intermediate. He completed his B.Sc., M.Sc., and Ph.D. in AMU and a second Ph.D. in zoology from Purdue University in 1958. As a student at AMU he supported the Muslim League. His siblings and parents all eventually migrated to Pakistan. He chose to remain in India and became a professor in AMU in 1977. He is retired and lives in Aligarh with his wife, fellow academic Dr. Zakia Siddiqi.

Siddiqi, Majid Ali
Location: Lucknow
Date: October 2, 2009
Biographical Notes: Majid Ali Siddiqi was born in 1935 in Gorakhpur, India. He arrived at AMU in 1952 to study engineering. He was also involved in sports: hurdles and hockey. He completed his B.Sc. in civil engineering in 1956. He was married in 1957. His first job was in the UP Irrigation Department as a Civil Engineer. He completed his postgraduate degree from Roorki University. Siddiqi still works after a long career with Jayaprakash Associates. He is now director, Jaypee Karcham Hydro, Corporation, Ltd.

Siddiqi, Professor Zakia
Location: Aligarh
Date: December 9, 2009
Biographical Notes: Zakia Siddiqi was born in Allahabad in 1936. Her father was an advocate who also served as an MLA. Her elder sister Saeeda Faiz was educated at Aligarh before her and went on to become a teacher. Zakia Siddiqi did her early education in her sister's school and then in Lucknow's Karamat Husain Girls' School, where she completed her intermediate in 1952. She then shifted to Aligarh's Women's College, where she lived in the hostel. She holds bachelor of education and M.Ed. degrees from the AMU. After her marriage to Ather Siddiqi, she moved to the United States and pursued an M.S.Ed. in guidance and counseling at Purdue University. After teaching for many years in the Aligarh Women's College, she became the principal and provost of Abdullah Hall. After retiring from that position, she established the Center for Women's Studies at Aligarh University and now she oversees the Aligarh Public School. She also enjoys caring for her garden.

Yunus, Mohammad
Location: Lucknow
Date: August 7, 2008
*In author's possession.
Biographical Notes: Mohammad Yunus is from Shahjahanpur. He studied at AMU from 1952 to 1955, but did not receive a degree. He opened an eyeglass lenses business in Lucknow with his brother and has made his home in Lucknow. His sons were educated at La Martiniere College and AMU.

Zaidi, Professor Zahida
Location: Aligarh
Date: November 20, 2009
*In author's possession.

Biographical Notes: Zahida Zaidi was born in Meerut on January 4, 1930. She was one of five sisters and one half-brother. Her family had deep roots in Aligarh and she was the granddaughter of both Maulana Khwaja Altaf Hussain Hali and noted social reformer Khwaja Ghulam-ul-Saqlain, but her father died when she was young. Her widowed mother and the family shifted to Panipat. Zaidi received her primary education in Panipat, and at that time she finished her Qur'an under the guidance of Maulana Hali's son, Khwaja Sajjad Husain. She earned degrees in English from AMU as well as B.A. and M.A. degrees from Cambridge University. She became a professor of English in AMU and was well known as a poet and a playwright. She died on January 11, 2011.

Bangladesh (2010)

Akhtaruzzaman, Professor Mohammad
Location: Dhaka
Date: March 10, 2010
*This interview was not recorded.
Biographical Notes: Akhtaruzzaman was born in Borguna, in southern Bangladesh (then East Pakistan), in 1961. His father was a teacher who later became a politician, and his mother was a housewife, but had a primary education. He has two brothers and three sisters. Akhtaruzzaman completed his B.A. and M.A. in Dhaka University before he went to AMU in 1995 to study Medieval History with Iqtidar Husain Siddiqi. He completed his Ph.D. in 1997. At the time of the interview, he was chair of the Department of Islamic History and Culture in Dhaka University, and in 2017 he became vice chancellor of the university.

Baaquie, Wing Commander M.A.
Location: Dhaka
Date: March 22 and April 7, 2010
*In author's possession.
Biographical Notes: M.A. Baaquie was born on December 28, 1917, in Fardabad, Pargana Bardakhat, in Comilla. He was born and brought up in East Bengal, and his father was Moulana Muhammad Ali Akbar. M. A. Baaquie holds an MSc degree in physics (gold medal) from AMU in 1941 and joined the Royal Indian Air Force in 1942; he went on to be one of the founding officers of the Pakistan Air Force in 1947. He resigned from the Pakistan Air Force in 1960 and joined Philips, retiring as chairman of Philips Bangladesh in 1975. In 1971, M. A. Baaquie was imprisoned due to his participation in the liberation war for Bangladesh. He died in Dhaka on August 10, 2014.

Choudhri, Saima
Location: Dhaka
Date: April 6, 2010
Biographical Notes: Saima Choudhri is a poet originally from Sylhet, where she was born in 1930. After fourth grade, she shifted to Calcutta and attended a Muslim girls' school. Her father was a Muslim League leader, and after partition the family shifted to Dhaka, where she completed her education in Eden College. She completed her

intermediate degree before marrying Waheeduddin Choudhri, and he supported her as she completed more education later. She has published several books of poetry. She lives in Dhaka.

Choudhri, Engineer Waheeduddin
Location: Dhaka
Date: April 6, 2010
Biographical Notes: Waheeduddin Choudhri was born in Sylhet. He attended Aligarh University for engineering from 1946 to 1949. He held leftist sympathies and was active in the student movement, even attending an All India Students' Federation rally in Delhi in January 1947. He settled in East Pakistan after completing his AMU education and became an engineer for the government. He later supported the movement for the independence of Bangladesh. He lives in Dhaka.

Chowdhury, Salahuddin
Location: Dhaka
Date: April 10, 2010
Biographical Notes: Salahuddin Chowdhury was born in Sylhet in 1928 and was the youngest of six siblings. He passed his matriculation from Sylhet Government High School in 1943 and got his intermediate degree from Sylhet College before setting out for Aligarh. In Aligarh, he lived in Sir Syed Hall, and he passed out in 1949. Chowdhury left for Scotland in 1949 to study jute technology at Dundee Technical College. When he returned to East Pakistan in 1953, he worked four years in the Adamjee Jute Mill. Then, from there, he went to Bhawani Jute Mill. Since his retirement he has consulted for the World Bank. He served as president of the Aligarh Old Boys' Association, Bangladesh, in 2009–10.

Khan, Mohiuddin
Location: Dhaka
Date: March 28, 2010
Biographical Notes: Mohiuddin Khan was born in Sylhet in 1924. His father was a police inspector, and as he was growing up, they lived in different places throughout Sylhet and Assam. He passed his matriculation in 1941 and his intermediate from Calcutta University. He completed his bachelor's degree in 1945 from M. C. College in Assam. Then, due to a shortage of seats for Muslims in engineering colleges, he applied to Aligarh University. During his stay at Aligarh, he was involved with the leftist Students' Federation and even attended conferences in New Delhi. He was also a supporter of Pakistan. After completing his engineering degree in 1949, he settled in East Pakistan. For most of his career, he served in the East Pakistan government in the Communications and Building Department. Until his retirement in 1982, he was a government engineer and, finally, chief engineer of the Public Works Department. At the time of our interview, he was serving as president of the Aligarh Old Boys' Association, Dhaka.

Rahman, Habibur
Location: Dhaka
Date: February 20, 2010, and April 9, 2010

Biographical Notes: Habibur Rahman was born in Dhaka on January 1, 1925. His father was in charge of the Lal Bagh Police Station, but his family belonged to village Munshiganj outside of Dhaka. He passed his matriculation from Calcutta University, and his father sent him on a tour of North India by train. After that, he began his education at Aligarh in 1944, and he lived in Sir Syed East. During his time at Aligarh, he tried to learn to fly in preparation for military service, and he was very involved in Muslim League activities. After he returned to East Pakistan in 1949, he tried to join the Air Force to become a pilot but he was deemed too small at only ninety pounds! He was later active in the Awami League and supported the independence of Bangladesh in 1971. Two of his brothers were killed during the war. He fled to India until Mujibur Rahman established his government in 1971. Rahman became an advocate and cared for his mother for much of his adult life, marrying quite late.

Rashid, Mohammad Abdur
Date: March 29, 2010
Location: Dhaka
*In author's possession.
Biographical Notes: M. A. Rashid hailed from Lucknow in North India; he was born in 1921. He studied in Amir Daula Islamia High School. At the age of seventeen, in 1938, he participated in the Lucknow session of the Muslim League, serving water to the delegates. He was the first in his family to attend AMU. After passing out from Aligarh in 1943, he took a job with M. M. Ispahani, Ltd. and settled in Calcutta. After communal riots in 1950, he fled to Dhaka, East Pakistan, and settled there, "because it was Pakistan." In the early 1950s, he started his own business trading in jute. In 1954, he joined the East Pakistan Stock Exchange. Though he planned to leave Dhaka in 1971 when Bangladesh became independent, his fellow Aligs, General M. A. G. Osmani (leader of Bangladesh Liberation Forces) and Captain Mansoor Ali (Bangladesh's first prime minister), and neighbors promised to protect him and prevented him from leaving, even getting police officers deputed to guard his house! The Stock Exchange was closed from 1971 to 1975 during which time businesses were nationalized. After liberalization, he returned to his work in the Stock Exchange. He long held a position as a director of the Stock Exchange.

Siddiqui, Masooda
Location: Dhaka
Date: March 12, 2010
*In author's possession.
Biographical Notes: Masooda Siddiqui was born in Faridpur in the early 1930s. She was seventy-seven at the time of this interview. She grew up in Faridpur and Calcutta but fled Calcutta in 1946. She was married in 1948. After her marriage, she moved with her husband to Kulna. I met her in Dhaka. She died on September 11, 2015.

Notes

Acknowledgments

1 https://kentuckyoralhistory.org/ark:/16417/xt7p2n4zkn0m

Preface

1 Wajahat Husain, Interviewed by Amber Abbas, Lahore, Pakistan, June 13, 2005, 2. Unless otherwise noted, interviews included in this book are archived in the *Partition's First Generation Oral History Project*, Louie B. Nunn Center for Oral History, University of Kentucky Libraries. https://kentuckyoralhistory.org/ark:/16417/xt7p2n4zkn0m
2 Ibid., 1–2. A version of this narrative also appears in his published memoir. Major General Syed Wajahat Husain, *1947: Before, During, After* (Lahore: Ferozsons, 2010), 16.
3 As a discipline, oral history seeks to preserve "an in-depth account of personal experience and reflections, with sufficient time allowed for the narrators to give their story the fullness they desire." Those whose memories are recorded in the oral history are usually referred to as Narrators. "Principles and Best Practices," *Oral History Association*, 2009. https://www.oralhistory.org/about/principles-and-practices-revised-2009/#best
4 The 1947 Independence and Partition of India and Pakistan, I will argue, is best understood as a long period of transformation in the subcontinent, of which the events of 1947 were only a part.
5 Wajahat Husain, Interview, June 13, 2005, 4.
6 Ibid., 18.
7 Husain, *1947*, 54–76.
8 Wajahat Husain, Interviewed, June 14, 2005, 15.
9 Ibid.
10 See the appendix for brief biographies.
11 The Oral History Association notes in its "Principles and Best Practices" that "Oral history interviews are historical documents that are preserved and made accessible to future researchers and members of the public." "Principles and Best Practices," *Oral History Association*, 2009.

Introduction

1 Throughout, I address the multiplicity of events that might be considered part of the history of partitioning the subcontinent. Therefore, unless I am referring to the

bureaucratic events that took place on August 14–15, 1947, I avoid setting "Partition" apart with a capital "P," as a unique and isolated event.

2 Arthur G. Neal, *National Trauma and Collective Memory: Major Events in the American Century* (Armonk: M.E. Sharpe, 1998), xi.

3 Tan and Kudaisya note the difficulty that both the Indian and the Pakistani states have in trying to incorporate partition and its violence into a continuous national history. In this context it seems fitting that during the fiftieth anniversary of partition, the dead were honored with a moment of silence. Tai Yong Tan and Gyanesh Kudaisya, *The Aftermath of Partition in South Asia* (London: Routledge, 2000), 2–3.

4 Even as a practical consideration, partition's migrations carried on in earnest through 1947 and 1948 (my own family left Aligarh, India, in October 1947) and up through the 1950s, and even into the 1960s in response to communal riots in both East (Pakistan) and West (India) Bengal. Willem van Schendel, *A History of Bangladesh* (Cambridge: Cambridge University Press, 2009), 132; Dipesh Chakrabarty, "Remembered Villages: Representations of Hindu-Bengali Memories in the Aftermath of Partition," *South Asia* 18 (1995): 109–29. Vazira Fazila-Yacoobali Zamindar, *The Long Partition and the Making of Modern South Asia* (New York: Columbia University Press, 2007). Sarmila Bose's work on the 1971 Bangladesh War demonstrates the danger of disconnecting the history of the war from its political antecedents. Sarmila Bose, *Dead Reckoning: Memories of the 1971 Bangladesh War* (New York: Columbia University Press, 2011).

5 Vazira Zamindar has used this strategy by examining the experience of "divided families." Zamindar, *The Long Partition*.

6 It is generally accepted that ten to fifteen million people migrated and up to a million died. Urvashi Butalia, *The Other Side of Silence: Voices from the Partition of India* (Durham: Duke University Press, 2000).

7 The official estimate of abducted women includes 50,000 women held in India and 33,000 Hindu and Sikh women held in Pakistan. The recovery numbers were much lower, "12,552 for India and 6,272 for Pakistan." Ritu Menon and Kamla Bhasin, *Borders & Boundaries: Women in India's Partition* (New Brunswick: Rutgers University Press, 1998), 70.

8 David Gilmartin, "Partition, Pakistan and South Asian History: In Search of a Narrative," *The Journal of Asian Studies* 57, no. 4 (November 1998): 1070.

9 Arthur Kleinman, "The Violences of Everyday Life: The Multiple Forms and Dynamics of Social Violence," in *Violence and Subjectivity*, ed. Veena Das, et al. (Berkeley: University of California Press, 2000), 228.

10 Gadi BenEzer, "Trauma Signals in Life Stories," in *Trauma and Life Stories: International Perspectives*, ed. Selma Leydesdorff, et al. (London and New York: Routledge, 1999), 30.

11 Tim Cole, "(Re)Placing the Past: Spatial Strategies of Retelling Difficult Stories," *The Oral History Review* Vol. 42, no. 1 (Winter/Spring 2015): 30–49.

12 Devika Chawla, *Home, Uprooted: Oral Histories of India's Partition* (New York: Fordham University Press, 2014), 38.

13 In both 2010 and 2019, as verdicts on the use of the land upon which the Babri Masjid stood—it was demolished by a Hindu mob in 1992—the *absence* of unrest in AMU stood in contrast to expectations that the verdicts could result in more communal violence of the kind that affected North India in the 1990s. "Aligarh Breathes Easy after Two Days of Anxiety," *The Asian Age Online*, October 1, 2010.

14 Though the narrative of rupture is powerful, some have recognized its generational impact. Purnima Mankekar, for instance, born after partition, has described herself

as a "second-generation survivor" and said "the violence never died down." Purnima Mankekar, *Screening Culture, Viewing Politics: An Ethnography of Television, Womanhood and Nation in Postcolonial India* (Durham, NC and London: Duke University Press, 1999), 289.

15 Joya Chatterji, "New Directions in Partition Studies," *History Workshop Journal*, Vol. 67 no.1 (Spring 2009): 213–20.

16 Gyanendra Pandey, "Partition and Independence in Delhi: 1947-48," *Economic and Political Weekly*, September 6–12, 1997: 2261–71. For other studies of "high-profile" sites, see Butalia, *The Other Side of Silence*. Veena Das, ed., *Mirrors of Violence: Communities, Riots and Survivors in South Asia* (Delhi: Oxford University Press, 1990); Menon and Bhasin, *Borders & Boundaries*; Gyanendra Pandey, *Remembering Partition: Violence, Nationalism, and History in India* (Cambridge and New York: Cambridge University Press, 2001).

17 Ahmad Salim, *Lahore: 1947* (Lahore: Sang-e-Meel Publications, 2003). Ian Talbot, *Divided Cities: Partition and Its Aftermath in Lahore and Amritsar 1947-1957* (Oxford: Oxford University Press, 2006).

18 Tim Creswell, *In Place/out of Place: Geography, Ideology, and Transgression* (Minneapolis: University of Minnesota Press, 1996).

19 Paul Brass's work on riots in Aligarh argues that violence became more frequent in Aligarh city after 1947 (and as a result of it), but notes the absence of violence there during partition. Paul R. Brass, *The Production of Hindu-Muslim Violence in Contemporary India* (Seattle: University of Washington Press, 2003).

20 Meghna Guha Thakurta, "Uprooted and Divided," *Seminar: Porous Bodies, Divided Selves*, no. 510 (February 2002): 55.

21 Wajahat Husain, Interview, June 13, 2005, 17.

22 This story about opportunity and the lack of it is remarkably similar to many told by Aligarh graduates who settled in Pakistan and remarkably different from the majority of the best-known stories of partition displacement. The only case I can recall: Urvashi Butalia recounts the story of her uncle who remained in Pakistan, converted to Islam, married, and raised his children there. When he explained his reasoning, he was not motivated by a desire to profit from the family's abandoned property as his sister suspected, rather he said, "I'd had little education. What would I have done in India? I had no qualifications, no job, nothing to recommend me." Butalia, *The Other Side of Silence*, 28.

23 Guha Thakurta, "Uprooted and Divided," 54.

24 Ather Siddiqi, Interviewed by Amber Abbas, Aligarh, India, May 11, 2009, 7.

25 Irfan Habib, Interviewed by Amber Abbas, Aligarh, India, June 28, 2009, 11.

26 Zafar Mohammad Khan, interviewed by Amber Abbas, Lucknow, India, April 4, 2009, 7.

27 The intimate orbit of the Aligarh campus, however, has not been free from conflict in independent India. Inside the campus, it has been plagued by competition between conservative Muslim and Marxist elements, and outside, both its minority and nationalist character have been challenged. Fatima Fari Rahman, Interviewed by Amber Abbas, Lahore, Pakistan, January 4, 2008. Ather Siddiqi, Interview, May 11, 2009. Iqtidar Alam Khan, Interviewed by Amber Abbas, Aligarh, India, May 31, 2009.

28 Khadija Minhaj Umar, Interviewed by Amber Abbas, Lahore, Pakistan, January 4, 2008. Fatima Fari Rahman, Interview, January 4, 2008. Ather Siddiqi, Interview, May 11, 2009. The film *Garam Hawa* (1973) portrays the terrible tension for a young Indian Muslim girl betrothed to her cousin who moved to Pakistan as she waits for

him to return for her. The film was based on a short story by Ismat Chugtai, who attended the Aligarh Women's College and was adapted for film by Kaifi Azmi.

29 Abdul Rasheed Khan, Interviewed by Amber Abbas, Karachi, Pakistan, August 10, 2006, 1. Sarfaraz Husain Mirza, at that time a child, remembered violence in the East Punjabi city of Ferozepur. Sarfaraz Husain Mirza, Interviewed by Amber Abbas, Lahore, Pakistan, July 21, 2006, 3. See also Amber Abbas, "Thinking through Partition: Finishing the Narrative (Unpublished Master's Thesis)," (Austin: The University of Texas at Austin, 2006).

30 Ather Siddiqi, Interview, May 11, 2009, 5. Zahida Zaidi, Interviewed by Amber Abbas, Aligarh, India, November 20, 2009, 7. Interview in author's possession. On disruptions in Meerut, see: Mansoor Qamar, Interviewed by Amber Abbas, Karachi, Pakistan, May 18, 2010. Mrs. I. S. (Anonymized), Interviewed by Amber Abbas, Karachi, Pakistan, May 28, 2010. Interview in author's possession. Anis Zaidi and Rais Sultana, Interviewed by Amber Abbas, Karachi, Pakistan, May 20, 2010.

31 Sindhi Voices Project www.sindhivoices.org

32 Uditi Sen, *Citizen Refugee: Forging the Indian Nation after Partition* (Cambridge: Cambridge University Press, 2018).

33 Anna Bigelow, "Punjab's Muslims: The History and Significance of Malerkotla," *International Journal of Punjab Studies* 12, no. 1 (2005): 63–94.

34 Ilyas Chattha, *Partition and Locality: Violence, Migration, and Development in Gujranwala and Sialkot, 1947-1961* (Karachi: Oxford University Press, 2011).

35 Pradeep Kumar Bose, "Partition—Memory Begins Where History Ends," in *Reflections on Partition in the East*, ed. Ranabir Samaddar (Calcutta: Vikas Publishing House, 1997), 78.

36 Pippa Virdee, "Remembering Partition: Women, Oral Histories and the Partition of 1947," *Oral History* 41, no. 2 (Autumn 2013): 49–62. Furrukh Khan, "Speaking Violence: Pakistani Women's Narratives of Partition," in *Gender, Conflict and Migration*, ed. Navnita Chadha Behera (New Delhi: SAGE Publications Pvt., Ltd., 2006). Nighat Said Khan, Rubina Saigol, and Afiya Shehrbano Zia, *Locating the Self: Perspectives on Women and Multiple Identities*, Women's Studies Journal Series (Lahore: ASR Publications, 1994).

37 Chawla, *Home, Uprooted*. Ravinder Kaur, *Since 1947: Partition Narratives among Punjabi Migrants of Delhi* (Delhi: Oxford University Press, 2007).

38 M. A. Jinnah, "Message to the Musalmans of the Frontier Province, November 27, 1945," in *Speeches and Writings of Mr. Jinnah* ed. Jamil-ud-din Ahmad, 2 vols., vol. 2 (Lahore: Sh. Muhammad Ashraf, 1964), 247. Iqbal Shafi, Interviewed by Amber Abbas, Rawalpindi, Pakistan, May 9, 2010, 13.

39 G. D. Khosla, *Stern Reckoning: A Survey of the Events Leading up to and Following the Partition of India* (Delhi: Oxford University Press, 1989 [1949]). Penderel Moon, *Divide and Quit: An Eye-Witness Account of the Partition of India* (Delhi: Oxford University Press, 1998 [1961]).

40 Sukeshi Kamra, *Bearing Witness: Partition, Independence, End of the Raj* (Calgary: University of Calgary Press, 2002), 11.

41 Nicholas Mansergh, ed., *The Transfer of Power 1942-7*, Transfer of Power (London: Her Majesty's Stationary Office, 1970-1982).

42 Saadat Hasan Manto's short story "Mishtake" encapsulates the consequences. In its entirety: "Ripping the belly cleanly, the knife moved in a straight line down to the midriff, in the process slashing the cord which held the man's pajamas in place. The one with the knife took one look and exclaimed regretfully, 'Oh no! . . . Mishtake!'"

Saadat Hasan Manto, *A Manto Panorama: A Representative Collection of Saadat Hasan Manto's Fiction and Non-Fiction*, trans. Khalid Hasan (Lahore: Sang-e-Meel Publications, 2000), 62.

43 Pandey, in particular, deploys literature on memory and trauma from the Holocaust to suggest that similarly Partition may be a "limit case" of historiography, an episode so horrifying it is unique. Pandey, *Remembering Partition*, 45.

44 "Principles," OHA.

45 Lewis A. Coser, "Introduction to on Collective Memory by Maurice Halbwachs," in *On Collective Memory*, ed. Lewis A. Coser (Chicago and London: University of Chicago Press, 1992), 26.

46 Alessandro Portelli, "The Peculiarities of Oral History," *History Workshop Journal*, Vol. 12, no. 1 (Autumn 1981): 100.

47 Ibid. As Dipesh Chakrabarty evocatively argued with regard to the essays he analyzed: "These are undoubtedly essays written in the spirit of mourning, part of the collective and public grieving through which the Hindus who were displaced from East Bengal came to terms with their new conditions in Calcutta. Yet we have to remember that this grieving was being publicized in print, perhaps in the cause of the politics of refugee rehabilitation in West Bengal in the 1950s." Thus, even in the newspaper, a fact can be much more than just a fact. Chakrabarty, "Remembered Villages," 322.

48 And, as I discuss in Chapter 3, they did talk about trains, but not trains crossing the Punjab border. Many narrators talked about the importance of trains in connecting them to other places in UP where they engaged in electioneering, and showed how trains became particularly volatile places for Muslims after Partition.

49 Susan Crane, "Writing the Individual Back into Collective Memory," *The American Historical Review* 102, no. 5 (December 1997): 1373.

50 Ibid., 1378.

51 Michel-Rolph Trouillot, *Silencing the Past: Power and the Production of History* (Boston: Beacon Press, 1995), 16.

52 Pandey, *Remembering Partition*, 6–7.

53 Philip Oldenburg, "'A Place Insufficiently Imagined': Language, Belief, and the Pakistan Crisis of 1971," *Journal of Asian Studies* 44, no. 4 (August 1985): 711–33.

54 Ayesha Jalal, "Conjuring Pakistan: History as Official Imagining," *International Journal of Middle East Studies* 27, no. 1 (February 1995): 73–89.

55 Menon and Bhasin, *Borders and Boundaries*.

56 In Intizar Husain's novel, Ammi locked the storeroom in the abandoned home, in India, but once she realized the key might be lost (twenty-five years after partition), she experienced a sense of partition's finality that she tied to her own mortality. The key was lost, and she would die in Pakistan. Intizar Husain, *Basti*, trans. Frances W. Pritchett (New Delhi: Indus, 1995), 147.

57 Butalia, *The Other Side of Silence*, 5.

58 Venkat Dhulipala's recent work has suggested that despite the messiness of the public sphere, by the mid-1940s a clear vision had emerged for Pakistan as "a sovereign Islamic state, a New Medina," even "an Islamic utopia that would be the harbinger for renewal and rise of Islam in the modern world." I suspect he both overstates the case for Islam and, despite his assiduous research, neglects the persistence of multiple imaginings that I analyze here. Venkat Dhulipala, *Creating a New Medina: State Power, Islam and the Quest for Pakistan in Late Colonial North India* (New Delhi: Cambridge University Press, 2015), 4.

59 These groups were supported by Yahoo Groups listservs.

60 I have also written about this in my M.A. Thesis submitted to the University of Texas in 2006. Abbas, "Thinking through Partition." See also Amber Abbas, "Belonging and the Beginning of the Past in Pakistan," in *Hidden Histories: Religion and Reform in South Asia*, ed. Syed Akbar Hyder and Manu Bhagavan (Delhi: Primus Books, 2018), 27–47.

61 Pandey, *Remembering Partition*, 4–5.

62 Some narrators described their efforts to hide this identity, especially on trains, by not wearing the Aligarh sherwani in public, or by inscribing a marked Hindu name into the books they carried. See Chapter 4. Waheeduddin Choudhri, Interviewed by Amber Abbas, April 6, 2010, 5. Mohammad Amin, Interviewed by Amber Abbas, New Delhi, India, November 5, 2009, 6.

63 See Appendix for biographical data on each of the narrators and for abstracts of the interviews.

64 Throughout the body of this book, the first time I cite a narrator, both in text and in citation I reference their full name and, where appropriate, their rank. I have also included one- to two-sentence biographies in the footnotes the first time a narrator is quoted. The question of a professional rank seems to interfere with the fact that at the time of the stories they are recounting, they were all students, not differentiated by rank. The risk of including their rank is to unwittingly authorize certain narratives over others, and this is certainly not my intent. Thus, in the body of the text, I have tried to be consistent in naming the narrators without their rank. This should not be construed as a lack of respect for their status. During our interviews and conversations, I would address people, as is customary in the Indian subcontinent, by their least common name. On norms of naming, see Marshall G. S. Hodgson, *The Venture of Islam: Conscience and History in a World Civilization*, 3 vols., vol. 1, The Classical Age of Islam (Chicago and London: University of Chicago Press, 1974), 17.

65 A. K. Mathur is an exception as the only non-Muslim Alig I was able to interview. A. K. Mathur, Interviewed by Amber Abbas, Lucknow, India, September 30, 2009.

66 Yasmin Saikia, "Strangers, Friends and Peace: The Women's World of Abdullah Hall, Aligarh Muslim University," in *Women and Peace in the Muslim World: Gender, Agency and Influence*, ed. Yasmin Saikia and Chad Haines (London: I.B. Tauris, 2015), 298.

67 Iqtidar Alam Khan, Interview, May 31, 2009, 8. Zafar Mohammad Khan, Interview, April 4, 2009, 3.

68 Though his father was Sunni, his uncle Fasahat was Shi'i, so Wajahat attended whichever service was most convenient! Wajahat consistently sought to undermine the need to ascribe to sectarian divisions, arguing that "it has been made quite a subject which it need not be and should not be." Wajahat Husain, Interview, June 13, 2005, 12.

69 This was especially true of Y. M. and Colonel Shamsi in Lucknow. Y. M. (Anonymized), Interviewed by Amber Abbas, Lucknow, India, 2008. Interview in author's possession. Mohsin Jalil Shamsi, Interviewed by Amber Abbas, Lucknow, India, August 11, 2008.

70 Business cards often identify people as "Alig" as an Oxford graduate might be "Oxon." In secondary scholarship, they are sometimes called "Aligarian" or "Aligarh Old Boys" (even if they are women).

71 There are a handful of exceptions: Pakistani scholars Ahmad Rafique, Ahmed Saeed, and Sarfaraz Hussein Mirza; Bangladeshi professor of English Akhtaruzzaman;

Indian engineer A. K. Mathur, Lucknow bookstore owner Ram Advani; and Indian communist S. M. Mehdi.
72 For more on the Women's College, see Gail Minault, *Secluded Scholars: Women's Education and Muslim Social Reform in Colonial India* (Delhi and New York: Oxford University Press, 1998).
73 As David Lelyveld and Gail Minault have shown, in its early years, AMU students primarily came from prominent princely, landed, or service gentry families. David Lelyveld, *Aligarh's First Generation: Muslim Solidarity in British India* (Princeton: Princeton University Press, 1978). Gail Minault and David Lelyveld, "The Campaign for a Muslim University, 1898-1920," *Modern Asian Studies* 8, no. 2 (1974): 145–89; "The Campaign for a Muslim University, 1898-1920," in *Gender, Language and Learning: Essays in Indo-Muslim Cultural History* (Ranikhet: Permanent Black, 2009).
74 A. K. Mathur also came from an educator's family. His father was the principal of a Hindu college in Aligarh city. Mathur enrolled at Aligarh for his Intermediate in 1957, and passed out with his M.Sc. in 1965. After his marriage, his wife taught in Aligarh and so they remained in the city until 1978. However, because he is Hindu and so much younger than the majority of informants, his interview figures only minorly here. A. K. Mathur, Interview, September 30, 2009.
75 The Aligarians I interviewed at the Sir Syed University of Engineering and Technology in Karachi, Pakistan (including Z. A. Nizami, Abdul Rasheed Khan, Zakir Ali Khan and others), are indeed educationists now, but began their careers in other professions.
76 Saeeda Kidwai, Interviewed by Amber Abbas, Aligarh, India, June 17, 2009. Khaliq Ahmad Nizami, *History of the Aligarh Muslim University (1920-1945)* (Karachi: Sir Syed University Press, 1998). See also Shan Mohammad, *Glimpses of Muslim Education in India: Peeping through the Convocation Addresses of the Aligarh Muslim University*, 2 vols., vol. 2 (New Delhi: Anmol Publications Pvt. Ltd., 2006), 150–6.
77 Niha Masih, "Why Some Women Can't Enter the Aligarh Muslim University Library," *NDTV (online)*, November 11, 2014. https://www.ndtv.com/india-news/why-some-women-cant-enter-the-aligarh-muslim-university-library-691874. Library Brochure https://www.amu.ac.in/pdf/amulib/brochure_new.pdf Opening Hours https://www.amu.ac.in/pdf/amulib/opening_hours.htm. Last Accessed September 2019.
78 Wazir Ahmad Razzaqi, Interviewed by Amber Abbas, Karachi, Pakistan, May 21, 2010.
79 Khadija Minhaj Umar, Interview, January 4, 2008. Fatima Fari Rahman, Interview, January 4, 2008.
80 Majid Ali Siddiqi laid the blame for status disparity between Muslims and Others on the caste system, corruption, and communalism, all of which, he said, have intensified since 1947. Mohammad Amin told me that association with Aligarh was a "black mark" on your record in the years after 1947. Majid Ali Siddiqi, Interviewed by Amber Abbas, Lucknow, India, October 2, 2009, 7. Mohammad Amin, Personal Communication with Amber Abbas, November 1, 2009.
81 Only M. A. Rashid originally hailed from Lucknow, in UP, and was a native Urdu speaker.
82 As I discuss further in Chapter 5, food was a frequent source of discontent for students. Bengali students especially missed the rice and fish that were typical of their diets at home, and lamented the bread (*roti*)-heavy diet in Aligarh.
83 Irfan Habib, "Irfan Habib: The Indian Variant of Secularism Opens the Door to Majority Communalism," ed. Ajaz Ashraf (Scroll.In, 2015). http://scroll.in/article/

748241/irfan-habib-the-indian-variant-of-secularism-opens-the-door-to-majority-communalism

84. Amber Abbas, "A Living Legacy: Sir Sayyid Today," in *The Cambridge Companion to Sir Sayyid Ahmed Khan*, ed. Yasmin Saikia and M. Raisur Rahman (Cambridge: Cambridge University Press, 2019), 255–72.
85. David Lelyveld, "Three Aligarh Students: Aftab Ahmad Khan, Ziauddin Ahmad, and Muhammad Ali," *Modern Asian Studies* 9, no. 2 (1975): 232. See also Minault, *Secluded Scholars*.
86. Ahmad Saeed, Interview with Amber Abbas, Lucknow, India, October 10, 2009, 8.
87. Riazur Rahman Sherwani, Interview with Amber Abbas, Aligarh, India, November 20, 2009.
88. Irfan Habib, Interview, June 28, 2009, 8.
89. Sarfaraz Husain Mirza, Interview, July 21, 2006, 6.
90. Tariq Abbas, Interviewed by Amber Abbas, Austin, United States, May 21, 2011, 4. https://www.saada.org/item/20110918-363
91. Alessandro Portelli, *The Death of Luigi Trastulli and Other Stories: Form and Meaning in Oral History* (Albany: State University of New York Press, 1991), 61.
92. My father left Pakistan in 1959 for the United States and lived the rest of his life abroad, though we visited Pakistan frequently. Tariq Abbas, Interview, May 21, 2011.
93. Portelli, "The Peculiarities of Oral History," 102.

Chapter 1: Defining the Aligarh Muslim University

1. Syed Ahmad Khan, "Translation of the Report of the Members of the Select Committee for the Better Diffusion and Advancement of Learning among the Muhammadans of India, April 15, 1872," in *The Aligarh Movement: Basic Documents, 1864-1898*, ed. Shan Muhammad (Meerut and New Delhi: Meenakshi Prakashan, 1978), 373.
2. Lelyveld, *Aligarh's First Generation*, 318.
3. Asloob Ahmad Ansari, Interviewed by Amber Abbas, Aligarh, India, July 5, 2008, 14. Interview in author's possession. Asloob Ahmad Ansari joined AMU in 1937 and completed his B.A. in 1943. In 1946, he completed his M.A. in English and became a Lecturer in 1947. He went to Oxford where he received an honors degree in English Language and Literature. He became a professor of English in AMU and retired in 1987. He died in 2016.
4. Abbas, "A Living Legacy: Sir Sayyid Today," 255–72.
5. Zakir Ali Khan, Interviewed by Amber Abbas, Karachi, Pakistan, August 10, 2006, 10. Zakir Ali Khan was born in Rampur in 1926 and graduated from Aligarh in 1948 with a degree in Civil Engineering. He migrated to Pakistan in 1949 where he served as first assistant and later chief engineer in the Karachi Metropolitan Corporation. He was a founder and vice chancellor of the Sir Syed University of Engineering and Technology in Karachi. In 2008, he was awarded the inaugural Sir Syed Ahmad Khan International Award of AMU. He died in 2012.
6. In 2005, as Zakir Ali Khan presented me a copy of his book *Riwayat-e-Aligarh* (The Traditions of Aligarh), he told me that the book was given to every incoming student at the Sir Syed University of Engineering and Technology in Karachi so that "He may become Aligarian." Zakir Ali Khan, Interview, August 10, 2006, 5.

7 The university was exclusively male until the late 1930s when a few women were admitted to postgraduate classes, and even until after independence, female students did not reside on the same campus as men.
8 The standard (and best) history of the early years of the institution is Lelyveld, *Aligarh's First Generation*. For the history of its transformation from the Muhammadan Anglo-Oriental College to the AMU, see Minault and Lelyveld, "The Campaign for a Muslim University, 1898-1920," *Modern Asian Studies*; "The Campaign for a Muslim University, 1898-1920," in *Gender, Language and Learning*.
9 Dominique-Sila Khan, *Crossing the Threshold: Understanding Religious Identities in South Asia* (London: I.B. Tauris, 2004), 70.
10 Minault, *Secluded Scholars*, 50.
11 For an in-depth examination of women's education in India, see ibid.
12 Ibid., 17.
13 Rafi Ahmad Alavi, *Translation of Hayat-I-Jawed: A Biographical Account of Sir Syed Ahmad Khan by Altaf Husain Hali* (Aligarh: Aligarh Muslim University Press, 2008), 6.
14 Ibid., 18.
15 Khalid Bin Sayeed, *Pakistan: The Formative Phase, 1857-1948*, 2nd ed. (London and New York: Oxford University Press, 1968), 13.
16 Neal, *National Trauma and Collective Memory*, xi.
17 Ibid., 37.
18 Thomas R. Metcalf, *The Aftermath of Revolt: India, 1857-1870* (Princeton: Princeton University Press, 1964), 47.
19 Heather Streets, *Martial Races: The Military, Race, and Masculinity in British Imperial Culture, 1857-1914* (Manchester: Manchester University Press, 2004), 27.
20 Though Muslims in India do not adhere to a rigid "caste" system as it is perceived in the Hindu tradition, Muslim social hierarchy is marked by bloodlines that correspond to status, including "Sayyid," which indicates direct blood relation to Mohammad, the prophet of Islam. Nonetheless, the anxiety here was about pollution of the body, which would render it impure, and thus "outcast." This question of purity was as significant to Muslims with regard to pig fat as it was to Hindus with regard to beef fat. One narrator sought to fully absolve Muslims of their role in the Mutiny by suggesting that the Hindus duped them into believing that the Enfield bullets were packed in pig fat, when it was only beef fat. Javid Iqbal, Personal Interview with Amber Abbas, Lahore, Pakistan, July 16, 2006, 13.
21 Metcalf, *The Aftermath of Revolt*, 46–91.
22 Pakistani nationalist historian, I. H. Qureishi, cites the elevation of the Mughal emperor as "proof of the popularity of the Mughal dynasty." This seems an inversion of priorities, as though the revolt was motivated by a determination to save the Mughal Empire from the British rather than by much more localized grievances. Ishtiaq Husain Qureshi, "The Causes of the War of Independence Excerpted from a History of the Freedom Movement Vol. 2 (1831-1905) Pt. 1," in *1857 in the Muslim Historiography*, ed. M. Ikram Chaghatai (Lahore: Sang-e-Meel Publications, 2007. Originally Published 1960), 286. Mahmood Farooqui, *Besieged: Voices from Delhi, 1857* (New Delhi: Penguin Books India, 2010).
23 Vinayak Damodar Savarkar, *The Indian War of Independence of 1857 by An Indian Nationalist* (Bombay: Phoenix Publications, 1947 [1909]), 7.
24 Savarkar himself is best known as the progenitor of the Hindu nationalist ideology of Hindutva. Though this work speaks to the value of the collaborations between

Hindus and Muslims in resisting British power, he emphasizes "Swadharma" (love of religion). Savarkar, *The Indian War of Independence of 1857*, 7–10.
25 In his explanation for the selection of Bahadur Shah as the figurehead of the revolt, Savarkar iterates his belief that Muslim rule was anathema to Indian civilization, "thrust upon India by sheer force," and had been defeated by the Mahrattas. Therefore, when "Bahadur Shah was raised by the free voice of the people, both Hindus and Mahomedans, civil and military, to be their Emperor and the head of the War of Independence," it was not a *restoration* of Muslim power, but a new agreement, a declaration that the war between Hindus and Mahomedans had ceased and with it, Mughal tyranny. Savarkar, *The Indian War of Independence of 1857*, 233–4.
26 Syed Ahmed Khan, "The Causes of the Indian Revolt Written by Sayyid Ahmad Khan Bahadur, C.S.I. In Urdoo, in the Year 1858 and Translated into English by His Two European Friends, Benares, Medical Hall Press. 1873," http://www.columbia.edu/itc/mealac/pritchett/00litlinks/txt_sir_sayyid_asbab1873_basic.html
27 George Farquhar Irving Graham, *The Life and Work of Sir Syed Ahmed Khan*, 2nd ed. (Karachi: Oxford University Press, 1974 [1885]), 22–3; 66–7.
28 Syed Ahmed Khan, "Translation of the Report of the Members of the Select Committee for the Better Diffusion and Advancement of Learning among Muhammadans of India," in *Sir Sayyid Ahmad Khan's Educational Philosophy: A Documentary Record*, ed. Hafeez Malik (Islamabad: National Institute of Historical and Cultural Research, 1872), 155.
29 W. W. Hunter, *The Indian Musalmans: Are They Bound in Conscience to Rebel against the Queen?* (London: Trubner and Co., 1871).
30 Syed Ahmad Khan, "Review on Hunter's *Indian Mussalmans*," in *Writings and Speeches of Sir Syed Ahmad Khan*, ed. Shan Mohammad (Bombay: Nachiketa Publications Limited, 1972), 66.
31 Sayyid Ahmad Khan, "An Account of the Loyal Mohomedans of India," in *Political Profile of Sir Sayyid Ahmad Khan*, ed. Hafeez Malik (Islamabad: Institute of Islamic History, Culture and Civilization, Islamic University, 1982), 268.
32 Ibid., 138.
33 Lelyveld, *Aligarh's First Generation*, 92.
34 Khan, "Review on Hunter's *Indian Mussalmans*," 67.
35 Anil Seal, *The Emergence of Indian Nationalism: Competition and Collaboration in the Later Nineteenth Century* (London: Cambridge University Press, 1968), 304–5.
36 Omar Khalidi, *Indian Muslims Since Independence* (New Delhi: Vikas Publishing House Pvt. Ltd., 1995), 107.
37 Paul Deslandes, *Oxbridge Men: British Masculinity and the Undergraduate Experience 1850-1920* (Bloomington: Indiana University Press, 2005), 5.
38 Streets, *Martial Races*, 8–11.
39 Philip Mason, *A Matter of Honour: An Account of the Indian Army, Its Officers and Men* (London: Jonathan Cape, 1974), 263. Cited in Kenneth Ballhatchet, *Race, Sex, and Class under the Raj: Imperial Attitudes and Policies and Their Critics, 1793-1905* (London: Weidenfeld and Nicolson, 1980), 3.
40 Thomas Metcalf has shown that Muslims disproportionately bore the brunt of Imperial retribution for the Mutiny. Metcalf, *The Aftermath of Revolt*, 298–305. On the gendering of Bengalis as "effeminate," and Sir Sayyid's rhetoric supporting it, see Mrinalini Sinha, *Colonial Masculinity: The 'Manly Englishman' and the' Effeminate Bengali' in the Late Nineteenth Century* (Manchester and New York: Manchester University Press, 1995).

41 Khan, "Causes of the Indian Revolt."
42 Khalidi, *Indian Muslims since Independence*, 108.
43 Francis Robinson, *Separatism among Indian Muslims: The Politics of the United Provinces' Muslims, 1860-1923* (London: Cambridge University Press, 1974), 85.
44 Lelyveld, *Aligarh's First Generation*, 116.
45 Deslandes, *Oxbridge Men*, 5.
46 Ibid.
47 Sir Sayyid believed that such superstitions were created and sustained by women and in the *zenanas* of *ashraf* households. They created a distraction from the values that should guide the community.
48 Alavi, *Hayat-I-Jawed*, 97.
49 Ibid., 98.
50 Lelyveld, *Aligarh's First Generation*, 102–3.
51 The Queen's Proclamation of 1858 that formalized British rule pledged that the Crown's duty to "Natives of Our Indian Territories" would be the same as to all other subjects. "Proclamation, by the Queen in Council, to the Princes, Chiefs, and People of India," ed. House of Commons Parliamentary Papers (Allahabad: Governor-General, November 1, 1858). DOI: http://gateway.proquest.com/openurl?url_ver=Z 39.88-2004&res_dat=xri:hcpp-us&rft_dat=xri:hcpp:rec:1876-052376
52 Deslandes, *Oxbridge Men*, 32.
53 John Tosh, *A Man's Place: Masculinity and the Middle-Class Home in Victorian England* (New Haven: Yale University Press, 1999), 176–81. Ronald Hyam has also argued that the empire provided a reservoir for the "export of surplus emotional energy." Ronald Hyam, *Britain's Imperial Century, 1815-1914: A Study of Empire and Expansion* (New York: Barnes and Noble, 1976), 135.
54 Theodore Beck to Oscar Browning, July 27, 1883. Cited in W. C. Lubenow, *The Cambridge Apostles, 1820-1914: Liberalism, Imagination, and Friendship in British Intellectual and Professional Life* (Cambridge: Cambridge University Press, 1998), 256.
55 Lelyveld, *Aligarh's First Generation*, 311.
56 Theodore Beck, "Native India and England," *The National Review* 24 (November 1894): 375–91. Cited in Lubenow, *The Cambridge Apostles*, 257.
57 Theodore Beck, "Principal's Annual Report, for 1895-86," in *Theodore Beck Papers from the Sir Syed Academy Archives*, ed. Khaliq Ahmad Nizami (Aligarh: Aligarh Muslim University, 1991), 86.
58 Theodore Beck to Oscar Browning, September 12, 1884. Cited in Lubenow, *The Cambridge Apostles*, 257.
59 Lelyveld, *Aligarh's First Generation*, 220.
60 "Address to the Right Hon. Edward Robert Lytton Bulwer-Lytton," cited in Graham, *The Life and Work of Sir Syed Ahmed Khan*, 179.
61 Kenneth W. Jones, "Religious Identity and the Indian Census," in *The Census in British India*, ed. N.G. Barrier (Delhi: Manohar, 1981), 89.
62 Faisal Devji, *Muslim Zion: Pakistan as a Political Idea* (Cambridge, MA: Harvard University Press, 2013), 51.
63 Hafeez Malik, ed., *Sir Sayyid Ahmad Khan and Muslim Modernism in India and Pakistan* (New York: Columbia University Press, 1980), 250.
64 Robinson, *Separatism*, 125.
65 Lelyveld, *Aligarh's First Generation*, 317.
66 Despite its lofty claims, Devji argues, the MEC was dominated by North Indian Urdu-speaking elites, and was not an All India organization. The geography of the

conference grew more inclusive after Sir Sayyid's death. Devji, *Muslim Zion: Pakistan as a Political Idea*, 57.

67 Benedict R. Anderson, *Imagined Communities: Reflections on the Origin and Spread of Nationalism* (London: Verso, 1983), 144. For a history of the transformation of the idea of *qaum* to communalism, see Ayesha Jalal, *Self and Sovereignty: Individual and Community in South Asian Islam since 1850* (London and New York: Routledge, 2000). Malik, *Muslim Modernism*, 231.

68 Faisal Devji, "Keywords in South Asian Studies: Qawm" (London: School of Oriental and African Studies, University of London, 2004).

69 For more on the British investment in the College, see Lelyveld, *Aligarh's First Generation*.

70 Minault, *Secluded Scholars*, 21.

71 Even after Partition, the future of Urdu was linked to the loyalty and future of the Muslim community remaining in India. See Jalal, *Self and Sovereignty*, 569–70.

72 Lelyveld, *Aligarh's First Generation*, 72.

73 Sayeed, *Pakistan: The Formative Phase, 1857-1948*, 18.

74 Mrinalini Sinha has explored the politics of race, caste, and class in late nineteenth-century colonial India in greater detail. See Sinha, *Colonial Masculinity*.

75 Khan, "Speech at Lucknow: December 28, 1887," in *Writings and Speeches of Sir Syed Ahmad Khan*, ed. Shan Mohammad (Bombay: Nachiketa Publications Limited, 1972), 209.

76 Sinha, *Colonial Masculinity*, 116.

77 Khan, "Speech at Meerut: March 16, 1888," in *Writings and Speeches of Sir Syed Ahmad Khan*, ed. Shan Mohammad (Bombay: Nachiketa Publications Limited, 1972), 180.

78 Graham, *The Life and Work of Sir Syed Ahmed Khan*, 176–7.

79 A peculiar feature of many reflections on Hindu-Muslim relations from Aligs in India, Pakistan, and Bangladesh is that almost all narrators emphasize good relations with their Hindu neighbors, classmates, and teachers prior to 1947. Yet, they also describe a pervasive mistrust of Hindus in matters of employment, equal treatment, and justice. Above all, they were not confident that a Hindu-dominated state would hold Muslim interests dear.

80 Mohamad Ali and his brother Shaukat remain two of the most prominent political and religious activists to emerge from the first generation of Aligarh graduates. They were both leaders of the anti-imperial Khilafat Movement, allies of Gandhi, and founders of the JMI. See Lelyveld, *Aligarh's First Generation*; "Three Aligarh Students."

81 Nizami, *History of the Aligarh Muslim University (1920-1945)*, 255.

82 Ibid.

83 This language became so deeply etched in the minds of some Aligs that they transposed it to other situations, creating affective political links between AMU and, for instance, Mohammad Ali Jinnah. Pakistani Brigadier General (Ret'd) Iqbal Shafi told me that in 1945 when Jinnah spoke to Aligarh students, he told them "Aligarh is the arsenal of Muslim India. I want you to fan out throughout the length and breadth of India and tell the Musalmans that they must vote for League ticket holders even if they are lamp posts!" I can find no evidence of Jinnah using this precise language at that time in Aligarh, though Jinnah did make the "lamp post" comment in a speech in the Frontier Province on November 27, 1945. It seems that Shafi has compressed several political strategies, and in so doing created immediate

links between AMU and the League. Jinnah, "Message to the Musalmans of the Frontier Province, November 27, 1945," 247. "Speech at the Muslim University Union, Aligarh, March 10, 1941," in *Some Recent Speeches and Writings of Mr. Jinnah*, ed. Jamil-ud-din Ahmad, 5th ed., 2 vols., vol. 1 (Lahore: Sh. Muhammad Ashraf, 1952), 268. Iqbal Shafi, Interview, May 9, 2010, 13. Iqbal Shafi was born in 1927; he started at Aligarh University in the mid-1940s and began military training in Dehra Dun in 1946. In 1947, he migrated to Pakistan, where he served in the army, retiring as a brigadier general. He cofounded the Sir Syed Memorial Society in Islamabad. He died in 2019.

84 Syed Ahmed Khan, "Excerpt: Lecture at Ludhiana," *The Aftab* Aftab Memoirs Special (January 23, 1883): 52.
85 The Aligarh Girls' College was founded by Sheikh Abdullah in 1906. See Minault, *Secluded Scholars*. Saikia, "Strangers, Friends and Peace," 308.
86 Ibid., 16, 67–9. As Minault has pointed out, the values of the North Indian *ashraf*, and particularly the attitude toward women, were similar to those of Victorian England. She does not believe them to be a product, however, of Sir Sayyid's international travels but simply the values of his own upbringing. Ibid., 15. See also Lelyveld, "Three Aligarh Students," 232–3.
87 Aftab Ahmad Khan, "Note by Aftab Ahmad Khan on His Work & Experience During the Last Three Years of His Office as Vice-Chancellor of the Aligarh Muslim University: Addressed to Members of the University Court" (Aligarh: Aligarh Muslim University, 1926), 54–5.
88 Ibid., 57.
89 Ibid., 90.
90 Ibid.
91 Theodore Beck, "Beck to Sir Sayyid, October 9, 1885," in *Theodore Beck Papers from the Sir Syed Academy Archives*, ed. Khaliq Ahmad Nizami (Aligarh: Sir Syed Academy, 1991), 13.
92 Beck, "The Principal's Annual Report 1895-6," 82.
93 Lelyveld, *Aligarh's First Generation*, 157. Theodore Beck, "Theodore Beck to Sir Sayyid Ahmad Khan, Letter No. 58, April 30, 1892," in *Theodore Beck Papers from the Sir Syed Academy Archives*, ed. Khaliq Ahmad Nizami (Aligarh: Sir Syed Academy, 1991), 53.
94 Zakir Ali Khan, Interview, August 10, 2006, 8. Also Habibur Rahman, Interviewed by Amber Abbas, Dhaka, Bangladesh, February 20, 2010, 5.
95 In both India and Pakistan today, universities have become key sites of recruitment for political parties and actors and many institutions, AMU included, have faced disruptive violence and academic decay as a result.
96 "The Proctorial Department," *The Aligarh Magazine: Union Jubilee Number*, Autumn 1934, 261.
97 Saikia, "Strangers, Friends and Peace," 287–8.
98 Ibid.
99 Ibid.
100 Yi-Fu Tuan, *Landscapes of Fear* (New York: Pantheon Books, 1979), 204.
101 Ibid., 206.
102 Tufail Ahmad Manglori, *Towards a Common Destiny: A Nationalist Manifesto (English Translation of Musalmanon Ka Roshan Mustaqbil)*, trans. Ali Ashraf (New Delhi: People's Publishing House for The Indian Council of Historical Research, 1994), 123.

103 Masood-ul Hasan, "Some Glimpses of the University in the Forties," *The Aftab* The Aftab Memoirs Special (1976): 68.
104 Zakir Ali Khan, Interview, August 10, 2006, 5.
105 Major General (Ret'd) Ghulam Umar, Interviewed by Amber Abbas, August 8, 2009, 13. Major General Ghulam Umar completed all of his education in Aligarh before joining the Indian Army in the early 1940s during the Second World War. He returned to India from Japan after the war and opted for Pakistan. He served in Pakistan's Army during both the 1965 and the 1971 wars (when he was a close associate of General Yahya Khan), and he also served as military secretary to King Faisal of Saudi Arabia. In his retirement he was involved in people-to-people diplomacy with India. He died in January 2009.
106 Iftikhar Alam noted that he "hated" the sherwani from the outset. His father was a Communist, but the party policy was to support Pakistan, which explains why he hosted AMU AIML activists. Iftikhar's uncle contested and won the 1945-6 election on the Muslim League ticket in their district. Around the time of independence, Iftikhar's father was arrested and jailed for six months. During that time, Iftikhar lived with his uncle in the village, and after his father's return, he and his brother Iqtidar were sent to Aligarh. His dislike for the sherwani could be related to these political tensions. As I discuss in Chapter 3, he arrived in AMU in 1949, when wearing the uniform potentially exposed students to anti-Muslim violence. Iftikhar Alam Khan, Interviewed by Amber Abbas, Aligarh, India, June 6, 2009, 3, 22. Iftikhar Alam Khan was born in 1938 and arrived in Minto Circle School in 1949. He completed High School in 1952. He completed all of his higher education in AMU and became a professor of museology there. He is an expert on Aligarh's architectural history and has written several books on the subject. He lives in Aligarh.
107 Iftikhar Alam Khan, Interview, June 6, 2009, 22.
108 Nasir Ali, "Aligarh- Then and Now," *The Aftab* The Aftab Memoirs Special (1976): 140.
109 Students were subjected to an initiation ritual known as "Introduction Night" for which they had to perform sometimes humiliating tricks. Discussions of Introduction Night featured a mix of trepidation and excitement. The boys knew they were being inducted, but they had no idea what they might be asked to do. Syed Saghir Ahmad Rizvi, Interviewed by Amber Abbas, Lucknow, India, October 6, 2009, 2-3. Interview in Author's Possession. See also Majid Ali Sidiqqi, Interviewed by Amber Abbas, October 2, 2009, 16.
110 Syed Saghir Ahmad Rizvi, Interview, October 2, 2009, 2. Syed Saghir Ahmad Rizvi is a native of Lucknow, where he completed his early education before studying Engineering in Lucknow. After completing his degree, he moved to the United States for several years before settling down in India in the late 1960s where he worked as an engineer.
111 Abdul Rasheed Khan, Interview, August 10, 2006, 7. Abdul Rasheed Khan is a native of Saharanpur. He actively fought the Muslim League elections in 1945-6 before settling in Pakistan. He served most of his career in the Karachi Development Authority and then served on the faculty of the Sir Syed University of Engineering and Technology.
112 A. B. A. Haleem, "Prof. Haleem's Address to Students," *Muslim University Gazette*, January 1, 1942, 5. This article is a report on Haleem's speech, not a verbatim transcript of it.
113 Zakir Ali Khan, Interview, August 10, 2006, 9. Zakir Ali Khan clearly associated this "can-do" attitude with the success of Aligs in Pakistan.

114 Lelyveld, *Aligarh's First Generation*, 30, 343.
115 Deslandes, *Oxbridge Men*, 28.
116 Deslandes shows how British undergraduate writings about the dons and instructors reviles them as not fully developed men, stuck as they are within the enclosed university environment. Ibid., 59.

Chapter 2: Self-Realization and the Nation

1 Doreen Massey, "Places and Their Pasts," *History Workshop Journal* 39 (1995): 183.
2 Sayyid Ahmad Khan et al., "To His Excellency the Viceroy and Governor General of India in Council: The Humble Petition of the British India Association, North West Provinces August 1, 1867," in *Sir Sayyid Ahmad Khan's Educational Philosophy: A Documentary Record*, ed. Hafeez Malik (Islamabad: National Institute of Historical and Cultural Research, 1989), 39–40.
3 Manglori wrote that by 1898 "a situation had arisen [sic] when the remaining supporters and co-workers of Sir Syed had decided even during his lifetime to place the entire situation concerning the College in the form of an appeal to the community." He cites an incident from the memoirs of Waqarul Mulk, a close associate of Sir Syed's, in which he details a plan to publish a series of articles criticizing Sir Syed's neglect of the Muslim community, having allowed Theodore Beck to take charge. However, Sir Syed died, and the articles were never published. Manglori, *Towards a Common Destiny*, 195.
4 Devji, *Muslim Zion: Pakistan as a Political Idea*, 56–63.
5 Mubarak Shah Zuberi, Interviewed by Amber Abbas, Karachi, Pakistan, May 26, 2010, 3. Mubarak Shah Zuberi was born in Meerut on October 7, 1935, and attended Aligarh University. After graduating from Aligarh, he remained in India until 1961, though much of his family migrated to Pakistan. At the request of his mother, he finally shifted in 1964. He has also lived and worked in the United States, both California and New York. He currently splits his time between Karachi and California.
6 Shaukat Ali, "The Late Mr. Beck and His Pupils," *Muslim Anglo-Oriental College Magazine*, June–July 1901, 27. Cited in Lelyveld, *Aligarh's First Generation*, 285.
7 Shan Muhammad, *Education and Politics: From Sir Syed to the Present Day the Aligarh School* (New Delhi: A.P.H. Publishing Corporation, 2002), 47.
8 The pamphlet was originally written in 1966 in response to the "injustice" of the amending of the Aligarh University Act in 1965 and intended for publication. Hameed-ud-Deen Khan gave a copy to Professor Theodore Wright in 1966, but it is unlikely that the pamphlet was ever published. Professor Wright passed on a copy to Naved Masood, son of retired Aligarh University professor Masood-ul Hasan, from whom I received a copy. Hameed-ud-Deen Khan, "Aligarh Muslim University: Attitudes and Trends of the M.A.O. College and the Aligarh Muslim University since 1909-Personal Observations and Revelations," (Aligarh, 1966), 1.
9 Emphasis in original. S. M. Tonki, *Aligarh and Jamia: Fight for National Education System* (New Delhi: People's Publishing House, 1983), 10. Minault and Lelyveld, "The Campaign for a Muslim University, 1898-1920," 265.
10 Khan, "Aligarh Muslim University: Attitudes and Trends," 1.
11 Non-cooperation organized resistance to British financing of public institutions. To understand the relationship between non-cooperation and the founding of AMU,

see the expanded and revised version of Minault and Lelyveld, "The Campaign for a Muslim University, 1898-1920."
12. Since its founding, the MAO College had been affiliated with Calcutta University, which was the degree-granting institution.
13. Minault and Lelyveld, "The Campaign for a Muslim University, 1898-1920," 268.
14. Allama Abdullah Yusuf Ali, "Human Factor in Education: Address to the Golden Jubilee Session of the University Section of the All India Muslim Educational Conference," *The Muslim University Gazette*, April 21, 1937, 7.
15. Barbara Daly Metcalf, *Islamic Revival in British India: Deoband, 1860-1900* (Princeton: Princeton University Press, 1982).
16. The phrase first appeared in a report by a special correspondent in the *Independent* on November 7, 1920. In Jawaharlal Nehru's letter on the occasion of the Jamia Jubilee in 1946, he admitted to having been that special correspondent. See Tonki, *Aligarh and Jamia: Fight for National Education System*, 94–5.
17. Minault and Lelyveld, "The Campaign for a Muslim University, 1898-1920," 271.
18. Muhammad, *Education and Politics*, 83.
19. Akhtarul Wasey and Farhat Ehsas, eds., *Education, Gandhi, and Man: Select Writings Khwaja Ghulamus Saiyyadain* (Delhi: Shipra Publications, 2008), 203.
20. M. A. Alavi, "A Plea for Sahibzada Memorial Fund," *Aligarh Magazine*, January–August 1930, 44.
21. During my interviews, I heard similar explanations for Aligarh's value, and the argument that real tolerance comes from understanding the culture and religion of another. Majid Ali Siddiqi, Interview, October 2, 2009, 12.
22. Crucially, Nehru's notion of India's "composite culture" rather preserves unique markers of identity, and has sometimes been compared to a salad bowl rather than a melting pot.
23. "New Bengal Pact," *The Muslim University Gazette*, January 22, 1937, 6.
24. "Ourselves," *The Muslim University Gazette*, January 8, 1937, 1. "Lessons from His Excellency's Visit," *The Muslim University Gazette*, February 5, 1937, 5.
25. Ishrat Ali Qureshi, *Aligarh Past and Present* (Aligarh: Aligarh Muslim University, 1992), 79–80.
26. Sherwani maintained nationalist sympathies, though his father was a prominent Muslim League politician. Riazur Rahman Sherwani, Interviewed by Amber Abbas, Aligarh, India, July 6, 2008, 3. Riazur Rahman Sherwani hails from a large UP landholding family. His early education was traditional, in Arabic, Persian, and the classical Islamic subjects, and he began his schooling in Minto Circle School in the 1930s. He went on to complete his M.A. and Ph.D. in Arabic and taught both in AMU and in Kashmir University. He still lives in his family home, Habib Manzil, in Aligarh.
27. Aziz Ahmad, *Islamic Modernism in India and Pakistan 1857-1964* (London: Oxford University Press, 1967), 170.
28. Considering the repeated and zealous involvement of Aligarh students in political activities, the "traditional" separation is flimsy at best, but it is frequently invoked as a critical pillar of Aligarh's identity. Indeed, although the Muslim League was founded largely by Aligarh men, Choudhry Khaliquzzaman wrote that four years after its founding, "The office of the Muslim League had already been removed to Lucknow from Aligarh in 1910 as a measure of policy, not to keep the political organization too close to the educational institution." Khaliquzzaman, *Pathway to Pakistan* (Lahore: Longmans Pakistan Branch, 1961), 18.

29 Original punctuation. "University and Politics," *The Muslim University Gazette*, May 5, 1937, 5.
30 Ibid.
31 A. B. A. Haleem, "A.B.A. Haleem to Maulavi Mohd. Ashiq Saheb Warsi: Report of the P.V.C. To the University Court," in *Freedom Movement Archives* (Islamabad: Pakistan National Archives, October 25, 1938).
32 "Muslim Education and the New Ministry in U.P.," *The Muslim University Gazette*, August 1, 1937, 5.
33 Sarvepalli Gopal, *Jawaharlal Nehru: A Biography*, 3 vols., vol. 1 (Cambridge, MA: Harvard University Press, 1976), 152.
34 Mushirul Hasan, "The Muslim Mass Contact Campaign: An Attempt at Political Mobilisation," *Economic and Political Weekly* 21, no. 52 (December 27, 1986): 2273.
35 Ibid., 2274.
36 Ibid., 2275.
37 Gyanesh Kudaisya, *Region, Nation, "Heartland:" Uttar Pradesh in India's Body Politic*, Sage Series in Modern Indian History, ed. Bipan Chandra, Mridula Mukherjee, and Aditya Mukherjee (New Delhi: SAGE Publications, 2006), 260–2.
38 "Mahatma Gandhi and Education," *The Muslim University Gazette*, August 24, 1937, 5. The Wardha Scheme of Education was designed in part by K.G. Saiyyadain, a distinguished Aligarh Old Boy.
39 "Prohibition or Education or Both," *The Muslim University Gazette*, October 24, 1937, 5.
40 "National Education," *The Muslim University Gazette*, December 24, 1937, 5.
41 "The Two Voices," *The Muslim University Gazette*, January 8, 1938, 6. Waheed Ahmad, ed. "M.A. Jinnah Addresses Muslim Students—'I Have Failed' with the Hindus, December 27, 1937," in *The Nation's Voice: Towards Consolidation; Quaid-i-Azam Mohammad Ali Jinnah Speeches and Statements March 1935-March 1940*, ed. Waheed Ahmad (Karachi: Quaid-i-Azam Academy, 1992), 202–4. Humayun Kabir, "Politics and Muslim Students: Presidential Address at the All India Muslim Students Conference December 1937," in *Muslim Politics 1906-1947 and Other Essays* (Calcutta: Firma K.L. Mukhopadhyay, 1969), 78–85.
42 Nripendra Nath Mitra, *The Indian Annual Register: An Annual Digest of Public Affairs of India 1937*, vol. 2 (Calcutta: The Annual Register Office, July–December 1937), 415–16.
43 Ahmad, "Jinnah: 'I Have Failed,'" 204.
44 Kabir, "Politics and Muslim Students," 85.
45 Ahmad, "Jinnah: 'I Have Failed,'" 203.
46 Ibid., 202–3.
47 "The Two Voices."
48 "All India Muslim League Resolution on the Congress Use of the 'Bande Mataram' Song Lucknow: 15-18 October 1937," in *Muslims under Congress Rule 1937-1939*, ed. Khursheed Kamal Aziz, 2 vols., vol. 1 (Delhi: Renaissance Publishing House, 1978), 150. "All India Muslim League Resolution on Hindu-Muslim Riots in Congress-Rule Provinces: Calcutta: 17 April 1938." in ibid., 157.
49 Mohammad Mujeeb, "The Partition of India in Retrospect," in *India's Partition: Process, Strategy and Mobilization*, ed. Mushirul Hasan (Delhi: Oxford University Press, 1993), 405.
50 Ibid.
51 Sarfaraz Hussain Mirza, *Youth & Pakistan Movement: History and Chronology* (Lahore: Nazaria-i-Pakistan Foundation, 2004), 2.

52 Zakir Ali Khan, Interview, August 10, 2006, 5.
53 Irfan Habib cited the Muslim League's "Pirpur Report of imaginary assaults against Muslims." Irfan Habib, Interview, June 28, 2009, 5. On the Aligarh riots, see Brass, *The Production of Hindu-Muslim Violence*.
54 Raja Syed Mohammad Mahdi, "The Pirpur Report: Delhi: End of 1938," in *Muslims under Congress Rule 1937-1939*, ed. Khursheed Kamal Aziz (Islamabad: National Commission on Historical and Cultural Research, 1978), 310.
55 Masood-ul Hasan, Interviewed by Amber Abbas, Aligarh, India, May 1, 2009, 19.
56 The present may have been weighing heavily on his memory. Arguably, the scale of the violence he described paled in comparison to attacks on Muslim communities after 1947, including in the city of Aligarh, where rioting after the 1992 destruction of the Babri Masjid was particularly severe. Masood-ul Hasan, Interview, May 1, 2009, 19. Masood-ul Hasan was born in Moradabad in 1928. He studied in the AMU from 1943 to 1947, where he completed his B.A. and M.A. in English Literature. He completed his Ph.D. in Liverpool while he was appointed as a Reader in the Department of English at AMU. He retired from AMU in 1988 after serving as Professor of English, Chair of Department of English, and Dean of the Faculty of Arts. He also served as the Proctor of the University. He died in 2019.
57 Ibid.
58 Mohammad Ali Jinnah, "Speech Delivered at the Muslim University Union, Aligarh on 6th March, 1940," in *Some Recent Speeches and Writings of Mr. Jinnah Vol. I*, ed. Jamil-ud-din Ahmad (Lahore: Sh. Muhammad Ashraf, 1952), 153.
59 Ayesha Jalal, *The Sole Spokesman: Jinnah, The Muslim League and the Demand for Pakistan* (Cambridge and New York: Cambridge University Press, 1985).
60 Ghulam Umar, Interview, August 8, 2009, 5. Note: Jinnah addressed the Union on March 6.
61 M. A. Dyan, "Whither Aligarh?," *The Muslim University Gazette*, November 1, 1940, 5.
62 Minault and Lelyveld argue this point in their assessment of Mohamad Ali's efforts to reform Aligarh and call Muslims to non-cooperation. See Minault and Lelyveld, "The Campaign for a Muslim University, 1898-1920," 253. Ayesha Jalal's biography of Jinnah is a detailed account of his efforts to solidify the League's monopoly. See Ayesha Jalal, *The Sole Spokesman: Jinnah, the Muslim League, and the Demand for Pakistan* (Cambridge and New York: Cambridge University Press, 1985).
63 Jinnah, "Speech at A.M.U. Union, 6th March 1940," in *Some Recent Speeches and Writings of Mr. Jinnah Vol. I*, ed. Jamil-ud-din Ahmad (Lahore: Sh. Muhammad Ashraf, 1952), 159.
64 "Presidential Address Delivered at the Special Pakistan Session of the Punjab Muslim Students' Federation, 2nd March 1941," in *Some Recent Speeches and Writings of Mr. Jinnah*, ed. Jamil-ud-din Ahmad (Lahore: Sh. Muhammad Ashraf, 1952), 247. See Mark Mazower, "Minorities and the League of Nations in Interwar Europe," *Daedalus* 126, no. 2 Human Diversity (Spring 1997): 47–63.
65 Jinnah, "Presidential Address at A.I.M.S.F. Nagpur," in *Some Recent Speeches and Writings of Mr. Jinnah*, ed. Jamil-ud-din Ahmad (Lahore: Sh. Muhammad Ashraf, 1952), 365.
66 "Presidential Address Punjab M.S.F.," in *Some Recent Speeches and Writings of Mr. Jinnah Vol. I*, ed. Jamil-ud-din Ahmad (Lahore: Sh. Muhammad Ashraf, 1952), 247.
67 Jalal, *The Sole Spokesman*. This is the centerpiece of Jalal's argument but there is also evidence in the Pakistan Freedom Movement Archives that scholars with League

sympathies continued to prepare plans well into the 1940s for "Muslim India" that included "safeguards and concessions" for a Muslim Minority. M. A. H. Qadri, "M.A.H. Qadri to M.A. Jinnah: Terms of Reference for Education Committee of All India Muslim League," in *Shamsul Hasan Collection* (Islamabad: Pakistan National Archives, December 19, 1943); A. B. A. Haleem, "Statutory Safeguards for Minorities," in *Freedom Movement Archives* (Islamabad: Pakistan National Archives, May 12, 1946).

68 Zakir Ali Khan Interview, August 10, 2006, 12.
69 The Nizam accepted his third term as chancellor and the Nawab accepted his second term as pro-chancellor in 1941–2. "Muslim University in the Year 1941–42," *Muslim University Gazette*, May 15, 1942, 4.
70 Khaliquzzaman, *Pathway to Pakistan*, 7.
71 Devji, *Muslim Zion: Pakistan as a Political Idea*, 85.
72 Nasim Ansari, *Choosing to Stay: Memoirs of an Indian Muslim*, trans. Ralph Russell (Karachi: City Press, 1999), 41–2.
73 Irfan Habib, Interview, June 28, 2009, 7. He repeated a version of this story in "Irfan Habib: The Indian Variant of Secularism." Irfan Habib was born in Baroda in 1931 but grew up primarily in Aligarh, where his father had been a professor since the mid-1920s. Habib began his education in Zahoor Ward and then onto Minto Circle and the Muslim University High School. He went on to become a professor of history at AMU after completing his D.Phil at New College, Oxford. He retired in 1991, but lives in Aligarh and continues to visit the university daily.
74 Riazur Rahman Sherwani, Interview, July 6, 2008, 6. Gandhi became the first lifetime member of the Union in 1920 during the non-cooperation movement. Mohammad Ali Jinnah was conferred with the honor in 1938.
75 Ibid.
76 "Faith in Quaid-e-Azam Reaffirmed," *The Muslim University Gazette*, November 1, 1941, 8.
77 Only during the League period, Khan writes, were students "used for political propaganda." Khan, "Aligarh Muslim University: Attitudes and Trends," 1–2.
78 Irfan Habib, Interview, June 28, 2009, 13.
79 Manzar-i-Alam was a lawyer from Gwalior, who practiced in Aligarh, but during this period dedicated much of his energy to organizing and leading the Muslim University Muslim League.
80 The vice chancellor was the executive head of the university.
81 Mukhtar Zaman, *Students' Role in the Pakistan Movement* (Karachi: Quaid-i-Azam Academy, 1978), 40–1.
82 "Revolutionary Activities by Congress in Punjab and U.P." August 13, 1942. Cited in P. N. Chopra, ed., *Quit India Movement: British Secret Documents*, 2 vols., vol. I (New Delhi: Interprint, 1986), 59.
83 Ziauddin Ahmad, "Using Students for Party Propaganda Deplored," *The Muslim University Gazette*, October 15, 1942.
84 Mohammad Ali Jinnah, "Speech at the Annual Session of the All-India Muslim Students' Federation, Jullundur, November 15, 1942," in *Some Recent Speeches and Writings of Mr. Jinnah*, ed. Jamil-ud-din Ahmad (Lahore: Sh. Muhammad Ashraf, 1952), 488–9.
85 "Presidential Address at A.I.M.S.F. Nagpur," 347. Wajahat Husain, Interviewed by Amber Abbas, Lahore, Pakistan, June 13, 2005, 8; Sarfaraz Hussain Mirza, ed.,

Muslim Students and Pakistan Movement: Selected Documents (1937-1947), 3 vols., vol. I (Lahore: Pakistan Study Centre, 1988), xlvi.
86 Mohammad Ali Jinnah, "Speech at the Annual Conference of the Punjab Muslim Students' Federation, Lahore, 18 March 1944," in *Speeches and Writings of Mr. Jinnah*, ed. Jamil-ud-din Ahmad (Lahore: Sh. Muhammad Ashraf, 1964), 22.
87 "Speech at A.M.U. Union March 10, 1941," 269.
88 *Daily Anjam* (Delhi), September 27, 1945, cited in Zaman, *Students' Role*, 145.
89 Mirza, *Muslim Students and Pakistan Movement: Selected Documents (1937-1947)*, lviii.
90 *Daily Anjam* (Delhi), September 27, 1945, cited in Zaman, *Students' Role*, 144–5.
91 Manzar-i-Alam, "Manzar-i-Alam to Qazi Isa," in *Freedom Movement Archives* (Islamabad: Pakistan National Archives, November 15, 1945).
92 From M.A. Jinnah to A.B.A. Haleem, February 26, 1945, in Mirza, *Muslim Students and Pakistan Movement: Selected Documents (1937-1947)*, 66.
93 Yi-Fu Tuan, *Space and Place: The Perspective of Experience* (Minneapolis: University of Minneapolis Press, 1977), 52.
94 Iqbal Shafi, Interview, May 9, 2010, 14. Sections in italics were translated from Urdu by the author.
95 The Frontier had a Congress government, and Punjab was under the control of the British loyalist Unionist Party.
96 Iqbal Shafi, Interview, May 9, 2010, 16. Zaman reports that students working in areas under the influence of the pro-Congress Jamiat-ul-ulema-e-Hind were "stoned and abused" and heard complaints that Muslim League workers denounced the Deoband ulema. See Zaman, *Students' Role*, 155.
97 Iqbal Shafi, Interview, May 9, 2010, 17.
98 Abdul Rasheed Khan, Interview, August 10, 2006, 3.
99 Zaman, *Students' Role*, 157.
100 Dhulipala, *Creating a New Medina*, 140–1.
101 Abdul Rasheed Khan, Interview, August 10, 2006, 3.
102 Mushirul Hasan, "Nationalist and Separatist Trends in Aligarh, 1915-1947," in *Myth and Reality: The Struggle for Freedom in India*, ed. Amit Kumar Gupta (New Delhi: Manohar, 1987), 130.
103 Ibid., 116.
104 One narrator even flatly denied involvement, though other documentary evidence suggested he had been an AIML supporter.
105 Masood-ul Hasan, Interview, May 1, 2009, 17.
106 Jinnah, "Speech at A.M.U. Union March 10, 1941," 268.
107 Masood-ul Hasan, Interview, May 1, 2009, 18.
108 Ibid.
109 Mohammad Amin, Interviewed by Amber Abbas, New Delhi, India, November 5, 2009, 5. Professor Mohammad Amin was born in 1928 in the United Provinces. He holds a master's degree in history and law from AMU in 1949, and became a professor in St. Stephen's College of Delhi University, where he taught for over forty years. He served as vice chancellor of Jamia Hamdard University from 1990–93. He was awarded the Padma Bhushan in 2010. He died in 2012.
110 Academic Council meeting notes read: "As a special case this year the shortage in attendance of the students appearing at the Intermediate B.A., B.Sc. (Pass & Hons.), MA. MSc (Previous & Final) and BT Examination of 1947 be condoned if they have put in 50% attendance till the end of March 1947." And there are further provisions

for the vice chancellor's discretion in matters of attendance. Ziauddin Ahmad and A. E. Zobairi, *Minutes of An Ordinary Meeting of the Academic Council* (Aligarh: Aligarh Muslim University, April 12, 1947).

111 It was well known that Ziauddin Ahmad and A. B. A. Haleem were bitter enemies. In 1937, Ziauddin had recommended abolishing the post of PVC, held by Haleem, which would concentrate both academic and executive powers in the hands of the VC himself. The post of PVC was abolished in 1944 at which time it had still been held by Haleem. "Muslim University Constitution: Need of Removing Certain Anomalies," *The Muslim University Gazette*, April 28, 1937.

112 Qazi Mohammad Isa, "Qazi Mohammad Isa to Chief Accountant, Muslim University Aligarh," in *Freedom Movement Archives* (Islamabad: Pakistan National Archives, November 22, 1945). Jamil-ud-din Ahmad, "Jamil-ud-din Ahmad to M.A. Jinnah: Election Work Committee Constituted," in *Shamsul Hasan Collection* (Islamabad: Pakistan National Archives, December 11, 1945).

113 "Jamil-ud-din Ahmad to M.A. Jinnah: Provincial Election Work and Committee," in *Shamsul Hasan Collection* (Islamabad: Pakistan National Archives, December 1, 1945).

114 Ali Ahmad Faziel, "Ali Ahmad Faziel to M.A. Jinnah: Provincial Election Work," in *Shamsul Hasan Collection* (Islamabad: Pakistan National Archives, December 2, 1945).

115 Manzar-i-Alam, "Manzar-i-Alam to M.A. Jinnah: Student Election Work and Need for Funds," in *Shamsul Hasan Collection* (Islamabad: Pakistan National Archives, December 3, 1945).

116 He had earlier spent several thousand rupees of his own money, and MUML received only Rs. 1000 from the Central Parliamentary Board. "Manzar-i-Alam to M.A. Jinnah: Letter of Support from Nawabzada Liaqat Ali Khan," in *Shamsul Hasan Collection* (Islamabad: Pakistan National Archives, December 3, 1945 (2)). Isa, "Qazi Isa to A.M.U. Accountant."

117 Ahmad, "Jamil-ud-din Ahmad to M.A. Jinnah: Provincial Election Work and Committee."

118 Mohammad Ali Jinnah, "M.A. Jinnah to Jamil-ud-din Ahmad: Need to Establish an Election Committee," in *Shamsul Hasan Collection* (Islamabad: Pakistan National Archives, December 5, 1945).

119 Jamil-ud-din Ahmad, "Jamil-ud-din Ahmad to M.A. Jinnah: Election Work Committee Constituted."

120 Manzar-i-Alam, "Manzar-i-Alam to M.A. Jinnah: Student Election Workers Sent out over Holidays," in *Shamsul Hasan Collection* (Islamabad: Pakistan National Archives, December 17, 1945), vol. 26/ 187–8.

121 Saiyed Mohammad Sarwar, "Letter from Saiyed Mohd. Sarwar to Nawabzada Liaqat Ali Khan January 19, 1946," in *Freedom Movement Archives* (Islamabad: Pakistan National Archives), vol. 26/ 214–15.

122 Irfan Habib, Interview, June 28, 2009, 19. Iqbal Shafi, Interview, May 9, 2010, 18.

123 Nizami, *History of the Aligarh Muslim University (1920-1945)*, 224.

124 Ghayurul Islam. Ghayurul Islam to M.A. Jinnah: Resignation of Ziauddin Ahmad. N.D. *SHC*, vol. 51/ 34–6. PNA, Habib, "Personal Interview with Amber Abbas."

125 Islam. Ghayurul Islam to M.A. Jinnah: Resignation of Ziauddin Ahmad.

126 Emphasis in original. Hasan, "Some Glimpses of the University in the Forties," 67.

127 Ziauddin Ahmad, "Ziauddin Ahmad to M.A. Jinnah: The Future of Muslims in India," in *Freedom Movement Archives* (Islamabad: Pakistan National Archives, January 2, 1947), vol. 591/ 3–4.

128 (Sd.) Shakir Husain Khan, "Shakir H. Khan to Liaqat Ali Khan," in *Freedom Movement Archives* (Islamabad: Pakistan National Archives, February 13, 1941), F 237/ 14-15.
129 Mohammad Ali Jinnah, "Pakistan, the Muslim Charter: Speech by Quaid-e-Azam M.A. Jinnah to Muslim University Union, Aligarh," in *Freedom Movement Archives* (Islamabad: Pakistan National Archives, November 2, 1941), F 237/ 19 (1–14).
130 "Muslim India Speaks: Speech Delivered by Quaid-e-Azam Mr. M.A. Jinnah President of the All-India Muslim League at a Meeting Held under the Auspices of the Muslim University Union," in *Freedom Movement Archives* (Islamabad: Pakistan National Archives, November 2, 1942), F 237/ 21 (1–25).

Chapter 3: Pushing the Boundaries

1 Mohammad, *Glimpses of Muslim Education in India*, vol. 1, 230.
2 Violette Graff details the long controversy over AMU's status in India and shows how its meaning has changed for Indians since independence. Violette Graff, "Aligarh's Long Quest for 'Minority' Status: A.M.U. (Amendment) Act, 1981," *Economic and Political Weekly*, August 11, 1990.
3 Ahmad Saeed, Interview, October 10, 2009, 10. Ahmad Saeed was born in Lucknow in 1927. He was primarily raised in Aligarh and attended the Muslim University High School. He got his degree in engineering from AMU, where he had served as a senior cabinet member of the Engineering College Union. He later served on the UP State Electricity Board from where he retired as director. Both of his children also attended AMU. He lives in Lucknow.
4 Emphasis in original. Arthur Kleinman and Veena Das, "Introduction," in *Violence and Subjectivity*, ed. Arthur Kleinman and Veena Das (Berkeley: University of California Press, 2000), 8.
5 There were no attacks on AMU during 1947 and 1948, though there were riots and communal disturbances in Aligarh city. There had been violence between city dwellers and students in 1946, and there were a number of riots in the 1950s. Brass, *Production of Hindu-Muslim Violence*. Pars Ram, "A UNESCO Study of Social Tensions in Aligarh, 1950-1951," ed. Gardner Murphy (Ahmedabad: UNESCO, 1955).
6 Tuan, *Landscapes of Fear*, 5.
7 *Aligarh Magazine,* Union Jubilee 1934, 261.
8 Guha Thakurta, "Uprooted and Divided," 55.
9 Salman Khurshid, *At Home in India: A Restatement of Indian Muslims* (New Delhi: Vikas Publishing House Pvt Ltd., 1986), 21.
10 Kleinman, "The Violences of Everyday Life."
11 Creswell, *In Place/out of Place: Geography, Ideology, and Transgression*.
12 Edward Casey, "Boundary, Place, and Event in the Spatiality of History," *Rethinking History* 11, no. 4 (December 2007): 508.
13 Yacoobali Zamindar, *The Long Partition*.
14 Casey, "Boundary, Place, and Event in the Spatiality of History," 508.
15 Emphasis in original. Ibid., 508–9.
16 Tuan, *Space and Place: The Perspective of Experience*, 179.
17 Neal, *National Trauma and Collective Memory*, xi. See also Kleinman, "The Violences of Everyday Life."

18 Mohiuddin Khan, Interviewed by Amber Abbas, Dhaka, Bangladesh, March 28, 2010, 8. Mohiuddin Khan was born in Sylhet in 1924. He passed his matriculation in 1941 and his intermediate from Calcutta University. He completed his bachelor's in 1945 from M.C. College in Assam and completed his engineering degree in AMU in 1949. He was a government engineer in East Pakistan and then Bangladesh, retiring as chief engineer of the Public Works Department. He lives in Dhaka.
19 Hasan, "Some Glimpses of the University in the Forties," 66.
20 Zakir Ali Khan, Interview, August 10, 2006, 10. An appendix to a meeting of the Academic Council in April 1946 resolves that two lorries will be made available and "one jeep can be made available with sufficient petrol for night duty." It must be noted that this was the first meeting of the Academic Council following the conflagration in the market covered below. Sh. Abdul (Proctor) Rashid, "Appendix F (Ref. No. A.C. Res. No. 3, Dated April 13, 1946): A Meeting of the Committee Appointed by the Academic Council to Devise Means for Patrolling the University at Night," in *Minutes of An Ordinary Meeting of the Academic Council* (Aligarh: Aligarh Muslim University, April 13, 1946).
21 Zakir Ali Khan, Interview, August 10, 2006, 9. Nizami, *History of the Aligarh Muslim University (1920-1945)*, 219.
22 Naved Masood argues that this deployment was the United Provinces Armed Constabulary. Personal Communication with Naved Masood who says this "on the twin authority of late Mr. Merajuddin Ahmad who was the Commandant of the troops (moved from Agra); and a very respectable lawyer of Aligarh, Maulvi Fazlur Rahman (also long deceased)." February 12, 2012.
23 Mohiuddin Khan, Interview, March 28, 2010, 8.
24 Irfan Habib, Interview, June 28, 2009, 19. The official reports cite four deaths. Pars Ram, in his UNESCO-funded study of Aligarh's riots, describes the location as a "Cotton and gur market." Ram, "UNESCO Study of Social Tensions," 172.
25 Iqtidar Alam Khan, Interview, May 31, 2009, 15. Iqtidar Alam Khan was born in a village near Qaimganj in District Farrukhabad in 1932. His father's family were landlords, though his father also maintained a small law practice and was a well-known poet. He first arrived in AMU in 1945, and then returned in 1950. Alam became a professor of history at AMU, from where he retired, though he still frequently visits campus.
26 Brass, *Production of Hindu-Muslim Violence*, 71-2.
27 A.P.I., "Punitive Police for Aligarh," *The Times of India*, April 25, 1946.
28 The British Government was ruling UP under Section 93, but preparing to hand governance over to the Congress, which had won a majority in the most recent elections. Pandit Govind Ballabh Pant and his ministry were sworn in on April 1 in Lucknow. "Late News," ibid. April 2, 1946.
29 United Provinces, Governor's Report, April 1, 1946. Brass, *Production of Hindu-Muslim Violence*, 72.
30 Home (Police) Box 378 File # 5004/1046 (Aligarh–Riot Scheme). Ibid., 71. My thanks to Steven Wilkerson, who also shared his notes on this source with me.
31 A.P.I., "Responsibility for Aligarh Riots: Official Inquiry Report," *The Times of India*, May 3, 1946.
32 Rashid, "Appendix F (Ref. No. A.C. Res. No. 3, Dated 13th April, 1946)."
33 "Aligarh Students' Rowdyism: Issue May Be Put before Viceroy," *The Times of India*, April 6, 1946.
34 Irfan Habib, Interview, June 28, 2009, 10.

35 *The Hindustan Times* of June 9, 1946, several months after the incident, reported that the vice chancellor had agreed to pay "compensation to damage done to Hindu property" but that his estimate was too low to cover all of it. Further, he also "gave assurance that in future the university will make genuine efforts to restore good relations between the students and the Hindu population of Aligarh. The town will be made out of bounds to students till good relations are restored." "University's Compensation Offer for Aligarh Riot Damage," *The Hindustan Times*, June 9, 1946.

36 Hasan, "Some Glimpses of the University in the Forties," 66.

37 It is worth remembering that the university was closed until September 15, 1947, though many students had already arrived there as early as July. The opening was delayed due to unrest in the country.

38 Mushirul Hasan is perhaps the most prominent scholar to take this approach. His articles on Aligarh during the 1940s have supported the idea that nationalism at Aligarh was more or less continuous and that the Pakistan period was an aberration that should be forgotten. In fact, this strategy, as I have shown, has altered the memory of the relationship between the city and the town and fortified the notion that Aligarh students were perpetually threatened by their city neighbors. It obscures the actions of Aligarh students that might have earned the ire of the non-Muslims living nearby. Mushirul Hasan, "Negotiating with Its Past and Present: The Changing Profile of the Aligarh Muslim University," in *Inventing Boundaries: Gender, Politics, and the Partition of India*, ed. Mushirul Hasan (New Delhi: Oxford University Press, 2000).

39 Guha Thakurta, "Uprooted and Divided," 55.

40 From the beginning of their careers at Aligarh, sportsmen received preferential entry: they were not required to meet as high an academic standard as other entrants. They also received special housing. Zakir Ali Khan remembered, "There were special seats reserved for the sportsmen. Special benefits and privileges were given to him. Those who were unable to pay the fees they were not charged the fees. Even meals were given to them free. Then they were decorated and looked up to by the boys." Zakir Ali Khan, Interview, August 10, 2006, 6.

41 Ibid., 10.

42 Masood-ul Hasan, Interview, May 1, 2009, 17.

43 K. P. S. (Anonymized), Interviewed by Amber Abbas, Lucknow, India, 2009, 10. Interview in author's possession.

44 Italicized sections are author's translation from Urdu. K. P. S. (Anonymized), Interview, 2009, 7.

45 Tuan, *Landscapes of Fear*, 204.

46 Majid Ali Siddiqi, Interview, October 2, 2009, 21. Majid Ali Siddiqi was born in 1935 in Gorakhpur, India. He arrived at Aligarh in 1952 to study engineering. He was also involved in sports, hurdles, and hockey. He completed his B.Sc. in Civil Engineering from Aligarh University in 1956. He had a long career with Jayaprakash Associates; he is now Director, JP Karsham Hydro, Corporation, Ltd. He lives in Lucknow.

47 Masood-ul Hasan, Interview, May 1, 2009, 14. Habibur Rahman, Interview, February 20, 2010, 5.

48 Italicized sections are author's translation from Urdu. Iftikhar Alam Khan, Interview, June 6, 2009, 5.

49 I have no specific evidence on whether people were killed in Aligarh's cinema houses in 1947. However, the impact of this knowledge/rumor affected Khan's behavior, and

left him fearful for his safety. This anxiety is what is at stake here, more than the facts of the violence in the city. In fact, he revealed, referring to the anxious days after 1947, "That fear is still with me."
50 Masood-ul Hasan, Interview, May 1, 2009, 14.
51 Ibid.
52 Iqbal Shafi, Interview, May 9, 2010, 10.
53 Massey, "Places and Their Pasts," 183.
54 Habibur Rahman, Interview, February 20, 2010, 5. Habibur Rahman was born in Dhaka on January 1, 1925. His family belongs to village Munshiganj outside of Dhaka. He passed his matriculation from Calcutta University, and his father sent him on a tour of North India by train. After that, he began his education at Aligarh in 1944, and he lived in Sir Syed East. Rahman became an advocate and cared for his mother for much of his adult life, marrying late. He lives in Dhaka with his wife and young daughter.
55 Wazir Khan, "Captain Wazir Khan: Interview with Unam Muneer, Citizens Archive of Pakistan," ed. Unam Muneer (Karachi, N.D.).
56 M. A. Bari, "Resolutions for 7th Annual Session of the All India Muslim Students' Federation," in *Freedom Movement Archives* (Islamabad: Pakistan National Archives, March 1945), F 961/ 17-21.
57 Iqbal Shafi Interview, May 9, 2010, 14.
58 Ziauddin Ahmad, "The Report of the Vice-Chancellor, Aligarh Muslim University for the Calendar Year 1945: Read at the Convocation Held on the 1st December, 1945" (Aligarh: Aligarh Muslim University Press, 1945).
59 Wazir Khan, Interview, 2. Train violence is a key theme in partition histories. See also Butalia, *The Other Side of Silence*; Menon and Bhasin, *Borders and Boundaries*; Khushwant Singh, *Train to Pakistan* (New Delhi: Roli Books, 2006); Husain, *1947*.
60 Marian Aguiar, *Tracking Modernity: India's Railway and the Culture of Mobility* (Minneapolis: The University of Minnesota Press, 2011), 172.
61 Waheeduddin Choudhri, Interviewed by Amber Abbas, April 6, 2010, 5. Waheeduddin Choudhri was born in Sylhet and attended AMU for engineering from 1946 to 1949. He held leftist sympathies and was active in the student movement. He settled in East Pakistan and became an engineer for the government but later supported the movement for the independence of Bangladesh.
62 Ibid.
63 These are distinctly Hindu names. Mohammad Amin, Interview, November 5, 2009, 6.
64 Saadat Hasan Manto's Short Story, "Mishtake" encapsulates this arbitrariness. In its entirety: "Ripping the belly cleanly, the knife moved in a straight line down to the midriff, in the process slashing the cord which held the man's pajamas in place. The one with the knife took one look and exclaimed regretfully, 'Oh no! . . . Mishtake!'" Manto, *A Manto Panorama*, 62.
65 I. H. Qureishi, "A Case Study of the Social Relations between the Muslims and the Hindus, 1935-1947," in *The Partition of India: Policies and Perspectives*, ed. C. H. Philips and M. D. Wainwright (London: Allen and Unwin, 1970), 368. Shahid Ahmad Dehlavi, "Dilli Ki Bipta [1948]," in *Zulmat-I-Nimroz*, ed. Mumtaz Shirin (Karachi: Nafiz Akademi, 1990), 188-9. Cited in Pandey, *Remembering Partition*, 133, 150.
66 A local bar serving homemade alcohol.
67 Mohammad Amin, Interview, November 5, 2009, 6.
68 Iftikhar Alam Khan, Interview, June 6, 2009, 7. Author's translation.

69 Or perhaps the other way around. Political power emanated from Delhi; it was there that the students traveled to seek guidance from Jinnah. However, the League's power was legitimated for the students by its presence on the campus at Aligarh. Prior to 1947, Aligarh's reputation "authorized" student travel to Delhi, but after 1947 this reciprocal relationship was disrupted.
70 Aguiar, *Tracking Modernity: India's Railway and the Culture of Mobility*, 76.
71 Pandey, *Remembering Partition*, 131–2.
72 Emphasis in original. Ibid., 140.
73 Ibid., 146.
74 "Great Killing" is the phrase used to describe the rioting that spread from Calcutta to Bihar and Noakhali in August 1946 in the wake of the Muslim League's "Direct Action Day." Hasan uses the term here to account for the rioting of both 1946 and 1947; it also shows the continuity he sees between these two events. Masood-ul Hasan, Interview, May 1, 2009, 22.
75 Ibid.
76 Zakir Ali Khan, Interview, August 10, 2006, 8.
77 As late as the 1990s, when a Ph.D. student at Aligarh University, Professor Akhtaruzzaman of Dhaka University, felt that when a Muslim went to AMU, he seemed to have "received more power," but when he went "outside," he was again "ordinary." Mohammad Akhtaruzzaman, Interviewed by Amber Abbas, Dhaka, Bangladesh, March 10, 2010, 4. Akhtaruzzaman was born in Borguna, in southern Bangladesh (then East Pakistan), in 1961. He completed his B.A. and M.A. in Dhaka University before he went to AMU in 1995 to study Medieval History with Iqtidar Husain Siddiqi. He is a professor of history in Dhaka University, Bangladesh.
78 Creswell, *In Place/out of Place: Geography, Ideology, and Transgression*, 12.
79 Massey, "Places and Their Pasts," 186.
80 K. P. S. (Anonymized), Interview, 2009, 7.
81 Asloob Ahmad Ansari, Interview, July 5, 2008, 4.
82 Cole, "(Re)Placing the Past."
83 Philip J. Ethington, "Placing the Past: 'Groundwork' for a Spatial Theory of History," *Rethinking History* 11, no. 4 (December 2007): 465–93.
84 Edward Casey, "Boundary, Place, and Event in the Spatiality of History," *Rethinking History* 11, no. 4 (December 2007): 509.
85 Devji, *Muslim Zion: Pakistan as a Political Idea*, 199.

Chapter 4: The Muslim Question in India

1 Justice Rajender Sachar, "The Sachar Committee Report: Social, Economic and Educational Status of the Muslim Community of India" (New Delhi: Prime Minister's High Level Committee, Cabinet Secretariat, Government of India, 2006).
2 Ibid.
3 Ather Siddiqi, Interview, May 11, 2009, 12. Ather Siddiqi is originally from Saharanpur. He was admitted to AMU in 1947 for his Intermediate. He completed his M.Sc. in AMU and his Ph.D. in Zoology in the United States and became a professor. He is retired and lives in Aligarh with his wife, fellow academic Dr. Zakia Siddiqi.
4 Sachar Committee Report.
5 Human Rights Watch has reported, based on data from Hate Crime Watch, a "collaborative database" compiled by FactChecker.in, that there were approximately

250 reported incidents of crimes targeting religious minorities from 2009 to 2018, with over 90 percent taking place after the BJP came to power in 2014. These attacks overwhelmingly targeted Muslims. "Report: Violent Cow Protection in India: Vigilante Groups Attack Minorities," Human Rights Watch, February 2019, 20. https://www.hrw.org/report/2019/02/18/violent-cow-protection-india/vigilante-groups-attack-minorities

6 William Gould, *Hindu Nationalism Ad the Language of Politics in Late Colonial India* (Cambridge: Cambridge University Press, 2004), 7.
7 Cited in Kudaisya, *Region, Nation, "Heartland,"* 349.
8 This effort was evident when I was conducting field research in Aligarh. As I explained my intention to study the 1930s and 1940s at Aligarh, many people directed me to literature on "The Aligarh Movement," the educational movement led by Sir Sayyid in the nineteenth century that ultimately led to the founding of the institution. This period is highly glorified in the Aligarh narrative, whereas study of the 1940s is absent.
9 Riazur Rahman Sherwani, Interview, November 20, 2009, 4.
10 However, Sherwani also pointed out that non-League politicians were not "allowed" to visit the campus in the 1940s. Ibid. Further, the minutes of the Executive Council Meeting of December 11, 1947, reflect that the university opened later than usual, on September 15, 1947.
11 Irfan Habib, Interview, June 28, 2009, 13.
12 Nawab Ismail Khan, "Application for Additional Grants-in-Aid Submitted to the Government of India by the Vice-Chancellor Aligarh Muslim University" (Aligarh: Maulana Azad Library, 1948).
13 Ather Siddiqi, Interview, May 11, 2009, 9.
14 Siddiqi first indicated that he was in AMU during partition, but when I pressed him for details, he noted that he had been there earlier in the year to apply for admission and returned to matriculate in the fall. Ibid.
15 K. P. S also told me, "These people who claim to be true Aligarians they joined Aligarh after post-independence era. So they are unable to locate what happened during that critical moments when Aligarh was on the major hit list." Here, Partition takes on the valence of a trial-by-fire through which true Aligs had to pass. K. P. S. (anon), Interview, 2009, 10.
16 Mohammad Obaidur Rahman Khan Sherwani, "Report of the Vice-Chancellor, Aligarh Muslim University for the Calendar Year 1946: Read at the Convocation Held on the 16th February, 1947" (Aligarh: Aligarh Muslim University Press, 1947).
17 Mohd. Ismail Khan, "Annual Report of the Vice-Chancellor Aligarh Muslim University for the Calendar Year 1947: Read at the Convocation Held on 24th January, 1948" (Aligarh: Aligarh Muslim University Press, 1948). The Annual Report from 1945 noted that "the centre of gravity of the University has shifted from Arts to Science, and the Strachey Hall now no longer occupies the central position which it had enjoyed for about sixty years." In addition, during the war there had been a rush of applications to the Engineering College. Ahmad, "The Report of the Vice-Chancellor, Aligarh Muslim University for the Calendar Year 1945: Read at the Convocation Held on the 1st December, 1945."
18 Mohiuddin Khan, Interview, March 28, 2010, 8.
19 Iftikhar Alam Khan, Interview, June 6, 2009, 4.
20 Mohiuddin Khan, Interview, March 28, 2010, 8.

21. K. P. S. (anon), Interview, 2009, 7.
22. David Lelyveld, "Places of Origin of Aligarh Students 1875-1895: Map by Joseph E. Schwartzberg," in *Aligarh's First Generation: Muslim Solidarity in British India* (Princeton: Princeton University Press, 1978); *Alumni Directory, Aligarh Muslim University*, 3 vols., Sir Syed House Publication (Karachi: Sir Syed University of Engineering and Technology, 1974?).
23. Sardar Vallabhbhai Patel, "Speech: You Cannot Ride Two Horses, January 6, 1948," in *For a United India: Speeches of Sardar Patel 1947-1950* (Delhi: Publications Division, Ministry of Information and Broadcasting, Government of India, 1967), 64.
24. Zakir Ali Khan, Interview, August 10, 2006, 4.
25. Roorki University reserved only a handful of places for Muslims. Zakir Ali Khan Interview, 8. Majid Ali Siddiqi, Interview, May 11, 2009, 5. Mohiuddin Khan, Interview, March 28, 2010, 2–3.
26. Siddiqi's brother and later his parents and sister migrated to Pakistan. Ather Siddiqi, Interview, May 11, 2009, 13.
27. Zamindar, *The Long Partition*.
28. Irfan Habib, Interview, June 28, 2009, 13.
29. He served as governor of Bihar from 1957 to 1962, as vice president of India from 1962 to 1967 and then as president from 1967 to 1969.
30. K. P. S. (anon.), Interview, 2009, 2.
31. Zakir Husain, "Application for Grants-in-Aid Submitted by the Vice-Chancellor Aligarh Muslim University to the Government of India" (Aligarh: Maulana Azad Library, January 1950).
32. Ahmad Saeed, Interview, October 10, 2009, 9.
33. Mohammad Amin, Interview, November 5, 2009, 4.
34. K. P. S. (anon.), Interview, 2009, 2.
35. Iftikhar Alam Khan Interview, 7. See also interviews with Ather Siddiqi and Zakir Ali Khan.
36. Ather Siddiqi, Interview, May 11, 2009, 7.
37. Ibid.
38. Iqtidar Alam Khan, Interview, May 31, 2009, 18.
39. Masood-ul Hasan, Interview, May 1, 2009, 17.
40. Syed Zainul Abedin, "In Memoriam," *Aligarh Magazine*, 1948, ii.
41. Anthony J. Parel, ed., *Gandhi: Hind Swaraj and Other Writings* (Cambridge: Cambridge University Press, 1997).
42. This effort was so successful that when I was researching at AMU, administrators at the university cautioned me against looking at materials from this period, sometimes refusing to make them available. Though the Maulana Azad Library maintains an archive of Sir Sayyid's writings from the late nineteenth century, the university registrar expressed his disbelief that I was asking to look at documents that were more than fifty years old! Hakeem Zillur Rahman told me, during a conversation, that the reason I could not find personal papers from this period was because after partition people held bonfires and burned them, fearing retribution should they be accused of disloyalty. Syed Mohammad Ali and Farrukh Jalali confirmed that many documents had been destroyed.
43. Syed Zainul Abedin, "The Flying Fez," *Aligarh Magazine*, 1948, xiii.
44. Syed Zainul Abedin, ed., "Our Prime Minister," *Aligarh Magazine*, 1948, vii–viii.
45. Jawaharlal Nehru, "Speech by the Hon'ble Pundit Jawaharlal Nehru, Prime Minister of India, at the Annual Convocation of the Muslim University at Aligarh on 24th

January, 1948," *Aligarh Magazine*, 1948, xvii. Mohammad, *Glimpses of Muslim Education Vol. 1*, 1, 229–33.
46 After independence, the convocation speeches delivered at Aligarh are overwhelming concerned with the responsibilities of citizenship. See Mohammad, ed. *Glimpses of Muslim Eudcation*.
47 Mohammad Iqbal, "Our New Vice Chancellor," *Aligarh Magazine*, 1949.
48 Mohammad Amin, Interview, November 5, 2009, 6.
49 I cite only a few here: S. M. Mehdi, Interviewed by Amber Abbas, Aligarh, India, June 15, 2009, 6. Ather Siddiqi, Interview, May 11, 2009, 14. Fatima Fari Rahman Interview, 9.
50 Ather Siddiqi, Interview, May 11, 2009, 14.
51 Masood-ul Hasan, Interview, May 1, 23.
52 Mehdi is one of the few non-Aligarians who I interviewed for the project. Though he was living in Aligarh to be close to his adult daughter, he said that in his younger years he had an "allergy" to Aligarh University! S. M. Mehdi, Interview, 1. S. M. Mehdi hailed from Bhopal State, and was born around 1924. He did his early education, through high school, in Bhopal before transferring to Christchurch College in Kanpur in 1939. He completed his M.A. from Lucknow University where he was involved in communist politics. He was a well-known Urdu author and playwright. He died in 2015.
53 Ibid.
54 Ibid.
55 S. M. Mehdi, Interview, June 2009, 8.
56 Irfan Habib, Interview, June 28, 2009, 14.
57 Iqtidar Alam Khan, Interview, May 31, 2009, 18.
58 Significantly, the RSS has continued to expand its influence and has been associated with anti-Muslim violence throughout India, including the destruction of the Babri Masjid in Ayodhya in 1991 and the Gujarat pogroms of 2002. Narendra Modi, head of the BJP, and a member of the RSS, was elected prime minister of India in 2014 and 2019.
59 Perhaps the most egregious example of this was the "Batla House Encounter" in which students from JMI were picked up on suspicion of having exploded bombs in crowded sections of New Delhi in September 2008.
60 Ashish Khetan, "In the Words of a Zealot," *Tehelka*, January 15, 2011.
61 Lalmani Verma, "After Aseemanand's Confession, A.M.U. Wants More Security," *Indian Express* January 12, 2011. At a time of external threat, it should be noted here, the Aligarh vice chancellor turned immediately to the civil authorities for protection.
62 Omar Khalidi reports that Vallabhbhai Patel labeled Maulana Azad's Education Ministry, staffed by Muslims including K. G. Saiyidain, as a "miniature Pakistan." Khalidi, *Muslims in Indian Economy* (Gurgaon, Haryana: Three Essays Collective, 2006), 39. Masood-ul Hasan Interview. Zakir Ali Khan Interview. Sayyid Hamid, Interviewed by Amber Abbas, New Delhi, India, October 29, 2009, 8. Sayyid Hamid was born in Faizabad near Lucknow in 1920. He attended Aligarh University 1937 to 1942, as a student, and later joined the Indian Administrative Service in 1943. In 1980, he was appointed by Prime Minister Indira Gandhi to serve as vice chancellor of AMU where he remained until 1985. He is currently chancellor of Jamia Hamdard University in New Delhi.
63 Pandey Gyanendra, "Can a Muslim Be an Indian?, *Comparative Studies in Society and History* 41, no. 4 (October 1999): 608–29.

64 Vallabhbhai Patel, "Speech: You Cannot Ride Two Horses, January 6, 1948," 64–9.
65 Ibid., 610.
66 Najeeb Jung, "Why Should a Muslim Have to Wear His Nationalism on His Sleeve?," *The Times of India* February 20, 2010.
67 Khalidi, *Indian Muslims since Independence*, 17.
68 Sachar, "The Sachar Committee Report," 2.
69 Seal, *The Emergence of Indian Nationalism*; Sachar, "The Sachar Committee Report." Khalidi, *Indian Muslims since Independence*.
70 Ibid., 67. Employment Statistics, 74.
71 16.4 percent of convicted prison inmates are Muslim according to the 2014 National Crime Records Bureau Report. The ten year average is 17.63 percent. In 2014, 21.1 percent of Undertrial prisoners and 20.3 percent of Detenues are Muslims. "Prison Statistics India 2014," (New Delhi: National Crime Records Bureau, 2014). http://ncrb.gov.in/PSI-2014rev1/PrisonStat2014rev1.htm
72 Khalidi critiques the government's transparency when he shows that since 1996 annual reports of the National Minorities Commission have not been made publicly available. He attributes this to the fact that the reports must be presented in the Lok Sabha alongside an Action Taken Report. He also reveals that other government-sponsored reports have languished for years (like the Gopal Singh Panel Report commissioned in 1983 that was not presented in parliament until 1990) before being presented in parliament. Khalidi, *Muslims in Indian Economy*, 5–6.
73 Ahmad Saeed, Interview, October 10, 2009, 21.
74 Thomas Blom Hansen described these artisans, traders, and farmers as "economically marginal." Thomas Blom Hansen, *The Saffron Wave: Democracy and Hindu Nationalism in India* (Princeton: Princeton University Press, 1999), 150.
75 Omar Khalidi reports that Vallabhbhai Patel labeled Maulana Azad's Education Ministry, staffed by Muslims including K. G. Saiyidain, as a "miniature Pakistan." Khalidi, *Muslims in Indian Economy*, 39. Brass, *Production of Hindu-Muslim Violence*, 36–7. See Preface.
76 Ibid., 21–3.
77 Khalidi, *Indian Muslims since Independence*, 114. See the Epilogue for a discussion of the most recent efforts of the Indian government to limit Muslim access to citizenship.
78 Khan, "Annual Report of the Vice-Chancellor Aligarh Muslim University for the Calendar Year 1947: Read at the Convocation Held on 24th January, 1948."
79 Salman Khurshid is a grandson of Dr. Zakir Husain, India's first Muslim president and former vice chancellor of AMU. Khurshid was born in Aligarh, but he attended St. Stephen's College, Delhi. He is a lawyer, writer, and politician, serving from the Farrukhabad Lok Sabha constituency. In 2009, he became the minister for minority affairs and in 2011 cabinet minister for law and justice, and minority affairs. Khurshid, *At Home in India: A Restatement of Indian Muslims*, 21.
80 In 1961, well after the major Partition-linked migration had ended, India's Muslim population was enumerated at 47 million, about 10 percent of the total population of 439 million. Sachar, "The Sachar Committee Report," 28. The most recent census data, from 2001, places the Indian Muslim Minority at approximately 13.4 percent of the population. http://www.censusindia.gov.in
81 Steven I. Wilkinson, *Votes and Violence: Electoral Competition and Ethnic Riots in India* (New York: Cambridge University Press, 2004), 109. See pages 108–22 for Wilkinson's discussion of the abolition of Muslim electorates, against the veto of

the few remaining Muslim League politicians. Begum Aizaz Rasul, apparently at the urging of Congress' Maulana Azad, Sardar Patel and K. M. Munshi, spoke only hesitantly in favor of the abolition with the logic that as "an integral part of the Indian nation" (121) Muslims should participate in the general electorate. For an assessment of Congress' failure to fulfill commitments to Aligarh, see also "A Wasted Generation at Aligarh" in Khurshid, *At Home in India: A Restatement of Indian Muslims*, 57–65.
82 Khaliquzzaman, *Pathway to Pakistan*, 394. M. Raisur Rahman, "UP Muslims: From Separate Electorates to Sachar Committee Report and After," Conference Paper at 48th Annual Conference on South Asia, October 18, 2019.
83 Christophe Jaffrelot and Gilles Verniers, "The Dwindling Minority," *The Indian Express (online)*, July 30, 2018. Last accessed November 17, 2019.
84 Ather Siddiqi told me that his parents took his sister to Pakistan in 1965 because it was too difficult to find a good "match" for their daughter in India as so many of the "good families" had migrated to Pakistan. Ather Siddiqi, Interview, May 11, 2009, 7.
85 This assessment came from an informal exchange with an AMU graduate who has family in Pakistan.
86 Zakia Siddiqi, Interviewed by Amber Abbas, Aligarh, India, December 9, 2009, 17. Zakia Siddiqi was born in Allahabad in 1936. She completed her Intermediate in 1952 in Lucknow's Karamat Husain Girls' School. She completed her bachelor's of education and M.A. in AMU and then earned an M.S. in Guidance and Counseling at Purdue University. She taught in the Aligarh Women's College, and became the principal and provost. She established the Center for Women's Studies at AMU and now oversees the Aligarh Public School.
87 Zakia Siddiqi, Interview, December 9, 2009, 17.
88 Hayatullah Ansari, "Mera Aftab Hall," *The Aftab* The Aftab Memoirs Special (1976).
89 Masood-ul Hasan, Interview, May 1, 2009, 21.
90 Only to narrators in India. Pakistani narrators make an effort to portray Jinnah as an insider, emphasizing his many visits to Aligarh during the 1940s. In a 2006 interview, General Ghulam Umar intimated a direct link between Aligarh and Jinnah by placing Mohammad Ali Jauhar and the *Khilafat* Movement leadership between them. Jinnah neither attended AMU nor supported the *Khilafat* Movement. However, General Umar easily incorporated him into Aligarh's narrative by identifying him as the heir to the legacy of Muslim reform in the period after 1857. The link was further solidified by Jinnah's commitment to the university and his belief that the young men educated there would go on to be leaders in Pakistan. Ghulam Umar Interview, 13. See also Abbas, "Thinking through Partition."
91 Translated from Urdu by author. Saeeda Kidwai, Interviewed by Amber Abbas, Aligarh, India, June 17, 2009, 12. Saeeda Kidwai, known to most as "Saeeda Apa," is originally from Delhi but was largely raised in Aligarh by an uncle after her father's death. She has three sisters. She was admitted to the Aligarh Women's College in 1926 and was the first woman to take graduate classes in Geography in AMU. She graduated in 1939 and began teaching in 1941. She taught in the Women's College and lives in Aligarh.
92 See Epilogue.
93 Dhulipala, *Creating a New Medina*.
94 Aamir Mufti, "Secularism and Minority: Elements of a Critique," *Social Text* 45 (Winter 1995): 84.
95 Ibid., 85.
96 Irfan Habib, Interview, June 28, 2009, 5.

97 Ibid., 9.
98 Salman Rushdie, *Shame* (New York: Alfred Knopf, 1983), Oldenburg, "'A Place Insufficiently Imagined': Language, Belief, and the Pakistan Crisis of 1971." See also Dhulipala, *Creating a New Medina*.
99 Saeed Naqvi, *Reflections of an Indian Muslim* (New Delhi: Har-Anand Publications, 1993), 14–15.
100 Masood-ul Hasan, Interview, May 1, 2009, 21.
101 Naqvi, *Reflections of an Indian Muslim*, 41. Ather Siddiqi, Interview, May 11, 2009.
102 Zamindar, *The Long Partition*.
103 Naqvi, *Reflections of an Indian Muslim*, 17. K. P. S also expressed anxiety on this point when he argued that "EVERY Muslim is a nationalist" by which he means that the Muslims who remain in India are there by choice, despite the presence of Pakistan and must be considered loyal Indians. As indicated in the preface, not all Indians share this conviction. K. P. S. (anon), Interview, 2009, 2.
104 For an exploration of the ways in which Pakistanis view their own history, see my chapter "Belonging and the Beginning of the Past," 27–47.
105 Gilmartin, "Partition, Pakistan, and South Asian History," 1090.
106 Saikia, "Strangers, Friends, and Peace," 287.
107 Tan and Kudaisya, *The Aftermath of Partition in South Asia*, 8.
108 Ather Siddiqi, Interview, May 11, 2009, 4.
109 Zamindar cites Arendt's 1951 *The Origins of Totalitarianism* as she examines the effects for minorities of the homogenizing narratives of South Asian nation-states. Vazira Fazila—Yacoobali Zamindar, "South Asia in Dark Times: Homogenizing Nation-States and the Problem of Minorities," *Current History* 114, no. 771 (April 2015): 153.
110 At one point, he told me, "Hindus will say this, that Muslims divided it. There were other reasons, but still." While he also blamed Muslims, he recognized the complexity of the identity politics, and acknowledged that the Hindu-Muslim relationship after 1947 has been dominated by the suspicion of Muslim separatism.
111 Ather Siddiqi, Interview, May 11, 2009, 4.
112 Mufti, "Secularism and Minority: Elements of a Critique," 85.

Chapter 5: Muslimness and Pakistan

1 Hasan, "Nationalist and Separatist Trends in Aligarh," 116.
2 Pandey, "Can a Muslim Be an Indian?"; Sachar Committee Report; Human Rights Watch Report.
3 Wajahat Husain, Interview, June 29, 2005, 14.
4 Mohammad Ali Jinnah, "Sacred Duty of Muslims to Protect Minorities," in *Quaid-i-Azam Muhammad Ali Jinnah (Speeches, Statements, Writings, Letters, Etc.)*, ed. Muhammad Haneef Shahid (Lahore: Sang-e-Meel Publications, 1976), 53. See also "Protection for Minorities in Pakistan," in *Quaid-i-Azam Muhammad Ali Jinnah (Speeches, Statements, Writings, Letters, Etc.)*, ed. Muhammad Haneef Shahid (Lahore: Sang-e-Meel Publications, 1976), 84.
5 Jane Perlez, "Pakistani Sentenced to Death May Get a Pardon," *The New York Times*, November 22, 2010. Dean Nelson, "Blog Shahbaz Bhatti Killing: What Hope Now for Pakistan's Christians?," *The Telegraph*, March 2, 2011. Theodore Gabriel, "The

Blasphemy Law and Its Impact on the Christian Community," in *Christian Citizens in an Islamic State: The Pakistan Experience* (Aldershot: Ashgate Publishing Ltd., 2007), 60.
6 As I discuss later, Ahmadis are forbidden from calling themselves "Muslims" or their places of worship "mosques."
7 Shemeem Burney Abbas, *Pakistan's Blasphemy Laws: From Islamic Empires to the Taliban* (Austin: The University of Texas Press, 2013).
8 Salman Masood and Carlotta Gill, "Killing of Governor Deepens Crisis in Pakistan," *The New York Times*, January 4, 2011. Ed Husain, "Explaining the Salman Taseer Murder," in *Expert Brief* (Council on Foreign Relations, January 7, 2011).
9 Shumaila Jaffrey, "Asia Bibi: Pakistan's Notorious Blasphemy Case," *BBC Online*. https://www.bbc.co.uk/news/resources/idt-sh/Asia_Bibi. Last accessed November 17, 2019.
10 Scholars have worked diligently to expose the diversity of the Muslim population of Pakistan and India. Richard Eaton, *India's Islamic Traditions, 711-1750* (Delhi: Oxford University Press, 2003), David Gilmartin, *Empire and Islam: Punjab and the Making of Pakistan* (Berkeley: The University of California Press, 1988), Peter Hardy, *Partners in Freedom and True Muslims: The Political Thought of Some Muslim Scholars in British India 1912–1947* (Westport: Greenwood Press, 1971), Mushirul Hasan, *Moderate or Militant: Images of India's Muslims* (Oxford: Oxford University Press, 2008), Akbar Hyder, *Reliving Karbala: Martyrdom in South Asian Memory* (Oxford: Oxford University Press, 2006), Jalal, *Self and Sovereignty*, Barbara Daly Metcalf, *Islamic Contestations: Essays on Muslims in India and Pakistan* (New Delhi: Oxford University Press, 2004). *Islam in South Asia in Practice* (Princeton: Princeton University Press, 2009). Annemarie Schimmel, *Mystical Dimensions of Islam* (Chapel Hill: The University of North Carolina Press, 1975), among many others.
11 Jacqueline Rose, "Nation as Trauma, Zionism as Question: Jacqueline Rose Interviewed," ed. Rosemary Bechler (OpenDemocracy.net, August 17, 2005). Rose is responding to the tension between the state of Israel and the potential threat of the Palestinians. She argues that Israel no longer has any concrete justification for feeling threatened as it possesses one of the most powerful militaries worldwide. Still, trauma is the foundation of its national identity and must be repeatedly enacted to fortify that identity.
12 Interview with Cecil Chaudhry, Rawalpindi, in Ahmad Salim, ed. *Reconstructing History: Memories, Migrants, and Minorities* (Islamabad: Sustainable Development Policy Institute (SDPI), 2009), 162.
13 Rose, "Nation as Trauma, Zionism as Question: Jacqueline Rose Interviewed." "Response to Edward Said," in *Freud and the Non-European* (London and New York: Verso in Association with the Freud Museum, 2003), 77.
14 Simon Ross Valentine, *Islam and the Ahmadiyya Jama'at: History, Belief, Practice* (New York: Columbia University Press, 2008), 228.
15 Metcalf, *Islamic Revival in British India*.
16 Spencer Lavan, *The Ahmadiyah Movement: A History and Perspective* (New Delhi: Manohar, 1974), 12.
17 Ibid., 164–85.
18 S. Abul A'la Maududi, *The Qadiani Problem* (Lahore: Islamic Publications Limited, 1979 [1953]).
19 In May 2010, two Ahmadi sites were simultaneously attacked in Lahore, part of a Sunni supremacist campaign of violence against those groups, including Shi'a, Sufis, and Christians, seen to be outside the Sunni fold. These sites, as well as Sufi shrines and Christian churches, were deliberately targeted as sites of plural or heterodox

practice. "International Religious Freedom Report-Pakistan," ed. Department of State (Washington, DC, July–December 2010), 2.
20 Devji, *Muslim Zion: Pakistan as a Political Idea*, 155.
21 Ibid., 244.
22 Abdul Rasheed Khan, Interview, August 10, 2006, 5.
23 Riazur Rahman Sherwani, Interview, November 10, 2009, 4.
24 Habibur Rahman, Interview, February 20, 2010, 4.
25 Salahuddin Chowdhury, Interviewed by Amber Abbas, Dhaka, Bangladesh, April 10, 2010, 4. Salahuddin Chowdhury was born in Sylhet and joined Aligarh in the mid-1940s, finishing his degree in 1949. He made his career in the jute industry in East Pakistan, later Bangladesh. After retiring from that industry, he provided consulting services for the World Bank.
26 Bangladesh, of course, did not exist then, so Chowdhury's statement betrays an explicit "reading back" of national history. It makes sense that he would associate the solidarity of Bengalis at AMU with Bangladesh, especially if he had felt most at home among other Bengalis in AMU itself. Ibid.
27 Habibur Rahman, Interview, February 20, 2010, 4.
28 Other narrators noted that "we were more friendly with the Southern Indian students and to some extent with Pathan students," in other words, with other non-Urdu-speakers suggesting that multiple minority communities within the university banded together. Mohiuddin Khan, Interview, March 28, 2010, 9.
29 Mohiuddin Khan, Interview, March 28, 2010, 17.
30 *Bhabi* means "brother's wife" in Urdu and Hindi.
31 Habibur Rahman, Interview, February 20, 2010, 6.
32 Mohiuddin Khan, Interview, March 28, 2010, 9.
33 Habibur Rahman, Interview, February 20, 2010, 4.
34 Salahuddin Chowdhury, Interview, April 10, 2010, 6.
35 An article on the session in *The Student* notes that "in the procession were a large contingent of Muslim students—many of them were from Aligarh in their black sherwanis and Jinnah caps. Together with the rest of the procession they joined their voices in the resounding slogans of: '*Hindu-Muslim nahi larenge!*' '*Angrezo-per war karenge!*' ('Hindus and Muslims will not fight each other!' 'Together we shall fight the British!'" "Forward to New Battles!: The A.I.S.F. Conference, Delhi," *The Student: Journal of the All India Students Federation* (January 1947).
36 Mohiuddin Khan, Interview, March 28, 2010, 7.
37 Waheeduddin Choudhri, Interview, April 6, 2010, 5.
38 M. A. Rashid, Interviewed by Amber Abbas, Dhaka, Bangladesh, March 29, 2010, 8. M. A. Rashid hails from Lucknow in North India; he was born in 1921. After passing from Aligarh in 1943, he settled in Calcutta, having taken a job with M. M. Ispahani, Ltd. He fled to Dhaka in East Pakistan in 1950 during communal riots in Calcutta. In the early 1950s, he started his own business trading in jute. In 1954, he joined the East Pakistan Stock Exchange. Today, he remains a director of the Stock Exchange and lives in Dhaka.
39 Ari Bassin, "Justice or Charade in Dhaka?," *International Justice Tribune*, no. 123 (March 2, 2011).
40 M. A. Rashid described the 1938 League session when Fazlul Haq was given this nickname. "He spoke in his speech 'If Hindus did something wrong with the Muslims of UP we will take revenge in Bengal where we have the same average of Hindus and Muslims as in UP. Muslims are here in majority, and Hindus were in majority in Lucknow.' On that point, the public of Lucknow uttered, '*Sher-e-Bengal Zindabad!*

(Long Live the Lion of Bengal!) Sher-e-Bengal Zindabad!' on this point. Since then, he became *Sher-e-Bangla*. And he is here also famous in this name, *Sher-e-Bangla, Sher-e-Bangla*. People know him as *Sher-e-Bangla* not as A.K. Fazlul Haq." M. A. Rashid, Interview, March 29, 2010, 3.

41 Rounaq Jahan, *Pakistan: Failure in National Integration* (New York: Columbia University Press, 1972), 22.
42 Mohiuddin Khan, Interview, March 28, 2010, 6.
43 Several narrators, on all sides of the borders, were sympathetic to the Cabinet Mission plan and blamed Congress intransigence for its failure. I. Q. (anonymized) argued "I think there was a glimpse of lightning when the Cabinet Mission was brought in ... And Quaid-e-Azam almost agreed to it. *Ke* 'Okay, where the Muslims are in the majority we'll form the government, where the Hindus are in the majority, they will form the government. There will be a few subjects which will be centered for both'. So Quaid-e-Azam almost agreed ... But the Congress they did not agree. Because they wanted to have overall supremacy. See that is where, that was a glimpse of where things could have settled down, and been sorted out." I. Q. (anonymized), Interviewed by Amber Abbas, Karachi, Pakistan, 2010, 20. Major General Ghulam Umar (Ret'd) said, "Up 'til 1946 this Mr. Jinnah was trying to find some understanding and when that understanding was no more possible, then it became obvious that you have to part company and that was how Pakistan came into being." Ghulam Umar, Interviewed by Amber Abbas, Karachi, Pakistan, August 8, 2006. Javid Iqbal, son of renown poet Mohammad Iqbal added, "Jinnah agreed with the Cabinet Mission plan ... Jinnah conceded. But Nehru under the influence of Patel refused to accept it. So actually Pakistan was created by the Congress. By the Hindu obstinacy!" Javid Iqbal, Interviewed by Amber Abbas, Lahore, Pakistan, June 13, 2006, 16.
44 Wajahat Husain, Interview, June 13, 2005, 10.
45 Habibur Rahman, Interview, February 20, 2010, 10.
46 Ibid.
47 "Six-Point Programme of Sheikh Mujib Ur Rahman," in *Banglapedia: National Encyclopedia of Bangladesh*, http://www.banglapedia.org/httpdocs/HT/S_0426.HTM.
48 Yasmin Saikia, *Women, War and the Making of Bangladesh: Remembering 1971* (Durham: Duke University Press, 2011), 39.
49 Saikia makes clear, too, that as the conflict developed, and especially with the intervention of India, vulnerable populations, including women, Urdu-speaking Biharis, and other minorities became targets of violence by different groups. "All groups involved in the wars were complicit in the violence." Saikia, *Women, War*, 46.
50 Although these interviews provide a diversity of views, Salim provides little to no biographical information on the informants, which compromises their value as "life history" interviews, in my opinion. I have used several excerpts from these interviews below, but in the absence of any contextualizing (age, profession, birthplace, etc.) information for each narrator's comments. Salim, *Reconstructing History: Memories, Migrants, and Minorities*.
51 "The Citizens Archive of Pakistan," http://www.citizensarchive.org/index.php.
52 Sinha, *Colonial Masculinity*; Streets, *Martial Races*.
53 The One Unit Scheme amalgamated all of the provinces of West Pakistan into one province, thus nearly equalizing the percentage of the population in each state, creating a false sense of West Pakistani regional unity and providing a bulwark against the possibility of a Bengali representative majority in government.
54 Saikia, *Women, War*, 36.

55 Wajahat Husain, Interviewed by Amber Abbas, Lahore, Pakistan, July 8, 2005, 3.
56 It is reasonable to characterize the relationship between West and East Pakistan, in fact as a "colonial" one, marked by the same exploitative commercial and political tactics of the recently deposed British Imperial regime. See also "Introduction" to Gail Minault, *Gender, Language, and Learning: Essays in Indo-Muslim Cultural History* (Ranikhet: Permanent Black, 2009), 5.
57 Husain, *1947*, 242.
58 Salim, *Reconstructing History: Memories, Migrants, and Minorities*, 74.
59 Guha Thakurta, "Uprooted and Divided," 59.
60 Remember the example of Salman Haider becoming "India's first Muslim Foreign Secretary" despite the fact that he selected "none" in the Religion Section of his Foreign Service Application. In all of these cases Muslimness is essentialized, in Pakistan it is synonymous with loyalty to the state, and in India it is proof of the state's affection for its minorities.
61 Saikia, *Women, War*, 48.
62 Sarmila Bose's 2011 book *Dead Reckoning* argues that more attention should be paid to the "civil war" that raged in Bangladesh between Bengali nationalists and non-Muslims and non-Bengalis. She argues that these minority groups were deliberately and aggressively targeted by Bangladeshi nationalists simply because they did not fit easily within the narrowly defined identity "Bengali." The work is highly problematic, but does shed light on this internal conflict which has, in turn, spawned racialized violence in independent Bangladesh. Bose, *Dead Reckoning*. See also Saikia, *Women, War*.
63 Mohiuddin Khan of Dhaka told me "Sylheti is not a language, it is a dialect of Bengali. It is Bengali." Mohiuddin Khan, Interview, March 28, 2010, 5.
64 He uses "East Pakistan" anachronistically here, referring to the period before 1947. Habibur Rahman, Interview, February 20, 2010, 7.
65 He uses the stereotype of Bengalis as "clever" to their advantage here, demonstrating the intellectual commitment of the Bengali students to the Pakistani cause.
66 Habibur Rahman, Interview, February 20, 2010, 7.
67 Ibid.
68 "Six-Point Programme of Sheikh Mujib Ur Rahman."
69 This was the term used by Indian Muslim Alig Masood-ul Hasan. Masood-ul Hasan, Interview, May 1, 2009, 18.
70 At Aligarh, the Union, led by Bengali A. T. M. Mustafa, initially rejected the Cabinet Mission Proposals outright, only withdrawing its vehement opposition when chided by Jinnah for not following the lead of the Muslim League Council. Ultimately, Mustafa assured Jinnah, "now that the Muslim League Council has declared that it accepts the Proposals [sic] only because they contain the germs of Pakistan . . . Aligarh stands solid behind the decision." A. T. M. Mustafa, "A.T.M. Mustafa to M.A. Jinnah: Muslim University Union Response to Cabinet Proposals-Full Account of the Meeting," in *Shamsul Hasan Collection* (Islamabad: Pakistan National Archives, June 12, 1946), Vol. 26/ 76–81. Mohammad Ali Jinnah, "M.A. Jinnah to A.T. M. Mustafa (Vice President Muslim University Union): Muslim University Union Response to Cabinet Proposals," *Shamsul Hasan Collection* (Islamabad: Pakistan National Archives, June 10, 1946), Vol. 26/ 75.
71 Mohiuddin Khan, Personal Communication.
72 Ibid.
73 Ibid.

74. An appraisal of Pakistan's economic policy reveals that it was overly concerned with protecting industry at the expense of agricultural development. Since East Pakistan's economy was driven by agricultural production, "a transfer of resources from agriculture to industry also implies a transfer from the East to the West Wing, since during the period under review more than 60 per cent of East Pakistan's gross output originated in agriculture and about 40 per cent in West Pakistan." Keith Griffin and Azizur Rahman Khan, eds., *Growth and Inequality in Pakistan* (London: Macmillan 1972), 29.
75. Mohiuddin Khan, Personal Communication.
76. See also Habibur Rahman, Interview, February 20, 2010, 8.
77. Mohiuddin Khan, Interview, March 28, 2010, 15.
78. Waheeduddin Choudhri, Interview, April 6, 2010, 6.
79. Neilesh Bose, *Recasting the Region: Language, Culture and Islam in Colonial Bengal* (Oxford: Oxford University Press, 2014), 189.
80. Ibid.
81. See also Amber Abbas, "The Solidarity Agenda: Aligarh Students and the Demand for Pakistan," *South Asian History and Culture Special Issue: Defying the Perpetual Exception: Culture and Power in South Asian Islam* 5, no. 2 (2014): 147–62.
82. Bose, *Recasting the Region,* 190.
83. Anwar Ahsan Siddiqui, Karachi in Salim, *Reconstructing History: Memories, Migrants, and Minorities,* 58.

Conclusion

1. Heads of state in all three countries, as well as other leaders, have passed through Aligarh University. Among the most influential have been, for example, India: Sheikh Mohammad Abdullah (prime minister and chief minister of Jammu and Kashmir), Hamid Ansari (vice president); Zakir Husain (president), Pakistan: Fazal Elahi Chaudhry (president); Liaqat Ali Khan (prime minister), Ghulam Mohammad (governor general); Khwaja Nazimuddin (governor general, prime minister), Bangladesh: Muhammad Mansur Ali (prime minister), M. A. G. Osmani (leader of Bangladeshi Liberation Forces); Maldives: Mohammad Amin Didi (president), among many other prominent literary and artistic personalities throughout the subcontinent.
2. By this I mean Victorian conservatism: concern with "proper" upbringing, elegance, and decorum that found sympathy with the traditional values of the Muslim elite. This conservatism was not necessarily religious. Though the institution's identity revolves around Muslimness, students were not driven by issues of faith and devotion. Many interacted with their faith largely through its public rituals. In other words, it was less important to pray as a spiritual imperative than it was to be *seen praying* as a disciplinary one.
3. So powerful was this agenda that as late as 1998 M. N. Farooqi reflected that "The maximum goal to be achieved was success in the IAS [Indian Administrative Service] and IPS [Indian Police Service] examinations, and it continues to remain so." M. N. Farooqi, *My Days at Aligarh* (Delhi: Idarah-i Adabiyat-i Delli, 1998), 20.
4. Devji, *Muslim Zion: Pakistan as a Political Idea,* 57.
5. Ibid., 60–1.

6 "Members of the Staff of Aligarh Muslim University to M.A. Jinnah." In *Freedom Movement Archives*, F 962/ 85–90 (Islamabad: Pakistan National Archives, N.D.).
7 Ibid.
8 Hasan, "Nationalist and Separatist Trends in Aligarh."
9 Graff, "Aligarh's Long Quest for 'Minority' Status: A.M.U. (Amendment) Act, 1981," 1771.
10 Ibid., 1779.
11 Violette Graff's close study of the Demand for Minority Character exposes many of the issues at stake. My review here is deeply informed by her study and by that of Theodore Wright. See also Theodore P. Wright Jr., "Muslim Education in India at the Crossroads: The Case of Aligarh," *Pacific Affairs* 39, no. 1/2 (Spring–Summer 1966): 50–63.
12 As I noted in the preface, most of the girls living with me in the private hostel in Aligarh were preparing for entrance exams to affiliated secondary institutions, all but guaranteeing their university admission when the time came.
13 Irfan Habib, Iqtidar Alam Khan, and K. P. Singh, "Problems of the Muslim Minority in India," *Social Scientist* 4, no. 11 (June 1976): 67–72.
14 Scheduled Castes/ Scheduled Tribes/ Other Backward Classes are officially designated groups that the Government of India has determined are socially and economically marginalized. The government maintains lists of castes, tribes, and other backward classes that meet its requirements and are eligible for reservations and associated services.
15 Minault and Lelyveld, "The Campaign for a Muslim University, 1898-1920."
16 K. N. Wanchoo et al., "S. Azeez Basha and Anr Vs. Union of India on 20 October, 1967" (New Delhi: Union of India, October 20, 1967).
17 Irfan Habib, Interview, June 28, 2009, 17. Graff, "Aligarh's Long Quest for 'Minority' Status: A.M.U. (Amendment) Act, 1981," 1771.
18 Khan was unable to get a seat reserved for Muslims or for Assamese or Sylhetis in Bengal Shibpur Engineering College. This, in part, he suggested, was because "[the seats] were limited and there was very hard competition . . . and there was again a difference between Assamese, Bengalis, Hindus and Muslims and all these combinations." Unable to find a seat in an Engineering College in Bengal that recognized either his ability or his religion or his region of origin, Mohiuddin set his sights on Aligarh, where he passed the competition and took his seat in 1946. Mohiuddin Khan, Interview, March 28, 2010, 2.
19 Wright Jr., "Muslim Education in India at the Crossroads: The Case of Aligarh," 61–2.
20 Aarti Dhar, "Jamia Millia Islamia Declared Minority Institution," *The Hindu-Online Edition*, February 23, 2011.
21 Justice M. S. A. Siddiqui, "Order in the Matters Of: Case No. 891 of 2006, Case No. 1824 of 2006, Case No. 1825 of 2006," ed. National Commission for Minority Educational Institutions (New Delhi, February 22, 2011), 52.
22 Dhar, "Jamia Millia Islamia Declared Minority Institution."
23 Ritika Chopra, "Centre Opposes Jamia Millia Islamia's Minority Status in Delhi High Court," *The Indian Express*, New Delhi, March 21, 2018. https://indianexpress.com/article/education/centre-opposes-jamia-millia-islamias-minority-status-in-delhi-high-court-5105217/
24 Krishnadas Rajagopal, "Government Backs Verdict Denying AMU Minority Status," *The Hindu*, New Delhi, April 5, 2016 (updated September 18, 2016). https://www.thehindu.com/news/national/other-states/Government-backs-verdict-denying-AMU-minority-status/article14219362.ece. Chopra, "Centre Opposes."

25 Mushirul Hasan, "Introduction," in *Knowledge, Power and Politics: Educational Institutions in India*, ed. Mushirul Hasan (New Delhi: Roli Books, 1998), 15–16.
26 Mushirul Hasan, "Partition Narratives: Presidential Address at the 31st Indian History Congress, Bhopal 28-30 December, 2001." *Social Scientist* 30, no. 7/8 (July–August 2002), 49.
27 Ritu Menon developed this terminology in her comment on Alok Bhalla's interview with author Bhisham Sahni. "His interview moves back and forth in time past and time present to highlight the present-tense-ness of Partition for many Indians." Ritu Menon, "Review of *Pangs of Partition: The Human Dimension* (Vol. 2)," *Seminar: Porous Bodies, Divided Selves*, no. 510 (February 2002): 84.
28 Iftikhar Alam Khan, Interview, June 6, 2009, 8.
29 Iftikhar Alam Khan was one of the youngest narrators, having arrived at the lower school Minto Circle, in 1949.
30 Nehru, "Speech by the Hon'ble Pundit Jawaharlal Nehru, Prime Minister of India." See also Mohammad, *Glimpses of Muslim Education Vol. 1*, 1, 230.
31 Mohammad, *Glimpses of Muslim Education Vol. 1*, 1, 230.
32 A. B. A. Haleem was appointed vice chancellor of Karachi University after partition and is remembered for his particularly harsh crackdown on the activities of leftists there.
33 Iqtidar Alam Khan, Interview, May 21, 2009, 23.
34 Mohammad Amin, Interview, November 5, 2009, 2.
35 Iqtidar Alam Khan Interview, May 21, 2009, 10.
36 Iqtidar Alam's father had been arrested in 1949 for his involvement in a "*kisan satyagraha* from a Communist platform," though he was a member of the Muslim League. Ibid.
37 Zahida Zaidi was also arrested during the same protest. Zahida Zaidi, Interview, November 20, 2009, 10.
38 B.T. Ranadive was elected as general secretary of the Communist Party of India in 1948 and served until 1950, during which time the party was actively encouraging revolutionary activities.
39 Iqtidar Alam Khan, Interview, May 21, 2009, 13.
40 Riazur Rahman Sherwani, Interview, July 6, 2008, 3.
41 Mohiuddin Khan, Interview, March 28, 2010, 9.
42 Habibur Rahman, Interview, February 20, 2010, 7.
43 Ibid., 9.
44 Pandey, "Can a Muslim Be an Indian?," 610.
45 "Jinnah Portrait at AMU Sparks Row," *The Hindu (online)*, Aligarh, May 1, 2018. https://www.thehindu.com/news/national/other-states/jinnah-portrait-at-amu-sparks-row/article23738686.ece
46 Shreya Roy Chowdhury, "Anatomy of AMU Attack: Why Aligarh's Hindutva Groups are Rankled by the University," *Scroll.in*, May 13, 2018. https://scroll.in/article/878700/anatomy-of-amu-attack-why-the-university-rankles-aligarhs-half-a-dozen-hindutva-groups
47 "AMU Jinnah Portrait Row: What has Happened so Far," *The Indian Express (online)*, May 5, 2018. https://indianexpress.com/article/india/amu-jinnah-portrait-row-what-has-happened-so-far-5164394/
48 Ibid.

Epilogue: The Babri Masjid, AMU, and Indian Muslims

1. Shoaib Daniyal, "The Hashimpura Massacre Is a Harsh Indictment of So-Called Secular Politics in India," *Scroll.in*, March 23, 2015.
2. Paul R. Brass, "Development of an Institutionalised Riot System in Meerut City, 1961 to 1982," *Economic and Political Weekly* 39, no. 44 (October 30–November 5, 2004): 4839–48.
3. Dhirendra K. Jha, "Attack on a Prominent Faizabad Mosque Ignites Fears of a Larger Communal Design," *Scroll.in*, August 20, 2015.
4. K. N. Panikkar, "A Historical Overview," in *Anatomy of a Confrontation: Ayodhya and the Rise of Communal Politics in India,* ed. Sarvepalli Gopal (London: Zed Books, 1993), 22.
5. Ibid., 30–3.
6. Rahat Abrar, "Appeal to Staff and Students for Communal Harmony" (Public Relations Office, Aligarh Muslim University, September 19, 2010).
7. Anwar Khursheed, "Past Tense-Future Perfect: Appeal for Forgiveness and Reconciliation" (YahooGroups: AligarhNetwork; TheAligarhForum; VoiceofAligs; WorldofAligs Listservs, September 19, 2010). Comments used with permission.
8. Islam Habib Khan (YahooGroups: VoiceofAligs Listserv, September 26, 2010). Comments used with permission.
9. "Aligarh Breathes Easy after Two Days of Anxiety."
10. Islam Habib Khan (YahooGroups: VoiceofAligs Listserv, September 27, 2010). Comments used with permission.
11. Hasan, "Partition Narratives," 52.
12. "Signal of Peace," *The Telegraph-Online Edition*, October 1, 2010. In November, the Vishwa Hindu Parishad said that it would not allow the construction of a mosque on the site and announced plans to build a temple there. "International Religious Freedom Report-India," 19.
13. Ibid.
14. Ramachandra Guha, "Life after Ayodhya," *The Hindustan Times-Online Edition*, September 30, 2010.
15. "Intriguing Compromise Could Work," *The Hindu-Online Edition*, October 1, 2010.
16. "Aligarh Breathes Easy after Two Days of Anxiety."
17. Nadeem F. Paracha, "Lessons from Ayodhya," *Dawn-Online Edition*, October 1, 2010.
18. "Aligarh Breathes Easy after Two Days of Anxiety."
19. Brass, *The Production of Hindu-Muslim Violence*.
20. Brass has argued that preelection communal violence consolidates communal voting patterns and benefits the Hindu parties. Brass, "Development of an Institutionalised Riot System in Meerut City, 1961 to 1982," 4847.
21. Foreign Policy South Asia Daily, December 10, 2014. Email publication. See also Niha Masih, "Mass Conversion in U.P. Sparks Outrage in Parliament, Government Asked to Explain," *NDTV (online)*, December 10, 2014.
22. Vasudha Venugopal, "R.S.S. Plans to Convert 4,000 Christian and 1,000 Muslim Families to Hinduism," *Economic Times*, December 10, 2014.
23. *The Times* quoted Aligarh-based pastor Samuel Shimon, who worried about his "flock" and added that "In such a suspicious environment, I have sent out instructions to priests in churches in rural areas of Aligarh for subdued Christmas celebrations. We do not want to appear as if we are making a mockery of the right-wing groups.

That may backfire." Hamza Khan, "Actual Ghar Wapsi Will Be Sending Muslims to Pakistan: Shiv Sena," *The Indian Express*, December 16, 2014.
24 Hamza Khan, "Actual Ghar Wapsi Will Be Sending Muslims to Pakistan: Shiv Sena" *The Indian Express*, December 16, 2014.
25 From Jinnah's Speech of March 23, 1940, "The Hindus and Muslims belong to two different religious philosophies, social customs, and literature[s]. They neither intermarry nor interdine together, and indeed they belong to two different civilisations which are based mainly on conflicting ideas and conceptions. Their aspects [=perspectives?] on life, and of life, are different. It is quite clear that Hindus and Mussalmans derive their inspiration from different sources of history. They have different epics, their heroes are different, and different episode[s]. Very often the hero of one is a foe of the other, and likewise their victories and defeats overlap. To yoke together two such nations under a single state, one as a numerical minority and the other as a majority, must lead to growing discontent, and final destruction of any fabric that may be so built up for the government of such a state." http://www.columbia.edu/itc/mealac/pritchett/00islamlinks/txt_jinnah_lahore_1940.html Indeed, V.D. Savarkar, the founder of the Hindu Mahasabha and a primary theorist of Hindutva, initially described the Two Nation Theory.
26 Sunil Prabhu, "Ayodhya Order 'Unjust,' Will Decide On Review Plea: Muslim Group Lawyer," NDTV, November 9, 2019. https://www.ndtv.com/india-news/ayodhya-verdict-muslim-group-lawyer-zafaryab-jilani-ayodhya-order-unjust-will-decide-on-review-plea-2129831. Last accessed April 15, 2020.
27 Wajahat A. Khan Yousef Zai (YahooGroups: VoiceofAligs Listserv, September 27, 2010). Comments used with permission.
28 "The Citizenship (Amendment) Act, 2019," Government of India, Ministry of Law and Justice (New Delhi: The Gazette of India Extraordinary, 2019), 2.
29 "India Plans to Deport Thousands of Rohingya Refugees," *Aljazeera.com*, August 14, 2017. https://www.aljazeera.com/news/2017/08/india-plans-deport-thousands-rohingya-refugees-170814110027809.html. Last accessed April 9, 2020.
30 Krishna, N. Das, "Hundreds of Rohingya Families Flee India after Deportations," *Reuters-Online*, January 17, 2019. https://www.reuters.com/article/us-myanmar-rohingya-india/hundreds-of-rohingya-families-flee-india-after-deportations-idUSKCN1PB1GS?feedType=RSS&feedName=&=worldNews. Last accessed April 9, 2020. India is not a signatory to the 1951 Convention or the update in 1967 that gave the convention universal coverage. Office of the United Nations High Commission for Refugees, "Introductory Note: Convention and Protocol Relating to the Status of Refugees," *The United Nations High Commission for Refugees* (Geneva, December 2010), 3. https://www.unhcr.org/en-us/3b66c2aa10
31 "What Is NRC?" Office of the State Coordinator of National Registration (NRC), Assam, Government of Assam. http://nrcassam.nic.in/what-nrc.html. Last accessed April 9, 2020.
32 Sanjoy Hazarika, "Assam's Tangled Web of Citizenship and the Importance of a Consensus," *The Hindu Center for Politics and Public Policy*, October 18, 2019. https://www.thehinducentre.com/the-arena/current-issues/article29724344.ece. Last accessed April 9, 2020.
33 In April 2020, the Indian government refined some categories of eligible property owners to include residents of longer than fifteen years, those who had studied in Kashmir for seven years, and the children of central government officials who had served in Jammu and Kashmir for ten years or more. Naveed Iqbal, "Centre Defines

New Domicile Rule for J&K, Includes those Who have Lived in UT for 15 years," *The Indian Express,* April 2, 2020. https://indianexpress.com/article/india/centre-defines-domicile-rule-for-jk-6341175/

34 The global coronavirus pandemic in 2020 that required lockdowns on movement around the world offered additional opportunities for the state to increase monitoring and surveillance of Kashmiris, as well as those entering and leaving the state. Samreen Mushtaq and Mudasir Amin, "Kashmir: Coronavirus Is a New Tool for India to Oppress Us," *Middle East Eye,* April 7, 2020. https://www.middleeasteye.net/opinion/coronavirus-kashmir-india-responds-more-violence. Last accessed April 9, 2020.

35 G. Sampath, "When the Students Rise," *The Hindu-online,* December 20, 2019. https://www.thehindu.com/society/when-they-rise-thousands-of-students-march-in-solidarity-with-jmi-and-amu-students-and-to-oppose-caa/article30358200.ece. Last accessed April 15, 2020.

36 Tariq Mansoor, "VC Appeal 17122019," https://www.amu.ac.in/. Last accessed April 9, 2020.

37 "AMU Students Continue Anti-CAA Protests Despite Administration's Warning," *India Today—online,* January 10, 2020. https://www.indiatoday.in/india/story/amu-students-continue-anti-caa-protests-despite-administration-s-warning-1635676-2020-01-10. Last accessed April 9, 2020.

Interviews Cited

Unless otherwise noted, all interviews have been archived in the *Partition's First Generation* Oral History Project, Louie B. Nunn Center for Oral History, University of Kentucky Libraries.
See Appendix for all interviews.

Pakistan (2005–2010)

Abbas, Tariq Azhar. Austin, Texas, May 21, 2011.
Fari Rahman, Fatima Minhaj. Lahore, January 4, 2008 and May 10, 2010.
Husain, Wajahat. Lahore, 2005–2008.
Iqbal, Javid. Lahore, July 13, 2006.
Khan, Abdul Rasheed. Karachi, August 10, 2006.
Khan, Zakir Ali. Karachi, August 10, 2006.
Mirza, Sarfaraz Hussein. Lahore, July 21, 2006.
Nizami, Zilley Ahmad. Karachi, May 24, 2010.
Qamar, Mansoor. Karachi, May 28, 2010.
Rashid, Shahid. Karachi, May 19, 2010.
Saeed, Ahmad. Lahore, July 20, 2006.
Shafi, Iqbal. Islamabad, May 9, 2010.
Umar, Ghulam. Karachi, August 8, 2006.
Umar, Khadija Minhaj. Lahore, January 4, 2008.
Zaidi, Anis and Rais Sultana, Karachi, May 20, 2010.
Zuberi, Mubarak Shah. Karachi, May 26, 2010.

India (2008–2009)

Amin, Mohammad. New Delhi, November 5, 2009.
Ansari, Asloob Ahmad. Aligarh, July 5, 2008.
Habib, Irfan. Aligarh, June 16, 2009.
Hamid, Sayyid. New Delhi, October 29, 2009.
Hasan, Masood-ul. Aligarh, March 20 and May 1, 2009.
Khan, Iftikhar Alam. Aligarh, June 6, 2009.
Khan, Iqtidar Alam. Aligarh, May 31, 2009.
Khan, Zafar Mohammad. Lucknow, April 4, 2009.
Kidwai, Saeeda Wahid. Aligarh, June 17, 2009.
Mathur, A. K. Lucknow, September 30, 2009.
Mehdi, Saeed Mirza. Aligarh, June 15, 2009.
Rizvi, Syed Saghir Ahmad. Lucknow, October 6, 2009.

Saeed, Ahmad. Lucknow, October 10, 2009.
Shamsi, Mohsin Jalil. Lucknow, August 11, 2008.
Sherwani, Riazur Rahman. Aligarh, July 6, 2008 and November 20, 2009.
Siddiqi, Ather. Aligarh, May 11, 2009.
Siddiqi, Zakia. Aligarh, December 9, 2009.
Zaidi, Zahida. Aligarh, November 20, 2009.

Bangladesh (2010)

Akhtaruzzaman, Mohammad. Dhaka, March 10, 2010.
Choudhri, Waheeduddin. Dhaka, April 6, 2010.
Chouwdhury, Salehuddin. Dhaka, April 10, 2010.
Khan, Mohiuddin. Dhaka, March 28, 2010.
Rahman, Habibur. Dhaka, February 20, 2010.
Rashid, M. A. Dhaka, March 29, 2010.

Several narrators in Karachi, Pakistan and Lucknow, India, requested anonymity. 2005–2010. Interviews in author's possession.

Bibliography

A.P.I. "Aligarh Students' Rowdyism: Issue May Be Put before Viceroy." *The Times of India*, April 6, 1946, 7.
A.P.I. "Punitive Police for Aligarh." *The Times of India*, April 25, 1946.
A.P.I. "Responsibility for Aligarh Riots: Official Inquiry Report." *The Times of India*, May 3, 1946.
Abbas, Amber. "Belonging and the Beginning of the Past in Pakistan." In *Hidden Histories: Religion and Reform in South Asia*, edited by Syed Akbar Hyder and Manu Bhagavan, 27–47. Delhi: Primus Books, 2018.
Abbas, Amber. "A Living Legacy: Sir Sayyid Today." In *The Cambridge Companion to Sir Sayyid Ahmed Khan*, edited by Yasmin Saikia and M. Raisur Rahman, 255–72. Cambridge: Cambridge University Press, 2019.
Abbas, Amber. "The Solidarity Agenda: Aligarh Students and the Demand for Pakistan." *South Asian History and Culture Special Issue: Defying the Perpetual Exception: Culture and Power in South Asian Islam* 5, no. 2 (2014): 147–62.
Abbas, Amber. "Thinking through Partition: Finishing the Narrative (Unpublished Master's Thesis)." Austin: The University of Texas at Austin, 2006.
Abbas, Tariq. Interviewed by Amber Abbas. Austin, Texas, May 21, 2011. The South Asian American Digital Archive. https://www.saada.org/item/20110918-363.
Abedin, Syed Zainul. "The Flying Fez." *Aligarh Magazine*, 1948, xiii.
Abedin, Syed Zainul. "In Memoriam." *Aligarh Magazine*, 1948, i–ii.
Abrar, Rahat. "Appeal to Staff and Students for Communal Harmony." Public Relations Office, Aligarh Muslim University, September 19, 2010.
Aguiar, Marian. *Tracking Modernity: India's Railway and the Culture of Mobility*. Minneapolis: The University of Minnesota Press, 2011.
Ahmad, Aziz. *Islamic Modernism in India and Pakistan 1857–1964*. London: Oxford University Press, 1967.
Ahmad, Jamil-ud-din. "Jamil-ud-din Ahmad to M.A. Jinnah: Election Work Committee Constituted." In *Shamsul Hasan Collection*, Vol. 26/ 180–1. Islamabad: Pakistan National Archives, December 11, 1945.
Ahmad, Jamil-ud-din. "Jamil-ud-din Ahmad to M.A. Jinnah: Provincial Election Work and Committee." In *Shamsul Hasan Collection*, Vol. 26/ 129–32. Islamabad: Pakistan National Archives, December 1, 1945.
Ahmad, Jamil-ud-din, ed. *Some Recent Speeches and Writings of Mr. Jinnah*. 5th ed. 2 vols. Vol. 1. Lahore: Sh. Muhammad Ashraf, 1952.
Ahmad, Jamil-ud-din, ed. *Speeches and Writings of Mr. Jinnah*. 2 vols. Vol. 2. Lahore: Sh. Muhammad Ashraf, 1964.
Ahmad, Waheed. "M.A. Jinnah Addresses Muslim Students--'I Have Failed' with the Hindus, December 27, 1937." In *The Nation's Voice: Towards Consolidation; Quaid-i-Azam Mohammad Ali Jinnah Speeches and Statements March 1935- March 1940*, 202–4. Karachi: Quaid-i-Azam Academy, 1992.

Ahmad, Ziauddin. "The Report of the Vice-Chancellor, Aligarh Muslim University for the Calendar Year 1945: Read at the Convocation Held on the 1st December, 1945." Aligarh: Aligarh Muslim University Press, 1945.

Ahmad, Ziauddin. "Using Students for Party Propaganda Deplored." *The Muslim University Gazette*, October 15, 1942.

Ahmad, Ziauddin. "Ziauddin Ahmad to M.A. Jinnah: The Future of Muslims in India." In *Freedom Movement Archives*, Vol. 591/ 3-4. Islamabad: Pakistan National Archives, January 2, 1947.

Ahmad, Ziauddin, and A. E. Zobairi. *Minutes of An Ordinary Meeting of the Academic Council*. Aligarh: Aligarh Muslim University, April 12, 1947.

Alam, Manzar-i-. "Manzar-i-Alam to M.A. Jinnah: Letter of Support from Nawabzada Liaqat Ali Khan." In *Shamsul Hasan Collection*, Vol. 26/ 152–3. Islamabad: Pakistan National Archives, December 3, 1945.

Alam, Manzar-i-. "Manzar-i-Alam to M.A. Jinnah: Student Election Work and Need for Funds." In *Shamsul Hasan Collection*, Vol. 26/ 146–8. Islamabad: Pakistan National Archives, December 3, 1945.

Alam, Manzar-i-. "Manzar-i-Alam to M.A. Jinnah: Student Election Workers Sent out over Holidays." In *Shamsul Hasan Collection*, Vol. 26/ 187–8. Islamabad: Pakistan National Archives, December 17, 1945.

Alam, Manzar-i-. "Manzar-i-Alam to Qazi Isa." In *Freedom Movement Archives*, F 237/ 71 (1–2). Islamabad: Pakistan National Archives, November 15, 1945.

Alavi, M. A. "A Plea for Sahibzada Memorial Fund." *Aligarh Magazine*, January–August 1930, 43–5.

Alavi, Rafi Ahmad. *Translation of Hayat-i-Jawed: A Biographical Account of Sir Syed Ahmad Khan by Altaf Husain Hali*. Aligarh: Aligarh Muslim University Press, 2008.

Ali, Allama Abdullah Yusuf. "Human Factor in Education: Address to the Golden Jubilee Session of the University Section of the All India Muslim Educational Conference." *The Muslim University Gazette*, April 21, 1937.

"Aligarh Breathes Easy after Two Days of Anxiety." *The Asian Age Online*, October 1, 2010.

"The Aligarh Muslim University Act (Act Xl of 1920)." Aligarh: Muslim University Press, 1920/1948.

Alumni Directory, Aligarh Muslim University. Sir Syed House Publication. 3 vols. Karachi: Sir Syed University of Engineering and Technology, 1974?

Amin, Shahid. *Event, Metaphor, Memory: Chauri Chaura 1922-1992*. Delhi and New York: Oxford University Press, 1996.

"AMU Students Continue Anti-CAA Protests Despite Administration's Warning," *India Today—Online*, January 10, 2020.

Anderson, Benedict R. *Imagined Communities: Reflections on the Origin and Spread of Nationalism*. London: Verso, 1983.

Ansari, Hayatullah. "Mera Aftab Hall." *The Aftab* The Aftab Memoirs Special (1976): 21–35.

Ansari, Nasim. *Choosing to Stay: Memoirs of an Indian Muslim*. Translated by Ralph Russell. Karachi: City Press, 1999.

Aziz, Khursheed Kamal, ed. *Muslims under Congress Rule 1937-1939*. 2 vols. Vol. 1. Delhi: Renaissance Publishing House, 1978.

Bagchi, Jasodhara, and Subhoranjan Dasgupta. "The Problem." *Seminar: Porous Bodies, Divided Selves*, no. 510 (February 2002): 12–14.

Bakhtin, Mikhail. *Rabelais and His World*. Translated by Helene Iswolsky. Bloomington: Indiana University Press, 1984.
Ballhatchet, Kenneth. *Race, Sex, and Class under the Raj: Imperial Attitudes and Policies and Their Critics, 1793-1905*. London: Weidenfeld and Nicolson, 1980.
Bari, M. A. "Resolutions for 7th Annual Session of the All India Muslim Students' Federation." In *Freedom Movement Archives*, F 961/ 17-21. Islamabad: Pakistan National Archives, March 1945.
Bassin, Ari. "Justice or Charade in Dhaka?" *International Justice Tribune*, no. 123 (March 2, 2011): 4.
Beck, Theodore. "Principal's Annual Report, for 1895-86." In *Theodore Beck Papers from the Sir Syed Academy Archives*, edited by Khaliq Ahmad Nizami, 82-111. Aligarh: Aligarh Muslim University, 1991.
BenEzer, Gadi. "Trauma Signals in Life Stories." In *Trauma and Life Stories: International Perspectives*, edited by Selma Leydesdorff, Graham Dawson, Natasha Burchardt and T. G. Ashplant, 29-44. London and New York: Routledge, 1999.
Bhalla, Alok, ed. *Stories on the Partition of India*. New Delhi: Indus, 1994.
Bhandare, Namita. "Better Off Than Dad." *India Today International*, February 19, 2001, 37-40.
Bigelow, Anna. "Punjab's Muslims: The History and Significance of Malerkotla." *International Journal of Punjab Studies* 12, no. 1 (2005): 63-94.
Blom Hansen, Thomas. *The Saffron Wave: Democracy and Hindu Nationalism in Modern India*. Princeton: Princeton University Press, 1999.
Bose, Neilesh. *Recasting the Region: Language, Culture and Islam in Colonial Bengal*. Oxford: Oxford University Press, 2014.
Bose, Pradeep Kumar. "Partition--Memory Begins Where History Ends." In *Reflections on Partition in the East*, edited by Ranabir Samaddar, 73-86. Calcutta: Vikas Publishing House, 1997.
Bose, Sarmila. *Dead Reckoning: Memories of the 1971 Bangladesh War*. New York: Columbia University Press, 2011.
Brass, Paul R. "Development of an Institutionalised Riot System in Meerut City, 1961 to 1982." *Economic and Political Weekly* 39, no. 44 (October 30-November 5, 2004): 4839-48.
Brass, Paul R. *The Production of Hindu- Muslim Violence in Contemporary India*. Seattle: University of Washington Press, 2003.
Brennan, Lance. "The Illusion of Security: The Background to Muslim Separatism in the United Provinces." In *India's Partition: Process, Strategy and Mobilization*, edited by Mushirul Hasan, 318-55. Delhi: Oxford University Press, 1993.
Bristow, Brigadier R. C. B. *Memories of the British Raj: Soldier in India*. London: Johnson, 1974.
Butalia, Urvashi. *The Other Side of Silence: Voices from the Partition of India*. Durham: Duke University Press, 2000.
Casey, Edward. "Boundary, Place, and Event in the Spatiality of History." *Rethinking History* 11, no. 4 (December 2007): 507-12.
Chakrabarty, Dipesh. "Remembered Villages: Representations of Hindu-Bengali Memories in the Aftermath of Partition." *South Asia* 18 (1995): 109-29.
Chatterjee, Partha. *The Nation and Its Fragments: Colonial and Postcolonial Histories*. Princeton Studies in Culture/Power/History. Princeton: Princeton University Press, 1993.
Chatterji, Joya. "New Directions in Partition Studies." *History Workshop Journal* 67 (Spring 2009): 213-20.

Chattha, Ilyas. *Partition and Locality: Violence, Migration, and Development in Gujranwala and Sialkot, 1947-1961*. Karachi: Oxford University Press, 2011.

Chawla, Devika. *Home, Uprooted: Oral Histories of India's Partition*. New York: Fordham University Press, 2014.

Chopra, Pran Nath, ed. *Quit India Movement: British Secret Documents*. 2 vols. Vol. I. New Delhi: Interprint, 1986.

"The Citizenship (Amendment) Act, 2019." Government of India, Ministry of Law and Justice. New Delhi. The Gazette of India Extraordinary, 2019.

Cole, Tim. "(Re)Placing the Past: Spatial Strategies of Retelling Difficult Stories." *The Oral History Review* 42, no. 1 (Winter/Spring 2015): 30–49.

Coser, Lewis A. "Introduction to on Collective Memory by Maurice Halbwachs." In *On Collective Memory*, edited by Lewis A. Coser. Chicago and London: University of Chicago Press, 1992.

Crane, Susan. "Writing the Individual Back into Collective Memory." *The American Historical Review* 102, no. 5 (December 1997): 1372–85.

Creswell, Tim. *In Place/out of Place: Geography, Ideology, and Transgression*. Minneapolis: University of Minnesota Press, 1996.

Daiya, Kavita. *Violent Belongings: Partition, Gender, and National Culture in Postcolonial India*. Philadelphia: Temple University Press, 2008.

Daniyal, Shoaib. "The Hashimpura Massacre Is a Harsh Indictment of So-Called Secular Politics in India." *Scroll.in*, March 23, 2015.

Das, Krishna, N. "Hundreds of Rohingya Families Flee India after Deportations," *Reuters-Online*, January 17, 2019.

Das, Veena, ed. *Mirrors of Violence: Communities, Riots and Survivors in South Asia*. Delhi: Oxford University Press, 1990.

Das, Veena, ed. "Specificities: Oral Narratives, Rumour, and the Social Production of Hate." *Social Identities* 4, no. 1 (February 1998): 109–30.

Dehlavi, Shahid Ahmad. "Dilli Ki Bipta [1948]." In *Zulmat-i-Nimroz*, edited by Mumtaz Shirin. Karachi: Nafiz Akademi, 1990.

Deslandes, Paul. *Oxbridge Men: British Masculinity and the Undergraduate Experience 1850-1920*. Bloomington: Indiana University Press, 2005.

Devji, Faisal. "Keywords in South Asian Studies: Qawm." London: School of Oriental and African Studies, University of London, 2004.

Devji, Faisal. *Muslim Zion: Pakistan as a Political Idea*. Cambridge, MA: Harvard University Press, 2013.

Dhar, Aarti. "Jamia Millia Islamia Declared Minority Institution." *The Hindu- Online Edition*, February 23, 2011.

Dhulipala, Venkat. *Creating a New Medina: State Power, Islam and the Quest for Pakistan in Late Colonial North India*. New Delhi: Cambridge University Press, 2015.

Dhulipala, Venkat. "Rallying the Qaum: The Muslim League in the United Provinces, 1937-1939." *Modern Asian Studies* 44, no. 3 (2010): 603–40.

Dyan, M. A. "Whither Aligarh?" *The Muslim University Gazette*, November 1, 1940, 4–6.

Ethington, Philip J. "Placing the Past: 'Groundwork' for a Spatial Theory of History." *Rethinking History* 11, no. 4 (December 2007): 465–93.

"Faith in Quaid-e-Azam Reaffirmed." *The Muslim University Gazette*, November 1, 1941, 8.

Farooqi, Mohammad Naseem. *My Days at Aligarh*. Delhi: Idarah-i Adabiyat-i Delli, 1998.

Farooqui, Mahmood, ed. *Besieged: Voices from Delhi, 1857*. New Delhi: Penguin Books India, 2010.

Faziel, Ali Ahmad. "Ali Ahmad Faziel to M.A. Jinnah: Provincial Election Work." In *Shamsul Hasan Collection*, Vol. 26/ 136-8. Islamabad: Pakistan National Archives, December 2, 1945.

"Forward to New Battles!: The A.I.S.F. Conference, Delhi." *The Student: Journal of the All India Students Federation* (January 1947).

Gabriel, Theodore. *Christian Citizens in an Islamic State: The Pakistan Experience*. Aldershot: Ashgate Publishing Ltd., 2007.

Gilmartin, David. "Partition, Pakistan and South Asian History: In Search of a Narrative." *The Journal of Asian Studies* 57, no. 4 (November 1998): 1068-95.

Gopal, Sarvepalli. *Jawaharlal Nehru: A Biography*. 3 vols. Vol. 1. Cambridge, MA: Harvard University Press, 1976.

Gould, William. *Hindu Nationalism and the Language of Politics in Late Colonial India*. Cambridge: Cambridge University Press, 2004.

Graff, Violette. "Aligarh's Long Quest for 'Minority' Status: A.M.U. (Amendment) Act, 1981." *Economic and Political Weekly*, August 11, 1990, 1771-81.

Graham, George Farquhar Irving. *The Life and Work of Sir Syed Ahmed Khan*. 2nd ed. Karachi: Oxford University Press, 1974 [1885].

Griffin, Keith, and Azizur Rahman Khan, eds. *Growth and Inequality in Pakistan*. London: Macmillan, 1972.

Guha, Ramachandra. "Life after Ayodhya." *The Hindustan Times- Online Edition*, September 30, 2010.

Guha Thakurta, Meghna. "Irfan Habib: The Indian Variant of Secularism Opens the Door to Majority Communalism." Edited by Ajaz Ashraf. *Scroll.In*, 2015.

Guha Thakurta, Meghna. "Uprooted and Divided." *Seminar: Porous Bodies, Divided Selves*, no. 510 (February 2002): 54-60.

Habib, Irfan, Iqtidar Alam Khan, and K. P. Singh. "Problems of the Muslim Minority in India." *Social Scientist* 4, no. 11 (June 1976): 67-72.

Halbwachs, Maurice. *On Collective Memory*. Translated by Lewis A. Coser. Heritage of Sociology. Edited by Lewis A. Coser. Chicago: University of Chicago Press, 1992.

Haleem, Abu Bakr Ahmad. "A.B.A. Haleem to Maulavi Mohd. Ashiq Saheb Warsi: Report of the P.V.C. To the University Court." In *Freedom Movement Archives*, F 1094/ 340-3. Islamabad: Pakistan National Archives, October 25, 1938.

Haleem, Abu Bakr Ahmad. "Statutory Safeguards for Minorities." In *Freedom Movement Archives*, F 1122/ 59-61. Islamabad: Pakistan National Archives, May 12, 1946.

Hasan, Masood-ul. "Some Glimpses of the University in the Forties." *The Aftab* The Aftab Memoirs Special (1976): 61-70.

Hasan, Mushirul. *Islam in the Subcontinent: Muslims in a Plural Society*. New Delhi: Manohar, 2002.

Hasan, Mushirul. "The Muslim Mass Contact Campaign: An Attempt at Political Mobilisation." *Economic and Political Weekly* 21, no. 52 (December 27, 1986): 2273-5, 2277-82.

Hasan, Mushirul. "Negotiating with Its Past and Present: The Changing Profile of the Aligarh Muslim University." In *Inventing Boundaries: Gender, Politics, and the Partition of India*, edited by Mushirul Hasan, 135-56. New Delhi: Oxford University Press, 2000.

Hasan, Mushirul. "Partition Narratives: Presidential Address at the 31st Indian History Congress, Bhopal 28-30 December, 2001." *Social Scientist* 30, no. 7/8 (July-August 2002): 24-53.

Hazarika, Sanjoy. "Assam's Tangled Web of Citizenship and the Importance of a Consensus." *The Hindu Center for Politics and Public Policy*, October 18, 2019.

Hodgson, Marshall G. S. *The Venture of Islam: Conscience and History in a World Civilization*. 3 vols. Vol. 1, The Classical Age of Islam. Chicago and London: University of Chicago Press, 1974.

Hunter, William Wilson. *The Indian Musalmans: Are They Bound in Conscience to Rebel against the Queen?* London: Trubner and Co., 1871.

Husain, Ed. "Explaining the Salman Taseer Murder." In *Expert Brief*: Council on Foreign Relations, January 7, 2011.

Husain, Zakir. "Application for Grants-in-Aid Submitted by the Vice-Chancellor Aligarh Muslim University to the Government of India." Aligarh: Maulana Azad Library, January 1950.

Hyam, Ronald. *Britain's Imperial Century, 1815-1914: A Study of Empire and Expansion*. New York: Barnes and Noble, 1976.

"India Plans to Deport Thousands of Rohingya Refugees." *Aljazeera.com*, August 14, 2017.

"International Religious Freedom Report- Pakistan." Edited by Department of State. Washington, DC, July–December 2010.

"Intriguing Compromise Could Work." *The Hindu- Online Edition*, October 1, 2010.

Iqbal, Mohammad. "Our New Vice Chancellor." *Aligarh Magazine*, 1949, iii.

Iqbal, Naveed. "Centre Defines New Domicile Rule for J&K, Includes those Who have Lived in UT for 15 years." *The Indian Express*, April 2, 2020.

Isa, Qazi Mohammad. "Qazi Mohammad Isa to Chief Accountant, Muslim University Aligarh." In *Freedom Movement Archives*, F 237/ 74. Islamabad: Pakistan National Archives, November 22, 1945.

Jahan, Rounaq. *Pakistan: Failure in National Integration*. New York: Columbia University Press, 1972.

Jalal, Ayesha. "Conjuring Pakistan: History as Official Imagining." *International Journal of Middle East Studies* 27, no. 1 (February 1995): 73–89.

Jalal, Ayesha. *Self and Sovereignty: Individual and Community in South Asian Islam since 1850*. London and New York: Routledge, 2000.

Jalal, Ayesha. *The Sole Spokesman: Jinnah, the Muslim League, and the Demand for Pakistan*. Cambridge and New York: Cambridge University Press, 1985.

Jha, Dhirendra K. "Attack on a Prominent Faizabad Mosque Ignites Fears of a Larger Communal Design." *Scroll.in*, August 20, 2015.

Jinnah, Mohammad Ali. "Full Text of the Presidential Address Delivered Extempore at the Fifth Annual Session of the All-India Muslim Students' Federation at Nagpur on December 26, 1941." In *Some Recent Speeches and Writings of Mr. Jinnah Vol. I*, edited by Jamil-ud-din Ahmad, 300–18. Lahore: Sh. Muhammad Ashraf, 1952.

Jinnah, Mohammad Ali. "M.A. Jinnah to A.T.M. Mustafa (Vice President Muslim University Union): Muslim University Union Response to Cabinet Proposals." In *Shamsul Hasan Collection*, Vol. 26/ 75. Islamabad: Pakistan National Archives, June 10, 1946.

Jinnah, Mohammad Ali. "M.A. Jinnah to Jamil-ud-din Ahmad: Need to Establish an Election Committee." In *Shamsul Hasan Collection*, Vol. 26/ 133. Islamabad: Pakistan National Archives, December 5, 1945.

Jinnah, Mohammad Ali. "Muslim India Speaks: Speech Delivered by Quaid-e-Azam Mr. M.A. Jinnah President of the All-India Muslim League at a Meeting Held under the Auspices of the Muslim University Union." In *Freedom Movement Archives*, F 237/ 21 (1–25). Islamabad: Pakistan National Archives, November 2, 1942.

Jinnah, Mohammad Ali. "Pakistan, the Muslim Charter: Speech by Quaid-e-Azam M.A. Jinnah to Muslim University Union, Aligarh." In *Freedom Movement Archives*, F 237/19 (1–14). Islamabad: Pakistan National Archives, November 2, 1941.

Jinnah, Mohammad Ali. "Presidential Address Delivered at the Special Pakistan Session of the Punjab Muslim Students' Federation, 2nd March 1941." In *Some Recent Speeches and Writings of Mr. Jinnah*, edited by Jamil-ud-din Ahmad, 210–24. Lahore: Sh. Muhammad Ashraf, 1952.

Jinnah, Mohammad Ali. "Protection for Minorities in Pakistan." In *Quaid-i-Azam Muhammad Ali Jinnah (Speeches, Statements, Writings, Letters, Etc.)*, edited by Muhammad Haneef Shahid, 82–9. Lahore: Sang-e-Meel Publications, 1976.

Jinnah, Mohammad Ali. "Sacred Duty of Muslims to Protect Minorities." In *Quaid-i-Azam Muhammad Ali Jinnah (Speeches, Statements, Writings, Letters, Etc.)*, edited by Muhammad Haneef Shahid, 52–3. Lahore: Sang-e-Meel Publications, 1976.

Jinnah, Mohammad Ali. "Speech at the Annual Conference of the Punjab Muslim Students' Federation, Lahore, 18 March 1944." In *Speeches and Writings of Mr. Jinnah*, edited by Jamil-ud-din Ahmad, 20–2. Lahore: Sh. Muhammad Ashraf, 1964.

Jinnah, Mohammad Ali. "Speech at the Annual Session of the All-India Muslim Students' Federation, Jullundur, November 15, 1942." In *Some Recent Speeches and Writings of Mr. Jinnah*, edited by Jamil-ud-din Ahmad, 488–9. Lahore: Sh. Muhammad Ashraf, 1952.

Jinnah, Mohammad Ali. "Speech Delivered at the Muslim University Union, Aligarh on 6th March, 1940." In *Some Recent Speeches and Writings of Mr. Jinnah Vol. I*, edited by Jamil-ud-din Ahmad, 153–9. Lahore: Sh. Muhammad Ashraf, 1952.

Jinnah, Mohammad Ali. "Speech at the Muslim University Union, Aligarh, on March 10, 1941." In *Some Recent Speeches and Writings of Mr. Jinnah*, edited by Jamil-ud-din Ahmad, 225–32. Lahore: Sh. Muhammad Ashraf, 1952.

Jones, Kenneth W. "Religious Identity and the Indian Census." In *The Census in British India*, edited by Norman Gerald Barrier, 75–101. Delhi: Manohar, 1981.

Jung, Najeeb. "Why Should a Muslim Have to Wear His Nationalism on His Sleeve?" *The Times of India*, February 20, 2010.

Kabir, Humayun. *Muslim Politics 1906-1947 and Other Essays*, 78–85. Calcutta: Firma K.L. Mukhopadhyay, 1969.

Kamal, Ahmed. *State against the Nation: The Decline of the Muslim League in Pre-Independence Bangladesh 1947-54*. Dhaka: The University Press Limited, 2009.

Kamra, Sukeshi. *Bearing Witness: Partition, Independence, End of the Raj*. Calgary: University of Calgary Press, 2002.

Kaur, Ravinder. *Since 1947: Partition Narratives among Punjabi Migrants of Delhi*. New Delhi: Oxford University Press, 2007.

Khalidi, Omar. *Indian Muslims since Independence*. New Delhi: Vikas Publishing House Pvt. Ltd., 1995.

Khalidi, Omar. *Muslims in Indian Economy*. Gurgaon: Three Essays Collective, 2006.

Khaliquzzaman, Choudhry. *Pathway to Pakistan*. Lahore: Longmans Pakistan Branch, 1961.

Khan, Dominique-Sila. *Crossing the Threshold: Understanding Religious Identities in South Asia*. London: I.B. Tauris, 2004.

Khan, Furrukh. "Speaking Violence: Pakistani Women's Narratives of Partition." In *Gender, Conflict and Migration*, edited by Navnita Chadha Behera, 97–115. New Delhi: SAGE Publications Pvt. Ltd., 2006.

Khan, Hameed-ud-Deen. "Aligarh Muslim University: Attitudes and Trends of the M.A.O. College and the Aligarh Muslim University since 1909- Personal Observations and Revelations." Aligarh, 1966.

Khan, Hamza. "Actual Ghar Wapsi Will Be Sending Muslims to Pakistan: Shiv Sena." *The Indian Express*, December 16, 2014.

Khan, Islam Habib. YahooGroups: VoiceofAligs Listserv, September 26, 2010.

Khan, Islam Habib. YahooGroups: VoiceofAligs Listserv, September 27, 2010.

Khan, Mohd. Ismail. "Annual Report of the Vice-Chancellor Aligarh Muslim University for the Calendar Year 1947: Read at the Convocation Held on 24th January, 1948." Aligarh: Aligarh Muslim University Press, 1948.

Khan, Moinuddin. Interview with Sara Ansari, Citizens Archive of Pakistan (Transcribed August 4, 2009). Karachi, N.D.

Khan, Nawab Ismail. "Application for Additional Grants-in-Aid Submitted to the Government of India by the Vice-Chancellor Aligarh Muslim University." Aligarh: Maulana Azad Library, 1948.

Khan, Nighat Said, Rubina Saigol, and Afiya Shehrbano Zia. *Locating the Self: Perspectives on Women and Multiple Identities*. Women's Studies Journal Series. Lahore: ASR Publications, 1994.

Khan, Sayyid Ahmad. "An Account of the Loyal Mohomedans of India." In *Political Profile of Sir Sayyid Ahmad Khan*, edited by Hafeez Malik. Islamabad: Institute of Islamic History, Culture and Civilization, Islamic University, 1982.

Khan, Sayyid Ahmad, Issen Chander Mookerjee, Mahomed Yosiff, Budree Pershad, and Others. "To His Excellency the Viceroy and Governor General of India in Council: The Humble Petition of the British India Association, North West Provinces August 1, 1867." In *Sir Sayyid Ahmad Khan's Educational Philosophy: A Documentary Record*, edited by Hafeez Malik, 133–80. Islamabad: National Institute of Historical and Cultural Research, 1989.

Khan, (Sd.) Shakir Husain. "Shakir H. Khan to Liaqat Ali Khan." In *Freedom Movement Archives*, F 237/ 14-15. Islamabad: Pakistan National Archives, February 13, 1941.

Khan, Syed Ahmad. "Review on Hunter's *Indian Mussalmans*." In *Writings and Speeches of Sir Syed Ahmad Khan*, edited by Shan Mohammad, 65–82. Bombay: Nachiketa Publications Limited, 1972.

Khan, Syed Ahmad. "Speech at Lucknow: December 28, 1887." In *Writings and Speeches of Sir Syed Ahmad Khan*, edited by Shan Mohammad. Bombay: Nachiketa Publications Limited, 1972.

Khan, Syed Ahmad. "Speech at Meerut: March 16, 1888." In *Writings and Speeches of Sir Syed Ahmad Khan*, edited by Shan Mohammad, 180–95. Bombay: Nachiketa Publications Limited, 1972.

Khan, Syed Ahmad. "Translation of the Report of the Members of the Select Committee for the Better Diffusion and Advancement of Learning among the Muhammadans of India, April 15, 1872." In *The Aligarh Movement: Basic Documents, 1864-1898*, edited by Shan Muhammad, 337–80. Meerut and New Delhi: Meenakshi Prakashan, 1978.

Khan, Syed Ahmed. "The Causes of the Indian Revolt Written by Sayyid Ahmad Khan Bahadur, C.S.I. In Urdoo, in the Year 1858 and Translated into English by His Two European Friends, Benares, Medical Hall Press. 1873." http://www.columbia.edu/itc/mealac/pritchett/00litlinks/txt_sir_sayyid_asbab1873_basic.html.

Khan, Syed Ahmed. "Excerpt: Lecture at Ludhiana." *The Aftab* Aftab Memoirs Special (January 23, 1883): 52.

Khan, Syed Ahmed. "Translation of the Report of the Members of the Select Committee for the Better Diffusion and Advancement of Learning among Muhammadans of India." In *Sir Sayyid Ahmad Khan's Educational Philosophy: A Documentary Record*, edited by Hafeez Malik, 133–80. Islamabad: National Institute of Historical and Cultural Research, 1872.

Khan, Wazir. Interview with Unam Muneer, Citizens Archive of Pakistan. Edited by Unam Muneer. Karachi, N.D.

Khan Yousef Zai, Wajahat A. YahooGroups: VoiceofAligs Listserv, September 27, 2010.

Khetan, Ashish. "In the Words of a Zealot." *Tehelka*, December 15, 2010.

Khosla, Gopal Das. *Stern Reckoning: A Survey of the Events Leading up to and Following the Partition of India*. Delhi: Oxford University Press, 1989.

Khursheed, Anwar. "Past Tense-Future Perfect: Appeal for Forgiveness and Reconciliation." YahooGroups: Aligarh Network; TheAligarhForum; VoiceofAligs; WorldofAligs Listservs, September 19, 2010.

Khurshid, Salman. *At Home in India: A Restatement of Indian Muslims*. New Delhi: Vikas Publishing House Pvt. Ltd., 1986.

Kleinman, Arthur. "The Violences of Everyday Life: The Multiple Forms and Dynamics of Social Violence." In *Violence and Subjectivity*, edited by Veena Das, Arthur Kleinman, Mamphela Ramphele, and Pamela Reynolds. Berkeley: University of California Press, 2000.

Kleinman, Arthur, and Veena Das. "Introduction." In *Violence and Subjectivity*, edited by Arthur Kleinman and Veena Das, 1–18. Berkeley: University of California Press, 2000.

Kudaisya, Gyanesh. *Region, Nation, "Heartland:" Uttar Pradesh in India's Body Politic*. Sage Series in Modern Indian History. Edited by Bipan Chandra, Mridula Mukherjee, and Aditya Mukherjee. New Delhi: SAGE Publications, 2006.

"Late News." *The Times of India*, April 2, 1946, 5.

Lavan, Spencer. *The Ahmadiyah Movement: A History and Perspective*. New Delhi: Manohar, 1974.

Lelyveld, David. *Aligarh's First Generation: Muslim Solidarity in British India*. Princeton: Princeton University Press, 1978.

Lelyveld, David. "Places of Origin of Aligarh Students 1875–1895: Map by Joseph E. Schwartzberg." In *Aligarh's First Generation: Muslim Solidarity in British India*. Princeton: Princeton University Press, 1978.

Lelyveld, David. "Three Aligarh Students: Aftab Ahmad Khan, Ziauddin Ahmad, and Muhammad Ali." *Modern Asian Studies* 9, no. 2 (1975): 227–40.

"Lessons from His Excellency's Visit." *The Muslim University Gazette*, February 5, 1937, 5.

Lubenow, William C. *The Cambridge Apostles, 1820-1914: Liberalism, Imagination, and Friendship in British Intellectual and Professional Life*. Cambridge: Cambridge University Press, 1998.

"Mahatma Gandhi and Education." *The Muslim University Gazette*, August 24, 1937, 5.

Mahdi, Raja Syed Mohammad. "The Pirpur Report: Delhi: End of 1938." In *Muslims under Congress Rule 1937-1939*, edited by Khursheed Kamal Aziz, 307–564. Islamabad: National Commission on Historical and Cultural Research, 1978.

Malik, Hafeez, ed. *Sir Sayyid Ahmad Khan and Muslim Modernism in India and Pakistan*. New York: Columbia University Press, 1980.

Manglori, Tufail Ahmad. *Towards a Common Destiny: A Nationalist Manifesto (English Translation of Musalmanon Ka Roshan Mustaqbil)*. Translated by Ali Ashraf. New

Delhi: People's Publishing House for The Indian Council of Historical Research, 1994. 1937 (Urdu).
Mansergh, Nicholas, ed. *The Transfer of Power 1942-7*. Edited by Nicholas Mansergh and E. W. R. Lumby, Transfer of Power. London: Her Majesty's Stationary Office, 1970-1982.
Mansoor, Tariq. "VC Appeal 17122019." https://www.amu.ac.in/
Manto, Saadat Hasan. *A Manto Panorama: A Representative Collection of Saadat Hasan Manto's Fiction and Non-Fiction*. Translated by Khalid Hasan. Lahore: Sang-e-Meel Publications, 2000.
Masih, Niha. "Mass Conversion in U.P. Sparks Outrage in Parliament, Government Asked to Explain." *NDTV (online)*, December 10, 2014.
Mason, Philip. *A Matter of Honour: An Account of the Indian Army, Its Officers and Men*. London: Jonathan Cape, 1974.
Masood, Salman, and Carlotta Gill. "Killing of Governor Deepens Crisis in Pakistan." *The New York Times*, January 4, 2011.
Massey, Doreen. "Places and Their Pasts." *History Workshop Journal* 39 (Spring 1995): 182–92.
Maududi, S. Abul A'la. *The Qadiani Problem*. Lahore: Islamic Publications Limited, 1979 [1953].
Mazower, Mark. "Minorities and the League of Nations in Interwar Europe." *Daedalus* 126, no. 2 Human Diversity (Spring 1997): 47–63.
Menon, Ritu. "Review of Pangs of Partition: The Human Dimension (Vol. 2)." *Seminar: Porous Bodies, Divided Selves*, no. 510 (February 2002): 84–5.
Menon, Ritu, and Kamla Bhasin. *Borders & Boundaries: Women in India's Partition*. New Brunswick: Rutgers University Press, 1998.
Metcalf, Barbara Daly, ed. *Islam in South Asia in Practice*. Princeton: Princeton University Press, 2009.
Metcalf, Barbara Daly, ed. *Islamic Contestations: Essays on Muslims in India and Pakistan*. New Delhi: Oxford University Press, 2004.
Metcalf, Barbara Daly, ed. *Islamic Revival in British India: Deoband*, 1860-1900. Princeton: Princeton University Press, 1982.
Metcalf, Thomas R. *The Aftermath of Revolt: India*, 1857-1870. Princeton: Princeton University Press, 1964.
Minault, Gail. *Gender, Language, and Learning: Essays in Indo-Muslim Cultural History*. Ranikhet: Permanent Black, 2009.
Minault, Gail. *Secluded Scholars: Women's Education and Muslim Social Reform in Colonial India*. Delhi and New York: Oxford University Press, 1998.
Minault, Gail, and David Lelyveld. "The Campaign for a Muslim University, 1898-1920." In *Gender, Language and Learning: Essays in Indo-Muslim Cultural History*, 220–73. Ranikhet: Permanent Black, 2009.
Minault, Gail, and David Lelyveld. "The Campaign for a Muslim University, 1898-1920." *Modern Asian Studies* 8, no. 2 (1974): 145–89.
Mirza, Sarfaraz Hussain, ed. *Muslim Students and Pakistan Movement: Selected Documents (1937- 1947)*. 3 vols. Vol. I. Lahore: Pakistan Study Centre, 1988.
Mirza, Sarfaraz Hussain. *Youth & Pakistan Movement: History and Chronology*. Lahore: Nazaria-i-Pakistan Foundation, 2004.
Mitra, Nripendra Nath. *The Indian Annual Register: An Annual Digest of Public Affairs of India* 1937. Vol. 2. Calcutta: The Annual Register Office, July–December 1937.

Mohammad, Shan, ed. *Glimpses of Muslim Education: Peeping through the Convocation Addresses of the Aligarh Muslim University*. 2 vols. New Delhi: Anmol Publications Pvt. Ltd., 2006.

Mohammad, Shan. *Glimpses of Muslim Education in India: Peeping through the Convocation Addresses of the Aligarh Muslim University*. 2 vols. Vol. 1. New Delhi: Anmol Publications Pvt. Ltd., 2006.

Mohammad, Shan. *Glimpses of Muslim Education in India: Peeping through the Convocation Addresses of the Aligarh Muslim University*. 2 vols. Vol. 2. New Delhi: Anmol Publications Pvt. Ltd., 2006.

Moon, Penderel. *Divide and Quit: An Eye-Witness Account of the Partition of India*. Delhi: Oxford University Press, 1998 [1961].

Mosley, Leonard. *The Last Days of the British Raj*. New York: Harcourt, Brace & World, 1962.

Mufti, Aamir. "Secularism and Minority: Elements of a Critique." *Social Text* 45 (Winter 1995): 75–96.

Muhammad, Shan. *Education and Politics: From Sir Syed to the Present Day the Aligarh School*. New Delhi: A.P.H. Publishing Corporation, 2002.

Mujeeb, Mohammad. "The Partition of India in Retrospect." In *India's Partition: Process, Strategy and Mobilization*, edited by Mushirul Hasan, 396–407. Delhi: Oxford University Press, 1993.

Mushtaq, Samreen, and Mudasir Amin. "Kashmir: Coronavirus Is a New Tool for India to Oppress Us." *Middle East Eye*, April 7, 2020.

"Muslim Education and the New Ministry in U.P." *The Muslim University Gazette*, August 1, 1937, 5.

"Muslim University Constitution: Need of Removing Certain Anomalies." *The Muslim University Gazette*, April 28, 1937, 5–6.

"Muslim University in the Year 1941-42." *Muslim University Gazette*, May 15, 1942, 4.

Mustafa, A. T. M. "A. T. M. Mustafa to M.A. Jinnah: Muslim University Union Response to Cabinet Proposals- Full Account of the Meeting." In *Shamsul Hasan Collection*, Vol. 26/76–81. Islamabad: Pakistan National Archives, June 12, 1946.

Naqvi, Saeed. *Reflections of an Indian Muslim*. New Delhi: Har-Anand Publications, 1993.

Nasreen, Taslima. *Aya Kashta Jhempe, Jibana Deba Mepe*. Dhaka: Jnanakosha Prakasani, 1994.

"National Education." *The Muslim University Gazette*, December 24, 1937, 5.

Neal, Arthur G. *National Trauma and Collective Memory: Major Events in the American Century*. Armonk: M. E. Sharpe, 1998.

Nehru, Jawaharlal. "Speech by the Hon'ble Pundit Jawaharlal Nehru, Prime Minister of India, at the Annual Convocation of the Muslim University at Aligarh on 24th January, 1948." *Aligarh Magazine*, 1948, xiv–xix.

Nelson, Dean. "Blog Shahbaz Bhatti Killing: What Hope Now for Pakistan's Christians?" *The Telegraph*, March 2, 2011.

"New Bengal Pact." *The Muslim University Gazette*, January 22, 1937, 6.

Nizami, Khaliq Ahmad. *History of the Aligarh Muslim University (1920- 1945)*. Karachi: Sir Syed University Press, 1998.

Office of the United Nations High Commission for Refugees. "Introductory Note: Convention and Protocol Relating to the Status of Refugees." *The United Nations High Commission for Refugees*. Geneva, December 2010.

Oldenburg, Philip. "'A Place Insufficiently Imagined': Language, Belief, and the Pakistan Crisis of 1971." *Journal of Asian Studies* 44, no. 4 (August 1985): 711–33.

"Ourselves." *The Muslim University Gazette*, January 8, 1937, 1.

Pandey, Gyanendra. "Can a Muslim Be an Indian?". *Comparative Studies in Society and History* 41, no. 4 (October 1999): 608–29.

Pandey, Gyanendra. "Partition and Independence in Delhi: 1947-48." *Economic and Political Weekly*, September 6–12, 1997, 2261–72.

Pandey, Gyanendra. *Remembering Partition: Violence, Nationalism, and History in India*. Cambridge and New York: Cambridge University Press, 2001.

Panikkar, Kavalam Narayana. "A Historical Overview." In *Anatomy of a Confrontation: Ayodhya and the Rise of Communal Politics in India*, edited by Sarvepalli Gopal, 22–37. London: Zed Books, 1993.

Paracha, Nadeem F. "Lessons from Ayodhya." *Dawn- Online Edition*, October 1, 2010.

Parel, Anthony J., ed. *Gandhi: Hind Swaraj and Other Writings*. Cambridge: Cambridge University Press, 1997.

Patel, Sardar Vallabhbhai. "Speech: You Cannot Ride Two Horses, January 6, 1948." In *For a United India: Speeches of Sardar Patel 1947- 1950*. Delhi: Publications Division, Ministry of Information and Broadcasting, Government of India, 1967.

Perlez, Jane. "Pakistani Sentenced to Death May Get a Pardon." *The New York Times*, November 22, 2010.

Portelli, Alessandro. *The Death of Luigi Trastulli and Other Stories: Form and Meaning in Oral History*. Albany: State University of New York Press, 1991.

Portelli, Alessandro. "The Peculiarities of Oral History." *History Workshop Journal* 12 no. 1 (Autumn 1981): 96–107.

Prabhu, Sunil. "Ayodhya Order 'Unjust,' Will Decide On Review Plea: Muslim Group Lawyer," *NDTV*, November 9, 2019.

Pred, Allan. "Place as Historically Contingent Process: Structuration and the Time- Geography of Becoming Places." *Annals of the Association of American Geographers* 74, no. 2 (1984): 279–97.

"Prison Statistics India 2014." New Delhi: National Crime Records Bureau, 2014.

"Proclamation, by the Queen in Council, to the Princes, Chiefs, and People of India." Edited by House of Commons Parliamentary Papers. Allahabad: Governor General, November 1, 1858.

"Prohibition or Education or Both." *The Muslim University Gazette*, October 24, 1937, 5.

Qadri, Mohammad Afzal Husain. "M. A. H. Qadri to M. A. Jinnah: Terms of Reference for Education Committee of All India Muslim League." In *Shamsul Hasan Collection*, Vol. 51/ 144–62. Islamabad: Pakistan National Archives, December 19, 1943.

Qasmi, Ali Usman, and Megan Robb, eds. *Muslims against the Muslim League*. Cambridge: Cambridge University Press, 2017.

Qureshi, Ishrat Ali. *Aligarh Past and Present*. Aligarh: Aligarh Muslim University, 1992.

Qureshi, Ishtiaq Husain. "A Case Study of the Social Relations between the Muslims and the Hindus, 1935-1947." In *The Partition of India: Policies and Perspectives*, edited by Cyril Henry Philips and Mary Doreen Wainwright, 360–8. London: Allen and Unwin, 1970.

Qureshi, Ishtiaq Husain. "The Causes of the War of Independence Excerpted from a History of the Freedom Movement Vol. 2 (1831- 1905) Pt. 1." In *1857 in the Muslim Historiography*, edited by M. Ikram Chaghatai, 281–304. Lahore: Sang-e-Meel Publications, 2007. Originally Published 1960.

Ram, Pars. "A UNESCO Study of Social Tensions in Aligarh, 1950-1951." Edited by Gardner Murphy. Ahmedabad: UNESCO, 1955.

Raman, Manjari. "Harvest Gold: Key to a Well-Bread Campaign?" *Indian Express Internet Edition*, February 23, 1998.

Rashid, Sh. Abdul (Proctor). "Appendix F (Ref. No. A.C. Res. No. 3, Dated 13th April, 1946): A Meeting of the Committee Appointed by the Academic Council to Devise Means for Patrolling the University at Night." In *Minutes of An Ordinary Meeting of the Academic Council*. Aligarh: Aligarh Muslim University, April 13, 1946.

Robinson, Francis. *Separatism among Indian Muslims: The Politics of the United Provinces' Muslims, 1860-1923*. London: Cambridge University Press, 1974.

Rose, Jacqueline. "Nation as Trauma, Zionism as Question: Jacqueline Rose Interviewed." Edited by Rosemary Bechler. OpenDemocracy.net, August 17, 2005.

Rose, Jacqueline. "Response to Edward Said." In *Freud and the Non-European*, edited by Christopher Bollas, 63–81. London and New York: Verso in Association with the Freud Museum, 2003.

Rushdie, Salman. *Shame*. New York: Alfred Knopf, 1983.

Sachar, Justice Rajender. "The Sachar Committee Report: Social, Economic and Educational Status of the Muslim Community of India." New Delhi: Prime Minister's High Level Committee, Cabinet Secretariat, Government of India, 2006.

Saikia, Yasmin. "Strangers, Friends and Peace: The Women's World of Abdullah Hall, Aligarh Muslim University." In *Women and Peace in the Muslim World: Gender, Agency, and Influence*, edited by Yasmin Saikia and Chad Haines, 275–308. London: I.B. Tauris, 2015.

Saikia, Yasmin, and M. Raisur Rahman, eds. *The Cambridge Companion to Sir Sayyid Amad Khan*. Cambridge: Cambridge University Press, 2018.

Salim, Ahmad, ed. *Reconstructing History: Memories, Migrants, and Minorities*. Islamabad: Sustainable Development Policy Institute (SDPI), 2009.

Sampath, G. "When the Students Rise," *The Hindu- Online*, December 20, 2019.

Sarwar, Saiyed Mohammad. "Letter from Saiyed Mohd. Sarwar to Nawabzada Liaqat Ali Khan January 19, 1946." In *Freedom Movement Archives*, F 237/ 80-81. Islamabad: Pakistan National Archives.

Savarkar, Vinayak Damodar. *Indian War of Independence, 1857*. Bombay: Phoenix Publications, 1947 [1909].

Sayeed, Khalid Bin. *Pakistan: The Formative Phase, 1857-1948*. 2nd ed. London and New York: Oxford University Press, 1968.

Seal, Anil. *The Emergence of Indian Nationalism: Competition and Collaboration in the Later Nineteenth Century*. London: Cambridge University Press, 1968.

Sen, Uditi. *Citizen Refugee: Forging the Indian Nation after Partition*. Cambridge: Cambridge University Press, 2018.

Sen, Uditi. "Dissident Memories: Exploring Bengali Refugee Narratives in the Andaman Islands." In *Refugees and the End of Empire: Imperial Collapse and Forced Migration in the Twentieth Century*, edited by Panikos Panayi and Pippa Virdee, 219–44. Houndmills, Basingstoke: Palgrave Macmillan, 2011.

Sherwani, Mohammad Obaidur Rahman Khan. "Report of the Vice-Chancellor, Aligarh Muslim University for the Calendar Year 1946: Read at the Convocation Held on the 16th February, 1947." Aligarh: Aligarh Muslim University Press, 1947.

Siddiqui, Justice M. S. A. "Order in the Matters Of: Case No. 891 of 2006, Case No. 1824 of 2006, Case No. 1825 of 2006." Edited by National Commission for Minority Educational Institutions. New Delhi, February 22, 2011.

"Signal of Peace." *The Telegraph- Online Edition*, October 1, 2010.

Singh, Khushwant. *Train to Pakistan*. New Delhi: Roli Books, 2006. 1981.

Sinha, Mrinalini. *Colonial Masculinity: The 'Manly Englishman' and the' Effeminate Bengali' in the Late Nineteenth Century*. Manchester and New York: Manchester University Press, 1995.

"Six-Point Programme of Sheikh Mujib Ur Rahman." In *Banglapedia: National Encyclopedia of Bangladesh*, http://www.banglapedia.org/httpdocs/HT/S_0426.HTM.

"Some Basic Data of the Economy of Pakistan." Lahore: Pakistan Administration Staff College, 1965.

Stallybrass, Peter, and Allon White. *The Politics and Poetics of Transgression*. Ithaca: Cornell University Press, 1986.

Streets, Heather. *Martial Races: The Military, Race, and Masculinity in British Imperial Culture, 1857-1914*. Manchester: Manchester University Press, 2004.

Talbot, Ian. *Divided Cities: Partition and Its Aftermath in Lahore and Amritsar 1947-1957*. Oxford: Oxford University Press, 2006.

Talbot, Ian. *Freedom's Cry: The Popular Dimension in the Pakistan Movement and Partition Experience in Northwest India*. Karachi: Oxford University Press, 1996.

Tan, Tai Yong, and Gyanesh Kudaisya. *The Aftermath of Partition in South Asia*. London: Routledge, 2000.

Tonki, Syed Mohammad. *Aligarh and Jamia: Fight for National Education System*. New Delhi: People's Publishing House, 1983.

Tosh, John. *A Man's Place: Masculinity and the Middle-Class Home in Victorian England*. New Haven: Yale University Press, 1999.

Trouillot, Michel-Rolph. *Silencing the Past: Power and the Production of History*. Boston: Beacon Press, 1995.

Tuan, Yi-Fu. *Landscapes of Fear*. New York: Pantheon Books, 1979.

Tuan, Yi-Fu. *Space and Place: The Perspective of Experience*. Minneapolis: University of Minneapolis Press, 1977.

"The Two Voices." *The Muslim University Gazette*, January 8, 1938, 6.

"University and Politics." *The Muslim University Gazette*, May 5, 1937, 5.

"University's Compensation Offer for Aligarh Riot Damage." *The Hindustan Times*, June 9, 1946, 3.

Valentine, Simon Ross. *Islam and the Ahmadiyya Jama'at: History, Belief, Practice*. New York: Columbia University Press, 2008.

van Schendel, Willem. *A History of Bangladesh*. Cambridge: Cambridge University Press, 2009.

Venugopal, Vasudha. "R.S.S. Plans to Convert 4,000 Christian and 1,000 Muslim Families to Hinduism." *Economic Times*, December 10, 2014.

Verma, Lalmani. "After Aseemanand's Confession, A.M.U. Wants More Security." *Indian Express*, January 12, 2011.

Virdee, Pippa. "Negotiating the Past: Journey through Muslim Women's Experience of Partition and Resettlement in Pakistan." *Cultural and Social History* 6, no. 4 (2009): 467–84.

Virdee, Pippa. "Remembering Partition: Women, Oral Histories and the Partition of 1947." *Oral History* 41, no. 2 (Autumn 2013): 49–62.

Wanchoo, Kailash Nath, Ranadhir Singh Bachawat, Veeraswami Ramaswami, Gopendra Krishna Mitter, and Kowdoor Sadananda Hegde. "S. Azeez Basha and Anr Vs. Union of India on 20 October, 1967." New Delhi: Union of India, October 20, 1967.

Wasey, Akhtarul, and Farhat Ehsas, eds. *Education, Gandhi, and Man: Select Writings Khwaja Ghulamus Saiyyadain*. Delhi: Shipra Publications, 2008.

"What Is NRC?" Office of the State Coordinator of National Registration (NRC), Assam, Government of Assam.

Wilkinson, Steven I. *Votes and Violence: Electoral Competition and Ethnic Riots in India*. New York: Cambridge University Press, 2004.

Wright Jr., Theodore P. "Muslim Education in India at the Crossroads: The Case of Aligarh." *Pacific Affairs* 39, no. 1/2 (Spring–Summer 1966): 50–63.

Zaman, Mukhtar. *Students' Role in the Pakistan Movement*. Karachi: Quaid-i-Azam Academy, 1978.

Zamindar, Vazira Fazila-Yacoobali. *The Long Partition and the Making of Modern South Asia*. New York: Columbia University Press, 2007.

Zamindar, Vazira Fazila-Yacoobali. "South Asia in Dark Times: Homogenizing Nation-States and the Problem of Minorities." *Current History* 114, no. 771 (April 2015): 149–53.

Index

Abdullah, Sheikh Mohammad   13, 199 n.1
Abedin, Syed Zainul   91
Account of the Loyal Mohomedans of India, An (Sir Sayyid)   24
Advani, L. K.   136
Advani, Ram   152–3
Ahmad, Farrukh Jalali   153
Ahmad, Ghulam   107
Ahmad, Hamida   153
Ahmad, Jamil-ud-din   59
Ahmad, Khwaja Fariduddin   22
Ahmad, Khwaja Shamim   153
Ahmad, Merajuddin   185 n.22
Ahmad, Qazi Moinuddin   143–4
Ahmad, Rafique   144
Ahmad, Syed Mohammad   153
Ahmad, Ziauddin   42–4, 54, 62, 68, 88, 91, 183 nn.110–11
   on AMU students' train travel without tickets   75
   Muslim League elections (1945–6) and   55, 58–61
Ahmadis   195 n.6
   in Pakistan   106–7, 196 n.19
Akhtaruzzaman, Mohammad   160, 188 n.77
Alam, Manzar-i-   58–60, 181 n.79, 183 n.116
Ali, Mohamad   44, 174 n.80
Ali, Muhammad Mansur   199 n.1
Ali, Nasir   36
Ali, Shaukat   43, 44, 174 n.80
Ali, Syed Mohammad   190 n.42
Aligarh Magazine, The   34, 45, 90, 91
Aligarh Movement   42, 46, 189 n.8
Aligarh Muslim University (AMU) (India)   xvi–xviii, 2. *See also individual entries*
Aligarh Union and   28

anti-CAA protests and   142
Babri Masjid verdicts and   136–9
Beck, Theodore at   27–8
brotherhood cultivation in   34
culture building at   37
discipline and place in   32–7
dress code at   35–6
foundation stone of   28–9
as hub of Muslim nationalism   65
identity of   20–1
in independent India   90–2
Introduction Night at   176 n.109
Minority Character, demand for   125–7
oral history of   1
origin of   17
partitioning and (*see* partitioning)
Sir Sayyid and   19–20
   context   21–6
sportsmen at   186 n.40
student activism (*see* student activism, of AMU)
Teachers' Association   132
voices from   9–14
Aligarh University Gazette   91
All-India Muslim League (AIML)   14, 38, 43, 48, 75, 124. *See also* Muslim League
All India Muslim Students Federation (AIMSF)   38, 48, 49, 75
   on AMU students' train travel without tickets   74
Amin, Mohammad   13, 57, 153–4, 169 n.80, 182 n.109
   on circles of safety during partitioning   77
   on Gandhi's assassination   92
   on leftism in AMU   130
   on Zakir Husain   88
Amritsar (India)   4

Anjuman-i-Ahrar-i-Islam 107
Ansari, Asloob Ahmad 12, 19, 154, 170 n.3
   on AMU's Minority Character demand 127
   on Delhi and circles of safety during partitioning 80
Ansari, Hamid 132, 199 n.1
Ansari, Hayatullah 98
Ansari, Nasim 53
anxiety and alarm, difference between 63-4
Arendt, Hannah 102, 194 n.109
Asbab-e-Baghavat-e-Hind (*The Causes of the Indian Revolt*) (Sir Sayyid) 23, 24
Aseemanand, Swami 95-6
ashraf Muslims 21, 24, 30, 32, 38, 173 n.47, 175 n.86
Awami League 113-15, 118, 132
Azad, Maulana Abdul Kalam 88, 100
Azeez Basha case 127-8
Azmi, Kaifi 166 n.28

Baaquie, M. A. 12, 160
Babri Masjid xv, 17, 99, 180 n.56
   verdicts and AMU 136-9, 164 n.13
Banaras Hindu University 43
Bangladesh 16, 196 n.26
Aligarh Old Boys' Association in 10, 16
   AMU and 12-14, 108-11
   independence of 107-8, 121
   Lahore Resolution and 112
   Pakistan and 111-14
Bangladeshi/East Pakistani narrators 13-14, 108-9, 112-15, 117, 119-21, 131, 160-2.
   See also individual Bangladeshi narrators
Bangla Language Movement 117
"Batla House Encounter" 191 n.59
Beck, Theodore 27-8, 31, 38, 43, 177 n.3
Begum, Jehan (Nawab Sultan of Bhopal) 13
belonging xvii, 122, 138
   collective identity and 34
   friability of 95
   guilt and 89
   legitimate, claim to 106

Muslimness and 131
   national xvii
   natural 30
   not 109, 131
      fear of 64, 133
   partition and 4, 84, 128
   place and 102
   safety and 65
   sense of 1, 11, 81, 109, 133
   shifting boundaries of 8, 11, 35, 64, 72, 76, 114, 117, 132
   tension over 103, 106, 107
   together, concept of 50
Bengal (India) 4, 31, 167 n.47. *See also* Bangladesh; *individual narrators*
Bengali Muslims, significance of 24, 31, 112, 114-18, 120
bhaichara (brotherly affection) 6
Bharatiya Janata Party (BJP) 83, 97-8, 125, 128, 132, 138
Bhasin, Kamla 7, 164 n.7
Bhatti, Shahbaz 105
Bhutto, Benazir 15
Bhutto, Zulfikar Ali 107
Bibi, Asia 105-6
Bigelow, Anna 6
biradari (brotherhood) 34, 38
blasphemy laws, in Pakistan 105-6
Bose, Sarmila 164 n.4, 198 n.62
boundary xvii, 2, 38, 89, 106, 133, 137, 142. *See also* partitioning
   belonging and 8, 11, 35, 64, 72, 76, 114, 117, 132
   inner circle of discipline and 66-72
   oral history and 6, 8, 9, 11
   outer circles and sites of disturbance and 72-80
   Partition and 6
   Two Nation Theory and 114-15, 117, 119
Brass, Paul 68, 165 n.19, 202 n.20
Butalia, Urvashi 3, 7, 164 n.6, 165 n.22

Cabinet Mission plan (1946) 112, 119, 197 n.43
Casey, Edward 64, 81
Chakrabarty, Dipesh 164 n.4, 167 n.47
Chatterji, Joya 4, 6
Chattha, Ilyas 6

Chaudhry, Cecil   106
Chaudhry, Fazal Elahi   199 n.1
Chaudhry, Mahmood Ali Khan   144
Chawla, Devika   3, 6
Chhatari, Nawab Sahib Ibn-e-Saeed   15
Choudhri, Saima   160–1
Choudhri, Waheedudin   12, 109, 161, 168 n.62, 187 n.61
  on AMU's protective capacity   110
  on Calcutta   110–11
  on circles of safety during partitioning   76, 77
  as leftist   120
Choudhury, Salahuddin   12, 57, 109, 110, 161, 196 nn.25–6
Chugtai, Ismat   166 n.28
circles of safety   72–80, 109
Citizens Archive of Pakistan   115
Citizenship Amendment Act (CAA) (2019) (India)   135, 139–42
collective memory   8, 22
community   1–2, 14, 55, 73, 78, 94, 97–8, 102–9. *See also* belonging; minorities
  backward   123
  boundaries and   8
  collective   4
  hostile   66
  minority   2
  moral   22, 29–32, 37, 42, 50–2, 84, 174 n.67
  religious   20
Cox, Harold   27, 28
Crane, Susan   8

Das, Veena   2
Dawn (newspaper)   137
Dead Reckoning (Bose)   198 n.62
Dehlavi, Shahid Ahmad   77
Delhi (India)   1–4, 6, 7, 110, 142, 188 n.69, 191 n.59
  AMU and   21–4
  boundaries and   64, 72–5, 77–81
  Muslim Question and   89, 92
Deoband Madrasa   44
Deslandes, Paul   27
Devji, Faisal   30, 42, 101, 108, 124, 173–4 n.66
Dhulipala, Venkat   100, 167 n.58

Didi, Mohammad Amin   199 n.1
discipline   xvii, 38
  in AMU   32–7
  partitioning and   64, 66–73, 75, 79, 81–2
  student activism   41, 47, 54, 55, 60–1
  moral   90, 91
  Muslimness and   109–11
displacement   xvi, xviii, 3, 4, 6, 8, 80, 82, 86, 109, 121, 128, 133, 140
  Babri Masjid issue and   137, 138
  Hindus in   167 n.47
  partition   165 n.22

East Pakistan. *See* Bangladesh
Eaton, Richard   195 n.10

Fatima, Aijaz   144–5
First War of Independence   22–3
"Flying Fez, The" (Abedin)   91
Foreign Policy South Asia Daily   138

Gandhi, Indira   7, 191 n.62
Gandhi, Mahatma   14, 42, 44, 78, 90–1, 101, 181 n.74
  assassination of   92–5
Garam Hawa (film)   165–6 n.28
Ghar Wapsi program   138
Gilmartin, David   2, 195 n.10
Godse, Nathuram   93
Graff, Violette   125, 184 n.2, 200 n.11
Guha Thakurta, Meghna   4, 5, 117
guilt sense, post-partition   85, 89, 128–30

Habib, Irfan   5, 12–14, 53, 54, 60, 154, 181 n.73
  on AMU
    after partitioning   86–8
    during partitioning period   67–70
    leftism   130
    Minority Character demand   126
  on Muslim League Muslims and Congress Muslims   100
  on redemption   129
  on RSS   94
Habib, Mohammad   45, 53, 68, 94, 100
Hadique, Mohammed   145

Haider, Salman   198 n.60
Haider, Zara   145
Haig, Harry   48
Halbwachs, Maurice   8
Haleem, A. B. A.   35, 37, 38, 47, 54, 129,
    176 n.112, 181 n.67, 183 n.111,
    201 n.32
  Muslim League elections (1945-6)
    and   58-61
Hamid, Sayyid   154-5, 191 n.62
Hansen, Thomas Blom   192 n.74
Haq, Fazlul   112, 196 n.40
Hasan, Masood-ul   12, 13, 50, 57,
    60, 155, 180 n.56, 188 n.74,
    198 n.69
  on AMU and partitioning period
    69-71
  on bloodshed of 1946-7   101
  on circles of safety during
    partitioning   73, 78-9
  on Gandhi's assassination   93
  on Khaliquzzaman   99
  on support for Pakistan as
    irrational   90
Hasan, Mushirul   48, 128, 186 n.38,
    195 n.10
Hate Crime Watch   188 n.5
Hazarika, Sanjoy   141
Hindu Jagran Manch   132
Hodgson, Marshall G. S.   168 n.64
hostage nation theory   56
Huda, Norul   116-17
Human Rights Watch   188-9 n.5
Hunter, W. W.   24-5, 95
Huq, Fazlul   120
Husain, Intizar   167 n.56
Husain, Iqtidar   145
Husain, Nayyar   146
Husain, Wajahat   xii-xiii, 9, 12, 146
  on alternate identities and
    fractures   104-5
  on Bangladesh   115-16
  during partition   xiv-xv
  early life of   xiii-xiv
  on future of Muslims during
    partition   4-5
  on his migration to Pakistan   14
  on partition reasons   112
  on religious inclination   11
  on sectarian divisions   168 n.68
Husain, Zakir   78, 128-9, 192 n.79,
    199 n.1
  as vice chancellor of AMU   85, 88-9,
    92, 111, 127
Hyder, Akbar   195 n.10

India. *See individual entries*
Indian narrators   14, 57, 65, 70, 98,
    152-60. *See also individual*
    Indian narrators
Indian Mussulmans, The (Hunter)   24
Indian National Congress   43, 45, 65,
    124, 135
Indian War of Independence of 1857, The
    (Savarkar)   22
"In the Words of a Zealot" (Khetan)   95
Iqbal, Javid   146, 171 n.20, 197 n.43,
    203 n.33
Islam, Ghayurul   60
Islamabad (Pakistan)   9

Jaffrelot, Christophe   97
Jafri, Alig Ali Sardar   93-4
Jahan, Rounaq   112
Jalal, Ayesha   174 nn.67, 71, 180 nn.62,
    67, 195 n.10
Jalali, Farrukh   190 n.42
Jamaat-i-Islami   107
Jamia Millia Islamia   38, 44-5, 88, 110,
    127
Jauhar, Mohamad Ali   32, 42, 44,
    193 n.90
Jilani, Zafaryab   139
Jinnah, Mohammad Ali   xvii, 6, 14,
    43, 48-51, 54-5, 62, 124, 132,
    174 n.83, 181 n.74, 193 n.90
  Cabinet Mission plan and   119,
    197 n.43
  on minorities in Pakistan   105
  Muslim elections (1945-6) and   55,
    58-61
  Mustafa and   198 n.70
  on Urdu as national language   114

Kabir, Humayun   48, 49
Karachi (Pakistan)   9
Kashmir, revocation of special status
    for   141, 203-4 n.33

Kaur, Ravinder 6
Khalidi, Omar 96, 97, 191 n.62, 192 nn.72, 75, 77
Khaliquzzaman, Choudhry 97, 99, 178 n.28
Khan, Abdul Rasheed 12, 37, 56, 108, 147, 176 n.111
Khan, Aftab Ahmad 32–3
Khan, Aga 42
Khan, Ali Hasan (Nawab of Bhopal) 52
Khan, Azizur Rahman 199 n.74
Khan, Furrukh 6
Khan, Hameed-ud-Deen 43, 44, 54, 60, 181 n.77
Khan, Iftikhar Alam 35–6, 128, 155, 176 n.106
   on AMU after partitioning 87
   on anti-communist sentiment on AMU campus 129–30
   on circles of safety during partitioning 72–3, 77–8
   on his sense of guilt 89
   on Nehru 129
   on Zakir Husain 129
Khan, Iqtidar Alam 11, 12, 155–6, 176 n.106, 185 n.25, 201 n.36
   jail experiences of 130
   on AMU
      during partitioning period 67
      leftism 130
      Minority Character demand 126
   on redemption 129
   on RSS 94
   on support for Pakistan as irrational 90
Khan, Islam Habib 136, 137
Khan, Ismaili Aga 124
Khan, Liaqat Ali 55–6, 58, 199 n.1
   on AMU students' train travel without tickets 75
Khan, Mohammad Ismail 189 n.17
Khan, Mohiuddin 12, 66, 161, 185 n.18, 196 n.28, 198 n.63, 200 n.18
   on AMU
      after partitioning 87
      protective capacity 110
   on discrimination at AMU 131

   on intimacy between food and home 109, 110
   on opposition to Pakistan's administration 119–20
   on support for League 119
   on support for partition of India 112
Khan, Nawab Ismail 111
Khan, Nighat Said 6
Khan, Sir Sayyid Ahmad 12–14, 17, 19–20, 50, 80, 123–4
   as *ashraf* 21
   on Bengali ascendance to power 31
   educational reform of 24–9, 37
   at England 26
   founding of Muhammadan Anglo-Oriental College 27
   on Hunter 24–5
   loyalty to British Crown 24
   Muslim Educational Conference and 29, 38
   on Mutiny of 1857 23
   on *qaum* 30
   on support of Urdu 30
Khan, Wazir 74–6
Khan, Yahya 117
Khan, Yaqoob Ali 147
Khan, Zafar Mohammad 5, 11, 156
Khan, Zakir Ali 12, 19, 34, 35, 37, 147, 170 nn.5–6, 176 n.113, 185 n.20, 186 n.40
   on AMU
      after partitioning 88
      during partitioning period 66, 70–1
   on circles of safety during partitioning 79–80
Khetan, Ashish 95
Khilafat Movement xvi, 42, 43, 48
Khurshid, Salman 64, 97, 192 nn.79, 81
Kidwai, Rafi Ahmad 68
Kidwai, Saeeda Wahid 12, 13, 156, 193 n.91
   on Babri Masjid mosque destruction 138
   on Muslim identity in Pakistan as communal 99
Kleinman, Arthur 2
Kothari, Rita 6
Kudaisya, Gyanesh 164 n.3

Lahore (Pakistan)   xii, xv, xvi, 2, 4, 9, 13, 15, 17, 50
Lahore Resolution (1940)   51, 52, 112, 113, 118
Lelyveld, David   26, 29, 38, 44, 169 n.73, 171 n.8, 174 nn.67, 81, 175 n.86, 178 n.11, 180 n.62
long partition, significance of   1
Long Partition, The (Zamindar)   64
Lytton, Governor-General Lord   28

mahol (atmosphere)   34, 90
Malaviya, Pandit Madan   48
Malerkotla (Indian Punjab)   6
Manglori, Tufail Ahmad   177 n.3
Mankekar, Purnima   164–5 n.14
Manto, Saadat Hasan   166–7 n.42, 187 n.64
martial races   25, 115
masculinity   17, 20
   change in conception of   25, 27
   conception at Oxford and Cambridge universities   26
Masood, Naved   185 n.22
Masooda, Siddiqui   162
Massey, Doreen   74
Mathur, A. K.   156, 168 n.65, 169 n.74
Maududi, Maulana   107
Mehdi, S. M.   93–4, 157, 191 n.52
memory   9, 11, 19, 56, 66, 67, 70, 78, 89, 109–11, 119, 121, 167 n.43, 180 n.56, 186 n.38. *See also* *individual narrators*
   collective   8, 22, 104
Menon, Ritu   7, 164 n.7, 200–1 n.27
Metcalf, Barbara Daly   195 n.10
Metcalf, Thomas   172 n.40
Minault, Gail   44, 169 nn.72–3, 171 nn.8, 11, 175 n.86, 178 n.11, 180 n.62, 198 n.56
minority   xvii, 2, 20, 29, 128, 194 n.109
   AMU and   17, 125–7, 165 n.27, 196 n.28
   belonging and   138
   CAA and   140
   Human Rights Watch and   188–9 n.5
   Jinnah's speech on   203 n.25
   Muslimness and   103–8, 113–15, 117, 120, 121, 198 n.60

   Muslim Question and   3, 83–4, 87, 91, 93, 95–7, 100, 102
   partitioning and   70, 78–9, 82, 132
   student activism and   43, 47–51, 56, 61, 62
   as targets of violence   135, 197 n.49, 198 n.62
   2001 census and   192 n.80
Mirza, M. B.   59
Mirza, Sarfaraz Hussain   14, 49, 148, 166 n.29
Modi, Narendra   16, 135, 138, 191 n.58
Mohammad, Ghulam   199 n.1
Mohammad, Shan   191 n.46
moral community   22, 37, 51, 84. *See also qaum* (Muslim moral community)
   pillars of   29–32
moral order, disruption of   65
Morison, Theodore   43
Mufti, Aamir   100, 102
Muhammadan Anglo-Oriental College. *See* Aligarh Muslim University (AMU)
Mujahid, Shariful   148
Mulk, Waqarul   177 n.3
Muslim education   22, 30, 46
   Victorian   26–9
Muslim League   47, 50. *See also* All-India Muslim League (AIML)
   elections (1945–6)   55–61
   Muslims, and Congress Muslims   100–1
   period of   53–5
Muslim Mass Contact Campaign (1937)   48, 49
Muslim minority   82, 83, 84, 87, 95, 132, 140, 181 n.67, 192 n.80. *See also* minorities
Muslim nationalism   xviii, 2, 6, 8, 17, 43, 47–51
   AMU as hub of   65
Muslimness   11, 76, 94, 101, 131, 198 n.60, 199 n.2. *See also under individual entries*
   AMU, Pakistan and Bangladesh and   108–14
   minority as majority and   104–8

Two Nation Theory and 114–20
Muslim Question 3–4, 83–5, 102, 113, 122
  AMU in independent India and 90–2
  continuity and slippage after 1947 85–90
  Gandhi's assassination and 92–5
  in India and 95–7
    Indian Muslims' view on migration to Pakistan 97–100
    Muslim League Muslims and Congress Muslims and 100–1
Muslim separatism 125, 128, 194 n.110
Muslim Students' Federation. *See* All India Muslim Students Federation (AIMSF)
Muslim University Gazette (AMU publication) 45–9, 54
Muslim University Muslim League (MUML) 58
Mustafa, A. T. M. 198 n.70
Mutiny of 1857 22–3, 25, 80, 171 n.20

Naqvi, Mukhtar Ahmad 148
Naqvi, Saeed 101, 194 n.103
National Commission for Minority Educational Institutions (NCMEI) 127
National Register of Citizens (NRC) (India) 140–1
Nazaria-e-Pakistan Foundation (Lahore) 9
Nazimuddin, Khwaja 199 n.1
Nehru, Jawaharlal 14, 48, 78, 88, 89, 92, 93, 101, 129, 178 nn.16, 22
1947: Before, During, After (Husain) xiii
Nizami, Zilley Ahmad 12, 148–9

Objectives Resolution (1949) (Pakistan) 100
One Unit Scheme 197 n.53
oral history 115, 116. *See also individual narrators*
  of AMU students 1
  partition and 6–9 (*see also individual entries*)
  significance of xvii, xviii, 2–3, 8, 16, 163 nn.3, 11

  as social justice practice 10
Oral History Association 163 n.11
Osmani, M. A. G. 116, 199 n.1

Pakistan. *See individual entries*
Pakistani narrators 5, 14, 16, 57, 65, 101, 103, 108–9, 112–13, 121, 131, 143–52. *See also individual Pakistani narrators*
Pakistan Movement 17, 81, 82, 86, 87, 132
  AMU student activism and 41, 56, 58, 61
  Muslimness and 113, 118, 119, 121
Pandey, Gyan 3, 7, 10, 132, 167 n.43
  on Delhi Muslims during partitioning 78
  on Muslims as Indians 95
  on Muslims as minorities 84
Pant, Govind Ballabh 47, 68, 130, 185 n.28
Partition xiv, 1–3, 6, 7, 9, 10, 123, 125, 128, 133, 163 n.4, 167 nn.43, 48, 174 n.71, 189 n.15, 201 n.27
  AMU and 64, 66, 73, 79, 81
  Muslim Question and 84, 85, 101
  Muslimness and 113, 122
Partition and Locality (Chattha) 6
partitioning xvii, 63–6
  inner circle of discipline 1946 and 66–72
  as lived experiences 9
  oral history and 6–9 (*see also individual entries*)
  outer circles of safety and 72–80
  present-tense-ness 128
  process of 1
Patel, Sardar 87, 93, 97, 191 n.62
Pathway to Pakistan (Khaliquzzaman) 97
patronage 24, 44
Pioneer, The (journal) 24
Pirpur Report (1938) 50, 63, 124
place xvii, 2, 4, 11, 21, 64–5. *See also belonging; boundaries*
  discipline and 32–7
  imagined 101
  importance and significance of 74, 80, 81, 102, 133

Punjab Muslim Students' Federation   52

Qadri, M. A. H.   181 n.67
Qadri, Mumtaz   105
Qamar, Mansoor   149
qaum (Muslim moral community)   30, 50, 52, 174 n.67. *See also* moral community
Qureishi, Ishtiaq Husain   77, 171 n.22

Raepuri, Akhtar   98
Raheja, Natasha   6
Rahman, Fatima Fari   12, 13, 149, 165 n.27
Rahman, Habibur   12, 74, 80, 131, 161–2, 187 n.54, 198 nn.64–5
   on AMU   108
      independence from government   110
   on discrimination of Bengali Muslims by Pakistan   115
   on League activity reasons   118
   on movement for Bangladesh   118, 132
   on mutual cooperation   113
   on nostalgia about food   109–10
   on Pakistan Movement   118
Rahman, Hakeem Syed Zillur   157, 190 n.42
Rahman, Maulvi Fazlur   185 n.22
Rahman, Mujibur   113, 117–19
Rahman, Sheikh. *See* Rahman, Mujibur
Rahman, Wasi ur   157
Raleigh, Walter   27, 28
Ram, Pars   184 n.5, 185 n.24
Ranadive, B. T.   201 n.38
   "Ranadive Period"   130
Rashid, Ahmad   13
Rashid, Anjuman   149–50
Rashid, M. A.   12, 162, 169 n.81, 196 nn.38, 40
   on critique of Pakistani values   111
Rashid, Shahid   12, 150
Rashtriya Swayamsevak Sangh (RSS)   93, 94, 132, 138, 191 n.58
Rasul, Begum Aizaz   193 n.81
Rawalpindi (Pakistan)   9
Razzaqi, Wazir Ahmad   12, 150
Reconstructing History (Salim)   115, 116
redemption, sense of   128–33
Reflections on Partition in the East (Samaddar)   6
relative deprivation/narrative of decline   20, 21, 42
Remembering Partition (Pandey)   3
Rizvi, Syed Saghir Ahmad   12, 13, 36–7, 109, 157–8, 176 n.110
   on AMU after partitioning   87
Robinson, Francis   29
Roorki University   190 n.25
Rose, Jacqueline   106, 195 n.11

Sachar Committee Report (2006)   96, 138
   Sachar, Rajinder   96, 192 n.80
Saeed, Ahmad   12, 14, 63, 64, 84–5, 150, 158, 184 n.3
   on discrimination on Muslims   96, 99
   on Zakir Husain   88, 89
Saharanpur (India)   5–6
Sahibzada (Aftab Ahamd Khan) Memorial Fund   45
Saikia, Yasmin   11, 34, 114, 117, 197 n.49
Saiyyidain, K. G.   45, 48, 191 n.62, 192 n.75
Salim, Ahmad   115, 116, 121, 197 n.50
Samaddar, Ranabir   6
Savarkar, V. D.   22, 171–2 n.24, 172 n.25, 203 n.25
Schimmel, Annemarie   195 n.10
Seal, Anil   25
self-manifestation   50, 57, 118
Sen, Uditi   6
seniority, significance of   36
Servaes, Tahira Minhaj   150–1
Shafi, Iqbal   12, 80, 151, 174–5 n.83, 182 n.96
   on circles of safety during partitioning   73–5
   on Muslim League elections (1945–6)   55–8
Shamsi, Mohsin Jalil   158
Sherwani, Khan Bahadur Obaidur Rahman Khan   58, 59
Sherwani, Riazur Rahman   12, 13, 14, 46, 158, 178 n.26, 189 n.10
   on AMU after partitioning   85–6
   Muslim League and   53–4

on non-discrimination in AMU 108
on redemption 130–1
sherwani dress 35–6, 38, 56, 91, 93, 168 n.62, 176 n.106, 196 n.35
  partitioning and 74–7, 79
Shiism 11, 107
Shiv Sena (India) 138–9
Siddiqi, Ather 5–6, 12, 13, 137, 158–9, 188 n.3, 189 n.14, 190 n.26, 193 n.84
  on AMU after partitioning 86–8
  on Ayodhya issue 139
  on discrimination on Muslims 96
  on Hindu tolerance 102
  on his guilt sense 89
  on Muslims in India after 1947 83
Siddiqi, Majid Ali 12, 13, 159, 169 n.80, 178 n.21, 186 n.46
  on circles of safety during partitioning 72
Siddiqi, Zakia 13, 98, 159, 193 n.86
Siddiqui, Anwar Ahsan 121
Singh, Manmohan 96
Singh, Rajeshwar 138
Sinha, Mrinalini 172 n.40, 174 n.74
Sir Syed Memorial Society (Rawalpindi) 9
"Six Points Programme" 113, 118, 119
solidarity 17, 124, 131, 136, 142, 196 n.26
  AMU and 20–1, 23, 37
  Muslimness and 104, 106, 108, 114, 117–19, 121
  Muslim Question and 89, 91–4, 99–100, 102
  partitioning and 70, 71, 74, 78–82
  student activism and 41–2, 49, 51–3, 57
Streets, Heather 25
structural violence 2
student activism, of AMU 41–3
  education and politics (1898-1937) and 43–7
  Muslim League period (1940-7) and 53–5
    1945–6 elections 55–61
  Muslim nationalism and 47–51
  Two Nation Theory and 51–3

Students' Role in the Pakistan Movement (Zaman) 56
subjectivity 8, 9
Sufism 107
Sultana, Rais 151–2
Sunni Muslim identity, in Pakistan 106
Sunni Waqf Board (India) 137, 139

Tan, Tai Yong 164 n.3
Tariq, Fayazuddin 52
Taseer, Salman 105
Tehelka (magazine) 95
Tehzib ul-Akhlaq (Social Reform) (journal) 26
territoriality 52. *See also individual entries*
Thakurta, Meghna Guha 117
Tonki, S. M. 43–4, 178 n.16
Tosh, John 27, 173 n.53
train journey xiv, 8, 65, 93–4, 111
  fear of 129, 168 n.62
  after Partition 167 n.48
  as sites of violence 73–9, 187 n.59
  without ticket 65, 73–5, 77
"Transfer of Power" 7
Trouillot, Michel-Rolph 8
Tuan, Yi-Fu 35, 63
Two Nation Theory 51–3, 89, 101, 103–4, 107–8, 114–20, 131, 140, 203 n.25
  challenge to 104, 121–2
  failure of 131

Umar, Ghulam 12, 14, 51, 57, 80, 151, 176 n.105, 193 n.90, 197 n.43
Umar, Khadija Minhaj 151
Unbordered Memories (Kothari) 6
UP Muslim League Parliamentary Board 60
Urdu, significance of 30, 38, 48, 101, 104, 114
  Urdu-speaking and 14, 51, 87, 104, 108–9, 114, 117, 131

van Schendel, Willem 164 n.4
Victorian conservatism 199 n.2
Victorian Muslim education, creation of 26–9
Vidya Mandir scheme (1921) 49

violence   xiv, xvii, 114, 121, 142
  absence of   3, 138, 165 n.19
  Ahmadis as victims of   107, 195–6 n.19
  in Aligarh City   64
  anti-Muslim   76, 79, 94, 96, 97, 176 n.106, 180 n.56, 191 n.58, 197 n.49
  anti-Sikh   7
  Babri Masjid issue and   136–9, 180 n.56, 164 n.13
  citizenship issue and   132, 140
  communal   2, 90, 129, 135, 164 n.13, 184 n.5, 202 n.20
  disruptive   175 n.95
  everyday   2, 3, 64, 81
  fear of   1
  partition and   10, 101, 164 n.3, 165 n.14
  Partition and   133
  physical   4
  Pirpur Report on   50
  racialized   198 n.62
  retributive   67
  social   65, 66
  student   69, 70
  terrorist   15
  trains as sites of   75, 187 n.59
  as unnatural   99
Violence and Subjectivity (Kleinman and Das)   2
Virdee, Pippa   6
Vishwa Hindu Parishad   202 n.12

Wardha educational scheme   48, 49
Wilkinson, Steven I.   192 n.81
Wright, Theodore   127, 200 n.11
Wylie, Francis   68

Yunus, Mohammad   159

Zafar, Bahadur Shah   22, 172 n.25
Zaidi, Anis   151–2
Zaidi, Zahida   5–6, 12, 13, 159–60, 201 n.37
Zaman, Mukhtar   54, 56, 182 n.96
Zamindar, Vazira   1, 64, 102, 164 nn.4–5, 194 n.109
Zardari, Asif Ali   15
Zia ul-Haq   105, 107
Zuberi, Mubarak Shah   42, 152, 177 n.5
Zuberi, Viqar Ahmad   152
Zuberi, Waqar Ahmad   152

www.ingramcontent.com/pod-product-compliance
Lightning Source LLC
Chambersburg PA
CBHW072146290426
44111CB00012B/1990